NEW WOMEN
OF THE NEW SOUTH

The Leaders of the Woman Suffrage
Movement in the Southern States

Marjorie Spruill Wheeler

Marjorie Spruill Wheeler

New York   Oxford

OXFORD UNIVERSITY PRESS

1993

Oxford University Press

Oxford   New York   Toronto
Delhi   Bombay   Calcutta   Madras   Karachi
Kuala Lumpur   Singapore   Hong Kong   Tokyo
Nairobi   Dar es Salaam   Cape Town
Melbourne   Auckland   Madrid

and associated companies in
Berlin   Ibadan

Copyright © 1993 by Marjorie Spruill Wheeler

Published by Oxford University Press, Inc.,
198 Madison Avenue, New York, New York 10016-4314

Oxford is a registered trademark of Oxford University Press

Library of Congress Cataloging-in-Publication Data
Wheeler, Marjorie Spruill.
New women of the new South: the leaders of the woman suffrage
movement in the southern states / Marjorie Spruill Wheeler.
p. cm.   Includes bibliographical references and index.
ISBN-0-19-507583-8—ISBN-0-19-508245-1 (pbk.)
1. Suffragists—Southern States—History.   2. Women—Suffrage—
Southern States—History.   I. Title.
JK1896.W48   1993
324.6′ 23′ 0973—dc20   92-27412

2   4   6   8   9   7   5   3

Printed in the United States of America
on acid-free paper

To David

Acknowledgements

There are many people I wish to thank for their assistance as I was researching and writing this book. First of all I thank Joseph F. Kett of the University of Virginia and Dorothy Ross of Johns Hopkins University (formerly of U.Va.) for directing this work while it was in the dissertation stage; I am grateful for their invaluable criticism and exacting standards as well as their encouragement and friendship. I also appreciate the time and considerable talent historians Nancy Hewitt, William Link, Edward Ayers, Anastatia Sims, Paul Fuller, Charles McCurdy, and Stephen Innes invested in this project; each read the manuscript carefully and offered very valuable suggestions. I owe a special debt to A. Elizabeth Taylor, Anne Firor Scott, and Paul Fuller, for both their exemplary scholarship on the Southern woman suffrage movement and their interest in and encouragement of my efforts.

It has been a great pleasure to discuss some of the ideas contained herein at conventions of the Southern Historical Association and the Organization of American Historians, as well as at conferences sponsored by the Southern Association for Women Historians. I profited a great deal from suggestions offered in these sessions by many of the scholars mentioned above and by still other insightful commentators, including Elsa Barkley Brown, LeeAnn Whites, Wayne Flynt, Rosalyn Terborg-Penn, Jaquelyn Dowd Hall, Joanne Hawks, Paula Baker, and Sidney Bland. Several of us with work in progress related to Southern suffrage or antisuffrage have met informally but regularly at these conferences to compare notes and discuss our theories; I learned much from Elizabeth Hayes Turner, Judith McArthur, Glenda Gilmore, Claudia Knott, Marlene Rikard, Mary Martha Thomas, Sarah Wilkerson-Freeman, and Elna Green, as well as Wayne Flynt, Anastatia Sims, and LeeAnn Whites.

A grant from the American Association of University of Women, the first annual Lucy Somerville Howorth Endowed Fellowship, made possible the extensive research in manuscript collections on which this study is based; I am grateful to the Mississippi Division of the AAUW (especially Cora Norman) for endowing this fellowship and their continuing interest in my work. Since receiving the fellowship I have come to know "Judge Lucy" well and to share the Mississippi AAUW's unstinting admiration for her. Indeed, Judge Lucy Somerville Howorth, now ninety-seven and thriving in Cleveland, Mississippi, has helped me in countless ways in addition to inspiring the creation of this fellowship. The daughter of Nellie Nugent Somerville, president of the Mississippi suffragists, she provided invaluable insight into the Southern suffrage movement through her recollections of her mother, Belle Kearney, Kate and Jean Gordon, Mary Johnston, Dr. Anna Howard Shaw, and other leading suffragists whom she brought to life for me. Indeed, all historians of the suffrage movement owe her a debt for collecting or causing to be collected the papers of her mother and of her friend Tennessee suffragist Sue Shelton White, papers now housed in the Arthur and Elizabeth Schlesinger Library on the History of Women in America at Radcliffe College.

I am also grateful to Mrs. Ralph Catterall of Richmond, Virginia, for permission to use the papers of Lila Meade Valentine (and to Anne Hobson Freeman for telling me about the papers and introducing me to Mrs. Catterall), and to Mr. and Mrs. John L. Hillhouse, Jr., of Birmingham for allowing me to read and quote from the diaries of Pattie Ruffner Jacobs, Mr. Hillhouse's grandmother. Thanks also to Captain John W. Johnston of Saratoga, California, for permission to quote from the papers of his great-aunt, Mary Johnston. Lee Anderson, editor of the Chattanooga *News-Free Press*, very kindly provided me with a copy of a special suffrage edition of his paper published in conjunction with an important suffrage convention there in 1914.

I am thankful for the assistance of the archivists and staff of: the Special Collections Department, University of Virginia; the Manuscript Division, Library of Congress; the Southern Historical Collection, University of North Carolina at Chapel Hill; the Arthur and Elizabeth Schlesinger Library on the History of Women at Radcliffe College; the Division of Manuscripts and Archives, Virginia Historical Society; the Virginia State Library and Archives; the Mississippi Department of Archives and History; the Valentine Museum, Richmond, Virginia; the Louisiana Collection, Tulane University Library; the Special Collections Division, University of Georgia Library; and especially William J. Marshall and the staff in Special Collections and Archives at the University of Kentucky Library and Teresa Ceravolo and Marvin Whiting at the Birmingham Public Library who provided assistance well beyond what I had any right to expect—or expected. I also appreciate the help my friend Bruce Ragsdale, Associate Historian, Office of the Historian, United States House of Representatives, provided in collecting the photographs for the book.

I am grateful for the support of many valued friends and associates here at the University of Southern Mississippi. My colleague in the history department, Neil McMillen, has been a wonderful source of information and encouragement and lent his expertise to the chapter on the race issue. Orazio Ciccarelli, history department chair, and Kim Nelson, department secretary, were also very helpful. A talented group of graduate students, including Audra Odom, Margery Geddes, Samantha LaDart, Dallas Criss, Chris Joyner, Sheryl Hansen, Karen Cox, and Lucy Gutman, and my friend Laurie Klinedinst, gave some of their valuable time to assist me with the proofreading. Karolyn Thompson, interlibrary loan librarian, was very patient and obliging in meeting my many requests. University support in the form of release time and funding for research was crucial to the undertaking; I am particularly grateful to Karen Yarbrough, Vice-President for Research and Planning; G. David Huffman, Vice-President for Academic Affairs; G. Terry Harper, Dean of Liberal Arts; and President Aubrey K. Lucas. In addition, former Assistant Vice-President for Academic Affairs David J. Bodenhamer (now at Indiana University at Indianapolis) and former Dean of the Honors College Peggy W. Prenshaw (now at Louisiana State University) provided essential support during the early stages of the project.

The editors at Oxford University Press have been a pleasure to work with. I have profited greatly from the talents of Karen Wolney and Gail Cooper; I am grateful to them and also to Sheldon Meyer for their enthusiastic shepherding of this book.

Finally, to my relatives and friends who provided hospitality while I was "on the road" conducting research, I am also very grateful, especially to my sister and brother-in-law Carol Spruill and Jack Nichols of Raleigh, North Carolina; Anne and Nick Read of Cambridge, Massachusetts; Cindy Aron of Richmond, Virginia; Chip and Jennifer Nichols of Washington, D.C.; and Frances Thompson of Paris, Kentucky. I am profoundly grateful to my mother, Edna Whitley Spruill of Washington, North Carolina, for all of her encouragement and assistance. On several occasions she came to Mississippi and helped me manage my busy life and still keep writing when my husband was teaching in England. I am thrilled by her interest in my work and in women's history; she has read this book more times than anyone and often goes with me to conferences on women's history. To my precious children, Scott (eleven) and Jesse (six), I am also thankful. I hope that their obvious pride in their mother for writing a book makes up for all those Saturdays I couldn't go to the park with them and their father; we'll all go now. Most of all I am grateful to my husband, David M. Wheeler, whose loving partnership has made it possible for me to have the things I want most—meaningful and intellectually satisfying work and a full and very happy personal life.

Hattiesburg, Mississippi   M. S. W.

Contents

Introduction

No stronger characters did the long struggle produce than those great-souled Southern suffragists. They had need to be great of soul.

Carrie Chapman Catt and Nettie Rogers Shuler
Woman Suffrage and Politics: The Inner Story of the Suffrage Movement (1923)

The story of the woman suffrage movement in the South and those who led it is intriguing and paradoxical. Southern suffragists sought major revisions in the rights and privileges of women in the region of the United States most devoted to preserving the traditional role of woman. The suffragists proposed a dramatic expansion of the suffrage in a time and place in which the political leaders sought increased restrictions on the electorate. Support for humanitarian reforms of the Progressive era led many Southern women into the suffrage movement while earning the movement powerful enemies among the South's leading industries. As a movement native to the North, with abolitionist roots, the woman suffrage movement was anathema to most Southerners. Yet women of the South's political and social elite stepped forward to lead the movement, and antisuffragists found it expedient to treat them decorously even while denouncing in no uncertain terms the suffrage cause and its Northern leaders. That these Southern women were at once devotees of the South and rebels against it, that they were proud to be both ``Southern Ladies'' and ``New Women,'' adds to the fascination of the story. Furthermore, while demanding an end to discrimination against women, many leading suffragists promoted woman suffrage as a means of preserving white supremacy and systematic discrimination against blacks. And some suffragists proved to be more devoted to preserving state sovereignty than to winning female enfranchisement.

The study of the Southern suffrage movement is not only intrinsically interesting, it is essential to a full understanding of the history of woman suffrage, of American women, of the South, of the Progressive era, and of American reform movements. Nevertheless, the woman suffrage movement in the South has never received the attention it deserves. The first scholars to study the suffrage movement focused on the women's rights movement in the Northeast where it originated, without investigating the significant regional variations in the suffrage campaign. Most Southern historians neglected the suffrage movement, perhaps concluding it was insignificant because it was largely unsuccessful. For many years, A. Elizabeth Taylor labored alone in this field, and her meticulous studies of the suffrage movement in most of the Southern states provide the point of departure for all of us who seek to understand Southern suffrage. Historians Aileen S. Kraditor (in *The Ideas of the Woman Suffrage Movement: 1890 to 1920* [1965]) and Anne Firor Scott (in *The Southern Lady: From Pedestal to Politics, 1830–1930* [1970]) also included chapters about the Southern suffrage movement in their well-known studies when few historians recognized its significance. Each provided important interpretations of the nature of the Southern movement. Professor Scott's account of the politicization of Southern women through voluntary societies remains indispensable to those who would understand the transformation of women in the postwar South and the conversion of some of them to the suffrage cause. Few biographies of individual suffrage leaders exist, but important works on two of the most prominent include Paul E. Fuller's *Laura Clay and the Woman's Rights Movement* (1975) and Kenneth R. Johnson's "Kate Gordon and the Woman Suffrage Movement in the South" in the *Journal of Southern History*, August 1972. There are numerous dissertations, theses, and articles on individual suffragists or on suffrage in various Southern states (see bibliography), and many others currently in progress; few of these studies, however, attempt to understand the movement as a regional phenomenon.

This is precisely what I have attempted in this study of the woman suffrage movement in the South. The primary focus is on the ideas and actions of the movement's most prominent leaders, the women who created and guided the movement and were thus primarily responsible for its tone, tactics, and strategy. Methodologically, I rely heavily on their private papers and published works as well as on the body of scholarship mentioned above. I discuss these women as suffragists but also as reformers, feminists, and political theorists and strategists. As this is a study of the Southern suffrage movement rather than of these individuals, however, the book is organized thematically. The six chapters explain the resistance of the South to the woman suffrage movement; the conversion (despite cultural barriers) of the elite corps of Southern women who assumed leadership of the movement; the ideas of these women concerning the relations between the sexes within the South and the extent of change they desired; the crucial role of the race issue in the woman suffrage movement in the South; the factionalization of the Southern suffrage movement as a result of differences of opinion over states' rights and the federal suffrage amendment; and finally, the suffragists' reaction to being enfranchised ``courtesy of Uncle Sam.''

Despite the widespread opposition in the South to expansion of woman's social role and hostility to the women's rights movement owing to its early association with the antislavery movement, a vigorous and systematic woman suffrage movement emerged in the South in the 1890s. Its aristocratic Southern leaders were committed to social reform in the tradition of *noblesse oblige*, and they were frustrated by their political impotence as they tried to wrest humanitarian reforms from the politicians who dominated the New South. In the area of women's rights, these women were radical for their culture, committed to winning widespread reform of the laws affecting women and children and recognition of women as equal and independent under the law. But despite their indignation at the powerlessness and degradation implicit in their own disfranchised state, many supported and none challenged the movement to restore white political supremacy that occurred simultaneously with the Southern woman suffrage movement.

Indeed, I argue that this Southern woman suffrage movement, with the full support of the National American Woman Suffrage Association, emerged in the 1890s *because* suffragists from both South and North believed the South's ``negro problem'' could be the key to victory for their cause. From the 1890s until approximately 1910, the argument that the enfranchisement of women (with qualifications that would in effect restrict the suffrage to white women) would restore white supremacy without the risks involved in disfranchising blacks was central to the strategy of Southern suffragists.

After 1910, the states' rights issue became all important in the debate over woman suffrage in the South as support for the federal suffrage amendment grew elsewhere in the nation. Southern suffragists tried to sidestep this thorny issue as they pressed for state suffrage amendments, but eventually they had to take a position on the federal amendment. By 1915, differences of opinion over states' rights shattered the internal harmony that had previously characterized the Southern suffrage movement as the National American Woman Suffrage Association, the Southern States Woman Suffrage Conference, and the National Woman's Party competed for the allegiance of

Southern suffragists. States' rights suffragists failed in their attempts to unify Southern women in a regional movement eschewing the leadership of the NAWSA and exploiting the Southern politicians' fear of the proposed Nineteenth Amendment. Before the suffrage struggle ended, the conflict over strategy strained and severed long-standing friendships within the movement and contributed to the problems it faced in the South.

When the Nineteenth Amendment was finally ratified in August 1920, Southern suffragists responded to the victory somewhat differently than their Northern counterparts. The states' rights suffragists, of course, were distraught that their enfranchisement had been won at the expense of state sovereignty. Yet even the Southern suffrage leaders (the majority) who actively supported the federal amendment greeted its success with mixed emotions. They were thrilled that their cause was victorious at last but deeply disappointed at the failure of most Southern states to ratify. Southern suffragists had greatly resented the NAWSA's lack of support after 1915 for state suffrage campaigns in the South. NAWSA president Carrie Chapman Catt was convinced that unsuccessful campaigns in these "hopeless" states would blunt the momentum of the federal amendment. Southern suffragists, however, wanted their states to contribute to the victory. They wanted their states and region to formally acknowledge woman's equality and individuality. To them, enfranchisement through federal "coercion"—as in the case of the Fifteenth Amendment—was a lesser victory indeed.

The eleven women I selected for study include most of the Southern suffragists prominent at the regional and national level: Laura Clay of Kentucky; Kate and Jean Gordon of Louisiana; Belle Kearney and Nellie Nugent Somerville of Mississippi; Rebecca Latimer Felton of Georgia; Madeline McDowell Breckinridge of Kentucky; Mary Johnston and Lila Meade Valentine of Virginia; Pattie Ruffner Jacobs of Alabama; and Sue Shelton White of Tennessee. I made it a point to include women active in each of the peak periods of suffrage activity in the South—the 1890s and the decade between 1910 and 1920; I refer to them as "first generation" and "second generation" suffragists. To facilitate comparison, I selected pioneers of the 1890s who remained active through 1920. I was also careful to include one or more representatives of each of the three major suffrage organizations that operated in the South: the massive, moderate National American Woman Suffrage Association (also called the NAWSA or "the National"); the Southern States Woman Suffrage Conference (the SSWSC or "the Southern Conference") that advocated the enfranchisement of women by state action only; and the relatively radical National Woman's Party (NWP). The eleven women represent seven states, including two of the four Southern states that ratified the Nine-teenth Amendment.

These suffrage leaders were well known to one another; within the group there were many close friends and co-workers who relied heavily on each other for advice on organization and strategy, assisted one another as lecturers and lobbyists, and provided greatly needed moral support for one another as they fought for years against great odds and with so little success. All of this is well documented in the extensive collections of papers and correspondence carefully pre-served by most of these women, their families, and their friends. Laura Clay's papers (at the King Library at the University of Ken-tucky) were of inestimable value in understanding, not only her own role in the movement, but those of all the principal players, Northern and Southern. Conscious of the importance of her work for women's rights, Clay saved her voluminous correspondence with national and Southern suffrage leaders; she also endeared herself to future genera-tions of historians by purchasing a typewriter almost as soon as they were invented, retaining not only the letters she received but carbon copies of her own outgoing letters, and holding on to correspondence marked ``read and destroy.'' The correspondence between Clay and Kate Gordon, extending from 1898 until 1923, was particularly valu-able.

Laura Clay was, of course, foremost among this group of Southern suffrage leaders. The able leader of Kentucky suffragists from 1888 to 1912, and an officer of the NAWSA from 1895 through 1911, Clay played a crucial role in bringing the national suffrage organization into the South and in recruiting and developing leaders indigenous to the region. She was a founding member and vice-president of the SSWSC, established in 1913 at the initiative of her friend Kate Gordon of Louisiana.

Kate Gordon and her sister Jean were the principal leaders of the suffrage movement in Louisiana from the late 1890s through 1920 and avid promoters of the suffrage movement, particularly in the Deep South. Of the Southern suffragists, Kate Gordon was second to Clay in national prominence. She served as NAWSA corresponding secretary from 1900 to 1909 and like Clay was an advocate and self-appointed watchdog for the South on the NAWSA board. Kate Gor-don is best known as the founder and president of the SSWSC, which she used to promote woman suffrage by state action only, and to oppose a federal suffrage movement. Indeed, toward the end of the long suffrage struggle, the Gordons and Clay— all firmly committed to preserving state sovereignty—became notorious among suffragists for working with antisuffragists against the Nineteenth Amendment.

Belle Kearney and Nellie Nugent Somerville of Mississippi were also Southern suffrage pioneers of the 1890s who remained active until the movement's conclusion. Kearney held office in the Mississippi Woman Suffrage Association and briefly in the SSWSC. Her greatest service to the movement in the South, however, was as an orator. A professional lecturer for the Woman's Christian Temperance Union in the 1890s, she promoted suffrage along with temperance, playing an important role in building support for woman suffrage in the South. More gifted as an orator than as an organizer, Kearney failed in her most ambitious effort, an attempt to establish a regional suffrage organization in 1906. But her efforts toward that end led to the reawakening of suffrage activity in Tennessee and Mississippi. Somerville was one of the most outstanding of the presidents of state suffrage organizations; she led the Mississippi Woman Suffrage Association in the 1890s and again after its reorganization in 1906. She was one of Gordon's key supporters in the establishment of the SSWSC and held office in the organization, but she resigned in 1915 to serve a term as an officer in the NAWSA and to help that organization promote the embattled federal suffrage amendment in the South. Despite the fact that Mississippi failed to ratify the Nineteenth Amendment, both Kearney and Somerville were elected to the state legislature in 1923, a testament to their personal prestige in the state.

Rebecca Latimer Felton added considerable prestige and talent to the suffrage cause in Georgia when she declared herself a suffragist shortly after 1900. Well known as the wife of a former congressman, she was also famous in her own right as a columnist for the Atlanta *Journal*. Her sister Mary Latimer McLendon presided over the Georgia suffragists, but Felton was highly visible as a forceful advocate of suffrage before the legislature and the public and was well known throughout the region.

Among the second-generation suffragists of the South, Madeline McDowell Breckinridge of Kentucky was the most prominent. In 1912 she succeeded Clay as president of the Kentucky Equal Rights Association and served as president or legislative chairman until 1920. Breckinridge was a NAWSA vice-president from 1913 to 1915; in this capacity she traveled extensively in the South, putting to use her considerable ability as an orator. A skillful politician, she was largely responsible for Kentucky's ratification of the Nineteenth Amendment in 1920.

Virginians Mary Johnston and Lila Meade Valentine also made tremendous contributions to the suffrage cause in the region. Johnston was quite famous in her day as the author of twenty-three novels, including *To Have and to Hold* (1900), which sold over 500,000 copies and was twice produced as a film. Southern suffragists admired her extravagantly; Johnston was elected honorary vice-president of the Equal Suffrage League of Virginia and honorary vice-president of the SSWSC. She was very valuable to the suffrage movement as an orator and a writer; a contributing editor to the NAWSA organ, the *Woman's Journal*, she was an important source of suffrage literature for the NAWSA as well as for Southern suffragists. Johnston also published *Hagar* (1913), a pro-suffrage novel based largely on her own experiences. Valentine (who served as Equal Suffrage League president from 1909 until 1920) was the principal leader of the Virginia suffragists. An active member of both the SSWSC and the NAWSA, she served the latter as a member of its Congressional Committee in 1916.

Pattie Ruffner Jacobs, president of the Alabama Equal Suffrage Association, founded the Birmingham suffrage organization in 1911, reactivated the state suffrage movement, and rose almost immediately to national prominence. Along with Breckinridge, Jacobs became increasingly important to NAWSA leaders as the states' rights views of Gordon and Clay created a rift between these Southern pioneers and national suffrage leaders. Jacobs served two terms as second auditor of the NAWSA and traveled widely throughout both South and North, promoting the federal suffrage amendment.

Tennessee's Sue Shelton White was the youngest of the prominent leaders of the woman suffrage movement in the South and was one of the minority of Southern suffragists who joined the National Woman's Party. White was an officer in the Tennessee Equal Suffrage Association (a NAWSA affiliate) from 1913 until 1918, when she agreed to chair the Tennessee branch of the Woman's Party. In 1919 she served as editor of the NWP national organ, *The Suffragist*, and was briefly imprisoned for taking part in NWP demonstrations in front of the White House. She won acclaim for her skillful coordination of suffragists of all factions during the successful ratification campaign in Tennessee in 1920. White earned a law degree shortly thereafter and enjoyed a distinguished career as a Democratic Party leader and a government official during the New Deal. But first she played a key role in another chapter of the women's rights movement in America as one of the authors of the Equal Rights Amendment, unveiled by Alice Paul in 1923 at the seventy-fifth anniversary of the 1848 Seneca Falls Convention, where American women had demanded the vote for the first time.

I do *not* claim that these women are typical of all Southern suffragists. Many, if not most, of their followers were middle-class and had neither the "plantation background" nor the extensive travel experience and contacts with Northern (or even British) feminists that influenced most of these leaders. Quite a few of the second-generation suffragists were better educated than these leading suffragists; and their ranks included both professional women and women who came to the South from other regions. Important work by Elizabeth Hayes Turner on the suffragists of Galveston, Texas, suggests that local leaders of whatever class often had political and social perspectives that were narrower, or at least different from, those of the regional leaders.

Finally, this study, while focusing extensively on race, does not tell the story of the African-American women of the South who supported woman suffrage. As described in the works of Rosalyn Terborg-Penn, Cynthia Neverdon-Morton, Adele Logan Alexander, and Glenda Gilmore (see bibliography), the educated black women who worked to improve conditions for their race through women's clubs recognized the need for the vote as a means of gaining justice for themselves and all African-Americans and promoted woman suffrage through the National Association of Colored Women's Clubs and other organizations. Transplanted Southerners including Ida Wells-Barnett and Mary Church Terrell actively promoted suffrage in the North; and, despite obstacles far more formidable than those faced by these elite white women, a few black women living in the South, including Margaret Murray Washington and Adella Hunt Logan of Tuskegee, were prominent suffragists. But these women were discriminated against by white suffragists of the North, who feared their participation would alienate potential support among white Southerners; and they were completely excluded from suffrage organizations in the South by white women who were either opposed to black suffrage or (at best) feared the participation of African-American women would totally discredit their cause in the minds of most Southern whites.

I *do* claim that these eleven women are representative of, and largely embody, the leadership of the mainstream, white Southern suffrage movement and that understanding them and their ideas and actions is crucial to understanding the Southern woman suffrage movement and the national woman suffrage movement as well.

I hope that the study adds to our understanding or sheds new light on a number of important subjects, including: the intransigence of Southern politicians on the suffrage issue; the crucial role of the South in the national movement; the personal relationships and lines of influence within the leadership of the Southern suffrage movement; the motives of these Southern women in becoming suffragists, in particular their low opinion of the current management of the New South; and the suffragists' extreme disillusionment with certain aspects of the traditional roles of men and women in the South. I document and attempt to explain the range of opinions within this group of Southern leaders on many subjects, but especially race and states' rights. I emphasize that the relationship between the Northern and

Southern leaders was one of mutual influence and that the Northern suffragists did not just *permit*, but encouraged and hoped to profit from, exploitation of the race issue in the South. The differences between "first-generation" and "second-generation" suffragists receive considerable attention, as do the important differences between the two peak periods of suffrage activity in the South. Most significant, perhaps, is a new theory concerning the role of the race issue in the suffrage movement that I believe explains the timing of the suffrage movement: why it emerged in the 1890s and why it was largely dormant between roughly 1900 and 1910.

New Women
of the New South

1

The Southern Lady: Hostage to "the Lost Cause"

May our Southern women remain on the pedestal, forever preserve that distinctive deference which is theirs so long as they remain as they are— our highest ideals of the true, the beautiful and the good. . . . Deference to its womankind has always been a distinguished characteristic of the Southern people. Southern men would perpetuate it. But foreign forces have invaded us, established branches over the South of a huge National Woman's Association whose ideals are not our ideals; whose women are not like our Southern women. They are women of a different clay, and are of different mould. Should these foreign crusaders succeed, pervert the tastes of our women, persuade them to abandon their old ideals and descend into the arena of politics . . . woe is the day for Southern civilization.

> James Callaway, Editor
> Macon (Georgia) *Telegraph*
> Antisuffrage pamphlet, 1919[1]

The women who are working for this measure [a state woman suffrage amendment] are striking at the principles for which their fathers fought during the Civil War. Woman's suffrage comes from the North and West and from women who do not believe in states' rights and who wish to see negro women using the ballot. I do not believe the state of Georgia has sunk so low that her good men can not legislate for the women. If this time ever comes then it will be time for women to claim the ballot.

> Mildred Rutherford, President
> Georgia Chapter, United Daughters
>   of the Confederacy
> Testimony to the Legislature, 1914[2]

The North was the birthplace of the woman suffrage movement and the home of most of its national leaders; the West furnished the movement its first crucial victories, eventually giving suffragists enough leverage in national politics to make an effective bid for a federal woman suffrage amendment; but the South was distinctive—indeed notorious—in the annals of the woman suffrage movement as the region that afforded the movement the greatest resistance and the least success.[3]

Southern hostility to the suffrage movement long prevented it from gaining a foothold in the region and frustrated Southern suffragists in their efforts to become enfranchised through state or federal action. Prior to the ratification of the Nineteenth Amendment in 1920, Southern women gained full enfranchisement in no Southern state and partial suffrage in only four. Southern politicians managed to block passage of the federal suffrage amendment in Congress for many years, and once it was submitted to the states made a concerted effort to prevent ratification—despite the pleas of regional favorite son President Woodrow Wilson to support the amendment for the sake of the national Democratic Party. Of the ten states that failed to ratify, nine were south of the Mason-Dixon line.[4]

The unyielding opposition of the majority of Southerners to the woman suffrage movement resulted from several interrelated cultural, economic, and political factors. The woman suffrage movement in the South took place in a period (1890 to 1920) in which many white Southerners were passionately devoted to the preservation of a distinct and, they believed, superior "Southern Civilization." A key element of this Southern civilization was a dualistic conception of the natures and responsibilities of the sexes that precluded the participation of women in politics and cast "the Southern Lady" in the role of guardian and symbol of Southern virtue. Charged with transmitting Southern culture to future generations, Southern white womanhood had a vital role to play in preserving the values of "the Lost Cause." That representatives of the burgeoning industry of the New South and particularly the textile industry wished Southern women to confine their beneficent influence to the home rather than vote for child labor legislation and other encumbrances was an additional and potent obstacle to the success of woman suffrage in the South.[5]

The so-called cornerstone of this "Southern Civilization" was white supremacy, and the determination of white Southerners to restore and then preserve it—and defend the "state sovereignty" thought necessary to protect white supremacy—also presented a tremendous obstacle to the Southern suffrage movement. Most white Southerners were contemptuous of the women's rights movement as yet one more unfortunate product of an inferior Northern culture, an offshoot of abolitionism led by women with the same "naïve" and dangerous belief in the equality of the sexes and disregard for vital social distinctions that characterized the abolitionists. Opponents of woman suffrage in the South considered the national woman suffrage movement, with its commitment to securing a federal woman suffrage amendment, one with the proponents of the Fourteenth and Fifteenth Amendments in their disdain for the sovereignty of the states and their eagerness to force change upon an unwilling South.[6]

Even after President Wilson became convinced that woman suffrage was inevitable and that the Democrats must not allow the Republicans to claim credit for the victory, he could not persuade most Southern congressmen or state legislators to support woman suffrage. Surrender of principle in anticipation of defeat was not an acceptable alternative to these children of the Confederacy who had grown up amidst tales of the heroic sacrifices of their ancestors.[7]

I

The commitment to preserving the traditional role of Southern womanhood was not just an isolated, idiosyncratic whim of nostalgic Southerners; it was part of an intense, conscious, quasi-religious drive to protect the South against the "ravages" of Northern culture during a period of massive and often unwelcome political, social, and economic change. Cultural leaders within the postwar South were committed to the preservation of the superior civilization for which they claimed to have fought the war. From Reconstruction well into the twentieth century, most white Southerners spoke of "the War" as a contest between a paternalistic, harmonious, homogeneous, and God-fearing South and a materialistic, competitive, heterogeneous, and atheistic North. As they struggled to cope with an increasingly competitive and individualistic society, they remembered "the War" as the height of Southern virtue, a period in which Southerners made undreamed-of sacrifices in defense of a just society.[8]

Reconstruction seemed to many a realization of their worst fears of chaos: "natural leaders" were disfranchised and Negroes out of control. Many feared that in defeat and despair white Southerners might become vulnerable to "foreign" influences from the North—as one Georgia minister put it, that "the victory over Southern arms is to be followed by a victory over Southern opinions." Southern leaders urged their constituents to consecrate themselves anew to preserving the values of "the Lost Cause." And Southerners responded to this call with such devotion and intensity that historian Charles Reagan Wilson speaks of the "postwar attitude" known as the Lost Cause as "a Southern civil religion."[9]

Through Lost Cause rituals and institutions, white Southern men and women tried to keep the memories of martyrdom alive and fortify themselves against erosion of values. Robert E. Lee, Jefferson Davis, Stonewall Jackson, and other leaders were virtually canonized as symbols of Christian and Southern values. Building monuments to them became an obsession, which peaked between 1890 and 1910; in 1907 a crowd of 200,000 gathered in Richmond for the unveiling of a statue of Davis as 12,000 Confederate veterans paraded down Monument Avenue. Organizations including the United Confederate Veterans and the United Daughters of the Confederacy were formed to insure remembrance of the "sacred principles" of the war. School textbooks, carefully monitored by the UDC and others, taught the "correct" version of the events of the war and Reconstruction, including that the South had a constitutional right to secede and that the war was fought to defend states' rights rather than slavery. Southern colleges stressed Southern and Christian values in their curricula; the University of the South (Sewanee, Tennessee), for example, required its students to drill in Confederate-gray uniforms until 1892. Universities were generally intolerant of any objective examination of the region's past by their faculty.[10]

Ministers joined lay leaders in assuring Southerners that the Northern victory was the result of the prosperity rather than the rectitude of the North, and explained the defeat and suffering of the South as a form of discipline from God, strengthening Southerners for the future. By the turn of the century, when some degree of sectional reconciliation had been effected (aided by Southern participation in the Spanish-American War), an additional theme appeared in the "theology" of the Lost Cause, that defeat had been necessary to keep the conservative, Anglo-Saxon influence of the South in the nation, as "the Lord could not trust the North to fulfill his great purposes on this continent without the aid of the Southern people." Indeed, the vogue enjoyed in the North by the plantation novels of Thomas Nelson Page and the Uncle Remus stories of Joel Chandler Harris in the 1880s suggests that the South had more influence on Northern culture in the late nineteenth century than the reverse. Page (to whom the famous saying that "even the moonlight was richer and mellower before the war" can be traced) and Harris painted such an attractive picture of an elegant and aristocratic society that reverence for antebellum Southern society became rampant in the North, where the reform impulse was rapidly fading.[11]

In this allegedly superior antebellum society and in the postwar South, the ideal Southern Lady had more than her famous ornamental role to play. Serene and compassionate, she cared for the health and welfare of her family, servants, and others in the community who needed her beneficence. But she played an even more important role as preserver of religion and morality, inspiration to her husband, and the conduit of Southern values to future generations of Southern statesmen. Convinced of her own (physical) weakness and the threat to her innocence if she ventured beyond home and hearth, the ideal Southern woman relied upon chivalrous Southern men to represent her interests in the outside world. And cognizant of her temperamental inability to deal with the harsh realities of business and government, she was grateful to men for sparing her these onerous duties. In reality, the elite Southern white woman had few alternatives to a domestic, subordinate role, since law as well as custom made it difficult for her to engage in business, and she was largely excluded from higher education and the professions, as well as politics. But she was taught not to question her "divinely appointed role" or to challenge the wisdom and authority of Southern males. Meanwhile, her "indirect influence" was constantly acknowledged as the source of the superior morality of Southern society.[12]

As Northern women's rights advocates resumed activity in the 1870s, Southern conservatives insisted that Southern white women continue to play this traditional role deemed so essential to the South's superior civilization. Indeed, in the postwar South, adherence to this ideal, which was originally associated strictly with upper-class women, was increasingly expected of all Southern white women who wished to be considered "respectable." Southern conservatives boasted of the traditional values and exemplary conduct of Southern women in comparison to those of the North. Indeed, as historian Gaines M. Foster writes, the support of white Southern women for their men during the war and in its grim aftermath, and their subsequent "failure to challenge the patriarchy," were accepted gratefully by the former Confederates and helped "ease their anxieties about their manhood" in the wake of their humiliating defeat on the field of battle. At their annual reunions, the United Confederate Veterans quite literally placed women on pedestals (in the role of "sponsors," young, socially prominent virgins representing each state) and eulogized the women of the South, who—long after the battles ended—remained as loyal and obedient and willing to sacrifice as ever, and who trusted their men to protect them.[13]

One of the most influential Lost Cause ministers, and founder of the *Southern Review*, Albert Bledsoe, proclaimed in his 1871 "Mission of Woman" that Southern women "still so live, and so act, in their own hallowed sphere, that they are sacred in our eyes, and an inspiration in our hearts." Bledsoe and other celebrants of Southern womanhood spoke with fear of the growing number of Northern women who, he said, despised the word of God and trampled underfoot the laws of nature as they eschewed their true mission. Like the prewar defenders of separate spheres for men and women, he insisted that woman's "frailer form, more delicate organs, timid nature . . . [and] the ease with which the balance of her judgement is disturbed by the impulses of kindness or cruelty (to enemies)," make her unsuited to the work of man, though in her "courage to endure" and "Christ-like capacity to suffer and to bear . . . she is more like the Lamb of God— a willing sacrifice for the good of man . . . well adapted to the sphere of private life, and, above all, to the home circle . . . her high and holy sphere."[14]

Referring to the formation in 1869 of the National Woman Suffrage Association and the American Woman Suffrage Association, Bledsoe challenged the women of the South to continue to shun the fruit offered by the women's rights movement and to remember the true source of woman's "glory":

> Be this your glory, then O ye blessed and beautiful women of the South!—not that you can vote, or beat a negro for Congress, but that you can point to your sons as *your* jewels. . . . Be this your glory, not that you can equal man in the might and the majesty of his intellectual dominion, but that you can surpass him in the sublime mission of mercy to a fallen world. Be this your glory, not that you can harangue a mob, or thunder in the Senate, but that you can wear "the ornament of a meek and quiet spirit, which, in the sight of God, is of great price. . . ." Be this your glory, in short, not that you can imitate a Washington, or a Lee, or a Jackson, but that you can rear, and train, and educate, and mould the future Washingtons, and Lees, and Jacksons of the South, to protect and preserve the sacred rights of woman as well as of man.[15]

Even the foremost advocates for change in the postwar South, spokesmen for the so-called New South Creed such as Louisville *Courier* editor Henry Watterson or Atlanta *Constitution* editor Henry Grady, were devoted to the preservation of the Southern Lady in her traditional role. These harbingers of an opulent, industrialized South frequently berated the region for its hostility to change (in the words of Walter Hines Page, for becoming intellectually "pickled" at about 1830). The New South boosters, however, under fire from critics wanting to preserve a traditional, pastoral Southern society and accusing them and Southern industrialists of mammonism and capitulation to Northern values, were eager to demonstrate their devotion to preserving Southern culture—even while transforming its economy. These men, says historian Paul Gaston, understood "that no program of reform could do violence to a universally cherished past and hope to succeed."[16]

Watterson and his associates thus rivaled Lost Cause ministers like Bledsoe in their adulation of the Southern Lady and her influence on Southern society. From 1881, when a woman suffrage convention strayed as far south as Louisville, until his retirement in 1919, "Marse Henry" Watterson opposed the coming of feminism with all of his editorial might. The woman suffrage movement, said Watterson, threatened "not only government and politics, but the whole human species." "Woman," he said, is "the moral light of the universe—man's only anchor to windward." The battle for woman (and against feminism) he considered to be his "supreme duty."[17]

Admirers of the traditional Southern Lady did not wish to recognize it, but in reality the Civil War and its aftermath had a profound impact on Southern white women; the war and Reconstruction initiated a series of social and economic changes that gradually altered Southern gender relations. From the vantage point of 1900, Mississippi suffragist and Woman's Christian Temperance Union organizer Belle Kearney observed that the expansion in the activities of Southern white women, from working for wages to seeking political equality, were all "the result of the evolution of events which was set in motion by the bombardment of Fort Sumter." During the Civil War, Southern white women were called upon to perform many tasks normally fulfilled by men, including meeting the needs of soldiers through soldiers' aid societies, managing plantations, mills, and stores in the absence of men, and in many instances "refugeeing" whole families—finding food and clothing for them when there was little to be found. After the war, Southern women rebuilt or aided husbands in rebuilding plantations, and often taught school or took in sewing to generate badly needed income. Many women had to support themselves or their families alone. Of the million men who served in the Confederate Army, at least one-fourth died in battle or of disease, and many more were incapacitated and unable to support their families.[18]

The shortage of men and the desperate plight of women and children in the immediate postwar period resulted in women's entering occupations previously held only by men. With the establishment of a public school system, the increased demand for teachers provided opportunities for paid employment and led to new educational opportunities for women of the South in the new normal schools created to train them. Many women who attended the normal schools then moved on to enroll in liberal arts colleges in the North, or one of the handful of such colleges opening in the South (such as Sophie Newcomb or Agnes Scott), or studied in one of the Southern universities that did not bar women. As conditions improved, Southern women with the leisure to do so became increasingly involved in voluntary associations, first in church and missionary societies (beginning in the 1870s), then in the Woman's Christian Temperance Union and women's clubs (1880s). Through employment or involvement in these organizations, Southern women gained new knowledge of conditions beyond the home and a new level of interest and involvement in public affairs.[19]

Many Southern men and women found these changes in the activities of women profoundly disturbing; but rather than revising their assessment of woman's role, they ignored, denied, or resisted new developments. They regarded the expansion of woman's role as another unfortunate consequence of the war and expected women to return to their traditional sphere as soon as possible. The taboo against women's working outside the home for wages lost some of its strength but never disappeared. Many Southern conservatives considered higher education for women unnecessary or downright dangerous. Women's clubs, even missionary societies, were regarded with suspicion by those who feared that the clubs might lead women to neglect their domestic duties or disdain their traditional role. Moreover, many of the men dedicated to economic development in the region feared that women would follow their moral and benevolent impulses to promote "unreasonable" and unwelcome reforms that would interfere with industrial development in the New South.

Religious leaders wanted women's aid in bringing the men in their lives to God and their assistance with the charitable enterprises of the church. But they were uneasy about the increased involvement of women in activities that took them beyond the home or the church basement, and feared that women would (as they soon did) demand greater authority in the church itself. Thus Southern ministers generally tried to turn back the tide of the increased assertiveness and independence of their female communicants. In 1893, the Southern Presbyterian Church issued a decree that "the session must absolutely enforce the injunction of Scripture forbidding women to speak in churches, or in any way failing to observe that relative subordination to men that is taught in I Corinthians 11:13 and other places." Women of the Methodist Episcopal Church, South, built and operated for twenty years effective foreign and home missionary societies largely independent of male control, only to have the church "fathers" move to place these organizations under an all-male board without even consulting the women. Individual ministers also used their considerable influence against the expansion of woman's role; a prime example was Bishop Warren Candler of Georgia, who opposed, and urged the Methodist ministers under him to oppose, a variety of developments, including WCTU women's speaking in public and getting involved in politics; the movement for laity rights within the Methodist Episcopal Church, South; and woman suffrage—which he denounced as against "both Reason and Revelation—a revolt against both Nature and God."[20]

Advocates of certain industries were also uneasy about the increased activism of Southern women and equally anxious to "protect" Southern woman's traditional role. During the Progressive era, which in most parts of the South began around 1900, the widespread assumption that women would be influenced by their natural affinity for religion and humanitarianism to support such reforms as prohibition, restriction of child labor, compulsory education, regulation of working conditions in industry, and abolition of the convict lease system made enemies as well as friends for the suffrage movement. Indeed, the determined opposition to woman suffrage of the leaders of the liquor and cotton textile industries made it clear that in some quarters the "direct influence" of enfranchised women was considered far more powerful and threatening than the celebrated "indirect influence" of the Southern Lady. If indeed the brewers and the cotton men admired woman's moral influence, they clearly wished to limit it to the domestic sphere, where woman would remain ignorant of wrongdoing—or at least powerless to correct it.[21]

Despite the fact that prohibition was "the most dynamic and passionately supported reform" in the South during the Progressive era, the assumption that enfranchised womanhood would support the curtailment of alcohol was of limited value to the Southern suffrage cause. For example, in Texas the prohibition forces gave the state's suffragists their most important allies; but the "Wets," led by Governor James E. Ferguson, became very formidable opponents. Records subpoenaed during an antitrust suit and published in 1916 by the Anti-Saloon League revealed that Texas breweries raised millions for fighting prohibition in their state through an assessment of sixty cents per barrel sold; a 1915 exposé in the *New Republic* provided evidence that the brewing industry distributed antisuffrage and anti-prohibition propaganda to newspapers all over the state through a publicity bureau called the "Texas Business Men's Association." Furthermore, the very breadth of the support for prohibition in the South meant that the association between the two reforms was less automatic than in other sections of the country: there were many Southern supporters of prohibition who did not support woman suffrage. Many WCTU members feared that association with the unpopular suffrage movement would undermine their own cause in the public mind. Furthermore, male prohibitionists were quite often conservative, antifeminist clerics, like the leading "Dry" of Virginia, Bishop James Cannon, Jr., who would not speak a civil word to the suffragists. On balance, the association between the two reforms probably did the suffrage cause more harm than good. The liquor industry, distressed by sentiment in favor of temperance and prohibition aroused by the WCTU, used their full resources to fight the enfranchisement of women. And particularly in large Southern cities such as New Orleans, Memphis, Nashville, and Louisville; in the state of Kentucky, famous for its breweries; and in heavily Catholic Louisiana, where Southern prohibitionism was weakest, the formidable influence of the brewers and distributors—and widespread public sentiment against prohibition—proved costly for woman suffrage.[22]

Similarly, the South's "cotton men" were very worried about the growing concern of organized Southern women for the plight of women and children in Southern industries and fearful that enfranchised womanhood would constitute a powerful base of support for reforms that as yet lacked widespread backing in the region. Most Southern Progressives were social conservatives who had only slowly come around to the view that private enterprises, such as railroads and Northern-based insurance companies, must be regulated by the government. Primarily middle- or upper-class in background and orientation, they seemed most concerned with their own protection, and were somewhat resistant to the idea that the lower classes needed substantial government intervention to protect them from Southern industrialists. According to one frustrated agent of the National Child Labor Committee in 1914, most Southern reformers showed some "disposition to cry out against the bad rich," but believed such people "lived next to Wall Street, and certainly north of the Mason-Dixon line." "To appoint an inspector to look into conditions in our mill villages" was considered to be "a reflection upon the word and character of good men."[23]

A minority of Southern Progressives, however, the "social justice" wing of the movement, actively supported humanitarian reforms such as child labor legislation, compulsory education, and regulation of working conditions; and of these "social justice Progressives," many were women. Thus Southern male Progressives who favored these reforms welcomed the increased social activism of women, and were eager for women to play an ever larger role in public affairs. Dr. Alexander McKelway of the National Child Labor Committee, and the leading North Carolina Progressive, Chief Supreme Court Justice Walter Clark, were among the strongest supporters of woman suffrage. At one time McKelway was actually employed by the National American Woman Suffrage Association.[24]

The Southern textile industry, which underwent a remarkable expansion beginning around 1890, was the jewel in the crown of the New South, one of the few Southern industries that seemed to be overtaking its Northern competitors. Promoters of the industry were well aware that cheap labor, particularly that of women and children, gave the South's burgeoning cotton textile mills their competitive edge. As the threat of woman suffrage materialized, therefore, these men became increasingly active in attempts to block female enfranchisement and prevent women from gaining the power to interfere with their exploitation of women and children. McKelway was regarded by the textile industry as a traitor to the region, turning public opinion against this so-called savior of the Southern economy—possibly at the behest of Northern manufacturers—and working against Southern interests in more ways than one.[25]

The cotton textile industry could hardly come out openly in favor of the exploitation of children or, for that matter, against the use of woman's moral authority in society. Spokesmen for the industry such as David Clark, editor of the *Southern Textile Bulletin*, tried to promote an image of cotton manufacturers as paternalistically protecting the interests of their employees, making protective legislation (and labor unions) unnecessary. In 1917, Clark, worried that "McKelway and his crowd have filled them [women's club members] full of stories of terrible conditions in our mills," began issuing special Welfare Editions of the *Bulletin* each December for the attention of the women's clubs, designed to pacify female critics by demonstrating the manufacturers' concern for the health and welfare of the operatives. According to McKelway, the cotton men pretended to favor child labor regulation and compulsory education "until the legislature meets."[26]

The textile industry was equally circumspect in its opposition to woman suffrage; indeed, Southern suffragists and national suffrage leaders were convinced that the textile industry, like the liquor industry, was among the leading corporate opponents of their movement and that the two were largely responsible for bankrolling the antisuffrage movement in the South. Damning testimony to that effect came from Walter Clark, none other than the father of editor David Clark. In a letter chastizing the well-known "Wet" Henry Watterson for opposing woman suffrage, Chief Justice Clark accused the "Whisky Interest" of being in league with the cotton men to finance the "real opposition" to woman suffrage.[27]

Unable to assail women openly for using moral influence in society, the threatened industries made their contributions to third parties—whether lobbyists or politicians—who spoke out against woman suffrage, emphasizing the harm that female enfranchisement would do to women and society rather than the harm that female enfranchisement would do to their industries. Casting himself in the role of defender of Southern womanhood, Watterson vigorously opposed "the dragging of women into the mire of politics; the diversion, if not the pollution of domestic interests; the coarsening . . . of the female character and fibre." "I would keep our women ignorant of dirt," he editorialized. "I would preserve in her the child unto the end."[28]

II

The campaign to restore and preserve white supremacy was a second aspect of the reactionary agenda of turn-of-the-century Southern whites. Like the effort to preserve the traditional role of woman, this movement had a profound impact on the woman suffrage movement in the South, delaying its development and impeding its progress.

Unlike the woman suffrage movement in the North, which commenced in 1848 in an era of widespread regional support for universal manhood suffrage, the woman suffrage movement in the South began in the 1890s during a region-wide movement to contract the electorate and limit the vote to the "better classes" of whites. After Reconstruction, upper-class Southern whites gradually regained control of Southern politics, at first by driving African-Americans from politics through violence or intimidation, manipulating election results, or paying blacks for their votes—blacks who would not have been allowed to vote otherwise. Yet upper-class whites found even these methods insufficient, as African-Americans and poor whites sometimes united against affluent whites, forcing the latter to accept black office-holders, judges, and juries; the whites also professed a distaste for "having to" stoop to violence and fraud. Furthermore, upper-class Southern whites were constantly in fear of new federal legislation requiring supervision of elections, a fear that nearly materialized in 1890 in the form of the famous (or infamous) "Lodge Elections Bill"—called by Southerners "the Force Bill."[29]

Thus upper-class Southern whites who led the Democratic Party were constantly searching for a means to restrict legally the votes of blacks. And owing to the agrarian revolt of the late 1880s and 1890s, they also sought to disfranchise as many lower-class whites as possible. Between the 1890 Mississippi Constitutional Convention—which established the much-emulated "Mississippi Plan," featuring poll taxes, residency requirements, and the "understanding clause" (allowing illiterates to register if they could prove to the registrar they understood the Constitution)—and the year 1903, every Southern state adopted legislation restricting the suffrage through legislation, dramatic disfranchising conventions, or both. Democrats employed a combination of chicanery and rhetoric to secure the support of poor whites for laws that disfranchised many of them along with blacks, though it was sometimes necessary to establish escape clauses such as the "understanding clause" or the "grandfather clause" that at least in theory would permit illiterate whites to circumvent the new restrictions. Democratic leaders countered Populist economic appeals with the warning that whites must band together within the party rather than divide and give blacks the balance of power. Thus the Democratic Party became firmly established as the "white man's party," and opponents were branded as "dangerous and insidious foes of white supremacy," "a grave menace to our civilization."[30]

The disfranchisers were highly successful in eliminating opposition to the Democratic Party. And the establishment of Democratic hegemony had a stultifying effect on Southern politics. Certainly it had profound consequences for woman suffrage: the salutary effect of two-party competition that so aided the progress of woman suffrage elsewhere in the nation could help the Southern suffrage movement only in a very few Southern states, such as Kentucky and Tennessee.[31]

The work of J. Morgan Kousser makes it clear that the Democratic leaders' goal was to re-create in the New South the paternalistic, oligarchical society of the Old South, which (in their memories) had been free of class conflict and racial tensions, a society in which the "best classes" of citizens ruled wisely for the sake of those incapable of understanding their true interests. For example, Ernest Kruttschnitt, President of the Louisiana Constitutional Convention of 1898 and nephew of Confederate Secretary of State Judah P. Benjamin, told the convention delegates:

> My fellow delegates, let us not be misunderstood! Let us say to the large class of the people of Louisiana who will be disfranchised under any of the proposed limitations of the suffrage, that what we seek to do is undertaken in a spirit, not of hostility to any particular men or set of men, but in the belief that the State should see to the protection of the weaker classes; should guard them against the machinations of those who would use them only to further their own base ends; should see to it that they are not allowed to harm themselves. We owe it to the ignorant, we owe it to the weak, to protect them just as we would protect a child and prevent it from injuring itself with sharp-edged tools placed in its hands.[32]

Kruttschnitt also predicted that the new constitution would "establish the relations between the races upon an everlasting foundation of right and justice." And the "best sort" of Negro was counted on to agree with Booker T. Washington, author of the famous "Atlanta Compromise" speech of 1895, who said that at least for the present, black Southerners should give up insistence on political rights, accepting property and educational restrictions upon the franchise as necessary. Blacks, said Washington, should concentrate on self improvement and economic development, counting on the support of upper-class white Southerners as they worked toward that end.[33]

The avowedly paternalistic disfranchisers generally did not live up to their promise of looking out for the interests of "the weaker classes," black or white. For example, the Alabama Constitutional Convention of 1901, led by Judge Thomas Coleman, ex-slaveholder, Princeton graduate, Confederate officer, justice of the Alabama Supreme Court, and banker; and by John B. Knox, possibly the state's richest railroad lawyer; was hostile to all proposals for social reform. These included efforts to strengthen the railroad commission, regulate various types of corporate activity, and abolish child labor and the convict lease system. The delegates also severely curtailed the government's ability to provide social services by cutting the maximum state tax rate. And even during the "educational awakening" of the New South, state policies led to improvement of schools for whites in urban areas and the Black Belt, while schools for blacks and hill-country whites deteriorated or lost ground compared with schools in wealthier counties. Progressivism in the South was not only "Progressivism for Whites Only," it was all too often Progressivism for upper-class whites only.[34]

Having disfranchised many illiterate whites and nearly all blacks and gained control of Southern politics, the Democrats remained anxious and watchful about the newly established political order. They were fearful of renewed federal efforts to protect black suffrage, a threat that failed to materialize owing to two factors: after 1894 the GOP no longer needed the votes of Southern Republicans in order to dominate national politics; and the growing xenophobia in the North in the wake of large waves of immigration from southern and eastern Europe made continued advocacy of black suffrage unpopular among Northern voters. Indeed, Northern voters in both political parties were increasingly sympathetic with white Southerners in regard to the "negro problem," and there was increased support for qualified suffrage in all parts of the nation. Southern politicians, however, continued to fear that the Supreme Court would question their disfranchising legislation, or that some unfortunate political development—such as success of the woman suffrage movement, with its demand for another federal suffrage amendment—would lead to a renewed demand for black suffrage.[35]

From the beginning of the women's rights movement in the antebellum period, white Southerners regarded it as threatening, not only to the relationship between men and women, but to the South's paternalistic, hierarchical social structure and to white supremacy. They were well aware that the women's movement was an offshoot of the despised abolitionist movement, which condemned the slave-based Southern society as immoral and labored for its destruction. Thus, even before the war, white Southerners came to think of the two movements as symbiotic and inseparable.

In the *Southern Quarterly Review*, *Debow's Review*, the *Southern Literary Messenger*, and other Southern periodicals of the 1840s and 1850s, there was a tremendous outpouring of articles and reviews attacking feminism along with abolitionism. Referring to feminists as "unsexed females," "female fanatics," and "men-women," Southern writers laid out their theories of the differences between the sexes and the necessity of women's remaining in the home and subordinate to their husbands. The Southern critics of feminism were particularly outraged that Northern feminists and abolitionists compared woman's status to that of the slave: her enforced dependence, her limited opportunities for education, the suppression of her power to dissent. Worse still, the Northern heretics even dared to urge Southern ladies to use their moral influence against slavery![36]

But defenders of Southern society generally accepted their adversaries' premise that the real issue in the controversy over the rights of blacks and women was the legitimacy of (in the words of a well-known apologist for slavery, George Fitzhugh) "a social status or condition in which the will of the superior stands for law to the inferior." Repeatedly, defenders of Southern society claimed that Northern reformers were out to destroy the family, that they threatened the patriarchical, hierarchical society of the South—and warned that one could not remove male authority over women without endangering the entire system. If the "Northern fanatics" had their way, they warned, the well-ordered Southern society would be destroyed; the family would be replaced by free love; "white integrity" would give way to amalgamation; and the Southland would fall victim to anarchy, rape, and pillage.[37]

In the postwar South, most white Southerners continued to regard the women's rights movement as an enemy of Southern culture, and the continued association in the minds of white Southerners between feminism and abolitionism made the woman suffrage movement anathema to many white Southerners. The association of the feminist movement with advocacy of the rights of blacks was strengthened when the first women's rights organizations of the postwar South were formed by "carpetbaggers" and "scalawags" in Virginia (1870) and carpetbaggers and the wives of black politicians in South Carolina (1870). And in 1878, even as white Southerners struggled against the results of the Fourteenth and Fifteenth Amendments, Northern feminists demanded a Sixteenth Amendment providing for woman suffrage.[38]

In the 1887 congressional debate over the proposed federal woman suffrage amendment (this was the first time the bill reached the floor, and was to be the last time until 1914), Southern Democrats pleaded with their Northern colleagues to remember that the South was already straining under the yoke of black male suffrage; the enfranchisement of "colored women . . . who are as much more ignorant than the colored men as it is possible to imagine" would further compound the "suffering" of the South. Senator John T. Morgan of Alabama insisted, as many others would after him, that "the ladies of the land" would remain in their "home circles" while the "ruder of the sex" would "fight their way to the polls through Negroes and others who are not the best of company even at the polls, to say nothing of the disgrace of association with them."[39]

Southern Democrats feared woman suffrage would complicate their drive to restore white supremacy partly because they believed it would be more difficult to exclude black women than black men from the polls. Senator John Sharp Williams of Mississippi—who was at least slightly sympathetic to the desire of elite white Southern women for the vote—claimed that Southern white men would be reluctant to use against black women the violence that they regularly employed against black men; "we are not afraid to maul a black man over the head if he dares to vote, but we can't treat women that way. No we'll allow no woman suffrage. It may be right, but we won't have it."[40]

Carrie Chapman Catt, later the successful President of the National American Woman Suffrage Association, recalled that in the late nineteenth century, "Senators from the seceding states would rather have committed hari kari than vote for any federal suffrage amendment, and border states were little less pronounced in their vindictive denunciation of suffrage by the federal amendment." She blamed Southern Democrats (and the Republicans who continuously assigned the chairmanship of the woman suffrage committee to Southern Democrats, knowing what they would do with the amendment) for the decades of congressional inaction on the bill.[41]

As the movement to disfranchise blacks legally was underway in the 1890s, a few Southern politicians favored the suggestion put forward by suffragists (see Chapter Four), that they solve "the negro problem" through woman suffrage. Assuming that either educational or property qualifications would be included in any woman suffrage bill, only white women would be enfranchised and the black vote could be overwhelmed without resorting to disfranchisement of voters and running the risk of congressional censure. Like a South Carolina politician who spoke against this idea, however, most of the disfranchisers preferred to "get out the shotguns and stand by the polls" rather than "use fair and lovely womanhood" to preserve white supremacy.[42]

Woman had a vital role to play in the restoration of white and Democratic supremacy in the South, but as a *muse*, not a direct participant. In seeking the support of the masses of white voters for the very legislation that would disfranchise many of them along with blacks, the disfranchisers manipulated voters by juxtaposing images of white womanhood with those of black men who allegedly threatened them. Charles Brantley Aycock of North Carolina, leader of the white supremacy campaign of 1898, campaigned successfully for governor in 1900 eulogizing the pure Anglo-Saxon heritage of his constituents, describing blacks (whose fusion with white Republicans had successfully challenged Democratic control) as rapacious "human fiends" and appealing for their disfranchisement in the name of "the White Goddess of Democracy—the White Womanhood of the State." According to one contemporary newspaper:

> In town after town, Aycock was met by huge processions with brass bands, floats of pretty girls dressed in white to symbolize the purity of white women, contingents of mounted Red Shirts, and occasionally as a special feature, the rapid-fire gun purchased in 1898 by anti-Fusion forces in Wilmington. At Roxboro, he appeared on a float surrounded by a bevy of Person County's most beautiful daughters, inscribed in large letters on each side of the float were the words, Protect Us.[43]

The white woman of the South could not be the savior of white political supremacy; she was the *reason* for it. The Southern Lady was a potent political symbol. And the more her purity and virtue were celebrated, the more fraud and violence could be justified in her name.

Once disfranchisement had been accomplished, suffrage proponents saw no reason why the race issue should further complicate the woman suffrage question; presumably the same laws that disfranchised black men would disfranchise black women. Suffragists often spoke of the "negro bogey" and its use by Southern politicians to conceal other reasons for opposition to the enfranchisement of women. No doubt this accusation was often warranted. As suffragists constantly pointed out, the Southern states were free to adopt woman suffrage through state legislation, apparently with whatever qualifications they deemed appropriate.[44]

The race issue was extremely important in Southern debate over the federal amendment. By 1910, as there had been no attempts to overturn the barriers to black suffrage they had erected, Southern Democrats assumed that most Americans now agreed with them that the Fifteenth Amendment had been a mistake and that the South should have been allowed to handle the crucial matter of suffrage without federal interference. They regarded a federal woman suffrage amendment as "an extension of the Fifteenth Amendment," as it had the same "Force Clause" giving the Congress the power to "enforce this article by appropriate legislation." Thus they perceived proponents of a federal woman suffrage amendment as threatening, since they clearly advocated federal regulation of the franchise, and thereby upheld the validity of the Fifteenth Amendment. Furthermore, assuming as they did the commonality of goals between advocates of woman suffrage and of the rights of blacks, Southern conservatives assumed (erroneously) that once enfranchised, Northern feminists would demand that the rights of their black sisters in the South be recognized.[45]

Southern Democrats were jubilant as their party recaptured control of national politics in 1912; the "racial settlement" they had established seemed far more secure. Lost Cause devotees celebrated the predicted return of Southerners to key positions of leadership; not only was Woodrow Wilson elected President (a man born in Virginia and claimed by Southerners as one of their own, and who promptly established segregation in federal agencies), but Southerners also served as Chief Justice of the United States Supreme Court and Speaker of the House of Representatives. Of the Democratic majority in the Senate, more than half were Southerners, and Southerners chaired all but two of the major committees in both houses of Congress. University of Virginia professor Edwin Alderman wrote to his friend Wilson that Wilson's rise to national prominence represented "a sort of fulfillment of an unspoken prophecy lying close to the heart of nearly every faithful son of the South." A Birmingham editor boasted that "the government of the United States is dominated by the South today as firmly as it was before the Civil War."[46]

Even as Wilson took office, however, the woman suffrage movement scored several key victories in the West and seemed to be gaining momentum in the North. As support grew for the federal suffrage amendment, Southern Democrats found themselves on the defensive in an increasingly sectional dispute over the extension of the suffrage through federal amendment. The West and North seemed ready to force upon them another federal amendment that, many feared, would take from them the power to protect white supremacy and "Southern Civilization." Most Southern Democrats believed this was a threat they must fight with all of the means at their disposal. Their constituents, they believed, expected it of them.[47]

III

Despite all of these formidable difficulties, a vigorous and systematic woman suffrage movement did develop in the South, and it gained a significant though insufficient degree of support. In the 1890s, small woman suffrage societies sprang up in nearly every Southern state, this time composed of native (Southern) white women of the "respectable" classes. Veterans of the reform-minded women's organizations, these women wished to expand woman's sphere, to make it possible for women to use their influence for good through the ballot. Accepting the nurturing role of the Southern Lady, they wished to be able to promote humanitarian reform through political activism; they did not believe the interests of women or of children were being adequately represented in the New South. Products of some of the South's most prominent families, the leaders of the Southern suffrage movement were imbued with a sense of *noblesse oblige*. They considered themselves more qualified than most men to determine the course of Southern society and claimed the ballot as their right.[48]

Southern suffragists of the 1890s worked very closely with representatives of the National American Woman Suffrage Association. Frustrated by the indifference or hostility of most congressmen, national suffrage leaders turned to the states, trying to build grassroots support for woman suffrage and to gain suffrage legislation in enough states that a federal amendment would in time become inevitable. Therefore, they were eager to have the help of prominent Southern white women, and were more than willing to work with Southern women who shared prevailing Southern attitudes toward black suffrage. Laura Clay of Kentucky played a crucial role in the development of the Southern suffrage movement during this period; she was an essential intermediary between Northern and Southern suffragists, convincing the Northerners that organization in the South was not only possible, but vital for the movement, and persuading Southern women to work with them.[49]

Most Southern Democrats never believed it, but Carrie Chapman Catt and the women who took over the leadership of the woman suffrage movement in the late nineteenth century shared many of their attitudes about black suffrage. And by 1890, even the aging Susan B. Anthony—who had supported abolition and black rights for decades—had concluded that the woman suffrage movement must drop all other causes and concentrate on gaining for American women the power to help themselves as well as others through the ballot. During the period in which an organized woman suffrage movement existed in the South, the National American Woman Suffrage Association (hereafter referred to as the NAWSA or "the National") not only disassociated itself from advocacy of rights for blacks, but used racist tactics quite openly in the effort to win support for their cause.[50]

Indeed, a distinguishing feature of the Southern suffrage movement in this early period was the centrality of racism in the suffragists' strategy and rhetoric (see Chapter Four). Both Southern suffragists and their Northern supporters believed there was an excellent chance that Southern politicians might resort to enfranchising white women as a means of solving the South's "negro problem."

Hence, in 1895, the NAWSA held its national convention in Atlanta (the first such convention to be held outside of Washington, D.C.) and, at the invitation of Louisiana suffrage leaders Kate and Jean Gordon, held its 1903 convention in New Orleans. In the intervening years, Southern suffragists and their Northern allies made pleas for woman suffrage at each of the state constitutional conventions held during the decade of disfranchisement. At first the suffragists were encouraged by the support they received, but their enthusiasm waned as one after another of their proposals was defeated. Their only success was a bill adopted by the Louisiana Constitutional Convention of 1898 giving partial suffrage to taxpaying women.[51]

Since the suffragists of the 1890s were few and had little chance of success, the reaction to them was mild relative to what was to come in the 1910s, when there were far more Southern suffragists and the threat of the federal amendment loomed large. Some editors, ministers, and politicians were very hostile to the suffragists, some ridiculed them, and a few supported them, but the movement was not generally treated seriously. It was common for editors to make patronizing remarks about the small numbers of Southern suffragists, and to discuss the absurdity of the demand for suffrage in the Southland, where women already ruled through "indirect influence." A handful of editors and politicians proclaimed their willingness to support woman suffrage when and if the majority of Southern white women wanted it, or if a way could be found to enfranchise them without enfranchising black women.[52]

Even the Northern suffragists operating in the South, those notorious representatives of an alien culture, met with more curiosity than hostility. One of the foremost Southern Baptist leaders, J. B. Hawthorne of Atlanta, outraged delegates to the 1895 NAWSA convention by publicly accusing them of defying divine law, outraging the social sentiment "which despises every woman who confesses to such an unwomanly aspiration [as suffrage]," and possessing "feeble-minded husbands." He warned the public to keep away from the suffragists' meetings, as their real purpose was to encourage the intermarriage of the black and white races, to break up the homes of America, and to degrade the morals of women. The delegates, however, were surprised and pleased by their reception; probably as a *result* of Hawthorne's diatribe the citizens of Atlanta packed lecture halls to catch glimpses of such creatures as Susan B. Anthony, Elizabeth Cady Stanton, Henry Blackwell, and the Reverend Dr. Anna Howard Shaw. Two thousand people filled DeGive's Opera House to hear Shaw speak of discrimination against women preachers. In New Orleans, a group of the Gordons' male supporters rented a hall for the NAWSA convention, and they even chartered a steamboat to entertain the Northern ladies with a Mississippi cruise.[53]

As the suffragists grew discouraged, the Southern movement diminished considerably. In the first decade of the new century, suffrage societies were dormant in some states, ceased to exist in several, and maintained intermittent activity in only a few, including Kentucky and Louisiana, where there were unusually strong leaders.

Around 1910, however, the suffrage movement in the South was revitalized, reflecting the renewed optimism of suffragists everywhere. The Progressive movement had breathed new life into the suffrage movement as many members of both national parties (men and women) recognized the commonality between their political agenda (honest government, pure food and water legislation, humanitarian reforms) and the traditional values, interests, and responsibilities of women (promoting morality, nurturing families, aiding the poor). Beginning with the adoption of a woman suffrage amendment in the state of Washington in 1910, the movement rolled up a long string of victories in Western and Midwestern states that encouraged suffragists in all parts of the nation.[54]

Southern suffrage pioneers of the 1890s renewed their activity, and the movement gained new converts from among the ranks of Southern Progressives: men like Alexander McKelway and Walter Clark who believed that women would support humanitarian reform and women who wanted the vote largely for that purpose. The latter group included Madeline McDowell Breckinridge of Kentucky and Lila Meade Valentine of Virginia, women who were among the most dedicated and able Progressive leaders in the New South and would now distinguish themselves as regional suffrage leaders. Significantly, there were large numbers of new followers, as well as new leaders. In state after Southern state, suffragists reported remarkable increases in the numbers of converts and organizations. The growth of industry and commerce and the rapid growth of cities and towns in the New South had led to an expansion of the region's middle class and a rise in the number of women's voluntary organizations through which women discovered a need for the ballot. An increase in the numbers of college-educated women and women professionals also aided the cause. Alabama, which had only two suffrage clubs in 1910, had eighty-one by 1917; the Equal Suffrage League of Virginia grew from twenty members in 1910 to seven thousand in 1915. In many places, men's suffrage clubs and college suffrage leagues were formed. With each passing year, more and more women's organizations formally endorsed woman suffrage.[55]

Southern opponents of woman suffrage watched all of these developments with apprehension and disdain. In March 1913, a large and enthusiastic crowd of suffragists, including many Southern women, participated in the first major American suffrage parade, a dramatic event that took place on the day of Woodrow Wilson's inauguration. The crowd, which included many Southerners there to celebrate the triumph of Wilson and the Democrats, assaulted the marchers; according to the NAWSA organ, the *Woman's Journal*, "rowdies seized and mauled young girls," "women were spat upon, slapped in the face, tripped up, pelted with burning cigar stubs and insulted by jeers and obscene language too vile to print or repeat." This shameful treatment and the failure of the Washington police to protect the marchers earned the suffrage movement a tremendous outpouring of sympathy, inspiring a congressional investigation, the dismissal of the Washington chief of police, and an outcry in the press—or at least, in the Northern and Western press. The Birmingham (Alabama) *Ledger* defended the crowd, saying that "our suffrage sisters must understand that when they cut away from the conventions of the ages they venture into untried fields and may find many rude men," and the "disorder is what the suffragettes should have anticipated. A majority of men still disapprove the movement and the very ideas underlying it and men are not always considerate in expressing their disapproval." Southern chivalry, apparently, was reserved for the exclusive protection of women who adhered to their traditional role.[56]

Like it or not, the Southern state legislators were soon besieged by suffragists demanding enfranchisement through state legislation; one of the best-organized and hardest-fought of these campaigns was in Alabama, led by Birmingham resident and Alabama Equal Suffrage Association President Pattie Ruffner Jacobs. In state after state, Southern suffragists petitioned for amendments to the state constitutions that would grant woman suffrage and, as suffragists often pointed out, make a federal amendment unnecessary. They had the support of a number of politicians, including former Virginia governor Andrew Jackson Montague and his son, Hill, a state legislator; Senator James K. Vardaman and Governor Theodore Bilbo of Mississippi; Governor Charles Brough of Arkansas; Secretary of the Navy Josephus Daniels; and John M. Parker of Louisiana (the national Progressive Party's candidate for Vice-President in 1916) who viewed woman suffrage as a boon to Progressive reform. They also had the support of many Progressive newspapers, including Daniels' Raleigh *News and Observer* (which along with the Charlotte *Daily Observer* was a staunch advocate of suffrage from 1913 on), the Memphis *Commercial Appeal*, the New Orleans *Times-Picayune*, and the Lexington *Herald*, owned and edited by Madeline McDowell Breckinridge's husband, Desha Breckinridge. Even the Louisville *Courier-Journal* was pro-suffrage after the retirement of Watterson. The suffragists celebrated "breakthroughs" in the South when Arkansas (1916) and Texas (1918) gave women the right to vote in primaries. Women also won partial suffrage in Tennessee where the legislature adopted a presidential suffrage bill in 1919.[57]

The suffragists were defeated, however, in every attempt to win full enfranchisement through state constitutional amendments. The nearest that any Southern full-suffrage campaign came to success was in Louisiana in 1918. In that state the oldest and most experienced group of suffragists, led by the Gordon sisters, had been working for many years in support of woman suffrage by state action exclusively. Indeed, in 1913, Kate Gordon had taken the lead in establishing the Southern States Woman Suffrage Conference, which she, as its president, used to promote state suffrage amendments in the South while opposing the federal amendment. Gordon enjoyed the support of many state politicians who also supported state but not federal enfranchisement of women, including Governor Ruffin G. Pleasant, whose wife, Anne, was one of Gordon's closest associates. Working together with Louisianans who favored suffrage by state or federal legislation, they came close to victory in the 1918 statewide referendum on a state constitutional amendment. The referendum was narrowly defeated, largely owing to the opposition of New Orleans mayor and machine-politician Martin Behrman. The referendum received a majority of the votes outside New Orleans but failed overall because of the votes cast in the city; said one newspaper, "the bar room and machine combination defeated it."[58]

As the pattern of defeat clearly indicated, conservatives outnumbered Progressives in legislatures throughout the South; antisuffragists were sufficiently alarmed, however, to organize in several Southern states. Most of these first "anti" organizations were composed of women, often wives or daughters of prominent male opponents, such as Marie Owen, daughter of Senator John H. Bankhead of Alabama. Suffragists regarded these women as pawns of antisuffrage men who prepared their literature and of the textile and other industries who funded their operations.[59]

Antis of both sexes were highly effective in exploiting the Southern prejudices against, and fears of, woman suffrage discussed above. They presented woman suffrage as a threat to Southern womanhood and the home and to white supremacy—indeed, as antithetical to Southern values. They depicted Southern suffragists as misguided and ungrateful. Female antisuffragists claimed that they, not the suffragists, were the true representatives of the wishes of Southern women and stressed their devotion to their traditional sphere. Anti women in Alabama once declined to take the podium at an open hearing before the legislature; instead they asked a senator to read their statement announcing they had no desire to "mix in politics" and pleading with legislators not to force them "from the quietude of our homes into the contaminating atmosphere of political struggle." Many ministers actively supported the antis; a Tennessee minister described suffrage as "a key that's going to unlock the gates of hell and turn the demons loose upon the human family." A Georgia anti warned that the "women who ask for [suffrage] are simply the unconscious agents of God's worst enemies."[60]

Suffrage opponents attacked suffragists as traitors to their region who would betray their birthright, the Lost Cause. Mildred Rutherford, the President of the Georgia United Daughters of the Confederacy, speaking for the state's chapter of the National Association Opposed to Woman Suffrage, told the Georgia legislature in 1914:

> The women who are working for this measure are striking at the principle for which their fathers fought during the Civil War. Woman's suffrage comes from the North and West and from women who do not believe in state's rights and who wish to see negro women using the ballot. I do not believe the state of Georgia has sunk so low that her good men can not legislate for the women. If this time ever comes then it will be time for women to claim the ballot.[61]

And, in a widely circulated pamphlet, "Politics and Patriotism" (1917), Alabama state senator J. B. Evans argued that Southern suffragists

> have allowed themselves to be misled by bold women who are the product of the peculiar social conditions of our Northern cities into advocating

a political innovation the realization of which would be the undoing of the South. . . . These misguided daughters of the South are endorsing the principles for which Thad Stevens, Fred Douglass, Susan B. Anthony and other bitter enemies of the South contended, and if they succeed then indeed was the blood of their fathers shed in vain.[62]

Antisuffragists constantly warned that woman suffrage would endanger white supremacy by calling into question the principles on which it rested or by tampering with election laws that now, at last, were successful guarantors of white supremacy. Virginia legislator Hugh White read to the House of Delegates from a black periodical in 1916 that declared that the same fight for recognition that faced the Negro race faced women: White concluded that every argument for woman suffrage was an argument for black suffrage. Without ever explaining why the laws that disqualified black men would not apply to black women, the Richmond *Times-Dispatch* warned that woman suffrage "would double the number of uncertain and dangerous votes and put the balance of political power in the hands of 165,000 colored women, only to gratify the whims of a small group of women who don't really know what they are about."[63]

A widely circulated reprint from the Richmond *Evening Journal* attacked Southern suffragists as illogical creatures accustomed to having their way, who had no real understanding of the stern realities of politics, and who were ungrateful to the men who had assumed this burdensome task for their sakes:

> Probably the ladies engaged in this suffrage movement are not very practical or very logical or very well informed or disposed to bother their heads with the actual facts of politics. Most of them, we surmise, hold the somewhat vague but firmly established feminine line of reasoning that when they want something, or think they want it, they ought to have it by all principles of wisdom and justice; and are prepared always to fall back on the traditional conclusive feminine argument "because."
>
> No other argument, however profound, is quite so convincing or fascinating as that word "because," accompanied by some pouting or alluring and scarlet lips—especially if there be dimples by way of re-enforcement [sic]. But men are compelled and accustomed to face and deal with hard facts when considering important affairs in business or in politics. It is a hard fact that twenty-nine counties of Virginia could be condemned by woman suffrage to colored rule and five others would be in serious peril of it with woman suffrage.
>
> We do not suppose, or imagine, that the suffrage ladies would suggest resort to counting out the colored people of their own sex or to stuffing the ballot boxes or padding registration lists. We wicked and inefficient and tyrannical men who are supposed to have made such a mess of government in Virginia, became ashamed of such methods and

alarmed by them and contrived to remove the necessity for them. Surely we are not to be incited to return to the slimepit from which we dug ourselves.[64]

Through such arguments and the behind-the-scenes assistance of the cotton men and other industrialist antis, the antisuffragists successfully held the line against woman suffrage in the Southern legislatures; but Southern Democrats were having less success in the halls of Congress. As the battle over suffrage in Congress grew increasingly sectional, Northern and Western supporters of woman suffrage increasingly accused Southern Democrats of being reactionaries who could only hope to delay the success of a movement whose time had come. A Republican congressman from Washington ridiculed the verbose Representative Thomas Heflin as "the brave and gallant Alabama warrior who has won world-wide fame for bravery fighting women, and who thinks that the great tide of woman suffrage can be stayed by stilted oratory." On the other hand, Southern Democrats opposing the amendment saw themselves, and were regarded by many of their constituents, as, in true Lost Cause style, keepers of tradition, level-headed conservatives who would save the United States from this "fad" that was sweeping the nation.[65]

Senator ("Pitchfork") Benjamin Tillman of South Carolina was a classic example of a Southern Democrat who assailed his colleagues for acting too hastily, for yielding to the pressures of the moment, for failing to stand up to the feminists. This aged senator, who had helped defeat woman suffrage during his state's constitutional convention in 1895, pleaded with his "rash, young colleagues" to be counseled and directed by "the wisdom of their seniors." Rather than rush "pell-mell, helter-skelter" into woman suffrage, he urged that Congress gather statistics in suffrage states "of the birth rate, death rate, divorces, and other things affecting the everyday social life of the people, which would *in a hundred years, say* [my emphasis], show us whether female suffrage has affected these things injuriously or not." Men from other parts of the nation, he said, should heed the example of the South, particularly South Carolina, where institutions regarding the relations between the sexes were beyond reproach: the lack of divorce that enabled men tired of their "skinny and shrunken" wives to go after "some young and buxom girl"; lynching, which makes "it dangerous to 'monkey with men's womankind'"; and the South's "unwritten law," which allowed men to shoot men who slept with their wives and daughters and go unpunished. He called the last "the best law to protect woman's virtue that I ever heard of."[66]

Though a storm of criticism from his colleagues from North and West caused Tillman to have it stricken, he introduced into the *Congressional Record* Dr. Bledsoe's 1871 "Mission of Woman" (quoted above) with its vicious attack on Northern feminists, and reasserted Bledsoe's contentions that equal rights for women had been the undoing of the Roman Empire and would lead America to a similar fate. He condemned as cowards the congressmen who were yielding to expediency, "trying to make peace with the women politicians and get on their good side now," and appealed to them to stand firm against this "craze" rather than "usher in another thousand years of moral blight, sexual depravity and degradation."[67]

Nothing infuriated the Southern Democrats more than the tactics of the National Woman's Party, the militant spin-off of the NAWSA that, following a strategy borrowed from British suffragists, tried to "punish the party in power" for its failure to secure a federal suffrage amendment. President Wilson, a champion of states' rights (at least in regard to suffrage), whose own wife was opposed to woman suffrage, insisted that the issue must be decided by the states. In 1912, and again in 1916, the National Woman's Party mounted offensives against Democrats in the West, trying to persuade women voters to unite against Democratic candidates. Furthermore, they behaved in a fashion that seemed to irritate the Democrats from the South above all others—picketing the White House and engaging in what one Democratic senator called "infantile and assinine bonfire performances" (i.e., burning Wilson's speeches in Lafayette Park). Southern suffragists loyal to the NAWSA were convinced that the behavior of the militant suffragists, antithetical to that of the Southern Lady, severely undercut their efforts to convert Southern senators and congressmen.[68]

The militants' campaign in the West against the Democrats failed; indeed, the opinion was widespread that women voters had furnished the narrow margin of victory for Wilson's re-election bid in 1916. Many assumed that women had responded most favorably to Wilson's campaign slogan, "He kept us out of the war." Yet the support of women voters for Wilson, again proving that the carrot is more effective than the stick, persuaded many national leaders, including the President, that woman suffrage was a force to be reckoned with, that it could, in fact, be crucial to success in the 1918 congressional and the 1920 presidential elections.[69]

Politicians did indeed, in Senator Tillman's words, want "to make peace with the women . . . and get on their good side now." The number of suffrage states grew. And finally both national parties capitulated. In 1916, the Democratic and Republican national conventions endorsed woman suffrage by state amendment. The Progressive Party, which had endorsed woman suffrage by state and federal action in 1912, did so again in 1916. The NAWSA was disappointed with the endorsements of suffrage by state action only, fearing this might give ammunition to opponents of a federal amendment. But the National's strategy of winning enough states to insure victory of a federal suffrage amendment was soon to succeed. With the suffrage victory in New York State in 1917, a victory in Congress seemed almost assured.[70]

In 1918 Wilson shocked and dismayed Southern opponents of the federal suffrage amendment by giving it his endorsement. Southern conservatives were outraged. They considered it bad enough that Wilson had endorsed woman suffrage by state action in 1915; he now compounded his crime by turning his back on what they believed to be a pillar of Democratic ideology—state sovereignty. But Wilson was the leader of the national party, not just of the Southern Democrats, and he felt it was essential that the Democrats not allow the Republicans to gain credit for what was certain to be the next great extension of the suffrage. He began to put pressure on Democratic opponents of suffrage to yield for the sake of the national party.[71]

In January 1918, the federal suffrage amendment was finally approved by the House of Representatives. But the Senate, thanks to the Southern Democrats, narrowly defeated it. According to David Morgan's *Suffragists and Democrats: The Politics of Woman Suffrage in America*, this defeat contributed to the Democrat's loss of control of Congress in 1918 and caused great dissension within the party. Angry Democrats from North and West accused Southern senators of being so secure in their states that they forgot other Democrats had to compete for votes within two-party systems. If Southern women were angry over the Democrats' failure to support woman suffrage, they would have no place else to turn once enfranchised. This would not be the case in the North and West.[72]

Having lost control of Congress in the November 1918 elections, national Democratic leaders were desperate to have the federal amendment approved early in 1919 before the new, Republican-controlled Congress would surely approve the amendment and gain credit for its passage. Wilson (through cables from Paris where he was taking part in the treaty negotiations) joined other Democratic leaders as they searched desperately for the two votes yet needed for Senate approval; they begged Southern Democrats to reconsider, to no avail. The Democrats had one last chance, when the measure came to a vote in February. They had gained only one additional vote in the Senate, ironically created by Tillman's death and his replacement by a suffrage sympathizer Senator William P. Pollock.[73]

Pollock, chosen to make the keynote speech before the February vote, said: "Some men have said that they do not want to force anything on the South. I tell you, speaking for the New South, speaking for the real South, we want this privilege. We feel that the women are entitled to it, and we know we can handle any race question."[74] Pollock and his recalcitrant colleagues knew perfectly well, however, that the new senator, a temporary appointee, did not represent the views of the majority of Southerners.

In caucus before the Senate vote, the Democrats decided to hold firm against the amendment on the grounds that expediency was not a good enough reason for amending the Constitution! In truth, they were convinced that, whatever might be expedient for the national Democratic Party, a vote for the federal amendment was anything but expedient for them as individual politicians from the South. Should they be turned out of office, other Democrats would no doubt be elected to replace them; but few of them were more concerned about the fate of the national party than their own political futures. Regional opposition to the woman suffrage amendment as a threat to the traditional role of woman and to white supremacy, now enhanced by years of antisuffrage rhetoric, made it virtually impossible for the Democratic senators who opposed the amendment to change their votes even if they had wished. And the senators from the major textile-producing states of North Carolina, South Carolina, Georgia, and Alabama, even men like North Carolina senator Lee Overman, who had been one of Wilson's key congressional supporters, knew that their political ascendency owed more to certain state constituents than to the national party or to the President.[75]

Thus, for a combination of reasons, most Southern Democratic senators believed they had no choice but to appear to die in the last ditch on this issue. As Senator John Sharp Williams said, when under intense pressure to change his vote on the suffrage amendment: "If they make me a party to it it is not my fault, but if I become a party to it of my own accord, it ceases to be rape and becomes fornication."[76]

In the new, Republican-dominated Congress, hearings were waived and a speedy vote called for: the suffrage forces were assured of success due to the replacement or conversion of antisuffrage senators from the Northeast, and Wilson's success in persuading one Southern senator, William J. Harris of Georgia, to support the resolution. The House adopted the amendment for the second time on May 21, 1919. And despite last-ditch efforts by individual Southern senators to amend the suffrage amendment to enfranchise white women only (Pat Harris of Mississippi), to allow the federal government to enforce the amendment only if the states failed to do so (Edward Gay of Louisiana), and to make the ratification process more involved and difficult (Oscar Underwood of Alabama), the amendment passed the Senate on June 4, 1919.[77]

The South now entered the last, nastiest, and most divisive phase of the suffrage struggle. Carrie Chapman Catt was speaking of Arkansas when she observed, "legislative debate brought into glaring relief the struggle between old-time Southern prejudice and the new spirit of

Southern progressiveness," but the description could have applied as well to any Southern state. In Texas and Arkansas (where the high turnout of women in the white primaries had called into question the old assumption that white women would not exercise the right to vote), "progressiveness" won out. Kentucky also ratified the amendment, and in August 1920, Tennessee was to be the state whose ratification supplied the necessary three-fourths majority and put the Nineteenth Amendment into effect. Most Southern states, however, united in opposition to the amendment, and Southern politicians made "heroic" efforts to block ratification.[78]

As Northern and Western states proceeded with ratification, there was in each Southern state a pitched battle between the suffragists and the conservatives. No longer willing to leave the fight in the hands of female antisuffragists (if indeed they ever had), male antis organized antisuffrage and "states' rights defense" leagues in many Southern states.[79]

Opponents continued to argue against female enfranchisement as a threat to Southern womanhood, an affront to God, and a danger to society; but antisuffragists now concentrated increasingly on the *method* of enfranchisement—the federal amendment—which, they insisted in the strongest of terms, was the greatest threat to white supremacy since the Fifteenth Amendment. Senator Overman issued a statement, just six days after the amendment was submitted to the states, that Catt considered the "keynote of the opposition":

> In my opinion, the Woman Suffrage Amendment just adopted by Congress is a reaffirmation of the Fifteenth Amendment. I wonder if this is appreciated throughout the South? This latter amendment simply goes a step further than the Fifteenth Amendment. In addition to saying that the right of suffrage shall not be abridged by reason of race, color or previous condition of servitude the new amendment adds the word "sex." The language is not identical, but it is evident that the Woman Suffrage resolution is a postscript to the former amendment, which we have always opposed in the South. . . . Congress reserves the right of "appropriate legislation" to enforce this mandate, regardless of the State. That is the condition in a nutshell. I wonder if woman suffrage advocates in the South have taken into consideration all the embarrassing features possible under such legislation.

Overman and other suffrage opponents turned the ratification fight into a full-scale battle over the survival of state sovereignty and the South's ability to preserve "the Southern Way of Life." Indeed, antis made it clear that, regardless of what others in the nation might say, they regarded support of the suffrage amendment as a litmus test of loyalty to the South and its values.[80]

Thomas Nelson Page summed up their argument elegantly, declaring that whatever the merits or demerits of woman suffrage,

I cannot imagine how any one, man or woman, who is in the least familiar with the history of suffrage in Virginia and in other States of the
South, could think for a moment of advocating placing the suffrage
under the control of the National Government. . . During more than a
generation the South lay in the throes of a great struggle to preserve its
local self-government and everything on which its civilization rested
from destruction, and it has only been in the last few years, since the
new constitutions of the several States were adopted and were held to be
constitutional by the highest courts in the land, that the people of
Virginia and of the other Southern States have been able to breathe
freely. To reopen this question now by an attempt to bring about a new
amendment to the Constitution of the United States, dealing with suffrage, would in my judgment, be an immeasurable injury to the South,
and indeed to the whole Nation.

The fundamental question underlying the federal suffrage amendment, Page insisted, "is that which the South fought against during
the entire generation following our war, the question not only of
equality of the sexes, but the equality of the races."[81]

Using every possible opportunity to remind Southerners of the
early connection between woman suffrage and radical feminism and
abolitionism, antisuffragists always spoke of the Nineteenth Amendment derisively as "the Susan B. Anthony Amendment," and attacked
national leaders of the movement as "nigger lovers" and enemies of
the South. They described Anthony as "a rabid hater of the Southern
people to the day of her death, and an absolute worshipper of the
negro." Dr. Anna Howard Shaw was singled out as "the bosom friend
of Miss Anthony" and "imbued with all of her South-hating, negro-
loving propensities." One anti brochure emphasized the friendship
between suffragists and Frederick Douglass and other blacks, while
another, entitled "Character of Robert E. Lee Defamed," accused
Anthony, Stanton, and Douglass of using "calumny and falsehood" to
"stab the name and fame of General Lee" and thus "commit so many
southern women to their creed—a creed that means wreck and ruin
of our southern ideals."[82]

NAWSA President Catt encountered such abuse personally and
publicly when she spoke before the Virginia House of Delegates to
urge ratification. According to the Richmond *Times-Dispatch*, prior to
her talk, "small memoranda" had been placed on the desks of each
legislator with the message that Catt "believed in free love and was
advocating interracial marriages." When Catt in her address remarked
that "there was a liar in Virginia," a "gentleman" jumped to his feet
saying that Catt "was no lady" because ladies did not use the word
"liar."[83]

In Alabama a senator referred to Catt as "that spawn of hell who
rules them [suffragists]," while in Tennessee a senator denounced
Catt as an "anarchist" who "would be glad to see the day when negro

men could marry white women without being socially ostracised."
"This is the kind of woman that is trying to dictate to us," he said.
"They would drag the womanhood of Tennessee down to the level of
the negro woman." Antisuffrage literature also condemned the movement's national leaders as pacifists and "bolshevists," and—emphasizing the connection between Elizabeth Cady Stanton's (1895) *Woman's
Bible* (which the NAWSA had refused to endorse) and the suffrage
movement—as heretics.[84]

Southern antisuffragists entered into a loose alliance with Southerners who favored woman suffrage but also interpreted the federal
amendment as a threat to regional self-determination, white
supremacy, and the rights of the states under the Constitution, and to
whom "states' rights" was a more important issue than woman suffrage. One of these, Louisiana governor Ruffin G. Pleasant,
telegraphed Southern governors three weeks after submission of the
amendment to the states, seeking an alliance of thirteen Southern
states to prevent ratification and to demand that suffrage be secured
only by state action.[85]

In true Lost Cause fashion, Southern opponents of ratification
were determined to block this error of national proportions, and por-
trayed the mission of the South as saving the nation from itself. Leading Southern anti James Callaway of Georgia wrote a pamphlet entitled "Will the States Consent to Blot the Stars from Old Glory, Leaving
Only a Meaningless Square of Blue" and subtitled "A Message from
the Old South to the Nation." Callaway and many antis believed most
Northerners now realized that the Fifteenth Amendment was an
error, a mistake owed to the passions of wartime. He warned that the
Nineteenth Amendment, like the Fifteenth, was being considered
during time of war when the "public mind is demoralized" and "when
passion and prejudice sway the thoughts of men." He urged that
opponents hold fast until this craze had passed, though its proponents
sought to take unfair advantage of a national emergency "once
again."[86]

Southern antis hoped to kill the federal suffrage amendment, not
just delay ratification. Their plan was to secure the adoption of rejection resolutions in thirteen states and then ask for a "Proclamation of
Defeat." By securing forthright rejection resolutions, they believed
they could prevent succeeding legislatures from approving an amendment that their predecessors had rejected. Georgia and Alabama, perhaps the states most hostile to the amendment, vied all summer for
the privilege of being the first to send a joint rejection resolution to
Congress. Georgia, Alabama, South Carolina, and Virginia passed such
resolutions, followed by Maryland, whose legislature even sent a delegation to West Virginia to urge rejection of the amendment. The
Maryland Senate also directed the state's attorney general to prevent
the United States Secretary of State from proclaiming the amendment

ratified until referenda were held in the states. The Jackson *Clarion-Ledger* celebrated Mississippi's rejection of the amendment, proclaiming "the vile old thing is as dead as its author [Susan B. Anthony], the old advocate of social equality and intermarriage of the races, and Mississippi will never be annoyed with it again."[87]

By March 1920, when the amendment had been ratified by thirty-five of the requisite thirty-six states, the Mississippi Senate, at the urging of Governor Theodore Bilbo and the national Democratic Party, sent shock waves through the nation by adopting a ratification resolution by a one-vote margin. In Mississippi as in most other Southern states, however, the "fight to the last ditch" mentality was far more prevalent than the impulse to yield for the sake of expediency. The Mississippi House cheered on the member who announced "he would rather die and go to hell" than vote for the amendment, and voted ninety to twenty-three against ratification.[88]

During the summer, as the nation wondered if women would win the vote in time for the November election and suffragists joined by the national leaders of both parties scrambled for the "Big Thirty-Six," suffragists hoped for a victory in either Florida, Louisiana, North Carolina, or Tennessee. But, Florida was prohibited from calling a special session of the legislature, and Louisiana and then North Carolina failed to ratify. Suffragists were desperate to claim their victory before the November 1920 elections, recognizing like their opponents that in the return to normalcy after the war, the widespread public sentiment in favor of extending the franchise to women could evaporate.[89]

Wilson, eager to have women participate in the November election, believing they would support Democratic Party candidate James M. Cox and the League of Nations, left no stone unturned in his efforts to secure ratifications from Democratic-controlled states. But suffrage opponents in the legislatures bitterly resented this pressure and denounced their former hero as a "meddler" and a "traitor to his section." The Alabama Association Opposed to Woman Suffrage now said that Wilson could not possibly understand the traditions they held so dear because he had only one native-born (i.e., Southern) ancestor![90]

Southern politicians who urged ratification out of expediency were also the targets of much abuse. Governor Thomas W. Bickett of North Carolina, by abandoning opposition to woman suffrage and urging ratification because the days of states' rights had passed away and "whatever the majority of the people of the nation want is going to be the supreme law of the land," only inflamed suffrage opponents and hardened their resistance. While Carrie Chapman Catt praised Bickett's courage in announcing "that the political faith handed down by their fathers and grandfathers and treasured by them as fundamental bases of government were but musty relics of bygone days," suffrage opponents in North Carolina pledged not to "sacrifice their honor upon the fickle altar of supposed political expedience." The state anti-suffrage newspaper, the *State's Defense*, asked:

Can a State which boasts of being "Last at Appomattox" run up the white flag and say, "It is coming, we surrender?" God grant that North Carolina has enough men with the spirit of the Old South left in them to go down with their backs to the wall fighting to preserve the last vestige of what their forefathers fought during four years of civil strife to preserve—the sovereignty of the State.

The legislature defeated the ratification resolution and urged Tennessee to "fight to the last ditch, and then some."[91]

In Tennessee, where the final showdown took place and where suffragists and antisuffragists from all over the nation gathered, opponents engaged in a no-holds-barred effort to block ratification. The Tennessee legislature, one-third Republican, had already extended presidential and municipal suffrage to women, and more than a majority had pledged to vote for ratification. The Senate ratified in a vote of twenty-five to four. But a formidable anti lobby, aided by lobbyists for liquor, railroad, and manufacturing interests, tried to break down suffrage support in the House. Catt claimed that before the struggle ended, every legislator on the pro-suffrage roster with a reputation of being "bribable" went over to the antisuffragists. Even the pro-suffrage Speaker of the House, Seth Walker, abandoned the suffragists and assumed leadership of the anti-ratification effort. Walker delayed the vote on ratification until confident of victory. But the amendment was ratified by a one-vote margin when a twenty-four-year-old Republican from the mountains, Harry Burn, acting on his aged mother's request, changed his vote.[92]

Desperate, Walker moved for reconsideration, and the opposition spent three days applying pressure to pro-suffrage legislators. Governor Pleasant's wife even visited the mother in the mountains; Mrs. Burn wired the Tennessee suffragists saying a woman who "claims to be the wife of Governor of Louisiana" tried "by every means to get me to refute and say that the letter I sent to my son was false." Indeed, said Burn, she was "very insulting to me in my home, and I had a hard time to get her out of my home." Failing to sway either of the Burns or to win any other new votes, thirty-eight anti legislators (the "red-rose brigade") fled to Alabama in the dead of night to prevent a quorum and buy time. The remaining legislators met without them, however, and reconfirmed the vote: Tennessee's ratification was forwarded to the United States Secretary of State, and the Nineteenth Amendment was declared to be in effect.[93]

Still the Southern antis continued to fight, even as the victory for woman suffrage was celebrated by supporters all over the nation.

Tennessee antis challenged the validity of the vote for ratification, and after pro-suffrage representatives went home, they adopted a rejection resolution. Walker and other antis went to Washington to entreat the Secretary of State to withdraw the proclamation, while the American Constitutional League (formerly the Men's Anti-Woman Suffrage League) and the Maryland League for State Defense publicly declared the Tennessee ratification invalid. Women antis announced that litigation would be initiated to invalidate the amendment and the entire presidential election would be challenged should women be allowed to vote in November. Only when Connecticut ratified in mid-September was the victory for woman suffrage clear and final.[94]

In conclusion, it is clear that the hold of traditional ideas about the relations between the sexes on Southerners was so great, and their commitment to preserving what the majority of Southern politicians regarded as "a superior civilization" was so strong, that Southern politicians felt they must defy their former hero Wilson and national Democratic leaders and resist the federal amendment until the bitter end. Those who were influenced further by the vested interests probably went through few crises of conscience; as David Morgan observed, "Here was an issue where spokesmen for southern industry could 'vote their pockets' and consciences together—a thing not always easy to do." Most Southern politicians agreed with the North Carolina legislator who said the woman suffrage movement originated in the North and "had no place in the sunny South, the land of chivalry and devoted respect for women." To them the feminist movement was a hostile, alien force, invading the South, "perverting the tastes of southern women," "persuading them to abandon their ideals" and, encumbered by all of their (albeit charming) naïveté, to interfere in the crucial and complex affairs of politics.[95]

After 1910, the suffrage movement made some progress in the South with the aid of the Progressive movement and national Democratic leaders. Yet, even as some politicians supported woman suffrage, believing it would increase the base of support for reform, others opposed woman suffrage for precisely the same reason. Many antis were more afraid that enfranchised women would clean up politics, support prohibition, and crack down on the exploitation of women and children laborers, than that politics would despoil women, lead to neglect of families, and bring discord to the home. Such men feared woman's moral and compassionate "influence" if women were allowed to exercise it directly rather than indirectly.

Furthermore, the pressure of national Democratic leaders meant little to the majority of Southern politicians who believed that resistance to woman suffrage—particularly when this "assault upon traditional southern values" was compounded with a threat to states' rights—was required of them. Even when pressured by the head of their party and threatened with the loss of the newly won Democratic ascendency in national politics, these men refused to embrace the amendment. They insisted that the fortunes of the party elsewhere in the nation meant nothing if they lost control over their own society. They claimed to be "resisting the lure of political gain." But individual politicians realized they had the most to gain by making a stand in the tradition of their forefathers for the values of the Lost Cause.

2

The Making of
Southern Suffragists

*The leisure class . . . is the pillar of the suffrage movement. If it wasn't
for them the suffrage movement would not have advanced as it has. The
women of the leisure class can afford to go around stirring up enthusiasm
for the movement which the women of other classes cannot do. The
suffrage movement is a great thing for the women of the leisure
class. . . . It gives the women . . . an opportunity to do something
for their less fortunate sisters that will be of benefit to the entire
feminine world.*

—Pattie Ruffner Jacobs
Speech to Birmingham Suffragists,
1913[1]

*We have learned that the interests of women and children will never be a
vital issue until made so by women for women. . . . And we also learned
(what we had suspected) that the much-boasted influence of the wife over
the husband in matters political was one of the many theories which melt
before the sun of experience. The wife of every representative present was
heartily in sympathy with the child labor bill, but, when the roll was
called, the husbands answered "no" and those wives realized how weak a
weapon was influence, and in that moment were sown the seeds of a
belief in the potency of the ballot beyond that of "woman's influence."*

—Jean Gordon, "New Louisiana Child
Labor Law," *Charities*, 1908[2]

Looking back on the woman suffrage movement from the vantage
point of 1923, Carrie Chapman Catt observed, "no stronger characters
did the long struggle [for woman suffrage] produce than those great-
souled southern suffragists. They had need to be great of soul." She

meant, of course, that advocacy of woman suffrage in such an inhospitable climate was character-building; but the leaders of the woman suffrage movement in the Southern states had to have unusual self-confidence and determination in order to take up this cause in the first place.[3]

Certainly it was no coincidence that most of the leaders of the Southern suffrage movement were descended from the South's social and political elite. Their privileged socioeconomic positions enabled them to have educational opportunities greater than those of most Southern women of their era and opportunities for travel outside the region that contributed to the undermining of provincial attitudes concerning woman's role. Exalted social position facilitated their suffrage work; it brought with it a certain familiarity with and access to the political process and a degree of immunity from criticism, or at least social ostracism, not enjoyed by Southern women of lesser social standing. Well aware of the particular importance of social position in the South, national suffrage leaders deliberately recruited Southern suffrage leaders from prominent families. These women could demand and receive, at the very least, a respectful hearing. Furthermore, economic security provided the leisure and the means for these women to assume leadership roles in the suffrage movement. Though a few were members of families that were experiencing financial distress, most were daughters of wealth and privilege who could hire maids, cooks, and baby-tenders, as well as personally finance most of the suffrage work in the South.[4]

As members of the dominant social class, these leaders of the Southern suffrage movement were raised with a sense of *noblesse oblige*; having internalized their society's expectations of them as Southern Ladies, they felt a special responsibility for guiding and nurturing Southern society. This led them, like many other upper-class Southern women, into women's clubs, church groups, and temperance societies in the 1880s and 1890s; and it led second-generation Southern suffragists to support Progressive reforms. Involvement in charitable work and reform societies led to a growing knowledge of social ills and a commitment to use their influence for good beyond the traditional limits of woman's sphere. They recognized that many of the social and economic problems that had traditionally been addressed by the private sector could now be resolved only through governmental action. And the women who became suffragists were convinced that woman's direct involvement in government was essential to insure that these problems would be resolved in a just and humanitarian fashion.

Obviously not all upper-class Southern women, nor all Southern women who were social activists, became suffragists. The decisions of these leading suffragists to embrace such a radical cause are attributable to a combination of personal characteristics and early experiences that made them receptive to feminism. The attitudes and example of family members were, of course, very important in shaping the attitudes of these women about the proper roles and duties of the sexes. And contacts with suffragists from the North and the West, from other countries, and with suffragists from other Southern states, led many of these women to regard feminism and woman suffrage favorably. Like all reformers, Southern suffragists came to feel themselves part of a supportive subculture, and to judge themselves according to the precepts of that group rather than those of the larger society they were trying to reform.

There was another important factor that explained, not only the conversion of these prominent Southern suffragists to woman suffrage, but the zeal with which they continued to press for it despite so many discouraging defeats; this was the disdain with which they regarded most of the men who were currently leading Southern society. Though all of the leading Southern suffragists had friends and relatives in high places, they believed that in general the New South was being poorly run, mismanaged by shortsighted, materialistic, and largely corrupt men who spoke often about the power of women behind the throne and turned their backs on them when it was time to make decisions. Even as Southern Democrats re-established their hegemony in Southern politics, the suffragists believed that all too often they failed to establish honest governments that protected the interests of those dependent upon their patronage—particularly women and children. And the suffragists' experiences as lobbyists led them to denounce emphatically the cherished myth that the Southern Lady was the true power in the region. Indeed, it was largely the perception that they—moral, God-fearing, intelligent women whose families had been largely responsible for settling and guiding the South— were being denied the right to vote while inferior men were not only voting but governing the South, that fueled their activism.

I

The women who led the Southern suffrage movement were indeed daughters of privilege. Laura Clay and Madeline McDowell Breckinridge were members of families that had been leaders in Kentucky since its earliest days. Clay was the daughter of Cassius Marcellus Clay, lord of a 2,500-acre estate, White Hall; lawyer and Kentucky legislator; Mexican War hero; Lincoln's Ambassador to Russia; and kinsman of Henry Clay. Her mother, Mary Jane Warfield Clay, was from a wealthy Lexington family. When Laura was only twenty-four, her father divided a part of his estate among his children, giving Laura a "farm" that she managed with great enthusiasm and ability, and the means to be financially independent and indeed affluent for the rest of her life. Madeline McDowell, the great-grandaughter of Henry Clay, grew up in Ashland, his famous Lexington home. She married into an equally distinguished family when she wed Desha Breckinridge: great-grandson of John Breckinridge, the Kentucky senator and attorney general under Jefferson; son of United States Congressman W. C. P. Breckinridge; lawyer; and owner and editor of the Lexington *Herald*.[5]

Nellie Nugent Somerville was also a member of a family that had played a key role in the settlement and development of her state. Her paternal great-grandfather was the Chief Justice for the Mississippi Territory and organized its judicial system, and her maternal grandfather was the first representative from her county in the Mississippi legislature. Her father was William Louis Nugent, a Confederate officer who played a leading role in restoring "home rule" to Mississippi. At the time of his death in 1897, he was one of the most prominent and wealthy lawyers in the state, and, according to several newspapers throughout the state, one of Mississippi's best-loved citizens. Nellie Nugent married Robert Somerville, a Virginian whose family fortune had been lost during the Civil War and who had come to Mississippi to work as a civil engineer.[6]

Belle Kearney was also the daughter of a Confederate officer, Walter Gunston Kearney. He served in the Mississippi legislature in the antebellum period and again in the 1880s and 1890s. She grew up at Vernon Heights, the family's splendid Greek Revival home in Madison County, and took annual trips to the Gulf Coast that were (according to Kearney) "heralded by outriders blowing bugles to announce the family's approach." Kearney's parents were, in her eyes, "tragic victims" of the war, "aristocrats" who failed to adjust to the economics of the postwar South and gradually lost everything. Their social standing, however, was unscathed: her autobiography, *A Slaveholder's Daughter*, contains accounts of Kearney earning wages by sewing for former slaves one day, and dancing as a young "belle" at the Governor's inaugural ball the next.[7]

Though we know less of the details of Kate and Jean Gordon's early lives, it is clear they were only moderately wealthy but very well connected. Their father had been a Scottish émigré and served as headmaster of a school for boys; but the prestige of their mother's family guaranteed their position in New Orleans society. The two sisters supported themselves with the income from inherited property.[8]

Rebecca Latimer Felton was the daughter of one prosperous planter and the wife of another. Her father, Charles Latimer, moved to Georgia with his family while a boy; they had been eminent planters in southern Maryland and were related to the Washingtons and Fairfaxes of Virginia. Her husband, Dr. W. H. Felton, was a physician and clergyman as well as a planter. Dr. Felton was elected to represent Georgia in the United States Congress (Independent, 1874–1880) and served three terms in the Georgia legislature in the

1880s. Rebecca Felton saw her fortunes wrecked by war and rebuilt in its wake, largely due to her own hard work and business acumen. At the time of her suffrage activity she was a wealthy widow.[9]

Mary Johnston and Lila Mead Valentine were also Southern aristocrats, members of families that prospered in the New South. Johnston's father was a major in the Confederate Army, a cousin of the famous General Joseph E. Johnston. He became a lawyer and state legislator and president of the Georgia Pacific Railroad Company, with interests in the Tennessee Coal and Iron Company and many other business enterprises. As an adult, Mary Johnston built her dream home, Three Hills, on a forty-acre tract in the Alleghanies near Warm Springs, Virginia, and supported herself and her two sisters largely from her earnings as a writer. Valentine was also from the ranks of the First Families of Virginia and married another FFV, Benjamin Batchelder Valentine. Ben Valentine was a banker and insurance company executive and an officer in his family's meat products company, a gentleman scholar who loved to dabble in archaeology and write poetry.[10]

Pattie Ruffner Jacobs moved to the South from West Virginia as a child, but her family originally came from Virginia, where her grandfather Lewis Ruffner was president of Washington and Lee University. She was raised in affluence in Nashville, where her father established a successful mercantile house. Her family fortunes collapsed just as she was to make her debut. But her marriage to a prosperous businessman, Solon Jacobs, saved her from the unwelcome prospect of supporting herself as a teacher. Solon Jacobs, a railroad executive and later founder and owner of the Birmingham Slag Company, provided for her handsomely, giving her the leisure for suffrage work.[11]

Even Sue Shelton White, who grew up in poverty, could trace her descent through her father to the Jeffersons and Marshalls of Virginia. Her mother was, in White's words, "from 'immigrant' non-slaveholding stock." Her father, a lawyer and Methodist minister, died when she was nine, and her mother had a difficult time providing for herself and her three children alone. White then lost her mother when she was thirteen and was taken in by an aunt, but soon had to become self-supporting. Yet White remained quite conscious of her father's family background, and wrote that she "had always understood that if I went to a certain distant country where my grandfather had worked his slaves, I would 'belong.'" She lacked the social prominence and wealth that made it possible for the other suffragists to assume the highest positions of leadership in the suffrage movement, however. Her social standing was modest, yet respectable. Her political contacts were largely the result of her acquaintance with the lawyers and politicians of Tennessee through her work as a "crack" court reporter.[12]

All of these suffrage leaders, including Sue White, enjoyed opportunities for education far above the norm for women of their region.

All attended private secondary schools for girls (variously called "academies," "institutes," or "finishing schools"). Laura Clay and Madeline McDowell Breckinridge went on to attend exclusive girls' schools in the North after graduating from local academies; Clay to a finishing school in New York, and Breckinridge to Miss Porter's School in Farmington, Connecticut. Several attended colleges for women: Felton graduated as valedictorian from the Methodist Female College in Madison, Georgia, in 1852; Somerville completed the limited offerings at Whitworth College in Brookhaven, Mississippi, in 1877, and then graduated from Martha Washington College in Virginia as valedictorian in 1880. Clay and Breckinridge both attended coeducational universities: Clay studied for a year at the University of Michigan in 1880, and later, briefly, at the Agricultural and Mechanical College of Kentucky (the University of Kentucky); Breckinridge took courses intermittently at the University of Kentucky between 1890 and 1894. Sue White and Pattie Ruffner Jacobs, whose financial circumstances indicated that they would have to become self-supporting, attended teacher-training "normal schools." White went on to attend a business college and become a court reporter, while Jacobs found the means to go to New York to study art and voice prior to her marriage. Valentine's dream of college was stifled by her family's traditions and finances; but after her marriage she was tutored in her home by professors secured from the faculties of the University of Virginia and the University of Richmond by her husband, who shared her love of learning and had the means to support it.[13]

Many of these women also had extraordinary opportunities for travel beyond the South. Clay spent a year in Russia at the age of twelve. Felton spent years in Washington as a congressional wife, meeting and talking with people from all over the world, and watching from the galleries of Congress as key historical events unfolded. Later she was appointed by the governor of Georgia to be the state's "Lady Manager" at the 1893 Chicago World's Fair. Mary Johnston traveled extensively in Europe and northern Africa with her father when she was in her early twenties. Kate Gordon and Pattie Ruffner Jacobs also spent considerable time traveling in Europe. Lila Meade Valentine accompanied her husband on many of his business trips to England. Madeline McDowell Breckinridge made many trips to New York and Colorado, seeking treatment for tuberculosis. And though her travels were owed to her position with the WCTU rather than personal affluence, as a young woman Belle Kearney traveled all over the United States, and, indeed, all over the world.[14]

That these travels made enduring impressions and stimulated thought about the condition of women is clear. Felton recalled becoming "well acquainted with Lucy Stone, Susan B. Anthony, and the other pioneers in the suffrage movement" while in Washington; in Chicago she was intrigued by the opportunity to meet such famous leaders of women as Isabella Beecher Hooker (who, unlike her sisters Catherine and Harriet, was an ardent suffragist) and the wealthy socialite and civic reformer Bertha Palmer, who chaired the World's Fair's Board of Lady Managers. Mary Johnston's speeches reveal that she was a student of woman's condition in the Arab states of northern Africa and other countries she visited, as does Belle Kearney's autobiography. Kearney's encounter with Susan B. Anthony at the Chicago World's Fair in 1893 made a lasting impression; Kearney was overwhelmed to "behold her receiving the homage of the public whose criticism and opposition had so persistently followed her in the earlier days." Such an experience was very important for a young woman like Kearney, who was hungry for approval and recognition and who had scant opportunities growing up to hear anything that was positive about feminists.[15]

Johnston and Valentine were strongly influenced by the British suffragists: they attended meetings and marches, gathered materials for use in Virginia, and corresponded with British suffragists after returning home to establish the Equal Suffrage League of Virginia. A few months before she and a handful of her Richmond friends met in Ellen Glasgow's parlor to commence their own suffrage work, Valentine wrote to Johnston from London: "The situation is intensely interesting. The question is no longer an academic one, but has entered the field of practical politics. . . . I find all my friends suffragists of one kind or another." She also wrote, "I trust I may be able to bring home something which may be of use to us in our work here [Virginia]." Breckinridge was greatly impressed by the participation of enfranchised women in Colorado politics. Her sister-in-law and biographer Sophonisba Breckinridge recalled that "Madge" "sent back reports on women voters in Colorado to those in Lexington interested in woman suffrage to help correct information appearing in the eastern periodicals who loved to attack them."[16]

Wealth was important in the making of Southern suffragists, not only because of the opportunities for education and exposure to new ideas about woman's role in society, but because Southern suffragists usually had to fund their own suffrage activities and those of their organizations. A few leaders of the suffrage movement, including Kearney and White, and many followers were women of moderate means. As Somerville's daughter, Judge Lucy Somerville Howorth, said, "The custom of the period was that if you had the background of loyalty to the Confederacy in your family, then you were accepted even if you couldn't always buy your own ticket." But she also emphasized the importance of money "back when you virtually had to foot the bills yourself." Suffrage associations often held fund-raisers and sought contributions, but they were always short on funds, and leaders were most certainly expected to donate their time and expenses.[17]

Laura Clay spent considerable money on suffrage work. She paid her own expenses when she attended state, regional, and national conventions and when she assisted in suffrage campaigns outside of Kentucky, including many months in Oregon, Arizona, and Oklahoma. She contributed to the Kentucky Equal Rights Association, the Southern States Woman Suffrage Conference, and to the NAWSA, and helped her friend Kate Gordon with the expense of suffrage work in Louisiana. In 1911, a year of financial distress for the National, she hospitably paid the hotel bills for all NAWSA officers attending the national convention in Louisville. In 1913, the NAWSA reported a debt to Clay of $1,000. Breckinridge was also generous in her contributions to suffrage work. Honoraria for her frequent "non-suffrage" speeches and suffrage speeches outside the South went "back into suffrage work"; she donated her time and expenses for speeches in "the states of the Old Confederacy for suffrage is very new and very weak in them and they need help very much." She was also highly skilled in extracting contributions for suffrage work from her wealthy acquaintances. A favorite technique of hers was to offer matching funds; in 1918 she wrote to the KERA treasurer and offered to give $100 if nine other persons outside the Clay family did likewise. During the winter of 1913–1914, when Mississippi suffragists brought up a suffrage amendment for the first time, Nellie Nugent Somerville sent copies of the *Woman's Journal* to all members of the state legislature for three months. At one time, her search for information about suffrage sentiment led her to subscribe to every county newspaper in Mississippi.[18]

Belle Kearney, who was totally self-supporting and made her living as a lecturer, encountered little sympathy when she periodically asked the NAWSA for financial support for her suffrage work in Mississippi. In 1907, she asked the National for $1,000 for her expenses and those of her secretary, claiming she would be sacrificing that much by giving up a lecture tour in Nebraska. When NAWSA President Anna Howard Shaw (who considered Kearney tactless and a poor organizer) solicited the opinion of Kate Gordon, the latter replied that she considered "Miss K's price outrageous," implied that Kearney was bluffing about the Nebraska engagement, and added, "it seems to me she shows very little suffrage feeling not to be willing to make somewhat of a sacrifice in behalf of her state."[19]

These leaders were quite conscious of the predominance of elite women in their movement; indeed, Pattie Ruffner Jacobs was somewhat defensive on the subject, insisting that "in our ranks there are no social lines drawn, the sweated worker and the idle woman being equally acceptable." But Jacobs fully understood the protection as well as the influence provided by high social position, and she criticized as "insane" the allegations of members of the press who suggested that the predominance of elite women was a problem for the suffrage movement:

> This element [the leisure class] is the pillar of the suffrage movement. If it wasn't for them the suffrage movement would not have advanced as it has. The women of the leisure class can afford to go around stirring up enthusiasm for the movement which the women of other classes cannot do. The suffrage movement is a great thing for the women of the leisure class. . . . It gives the women . . . an opportunity to do something for their less fortunate sisters that will be of benefit to the entire feminine world. I only wish that more women of the leisure class in Birmingham would take up equal suffrage as they can do so much for the movement.[20]

Madeline McDowell Breckinridge and Laura Clay also understood that women from prominent families could, as Jacobs said, "do so much for the movement" with their exalted social position and influential connections. Describing her speech to the North Carolina legislature, Breckinridge wrote: "As I spoke under the portrait of my great-grandfather [Henry Clay], and as he had dedicated the capitol in the forties, that lent respectability to me and suffrage." The fact that Laura Clay's cousin Cassius M. Clay was the president of the Kentucky Constitutional Convention of 1890 meant that she was allowed to address the convention on behalf of women's rights. By 1914, the suffrage movement in Kentucky reached what Breckinridge called "the pink tea stage"; indeed, in that state, which in 1920 ratified the Nineteenth Amendment, the movement actually became quite fashionable. In January 1914, Breckinridge and Clay together addressed the legislature in joint session—the first time women had ever been given that privilege. The evening was described as "a brilliant social occasion as well as a political innovation. The socially eligible came from many parts of the state, and the resulting publicity for the cause throughout the state was very great."[21]

The protection of lofty social position was essential in Virginia, where the announcement of the very existence of a suffrage organization caused, in Mary Johnston's words, a "hornet's nest" to descend around their ears; it was hard to understand, she said, "the shock of surprise, of more or less indignant incredulity with which Richmond received the intimation that within her walls were women who wished votes." That the suffragists included some of the state's most eminent daughters helped them weather the storm and expand their ranks. Norfolk suffragists pleaded with Mary Johnston to allow them to honor her with a tea that was actually a front for a reception for NAWSA President Dr. Anna Howard Shaw; people would come to pay homage to the famous Virginia gentlewoman, novelist, and relative of a Confederate hero who might be put off by association with

Dr. Shaw. Friendships with leading politicians were also useful; Lila Meade Valentine confided to Johnston that her close friend (former) Governor A. J. Montague and his son Hill helped her draft the suffrage petition the Virginia suffragists sent to Congress in 1910. And in 1912 Hill Montague introduced the first suffrage bill into the House of Delegates.[22]

The impeccable credentials of William Louis Nugent as a champion of "home rule" in Mississippi meant, according to Somerville's daughter Judge Lucy Somerville Howorth, that her mother "could do no wrong." Fellow citizens of Greenville might grumble about her support for suffrage and other reforms, but they would nevertheless contribute when she asked them for money for "her" causes. The wives of Louisiana governors Ruffin G. Pleasant and John Parker were among the Gordons' lieutenants. Southern suffragists often held their meetings in the state capitols; and newspapers that refused to endorse them would nevertheless grant them special privileges such as printing special suffrage sections with proceeds going to the suffrage coffers.[23]

Newspapers never failed to comment on the social standing of the suffragists. The Knoxville *Sentinel* described Clay as "belonging to one of the South's oldest families; the Clays have for generations held positions of dignity and honor in the nation," and as "the brilliant daughter of the late Cassius M. Clay, Sr., diplomat and soldier." The Charlotte *News* described Breckinridge's lecture as "characterized by the dignity of a woman of gentle birth and high refinement." A Birmingham paper described Jacobs as "one of the prominent social leaders of the city," while a Pensacola paper called her "one of the most brilliant club women in the United States and the South" as well as "eloquent, beautiful and gowned in perfect taste." The Nashville *Democrat* observed in January 1913 "that a young Southern woman of Miss Johnston's type, rearing, and environment should become an ardent advocate of equal suffrage is one of the most marked evidences of the growth of the sentiment. A speech from such a source before the Tennessee legislature twenty-five years ago would hardly have been conceivable."[24]

White, often the exception that proved the rule, realized that her lack of social contacts at times made her less effective than certain other suffragists in her state. Writing to Catt concerning an upcoming audience of prominent Tennessee suffragists with Senator John Shields, she observed: "Mrs. Warner [Kate Burch Warner, President of the Tennessee Woman Suffrage Association] . . . knows him quite well socially. I know him quite well also, but my acquaintance has been more political than social. There is sometimes a difference."[25]

Leaders of the suffrage movement in the South were selected and recruited by leaders from both North and South who understood the particular importance of family name and social standing in the region. In 1894, Susan B. Anthony wrote to Laura Clay, who was making arrangements for Anthony and Catt's sweeping tour of the South in 1895, expressing hopes that "our National Southern Committee will do all it can to open the way *for* us—by finding the most *influential* and *practical native* parties in each city—to *invite* us, and *chaperone* us, for us to go into any city *without* such parties to *herald* and *welcome* our coming—would be a *misfortune*—rather than a help to our cause!" NAWSA leaders who recruited Kearney and Somerville as leaders of the Mississippi Woman Suffrage Association in the 1890s were impressed by their standing in Mississippi society, as well as by the personal talents of the two women. Anna Howard Shaw, reporting on her visit to Mississippi (one of the places "where the workers were having the hardest struggle and where they were making the bravest fight"), wrote of Somerville: "her enthusiasm and tireless service, added to the prominence of her family in the state, make her an ideal president. If Mississippi does not show a marked increase in sentiment during the coming year it will not be the fault of Mrs. Somerville and her corps of splendid assistants." NAWSA Treasurer Harriet Taylor Upton was delighted at the recruitment of Madeline McDowell Breckinridge, who, because of her editorial connection with the Lexington *Herald*, "is one of the most useful members in the South."[26]

Southern suffragists confirmed the NAWSA leaders' assessment of the importance of recruiting eminent women as leaders in their region. Kate Gordon was highly conscious of social reputation, and as a NAWSA officer she stressed the need for the organization to consider whether or not a woman had "a name to conjure with" when selecting leaders for the South. And Belle Kearney, appealing to President Shaw to send Laura Clay to speak in Mississippi, said, "You could not do a greater kindness to this state than to send Miss Laura Clay here for one month if no longer. . . . The Clay name means power in the whole South."[27]

That social position afforded a degree of protection is evident in the fact that, though Southern suffragists endured a great deal of criticism, they were rarely, if ever, attacked as personally and as viciously as Catt, Shaw, Anthony, and other national leaders of the movement from North and West were attacked by Southern opponents. At the end of her long suffrage career, Laura Clay observed that she "was never heckled or treated rudely by an audience." Mary Johnston and Lila Meade Valentine received considerable criticism after declaring for woman suffrage in 1910, but according to Valentine the "storm" was soon over and they were "riding in smooth waters again." Criticism was generally guarded. For example, James Callaway of the Macon *News* wrote of Rebecca Latimer Felton:

> Mrs. Felton is one of Georgia's most remarkable women. She is a woman of pronounced intellectuality. Hers is a vigor and keenness of mind seldom

possessed by sisters of her sex of fewer years. And it is regrettable, therefore, that she, a woman of the old school by whom the traditions of Southern womanhood and womankind in general should be especially appreciated and understood, a woman of such unusual capacity should be stumping the state in behalf of the equal suffrage propaganda.

A society known for its violence produced only one known incidence of violence directed at a suffragist: in 1913 someone broke open a skylight and threw a can of vile-smelling chemicals at Jacobs and the other suffragists on the platform at the state suffrage convention in Tennessee.[28]

When opponents were abusive, suffragists and their families and supporters became highly indignant. On one occasion, Felton gave Callaway a thorough scolding in print for "unchivalrously" attacking her—a grandmother eighty years old. When the Jackson *Clarion-Ledger* criticized the Mississippi suffragists' 1907 plan to petition for woman suffrage, saying "the present legislature has the opportunity to administer to female suffrage the blow it deserves and should receive," Nellie Nugent Somerville; her son, attorney Robert Nugent Somerville; and several others fired off a letter to the editor stating:

> As to this, we have to say, the women and men of this state who are presenting this matter to the legislature are not a set of children coming here to be reproved for their temerity. We expect nothing but respectful treatment from the legislature, and do not believe the advice of the *Clarion-Ledger* will influence legislators to depart from their usual policy of consideration for all classes of people who appear before them.[29]

Like a knight charging off in defense of fair ladies, Desha Breckinridge publicly rebuked "Marse Henry" Watterson for the latter's attacks on Kentucky suffragists who were led by the women of his family. When Watterson complained of the *Herald*'s treatment of him, pronouncing Breckinridge "destitute of honor and courage" and saying he would "visit upon (Breckinridge) the physical chastisement an act so dastardly deserves" were he not so old and feeble, Breckinridge replied:

> You claim exemption from attack or insult because of your age and condition. You do not let sex, age, or conditions bar your brutal attacks on those who lead the movement for votes for women. . . . Your brutal, vulgar and mendacious characterization of those at the head of this movement put you beyond the pale of recognition by gentlefolk: you put yourself in the pillory of shame. . . . Your characterization, denunciation and slander of those the hem of whose garment you are not fit to touch demands that someone tell the truth to and about you.[30]

It was much safer for the opponents of the movement in the South to speak of Southern suffragists, as they usually did, as innocent victims who were being misguided and misled by Northern feminists.

Like Mary Johnston—who, in her speech to the Virginia House of Delegates entitled "Noblesse Oblige," emphasized that her family had helped establish the commonwealth, fight its wars, cultivate its soil, and build its public works—Southern suffragists deliberately highlighted the social standing of the movement's advocates and insisted that they were people to be reckoned with. In all of their dealings with the press, in their pleas to the legislatures, they insisted on, and usually received, respect—if not suffrage.[31]

II

If social position had its privileges, it also brought certain obligations; like many men and women who engaged in the reform activities of the South in the late nineteenth and early twentieth centuries, these women felt a special responsibility for the lower classes, along with a conviction that the masses should defer to their advice and leadership. In her 1921 biography, *Madeline McDowell Breckinridge: A Leader in the New South*, Sophonisba Breckinridge said of "Madge":

> She belonged to Kentucky by right of five generations of service and devotion. What interested Kentucky was her interest; what interested her must be of concern to the community with whose life her life was one. Only by understanding this reciprocal relationship is it easy to understand her. She was so modest, yet so aggressive; so humble-minded, yet so assured; so without claim for herself as an individual, so peremptory in demanding the best for the community.[32]

Lila Meade Valentine also believed that "of those to whom much is given, much is expected." Her 1921 obituary read, "This, then, was the aristocrat with her *noblesse oblige*, the democrat with her longing to give to the great body of unknown and undiscovered men and women the glow and potency of exalted ideals." Fulfilling their obligations under this aristocratic credo led the leaders of the Southern suffrage movement, like many other Southern women, into charitable and reform work that in turn led them to desire political power.[33]

While the traditional, sex-specific duties of aristocratic Southern men involved an obligation to govern, upper-class Southern women were charged with safeguarding the morals as well as the health and welfare of Southern society—though expected to stay out of politics. In the Old South, their responsibility was limited to their families and "extended families"—slaves, relatives living under their roofs, and to a certain extent, the poor whites nearby—though through their much-celebrated "indirect influence" they were said to exercise "an ameliorating influence" throughout Southern society. In the New South, however, middle and upper-class Southern women increasingly carried their social concern beyond "the individual home" to serve "the great social home" as well. Upper-class Southern women seemed to feel a sense of "maternalism" not unlike the "paternalism" characteristic of Southern men of their class, and they had little confidence in the ability of lower-class Southerners to solve their own problems. Yet the ideas of these altruistic women about how to help the less fortunate mainly involved amelioration of conditions, not alteration of the basic social and economic arrangements of the South.[34]

As Anne Firor Scott first described in the *The Southern Lady: From Pedestal to Politics*, Southern women gradually expanded their sphere through involvement in various groups, including church groups, charitable organizations, women's clubs, and reform associations such as the Woman's Christian Temperance Union. As these women became increasingly familiar with society's ills, many of them tried to use their influence to help resolve in a humane fashion the pressing social problems of their region. And as Southern society became increasingly urban and industrial in the late nineteenth and early twentieth centuries, these women were drawn into politics, just as changed methods of textile production led many women of lesser means to follow their traditional tasks of spinning and weaving out of the home and into the factories. It became clear to these Southern reformers that problems related to health, safety, and morality must be resolved by large-scale, government-directed efforts, not by altruistic individuals.[35]

These prominent leaders of the woman suffrage movement in the South all followed this path outlined by Scott. Many of them compiled splendid records of service, and in many cases they were as well known for their civic and reform work as for their involvement in the suffrage movement. Once converted to the suffrage cause, they used civic clubs and reform groups to promote (directly or indirectly) woman suffrage, and used suffrage organizations to promote reform.

Jean Gordon was one of the South's most notable reformers and a prime example of an affluent Southern woman whose charitable impulses led her into a career as an advocate of governmental protection of the poor. After the death of her fiancé in 1888, Gordon became a volunteer for the Charity Organization of New Orleans, through which she first learned of the extent and condition of child labor in the city. In 1896 she persuaded the Era Club (a women's club that she and Kate founded that same year) to investigate the problem of child labor in the city. Armed with its report, she began a ten-year battle for an effective child-labor law. In 1906, the child-labor law and a state constitutional amendment permitting women to serve as factory inspectors were adopted, and Jean Gordon was the first to serve—insisting on serving the full five years without pay. Gordon's concern about the children of the poor also led to the creation of a day nursery at Kingsley House, the New Orleans settlement house, and the establishment of a home for "feeble-minded" girls.[36]

Jean Gordon was a leading light in the Progressive movement in the South, even joining the Progressive Party (1912) and serving on its state committee. In 1909, she persuaded her friend Louisiana governor Jared Sanders to call a conference of Southern governors to address the problem of child labor in the region; the delegates formed an organization, "The Southern Conference on Women and Child Labor," which brought together child-labor reformers at annual conferences to share experiences and call for stronger state action. In 1912, Gordon joined forces with other Southern philanthropists and reformers (including Nellie Nugent Somerville, Mary Johnston, Madeline McDowell Breckinridge, and Sue White) in the Southern Sociological Congress, an organization dedicated to finding solutions for and coordinating efforts to solve a variety of social problems in the South.[37]

Sometimes called "the Jane Addams of the South," Jean Gordon admired and emulated the goals and methods of Addams and the genteel volunteer reformers who constituted our nation's first generation of social workers. She was one of the foremost Southern members of the predominately Northern National Consumers' League, a small, elite organization of well-educated, mostly upper-class women who used their influence to promote maximum-hour and minimum-wage legislation for working women. Gordon served as vice-president of the League from 1909 to 1911, and as secretary for the Southern states in 1912. She believed that wealthy, educated women should become increasingly involved in public service, and that they were uniquely qualified to serve, as she had, as public officials administering hard-won protective legislation. Indeed, in 1908, she gave an address, "Noblesse Oblige," at the NAWSA annual convention, in which she insisted such jobs should be *reserved* for upper-class female volunteers: "Instead of being regarded as only fitted for women of ordinary position and intellect," she said, "all offices such as superintendents of reformatories, matrons and women factory inspectors, should be filled by women . . . [who] would be above the temptation of graft or the fear of losing their positions."[38]

Jean's sister, Kate Gordon, became well known for her efforts in the field of public health. In 1899, she won the eternal gratitude of the civic-minded in New Orleans for leading a successful campaign for a water and sewage system for that flood-plagued city. Taking advantage of the 1898 constitutional amendment allowing women taxpayers to vote on tax issues, she organized a systematic campaign to put an initiative petition for the requisite bond issue on the ballot and then secured the votes to carry it. Kate Gordon was also credited with the establishment of the New Orleans Anti-Tuberculosis League in 1906, which later established a hospital for victims of that disease. She also aided in the establishment of the New Orleans Hospital and Dispensary for Women and Children, a juvenile court system, and a Society for the Prevention of Cruelty to Animals.[39]

Like her friends the Gordon sisters, Nellie Nugent Somerville was a prominent philanthropist and reformer. Her first ventures beyond the home were through the Methodist Episcopal Church, South, whose women compiled such a remarkable record of charitable and reform work in the region. In the 1890s she served as district secretary for Woman's Foreign Mission work, as the first president of the North Mississippi Conference Parsonage and Home Mission Society, and as a member of the Board of Home Missions. She also belonged to the Hypatia Club, a women's literary society. Before abandoning it in 1897 for suffrage work, Somerville was a leader in the Woman's Christian Temperance Union, serving as president of the Greenville chapter and as corresponding secretary of the Mississippi WCTU.[40]

Like Kate Gordon, Somerville was keenly interested in the issue of public health. Living in the Mississippi Delta, where periodic epidemics of malaria caused many deaths and led to closings of schools, evacuations (and even interruption of suffrage campaigns), Somerville was particularly concerned about this omnipresent threat to her community. And in this period before the advent of public-health professionals, people turned to this intelligent Southern matron to advise them on this problem. A Cleveland, Mississippi, newspaper noted:

> Mrs. Nellie Nugent Somerville of Greenville was the guest of her son, Attorney Robert Somerville, during the latter part of last week. She spent a portion of her time with the faculty and pupils of Cleveland High Schools, giving some very valuable and interesting talks to all grades, regarding neatness in person and dress, care in using a common drinking cup in schools, stores, etc. Her talks made a vivid impression on the children, and there is no doubt but that these good seeds sown in the fertile fields of the child mind will awaken many a mother and father to a sense of duty along these lines. She also visited among the representative women of the place, enlisting their co-operation in the betterment of conditions in the town. She was justly distressed at the condition of the bayou at and near the bridge, and attributed the greater part of the severe attacks of chills and fevers to that foul place. The refuse that is being dumped into the stagnant water cannot but cause illness.[41]

Eager for the local government to assume responsibility for public health and other community problems, Somerville was one of the founders of the Greenville Civic Club (1909), which vowed to work for "good government" that "protects public health, public morals, law and order, and which demands efficiency in public office." Resolving to "first learn the latest approved features and methods of civic betterment, and then to pass on to the community such information," the Civic Club was successful in establishing a public library and persuading the city to enact the first sanitation and health regulations in the city and to hire the first community health nurse in the state. These reformers also launched the state's first anti-tuberculosis campaign—including waging war on the tobacco-spitting habit widespread among Southern men and particularly offensive to these refined women. Indeed, the ladies carried cards to hand out to offenders reminding them that their expectoration posed a threat to public health.[42]

In addition to Somerville, Belle Kearney, Rebecca Latimer Felton, and (to a lesser extent) Laura Clay were active in the WCTU. Kearney, a brilliant orator, was a professional organizer with the Union; she was a protégée of Frances Willard, who greatly appreciated Kearney's contribution to making the organization so popular among Southern women in the 1890s. Kearney clearly recognized that the WCTU had awakened many women to social activism; she called it "the golden key that unlocked the prison doors of pent-up possibilities. . . . The generous liberator, the joyous iconoclast, the discoverer, the developer of Southern women." Alcohol abuse among men was a problem of major proportions in the late nineteenth century, and one that many Southern women like Kearney and Felton believed to be the root of a great many social evils. Between the time Felton joined the WCTU in 1886 and the adoption of statewide prohibition in Georgia in 1907, she used her considerable influence to demand the outlawing of liquor, which she believed brought untold suffering upon women and children.[43]

Felton was well known for her advocacy of a number of other reforms, notably the abolition of the convict lease system in Georgia, accomplished in 1908. She campaigned for twenty-five years for vocational training opportunities for poor white girls, and is given partial credit for the establishment of the state's Normal and Industrial College (1889) and training school for girls (1915). Felton saw herself as the champion of the "Georgia Crackers," the group that had made up her husband's constituency. But unlike the other leading suffragists, she opposed the restriction of child labor, saying that refusal to allow the children of poor widows to work in cotton factories would work a hardship on many needy families. When Northern reformers suggested the morality of the female millworkers was being compromised, Felton defended their honor. After her death the operatives showed their gratitude by raising sixty dollars for a marker to be placed on her grave.[44]

Few Southern Progressives of either sex achieved as much as Madeline McDowell Breckinridge and Lila Meade Valentine. Breckinridge was acclaimed by reformers throughout the nation for her work in Lexington and in Kentucky, and was consulted as an expert by leading educators and professionals in the fields of charity and corrections. She was an officer of the National Conference of Social Work and a member of the National Child Labor Committee. As legislative chairman of the State Federation of Women's Clubs of Kentucky (1908–1912), she rallied the state's women behind Progressive reform; and in 1910 she was elected to a two-year term on the General Federation of Women's Clubs' National Board of Directors.[45]

Through her sister-in-law and dear friend Sophonisba Breckinridge, a professor at the University of Chicago (1904–1933) and resident of Hull House (1908–1920), "Madge" had direct knowledge of the theories and methods of the nation's pioneering reformers and social scientists. She brought in many of them, including Jane Addams, Marion Talbot, Grace Abbot, and Charles Zueblin, to speak to reformers in Lexington. Breckinridge helped establish a rural adaptation of a settlement house in the Kentucky mountains. And as the leader of the Lexington Civic League, founded in 1900, she founded a playground for slum children that grew into a combined school and social settlement that was a model of its kind. While in Denver she learned of the work of Ben Lindsey, pioneer in the juvenile court movement; and upon her return to Lexington, she successfully campaigned for the establishment of a juvenile court system and the restriction of child labor. She served on the Executive Committee of the Kentucky Anti–Child Labor Association. Breckinridge was also extremely effective as a leader in the fight against tuberculosis, with which she and several members of her family were afflicted, and was largely responsible for the establishment of a state sanitorium.[46]

Breckinridge was unique among these "maternalistic" Southern ladies in her interest in the development of new, more "scientific" methods of administering charity that would help people break out of what is now known as the cycle of poverty. Toward this end she was a founder of the Lexington Associated Charities in 1900, which attempted to screen recipients of charity, identify the "truly needy," and work with them to help get them back on their feet. Believing that the indiscriminate distribution of largesse encouraged indolence, she did battle against the Salvation Army, a move that was applauded by exponents of "scientific charity" in Chicago but largely misunderstood in Lexington.[47]

Lila Meade Valentine was especially notable for her contributions in the fields of education and public health. After a prolonged visit to England in 1892, where she witnessed "Gladstonian liberalism" at high tide, she returned to Virginia determined to awaken the social conscience of the South. In 1900, she played a leading role in establishing the Richmond Education Association, an organization of lay people with the goal of convincing the people of Richmond

that although we are growing in wealth, that growth will be greater and its foundations surer, if our children, all of them, white and black, are trained in head and heart and hand, not only to do the work that cries out to be done in the material upbuilding of our city, but also to become the intelligent, self-respecting, law-abiding citizens who shall make impossible the inefficiency, bribery, and corruption that are disgracing so many American communities today.[48]

Valentine and her co-workers launched a campaign for public kindergartens and in 1901 founded a school to train teachers for them. They were also responsible for the construction of a new high school, complete with vocational education. Increasingly aware of the poor state of health of most of the schoolchildren, Valentine assisted a group of nurses who were struggling to keep open a settlement house. She also helped the nurses establish the Instructive Visiting Nurses Association, which sent nurses into the public schools and set up tuberculosis clinics for each race. Valentine was also instrumental in the establishment of the Anti-Tuberculosis Auxiliary and a hospital for victims of the disease. She was quite successful in mobilizing the leading ladies of Richmond society in support of her causes. When campaigning for the new high school, she found them totally ignorant of the wretched state of the existing school; so she led a group of them on a tour of the decaying, rat-invested facility—in the company of a reporter who publicized their horrified reaction and thus committed them to action.[49]

In 1902, the founders of the Southern Education Board, a group that in 1901 began what Dewey Grantham describes as "a spectacular campaign" to stimulate public sentiment in favor of universal public education, sought out Lila Valentine. Organized initially by Northern philanthropists, the SEB worked through local leaders to enlist the cooperation of government officials in the Southern states. Valentine signed on enthusiastically, inviting the SEB to hold its next conference in Richmond—the first interracial gathering in the city since the Civil War. An energetic and highly successful statewide educational crusade followed, directed by a new "Cooperative Education Association" of which Valentine and her friend Virginia's "educational governor" Andrew J. Montague were leaders.[50]

Mary Johnston's travels, including four years in New York, exposed her to the full range of reforms being discussed in England and America at the turn of the century. As a result she supported many causes, including protective legislation for women and children, compulsory education, the peace movement, and eugenics. Such was her sympathy for the working class and her disgust with those who exploited them that she called herself a socialist, though she was never a "card carrying" member (her words). As chair of the Legislative Committee of the Equal Suffrage League of Virginia, Johnston led the organization to victory in securing bills concerning juvenile delinquency and child neglect, and helped defeat legislation to lower standards for milk and increase the working hours of women and children in factories.[51]

Johnston and Valentine were unusual in their support for organized labor; under their leadership the Board of Directors of the Equal
Suffrage League of Virginia passed resolutions patterned after those of
a New York City suffrage organization in support of labor's right to
organize and calling on the labor movement in Virginia to support
woman suffrage. Johnston was appointed by the governor as a delegate to the National Child Labor Committee conference in 1916. She
belonged to the American Association for Labor Legislation, the
National Consumer's League, the Southern Sociological Congress, and
the National Institute of Social Sciences, and contributed to the International Congress of Working Women.[52]

Though none of the other leading Southern suffragists under consideration had a record of service quite as extensive as those listed
above, all were actively involved in reform work that stimulated their
desire for woman suffrage. Jacobs was a leader in the movement for
effective child-labor legislation in Alabama (and in the 1920s in the
campaign against the convict lease system). White championed state
support for the blind and served as executive secretary of the Tennessee Commission for the Blind when it was established in 1918. She
helped draft and push through the state legislature the state's first
married women's property bill, a mother's pension act, and an old-age
pension act. Laura Clay, though interested in a wide variety of causes,
was first and foremost a feminist; and most of the reforms she promoted had to do with women's rights (see Chapter Three). Under her
leadership the Kentucky Equal Rights Association secured important
revisions in many Kentucky laws affecting women and children, and
improvements in women's educational opportunities.[53]

The participation of the leaders of the Southern suffrage movement in
this wide range of organizations and activities aimed at improving
Southern society led them to a heightened awareness of the problems
of their section and the need for governmental action to solve them.
But in itself this does not explain their decision to take up the suffrage
cause. Though over time a growing number of organized women in
the South—probably a majority by 1918—endorsed the suffrage movement, there were many Southern women who worked long and hard
for all of these causes without affiliating with the suffrage movement.[54]

Many Southern women who were actively engaged in reform
were content to accept the traditional definition of woman's sphere,
now expanded to include social activism short of direct involvement
in politics. Some no doubt lacked the courage to defy convention in
support of such a radical cause. Others rejected the suffrage cause for
religious reasons; as Jean Friedman described in *The Enclosed Garden:
Women and Community in the Evangelical South*, the South's evangelical
churches, which promulgated conservative definitions of gender roles,
exerted a powerful influence that diminished only very slowly and

gradually in the postwar South. Many women believed that their sex could be more effective using "indirect influence" than as full-fledged participants in the unsavory world of Southern politics. Lucinda Helm, a high-ranking official within the Women's Department of the Methodist Episcopal Church, South, responded negatively to Clay's recruitment efforts, saying she and Clay "differ in regard to the *methods* by which God intended woman to work and I cannot see differently yet." Other female reformers (perhaps advocates of fewer, or relatively uncontroversial reforms) believed that their legislators had responded affirmatively to many of the requests of organized womanhood, and that they would continue to do so if not insulted by a demand for female enfranchisement. The president of the Georgia Federation of Women's Clubs, Mrs. Z. I. Fitzgerald, used her influence to prevent consideration of a suffrage resolution at the Federation's 1914 state convention, saying, "I am against woman suffrage. Women's clubs of Georgia have had no difficulty in getting their measures passed by the legislature. We are the power behind the throne now, and would lose, not gain, by a change."[55]

The women who stepped forward to lead the suffrage movement, however, were prepared by temperament and experience for this bold adventure. And they were convinced that the reforms they supported would never be fully implemented, nor the needs of women and children adequately represented, until women were enfranchised.

III

To a certain extent, personal characteristics, including courage and confidence, even stubbornness, always play a role in an individual's decision to work for a reform long before there is widespread support for it in his or her community and to continue working for it against such strong opposition and with so little success. These "great-souled southern suffragists," as Catt called them, were so armed. These were formidable individuals with strength of will either innate or acquired —sometimes quite deliberately—through experience. Part of their confidence was due to their social position; after all, most of them came from families accustomed to shaping rather than being shaped by public opinion in their communities. The early experience of these women led them to reject the traditional assessment of woman's nature and potential and made them receptive to feminism. And years of frustration in advocating various reforms before Southern politicians, most of whom the suffragists held in slight regard, convinced these women of their own impotence without direct political power.[56]

The Gordon sisters and Nellie Nugent Somerville had more than their share of self-assurance. Kate Gordon once said, "the reason that Jean and I have accomplished so much is that we never cared what people thought." Highly elitist, the Gordons did not expect the masses to support the "correct" course of action. "Review every advance, moral or otherwise," said Kate. "Have the majority ever desired the advance? The great earnest minority always shapes thought and leads the van." Kate Gordon never doubted her own views, even in the final years of the suffrage struggle when scores of suffragists begged her to reconsider her opposition to the federal amendment (see Chapter Six). The fact that Nellie Nugent Somerville and her associates named their literary society after Hypatia, a learned woman stoned to death by a mob in ancient Egypt, was indicative of their attitude toward public opinion.[57]

Young Pattie Ruffner's diary reveals a mischievous desire to be distinctive if not distinguished: "I wish I was phenomenally brilliant or else stupid or something or other different from everybody else—I do detest with my whole soul mediocre people and things." Shortly thereafter, she continued along the same lines: "I am sorry not to be odd and eccentric, and it would be senseless to affect it as folks do frequently. It is dreadful to be like everybody else and express the same opinions and views about everything that people thought and said before your grandmother was born." Not at all intimidated by their opponents, Jacobs and her associates in Birmingham held as a fundraiser a mock session of the legislature in which they ridiculed suffrage opponents for "propaganda and profit": her imitation of the bombastic Alabama congressman Thomas Heflin at the 1913 NAWSA convention "brought down the house."[58]

Laura Clay's extraordinary character was evident at an early age. Even as a schoolgirl of fifteen years she was consciously trying to develop courage through the exercise of it. She wrote in her diary: "Today I took a galvanic shock. Mrs. Williams was showing experiments to the girls, and gave those who wished it, shocks. I was a good deal afraid, though I have taken one before; but I determined to overcome this fear, so took two, one severer than the other. By constantly resisting fear, I hope finally to become courageous. I think it is becoming too, for a Christian not to be a coward." Clay felt an obligation to society attributable not only to a sense of *noblesse oblige*, but to her awareness of her own extraordinary ability: "From my early youth I have been told that I possessed more than ordinary mental abilities. I have them, I owe more than ordinary service to myself and others."[59]

For Clay, as for several of these leading suffragists, religious conviction was a source of strength and confidence. They rejected the religious conservatism in regard to gender so pervasive in their region, instead embracing the view common among nineteenth-century women's rights advocates that Christianity elevated the position of women. To them, work for greater influence for women was quite in keeping with God's will. Efforts by conservative male leaders of their denominations to rein in the growing activism of women only increased their commitment to women's rights (see Chapter Three). Laura Clay was convinced that God had called her to serve the "great cause of women's rights," and that he would give her the courage to go against the grain:

> Instead of the morbid craving for the admiration and affection of others, these ten years have taught me to strive more to follow that which is right according to my best judgement, and I have found that this will in this life produce cold esteem and repel affection as often as otherwise. Nevertheless, God sees and approves, and may He grant that this may daily become more and more sufficient incitement to me to fulfill all that He seems to set before me.[60]

Belle Kearney also believed she had been called by God to serve the cause of woman suffrage. Armed with the martyr's conviction of eventual vindication, Kearney defined her "radicalism" as "Christianity brought down into daily life—against conservatism which often means selfishness." And Somerville inspired her followers in her first presidential address in 1898 by proclaiming that: "The strength of any movement lies not in its notoriety or popularity but in its justice. 'Thrice armed is he who hath his quarrel just.' Think today, not of the difficulties and opposition but of the truth and righteousness of our cause."[61]

The early experiences of these women who became leaders of the Southern suffrage movement were of crucial importance in making them more susceptible to feminism than other women of similar social and economic backgrounds. The examples and attitudes of family members were especially important. Laura Clay's childhood experience was such that it would have converted almost anyone to feminism, and it had that effect on all of the women in her family. Upon his appointment to Russia, Cassius Clay took his family with him to St. Petersburg, but when living with six children and in the style expected of an ambassador proved too costly, he sent them back home. Mary Jane Clay managed to get her brood back to Kentucky, despite the hazards of travel in the midst of the Civil War, and to manage the plantation and multitude of children by herself for eight years. A talented businesswoman, she was able to pay off a large debt on the property and remodel and expand White Hall even during wartime, and to provide her daughters with a formal education despite her husband's opposition. Meanwhile, Cassius Clay became involved in a well-publicized scandal with a notorious St. Petersburg courtesan and then returned to Kentucky with an illegitimate son, whom he legally adopted. Advanced in his thinking when it suited his own desires, Clay divorced his wife, who lost the plantation she had tended so carefully. Mary Jane Clay, her daughters Mary Barr Clay (who resumed her original name after a divorce), Sallie Clay Bennett, and Annie Clay all became suffragists and advocates of women's rights.[62]

Like Laura Clay, whose feminism resulted from admiration for her unimpeachable mother and disgust with her errant father, many suffrage leaders were open to feminism owing to a combination of positive and negative experiences. Sue White greatly admired her Baptist mother for refusing to be intimidated by "baiting and harrassment" from her Methodist husband's congregation because she refused to change her affiliation; and White was equally proud of her father for upholding his wife's right to choose. White also admired her mother for her resourcefulness as she struggled to bring up her three children after her husband's death. White was influenced as well by the fact that her mother "drew few distinctions between" her son and her daughters in rearing her children. On the negative side, White saw many examples of the mistreatment of women and of their disadvantages under the law during her ten years as a court reporter. And she was bitter that the attorneys and judges who thought so highly of her as a scribe ridiculed her desire to become a lawyer.[63]

Kearney recalled that her "mother and father reared me in a very liberal atmosphere concerning the intellectual and political status of women" and was enormously proud that late in life her parents both became suffragists. At seventy-one, Walter Kearney even accepted the presidency of an Equal Rights Club Belle helped organize. But "notwithstanding father's broad-minded position," Belle recalled, "in the earlier days it did not occur to him that *his* daughter might desire to enter the field of active modern workers." He even opposed her becoming a public school teacher, and when she was nineteen they had an enormous "clash of ideas," as he could not endure the humiliation of having his daughter work for wages. But finally recognizing in his daughter "a certain will-force" and "an indomitable energy which he began to respect," he allowed her to open a private school in his own home. He dismissed her desire to study law as absurd, however, and never relented on that point.[64]

Somerville's formative experiences in regard to her views on sex roles were all positive; she was the descendent of several generations of well-educated women as well as educated men. Her grandmother, who was the most important female figure in Nellie's life after her mother's early death, was a wise and strong-willed woman to whom Nellie was totally devoted. Her father, well aware of the remarkable intelligence of his daughter, gave her the best education available for women, and then invited her to read for the law in his office. Nellie declined; according to her daughter (who became a distinguished lawyer and judge), Nellie was more inclined to "do good" than read law, which "was a little more on the side of pure business than her nature would respond to."[65]

The Gordon sisters also grew up in a family environment that encouraged a liberal interpretation of woman's proper activity. They traced their disregard for traditional limitations on woman's role (as well as their "hatred of suffering") to their mother who, "strange for that day, believed it was all right for a lady to go up to a city hall or a newspaper office. In fact, she believed that a lady might do anything if it were for good."[66]

Once they espoused the suffrage movement, these leading suffragists had considerable support from their families. The women of the Clay family, of course, had one another for support, as did the Gordon sisters. The Gordons were also encouraged by their sister Fannie, a teacher and then principal in the New Orleans Public Schools; more domestically oriented than her prominent sisters, she managed the household for the three women. Mary Johnston lived with her two sisters, who were also suffragists. Indeed, Anna Howard Shaw once said, in reference to the Clays, the Gordons, the Johnstons, the three Howard sisters of Georgia, and the three Finnegans of Texas: "We used to say, laughingly, if there was failure to organize any state in the South, that it must be due to the fact that no family there had three sisters to start the movement."[67]

Madeline Breckinridge, Pattie Jacobs, and Lila Valentine all enjoyed the enthusiastic backing of their husbands. Despite the fact that Desha Breckinridge engaged in a long love affair that caused his wife considerable heartache, the Breckinridges continued to live together in a surprisingly amicable fashion, with Madge even recruiting her husband's lover into suffrage work. Desha put the Lexington *Herald*, in which Madge had a weekly women's page, at his wife's disposal, and he wrote countless editorials in support of her suffrage work, of which he was very proud. Solon Jacobs took great pride in the prominence of his attractive wife; he fully supported Pattie's suffrage work, even attending occasional meetings and offering advice and suggestions. Ben Valentine was passionate (indeed poetic) in support of woman suffrage; his death in June 1919 was a great blow to Lila, though, since he had shared her commitment to woman suffrage, she found comfort in the work. In a letter to a co-worker, she wrote:

> He left me a precious letter in which he urges me to go on with the work we both so ardently believed in, and I feel him near me all the time. I have been blessed beyond compare in having such perfect companionship all these years. I thank God for it and try to say, "Thy will be done." I pray that I may be given the strength to face life as a Christian . . . and if I can go on working with all of you in our woman's movement and in the church I shall feel that there is a chance of "carrying on" a little longer, even without the sunshine of his bodily presence, which has so powerfully sustained me hitherto.[68]

Somerville's husband was a rather conventional man who, according to his daughter, did not really understand the basic reasons for the women's movement, but did not oppose it. "He thought women had everything. He lacked the imagination to really understand people." But he "never lifted a finger in opposition," and husband and wife presented a united front to the community. Their four children, however, actively supported the suffrage cause, especially their son Robert and daughter Lucy; she attended suffrage conventions with her mother and founded an Equal Rights Club while at Randolph-Macon College in Lynchburg, Virginia.[69]

Personality and family background contributed to the conversion and dedication of these women to woman suffrage, but the recruiting efforts of Northern feminists were essential in their decisions to become suffragists and assume leadership roles in the controversial movement. The overtures of Northern women were crucial in the decisions of Clay, Kearney, Somerville, and the Gordons to become suffrage leaders; and once converted, these Southern suffragists helped recruit others. Clay, who was recruited into the movement along with her mother and sisters in the 1880s by the combined efforts of Susan B. Anthony and Lucy Stone, in turn converted many other Southern women. As head of the NAWSA's Southern Committee, she brought together the handful of Southern suffrage pioneers of the 1890s and wrote countless letters in an effort to identify and recruit other potential leaders. Naturally Clay looked for supporters within the ranks of Southern reformers. For example, in 1892 she requested and received suggestions from Belle Bennett, one of the foremost leaders of women in the Methodist Episcopal Church, South. Shortly thereafter, Clay wrote to Somerville.[70]

The Woman's Christian Temperance Union was a prime target for Northern feminists in search of converts. In 1891, Belle Kearney and other delegates to the national WCTU convention in Boston were invited to a reception by the Massachusetts Woman Suffrage Association; Lucy Stone spoke and invited the guests to make brief speeches on woman suffrage and public attitudes in their sections. In 1897, the NAWSA sent two professional organizers on a tour of Mississippi, who concluded their series of speeches in various towns by calling a convention immediately following the state WCTU convention; a state suffrage organization was established with Somerville as president and Kearney as vice-president. In 1899, Kearney was invited to be a guest in the home of Susan B. Anthony (who installed Kearney, the "slaveholder's daughter," in a bedchamber decorated with "time-faded pictures illustrating the horrors of the slave trade") and urged her to "devote yourself wholly to getting the ballot into the hands of the women of Mississippi that they might make of themselves a power to bring about the good they so much desire."[71]

The same NAWSA organizers who helped establish the Mississippi Woman Suffrage Association went on to New Orleans, where they converted the Gordons. Kate Gordon recalled the experience as "a great epoch in my life. I saw how women could help women at every point." The following year Laura Clay and Carrie Chapman Catt came to Louisiana to help the Gordons seek suffrage from the Louisiana Constitutional Convention. Kate Gordon's mobilization of women in the successful campaign for the water and sewerage system so impressed NAWSA leaders that Gordon was invited to describe it before the 1901 NAWSA convention, and was elected a national officer.[72]

Catt and Alice Stone Blackwell, editor of the Boston-based *Woman's Journal*, both courted Mary Johnston—already inclined toward suffrage work as a result of her British contacts. And Clay's speech during a tea in her honor in 1909, hosted by Ellen Glasgow, also helped inspire Johnston to enter the suffrage work. Both Jean Gordon and Mary Johnston were instrumental in Jacobs' conversion: while in Birmingham for a meeting of a child-labor league, Gordon gave a public address on suffrage and met with Jacobs and other interested women in a private home. Soon afterwards Jacobs hosted a tea for Mary Johnston, who with her "exquisite diction" gave the Alabama women advice based on her experience in Virginia. Both Jean Gordon and Mary Johnston stayed in close touch with the suffrage league they helped establish, and both Gordon sisters assisted the Alabama suffragists often as speakers.[73]

Through their contacts with suffragists from the North, the West, or Great Britain, or with Northern suffragists working within the South, the women who became the leaders of the Southern suffrage movement came to measure themselves by their own standards, not by the conservative standards of their region; and to delight in and thrive on the support and encouragement of a network of feminists that transcended state and regional boundaries. Laura Clay and her mother and sisters enjoyed a close and affectionate friendship with Susan B. Anthony until Anthony's death in 1906. Clay and Gordon were also good friends with Lucy Stone's husband, Henry Blackwell, and daughter, Alice Stone Blackwell (Lucy Stone died in 1893). Henry Blackwell was a great admirer of Belle Kearney's *A Slaveholder's Daughter* and reviewed it very positively in the *Woman's Journal*. And within this group of eleven Southern leaders, there were many close friends and co-workers who corresponded with each other offering advice and encouragement, consulted with one another about strategy and organizing techniques, served one another as guest lecturers, visited in one another's homes, and met frequently at regional and national suffrage conventions. Nellie Nugent Somerville and the Gordons, Kate Gordon and Laura Clay, Mary Johnston and Lila Meade Valentine, Valentine and Breckinridge—all enjoyed warm personal friendships as well as a common interest in the suffrage movement. For examples: Mary Johnston once wrote to her "Dear Lila," urging Valentine to come and visit her in the mountains and escape the political fray in Richmond: "I am sorry for this hornet nest around your

ears. Come and rest on my sofa and tell me all about it." Breckinridge
wrote to Valentine just before the NAWSA convention in which Alice
Paul's "militant" faction was expelled, saying, "Please do go to the
convention. We can get a lot of fun out of it in spite of the strains and
fights that are to be going on. One rumor is that Alice Paul is going to
run for President!" During the twenty-odd years in which Laura Clay
and Kate Gordon were acquainted, a constant stream of correspondence passed between the two women, letters carefully preserved by
Clay and now an historian's delight.[74]

Another important characteristic shared by all of the leading suffragists, which inspired them to take up the suffrage cause and persist in
fighting for it despite so many discouraging defeats, was their low
opinion of the current management of the New South. All of these
women had friends or relatives in public office, but they believed the
world of politics had degenerated to the point that too few honest and
intelligent men were willing to serve. They supported wholeheartedly
the campaign by the men of their class to return government to the
"best people," and at times they were critical of the disfranchisers for
not going far enough in taking the vote away from "debased" and
"ignorant" Southerners—white as well as black (see Chapter Four).
Some, including Kate Gordon, assumed that the vote of the poor and
ignorant was nearly always corrupt, as such people were easily misguided by those who would exploit them; others, including Breckinridge, believed that the poor could do little to prevent "the daily suck-
ing of [their] blood . . . by the great corporations" as the "whole
energy" of the working class "is consumed in the struggle merely to
maintain existence." In either case, these suffragists believed that fair
and honest government depended on the control of government by
well-bred (i.e., honest and compassionate), well-educated citizens.
Their experiences promoting reform as well as suffrage suggested to
them that the South was generally poorly run by men who either
failed to understand the crucial need for reforms such as improved
public education and community health programs, or preferred to use
their offices to line their pockets. It seemed clear to the suffragists that
many Southern legislators were failing to live up to their responsibilities under *noblesse oblige*, and needed to be reminded of their moral
obligations by the citizens to whom such concerns were paramount—
women. The suffragists were particularly disgusted with politicians for
promoting economic development by offering up the Southern working class for exploitation.[75]

Nellie Nugent Somerville, truly a "strong-minded woman" of
strong moral conviction, was disgusted by the corruption rampant in
the South and indeed throughout the nation in the 1890s. In her
speeches of that decade she spoke nostalgically of the character and
quality of the leaders of bygone days, from the founding fathers to

Robert E. Lee. She spoke of the "boys" of the Confederacy who "gave
up prospects of material advancement to fight for principle"—con-
trasting them with the politicians of the present who spoke of the
rampant chaos and corruption in government as "practical politics,"
which if deplorable was nonetheless inevitable. And she insisted that
if "good men" continue to say "no man can go into politics and maintain his integrity . . . and therefore hold themselves aloof and do not
even vote," the hope for the restoration of morality and thus the
preservation of the republic must rest in the women. Speaking to the
Mississippi Woman Suffrage Association in 1898, she said: "Among
thoughtful people there is a growing belief that American institutions
can not be preserved without the infusion into the body politic of a
new moral force and there are not a few who think that only the
womanhood of the nation can furnish that moral fervor." Influenced
by Frances Willard, who insisted that the causes promoted by the
WCTU would never be fully successful until women were enfranchised, and angered by the overt bribery and coercion used by Wets in
her county—with the knowledge and the cooperation of local
officials—Somerville was ripe to be recruited into the suffrage movement when the NAWSA recruiters arrived in 1897.[76]

Rebecca Latimer Felton's long struggle for prohibition and against
the convict lease system convinced her that women must be enfranchised; she was well aware how much the "Liquor Interest" wanted to
keep women in the home. Criticized for meddling in politics, she said
that the failure of men to give "sober homes to women and children"
made it necessary for women to become involved. When politicians
accused her of injecting politics into moral issues, she said: "It's not
carrying politics into moral issues, it's injecting morality into politics,
and I don't know where else a little morality could do more good. It's
a mighty dirty house you men have made of politics and you are not
willing for the ladies to sweep up after you."[77]

Felton carried with her a lingering bitterness and passionate distrust of Southern male politicians traceable to her tragic Civil War
experience: she lost two of her children from malaria and measles as
the family camped in Georgia's Piney Woods, fleeing the embattled
armies. "If women had been allowed the ballot in 1861, there would
have been less haste and more judgement, for the mother heart beats
true to her innocent children. . . . [Men] need the help we can give
you more than we need the ballot," she wrote in one of her suffrage
speeches.[78]

Decades of combatting the establishment in the Georgia Democratic Party gave Felton a good education about the graft and corruption
in Georgia politics; and she despised many of the state's leading
Democratic politicians for their demagoguery. She had been a loyal
supporter of the Confederacy after secession, but she deplored the

ceaseless glorification of the Civil War and accused Democratic politicians of extolling "the Lost Cause" and "waving the Bloody Shirt" to perpetuate their own power even as they got rich from public office:

> The children of the Southern States are being unwisely taught by Southern agitators, women as well as men, that the political issues of the Civil War are still germane and worthy of adoration. They are instructed to call the Lost Cause a glorious cause. They resent any change in public opinion, because the change would mean their own retiracy to back seats in politics and from public attention. They are barnacles on the ship of state, and they have inoculated hatred to "D__n Yankees" as a creed to be eulogized and fostered.[79]

The Gordon sisters also found themselves locked in political battle against politicians they despised. Jean and Kate Gordon were allied with what Dewey Grantham refers to as New Orlean's "silk-stocking" reformers, a group that in the 1890s and then again in the 1910s fought with the Democratic machine for control of the city's politics. The Democratic machine led by Mayor Martin Behrman held power by manipulating the immigrant and lower-class vote, cooperated with financial and corporate interests and opposed labor legislation and regulation of business, and assumed a "let live" attitude toward gambling, drinking, and prostitution. Patrician, moralistic, and confident of the rectitude of their views, these New Orleans reformers fought for the adoption of an Australian (secret) ballot that would heighten their influence as it disfranchised illiterates and thus undercut the base of support of the machine; and they fought against the corruption in Louisiana politics typified by the state lottery.[80]

Jean Gordon was supremely disgusted by the crudeness as well as the corruption of the state's legislators, who spat streams of tobacco juice all over the carpets of the State House even as they denied the "dignified requests" of the women in "scenes which might be likened to a vaudeville show." She concluded that in an ideal world, all legislators would be over thirty years old, sober, and possessed of "a certain dignity which comes only from an innate gentility and good breeding." Like Somerville, the Gordons were appalled that so many politicians had accepted graft and corruption as a routine part of their world—even going so far as to use this corruption as an excuse for keeping women out of politics. Like Breckinridge, who said that men did not want politics "in its present unsavory sense to be cleaned up," they were convinced that Behrman "ordered out his slaves" to jettison the 1918 Louisiana referendum on woman suffrage because he "feared the votes of the reputable women of this city." Said Jean Gordon, "For perpetuation in power we have been sacrificed."[81]

It was a series of political murders in 1899 and 1900, including the shooting of a gubernatorial candidate by a member of a rival "gang" in the yard of the state capitol, that first prompted Madeline

McDowell Breckinridge to become involved in political activity. Shocked by what she perceived as a general atmosphere of lawlessness in her state, Breckinridge organized a women's committee that passed resolutions protesting the corruption of the ballot box and the bribery of public officials and called for laws against the carrying of concealed weapons. The women pledged themselves "to make every effort in our power for the overthrow of lawlessness and crime, and for the establishment of that social and political purity of righteousness which makes for good citizens and exalteth a nation."[82]

Many of these suffragists feared that the health, education, and welfare of the people were far less important to those shaping the New South than the growth of the region's economy, and that the politicians failed to understand the relationship between public education and healthy economic development. Said Breckinridge:

> The South after the years of war and destruction and the succeeding years of despair and struggle is on its feet and she is on fire with the goal of material development. The dream of commercial advance is filling her brain and a new activity is abroad in the land. [But] more than ever it needs to be reminded . . . that this very commercial advancement must rest upon the foundation of an educated and not an illiterate people. . . .

Breckinridge warned against trading "ideals of the past" for material prosperity, and expressed disgust at attempts to attract Northern manufacturers by advertising "that we have not only the cotton and the fuel . . . but the cheap child labor as well."[83]

The Gordons were likewise disgusted by the mill owners and representatives of the canning companies, who, at legislative hearings, described conditions in their plants in such glowing terms that (as Jean said sarcastically) "one, not knowing any better, would have been convinced that the most healthful, renumerative, educational place in the entire world in which to develop children was in a mill or oyster cannery. One fairly tingled to spend the rest of life shucking oysters or peeling shrimp."[84]

The restriction of child labor was an issue about which all of the leading suffragists, excepting Felton, were passionate. They shared the belief, expressed by Somerville, that "the corporate conscience, which means lack of conscience, will sacrifice children to increasing dividends," and that "the poverty or the selfishness of parents will too often assist in that sacrifice." As neither parents nor industrialists could be trusted to do the job, "it is evident that the State must look to the protection of its future citizens."[85]

Many a child-labor advocate became a suffragist after being shocked into an awareness of her political impotence by the defeat of a child-labor bill. Jean Gordon described the impact of the defeat of an Era Club–backed child-labor bill on its female supporters in New Orleans:

> We have learned that the interests of women and children will never be a
> vital issue until made so by women for women. . . . And we also
> learned (what we had suspected) that the much-boasted influence of the
> wife over the husband in matters political was one of the many theories
> which melt before the sun of experience. The wife of every representa-
> tive present was heartily in sympathy with the child labor bill, but, when
> the roll was called, the husbands answered "no" and those wives realized
> how weak a weapon was influence, and in that moment were sown the
> seeds of a belief in the potency of the ballot beyond that of "woman's
> influence."

It was frustration with the opposition to effective child labor legislation in Alabama that made Jacobs and her associates so open to Jean
Gordon's message in 1911. Jacobs recalled: "Those of us who heard
the speakers on this occasion, became convinced that if the child
labor problem could be solved, the mother's voice must be heard
politically."[86]

Though the antisuffrage president of the Georgia Federation of
Women's Clubs insisted that the state's women's clubs had "no
difficulty getting their measures passed by the legislature" through
their powers of persuasion, Breckinridge, the leader of the Kentucky
Women's Clubs, was profoundly disgusted with having to rely on
"indirect influence." She pointed to the impressive list of legislative
victories of the Kentucky Equal Rights Association and declared: "This
looks like a considerable accomplishment. But when one remembers
that it is the result of twenty-five years of work of a group of able and
determined women, it is seen to be small. If these women in that time
with the ballot in their hands had been able to do for Kentucky the
things that Kentucky needed to have done, the accomplishment
would have been much greater."[87]

Mary Johnston also spoke angrily of "indirect influence," saying,
women are fighting "but their arms are antiquated. If they had even
an old smoothbore musket or a Revolutionary flintlock! But they
haven't any weapon at all—not what a man would call a weapon.
They have a thing called 'Indirect Influence,' the indirection of which
is extreme indeed."[88]

Despite the anger that fueled their protests, when speaking to the legislators the suffragists tried to be diplomatic. To those who said that
they wanted the women of the South to stay as they had been,
devoted exclusively to home and family and out of politics, these
women insisted that the women of the South had *already* changed,
though through no fault of their own. Like Belle Kearney, writing in
her 1900 *A Slaveholder's Daughter*, they nearly always emphasized that
change had been "thrust upon them" by the Civil War and by the
"changed social and economic environment" of the New South. The
women of the region had been forced into new responsibilities,

including participation in public affairs, but now they would not shrink from the challenge. Somerville wrote: "The civic conscience has been awakened in Southern women, and they are not going to dwindle and shrivel into a selfish, ease-loving way of living. . . . The woman who takes absolutely no interest in any political questions is no longer typical or the ideal Southern woman."[89]

In 1917, when yet another war disrupted the lives of American women, Pattie Jacobs told a Florida audience, "Some state that the woman's place is in the home, and yet the war is thrusting them into fields they never occupied before. . . . It was not from choice but necessity. We agree that woman's place is the home, but not in the home. We regard the world as the home, and we want the ballot to protect the home."[90]

In a frequently quoted address before the 1911 NAWSA Convention in Louisville, Breckinridge claimed that "it is really now too late to speak of the admission of Southern women into public affairs. In the community business of caring for the sick, the incurable, the aged, the orphaned, the deficient and the helpless the women of the South bear already so important a part that to withdraw them from public affairs would mean sudden and widespread calamity." She predicted that after Southern men "swallowed the pill" of officially admitting women to politics, they would find their participation neither "uncomfortable nor particularly strange."[91]

Like suffragists all over the nation, the leaders of the Southern suffrage movement pointed out that industrialization and urbanization had changed domestic life, and that women no longer cared for their families in isolation. Lila Meade Valentine wrote: "There is a whole group of interests which belong peculiarly to women and which with the expanding functions of government have become political questions. . . . Questions concerning food, water, sanitation, education, light, heat, plumbing, treatment of diseases, child labor, hours of labor for women and children . . . all these questions nearly concern the home and the child." And they pleaded for equal partnership with the men of their class in government by emphasizing the differences in interests and responsibility for the sexes—a tactful way of saying that the interests of women and children would never be adequately represented so long as women were relying on men to protect them. "We wish to take from men not one right or privilege which they now possess nor do we claim that woman suffrage would at once cure 'all the ills that flesh is heir to,'" said Somerville. "We only ask at your hands an undivided half in all the affairs of life and we claim that woman's influence in politics would be for good, not evil."[92]

The women who led the woman suffrage movement in the South, then, were women of the South's social and political elite, who followed their traditional responsibilities for the morals and the health and welfare of the people, particularly women and children, beyond the home. Disillusioned with the failure of Southern politicians to deal in an adequate and humane fashion with the pressing social problems of the New South, unwilling to rely on obviously unreliable "indirect influence," and inspired and encouraged by suffragists of the North, the West, and Great Britain, they sought to inject the direct influence of women into the politics of the South.

3

Respectable Radicals: Southern Suffragists As Champions of Women's Rights

Southerners, though tenacious of social traditions . . . are chivalrous toward a woman who wishes their cooperation provided that she comes to them as a lady.

—Belle Kearney
A Slaveholder's Daughter, 1900[1]

It is quite common for men to say . . . that women should not vote because they are too good and must not be degraded to the level of men. . . . Now the facts in the case are that there is not a word of truth in this proposition. It is exasperating because it is short-sighted, unreasonably and historically false. . . . Exclusion from the right to vote is a degradation—always has been, always will be, never was intended as anything else, can not be sugarcoated into anything else. The age-long cause of all these things [discrimination against women in education, in industry, in property rights and political rights] has been the theory that women were too bad and too incompetent.

—Nellie Nugent Somerville
"Are Women Too Good to Vote?"
Newspaper article, ca. 1914[2]

The leaders of the Southern suffrage movement understood all too well that theirs was the region of the United States most hostile to the women's rights movement, and they made every effort to present

72

themselves and their cause as nonthreatening and in accord with traditional Southern values. Proud to be Southern Ladies, these women took care to look and act the part; publicists for the suffrage movement deliberately celebrated the femininity as well as the social prominence of their leaders. Like most suffragists throughout the nation, Southern suffragists believed that there were innate differences between the sexes, and promoted suffrage by emphasizing these differences and the benefits to society of female enfranchisement. They denied that enfranchisement would lead women to neglect their traditional duties, but insisted that changed social and economic conditions now required women to have the vote in order to carry out these responsibilities.

The record of reforms championed by Southern suffragists makes it clear, however, that these women were feminists who sought many changes in woman's role in the South in addition to suffrage. They supported a wide variety of reforms in the industrial, educational, and legal rights of women that would benefit both women of privilege and their less fortunate sisters. Indeed, suffragists succeeded in bringing about a number of significant changes in women's status and opportunities, though they failed to persuade most Southern legislators to support female enfranchisement.[3]

The private papers and more candid public statements of the Southern suffrage leaders provide further evidence that the women who led the Southern suffrage movement were profoundly unhappy with the traditional role of women in the South and impatient for change. They bitterly resented the restraints Southern society imposed upon the women of their class and expressed considerable indignation at the treatment Southern women of all classes received at the hands of men. As they became increasingly frustrated by legislative resistance to the reforms they supported, these suffrage leaders grew more and more cynical about the celebrated chivalry of Southern men, and denounced the Southern woman's enforced reliance on "indirect influence" as degrading as well as inefficient.

Indeed, though they shared many of the ideas of Southern men of their class and race and were quite conservative compared to some women's rights advocates of their era, particularly those in Northeastern cities, these suffragists were clearly radical for their section on the subject of women's rights. They were self-consciously "New Women" who believed the traditional roles and duties of the sexes needed to be re-examined in the New South. Not believing that women's interests were being fully represented in politics by Southern men, these leaders were indignant that Southern men so often denied women the right to vote in the guise of protecting them. Consistent with their belief in female uniqueness, the suffragists insisted that men *could not* fully comprehend the needs of women and children, and demanded the vote in order to protect their own interests and those of the less fortunate women and children of the South.[4]

Winning the vote was very important to these leaders of the Southern suffrage movement for symbolic as well as utilitarian reasons. Throughout the thirty-year history of the Southern suffrage movement, the primary objective of the suffragists was to win recognition of women's status under the law as individuals with full rights and privileges, and they interspersed "natural rights rhetoric" freely among their "arguments from expediency." Living in a society in which the dominant class believed in the right of the "best people" to govern the rest, they understood all too well the symbolism of the ballot. Though they agreed that suffrage should be restricted, they wanted, and believed that they (if not all women) deserved, in Mary Johnston's words, "the dignity of citizenship."[5]

Southern suffragists recognized that they were a minority among Southern white women, but the leaders of the movement believed it to be their duty to awaken other women to new ambitions. They challenged them not to be bound by Southern conservatism but to become a part of a vast awakening of women throughout the world, and they promised that their movement would one day be viewed by society in a different and much more positive light.

I

In the effort to present themselves and their cause as "respectable," the leaders of the suffrage movement generally avoided association with unpopular causes and any tactics that smacked of radicalism. Suffragists like Lila Meade Valentine and Mary Johnston, who sympathized with movements deemed suspect by fellow Southerners, soon learned to play down the fact. Valentine sent shock waves through her social circle early in her suffrage career by accepting an invitation to address the Central Labor Council of Richmond, but apparently she had no desire to repeat the experience. By 1914, she concluded: "the more I study the situation in Virginia, the more convinced I am of the necessity of quiet, educational propaganda with an entire elimination of the spectacular for the present at least. The latter method simply shocks the sensibilities of most people without convincing them of the truth of our movement." Valentine took action to prevent any association in the eyes of the public of woman suffrage with organized labor, and especially with socialism; for example, on separate occasions she instructed the leader of the Norfolk suffragists not to publicize any alliance between the Equal Suffrage League and the National Women's Trade Union League and to remove socialist literature from the window of the Norfolk suffrage shop. Mary Johnston refused the request of a Virginia socialist leader to publicly declare her support for socialism, saying "to enter the papers—or to try to enter them—on this other issue, would, I think, be disastrous to my immediate cause without doing much good to yours."[6]

Laura Clay experienced at first hand the repercussions of the association of woman suffrage and radical causes during the 1895 suffrage campaign in South Carolina, when the newly published *Woman's Bible* (a book edited by Elizabeth Cady Stanton, which criticized the Old Testament as derogatory to women) was used to great effect by her opponents. The following year Clay played an important role in securing the NAWSA resolution disassociating the organization from this notorious publication. Clay declared, optimistically, "when we go through the South advocating woman suffrage without attaching it to dress reform, or bicycling, or anything else, but asking the simple question, why the principles of our forefathers should not be applied to women, we shall win."[7]

With equal determination, these leaders of the Southern suffrage movement tried to link the suffrage cause with popular causes. For example, during World War I, most threw themselves wholeheartedly into the war effort, seeking to avoid the stigma of pacifism and demonstrate their patriotism. Of those who had been associated with the prewar peace movement, among them Clay, Rebecca Latimer Felton, Pattie Ruffner Jacobs, and Mary Johnston, only Johnston continued to be a (self-professed) "conscientious objector." Clay recommended that Kentucky suffragists publicly support Wilson's plan to call for prohibition as a war measure, saying it would be "both politic and patriotic" for them "to throw themselves" behind it. Like many Americans caught up in the fever of war, she questioned the Americanism of the Woman's Peace Party led by Jane Addams, and asked that her own name be dropped from its roll. Madeline McDowell Breckinridge also parted company with her mentor Addams on this issue, and refused to be recruited into the peace movement, saying she considered "whipping Germany to a finish" to be "entirely peaceful." Jacobs and Nellie Nugent Somerville served as officers of the Woman's Council on Defense, and Valentine was the first person in Virginia to speak on the streets for recruits.[8]

Above all, these women understood that their movement, which sought to modify the traditional relationship between the sexes by involving women in politics, must not appear to threaten other cherished ideas concerning Southern womanhood. Drawn from the social and political elite of the region, the leaders of the woman suffrage movement in the South were proud of the image of the Southern Lady, and—at least in the early days—believed it could work to their advantage. In 1900, Belle Kearney observed, "Southerners, though tenacious of social traditions . . . are chivalrous toward a woman who wishes their cooperation provided that she comes to them as a lady." They took care to look and act as such. Kearney always wore dresses with trains that swept the floor in an era when most women had long since given them up. Laura Clay often carried that emblem of femininity, the parasol. And Nellie Nugent Somerville, newly elected as president of the Mississippi Woman Suffrage Association, wrote to "members and friends" of the organization saying, "The public, and especially the editorial public, will be quick to see and use against us any mistakes that may be made. An unpleasant aggressiveness will doubtless be expected of us. Let us endeavor to disappoint such expectations."[9]

All over the South, chairs of publicity committees celebrated the beauty, femininity, and domesticity of the movement's leaders, as well as their social prominence. The handsome and stately Somerville was herself described in the press as "gentle and attractive," "entirely refuting the idea that a suffragist is not the sweetest and most womanly woman imaginable. She is the mother of four charming children, and her home life is beautiful and tender. In all her work on behalf of women and the church she has the earnest and cordial support of her husband." Suffrage columns in the Alabama papers literally gushed over Pattie Ruffner Jacobs, who had, they said, "one of the prettiest, most exquisitely feminine, most comfortable, most practical and best ordered homes in the South, and two of the loveliest, best trained children that any one ever knew. Her political interests do not interfere with her housekeeping." Furthermore, in 1918, she had the "best war garden produced by any woman in Birmingham."[10]

In Virginia, Georgia, and Tennessee, suffragists sold home-baked cakes and bread and fancy needlework to demonstrate their domestic accomplishments while making money for the cause. Suffragists in Tennessee tried to provide an attractive impression of their organization (and demonstrated an understanding of the proper method of caring for upper-class babies of the South) by sponsoring a "baby rest tent" at a Chautauqua, complete with "freshly kept baby beds," and "a good 'black mammy' to attend the babies and distribute literature." During World War I, Birmingham suffragists disseminated household tips for the wartime economy in regular suffrage columns and published a special cookbook, *A Hoover Helper*.[11]

The tactics employed by the "militant" suffragists in England and America were anathema to most Southern suffragists. In addition to being directed against the "party in power," the Democratic Party so beloved by white Southerners, such tactics were profoundly unladylike and "unworthy of southern women." Sue Shelton White obviously chose to disregard such widespread sentiments and cast her lot with the militants; and Madeline McDowell Breckinridge defended Emmeline Pankhurst and her followers, contending that Americans should not applaud militance for the sake of a righteous cause in men while expecting women to suffer quietly. But most Southern suffragists roundly denounced the militants. Clay was highly indignant when a reporter addressed her as "a suffragette," saying "the term is confined to the element that is now gaining notoriety in England by their acts of violence and lawlessness. I have no sympathy with such exponents of our theory, and believe they hurt the cause rather than further it."[12]

The Equal Suffrage Association of Virginia released a statement signed by its president, Lila Meade Valentine, "condemning the folly of the fanatical women who are picketing the White House" and agreeing with the leaders of the NAWSA that such actions were "unwise, unpatriotic and injurious to the cause of woman suffrage." They continued: "We utterly repudiate such methods and deeply regret that any citizen of the United States should seek to embarrass the President or the government at such a crisis." They pleaded that the public not "condemn the suffrage cause as a whole because of the folly of a handful of women." Alabama suffragists were "considerably embarrassed" when Sue White and several members of the National Woman's Party appeared in their state to lobby, and tried to avoid being associated with them.[13]

Like Valentine, most leaders of the woman suffrage movement in the South preferred to avoid "spectacular tactics" and concentrate on "quiet, educational" campaigns. Along with the majority of suffragists nationwide, they emphasized the differences between the sexes and the potential benefits to society if women could add their special insight and perspective to politics. They embraced woman's assigned role as custodian of morality in society, as well as her "god-given" mission to care for children and the home. Emphatically they denied that woman suffrage would lead women to neglect their duties: indeed, under the changed conditions of the industrial age, the opposite was true. Mary Johnston stated in 1913:

> The home will not be destroyed by woman's participation in government, for nothing can destroy the individual home. But the whole concept of home is being changed. The government is taking over the functions that once belonged to the home—health, education, sanitation and a score of other matters. We are beginning to live in a great social home, as it were. And you can no more keep woman out of the affairs of this larger home than you could do without her in the smaller one.[14]

Pro-suffrage leaflets widely used in the South declared that "the place of the Woman is in the Home. But merely to stay in the Home is not enough. She must care for the health and welfare, moral as well as physical, of her family." To carry out these duties, a woman must be able to help elect the officials who set the standards for the health, safety, and morality of her community. And to Progressive-era voters eager to clamp down on public corruption, suffragists promised that women would help in the task. Since "women are by nature and training housekeepers, Let them help in the city housekeeping. They will introduce an occasional spring cleaning."[15]

Suffragists from other regions of the United States were often astonished at the "honey-tongued charm" exuded by their Southern co-workers. Pattie Ruffner Jacobs, Belle Kearney, and even Mary Johnston were particularly adept at the use of this traditional technique of the Southern Lady. Jacobs wrote to the editor of the Birmingham *Ledger* in 1912:

> There may be some women who have "made foolish and bitter attacks upon men" but the vast majority of women interested in the [suffrage] movement are so by reason of their desire to help men. They hold that men have done remarkably well to have battled so many foes of the human race and its progress. They think the time has come when men should demand that women share their responsibility. They now offer their assistance which some wise, forsighted [*sic*] men are accepting believing that a highly developed moral nature and an intimate knowledge of conditions governing the welfare of women and children (which women possess) would ultimately result in great good to the state, the nation and the race. . . . It may take years, undoubtedly it will, for woman to have the largeness of outlook . . . that men have . . . but she can learn in small degrees.

And Mary Johnston, speaking to a Richmond audience, said, "men have their minds too much fixed on the large political issues, and there are a multitude of details that slip through their fingers, so to speak, and which women can better attend to. This is especially true of legislation concerning schools and children. . . ."[16]

Particularly in the early years of their suffrage work, before personally experiencing defeat and frustration, many of these Southern suffragists optimistically predicted that the chivalry of Southern men would be a boon to the cause. Kearney, who got along famously with men, wrote in 1900:

> I have always maintained, and do now insist, that Southern men, as a rule, are stronger advocates for the enfranchisement of women than men in any other section of the United States except certain portions of the West. The old-time element of chivalry, which constituted so largely the make-up of the Southern gentleman, has been handed down through the generations and now begins to crystalize in the direction of equality before the law for men and women. . . . For years, in different Southern states I have heard prominent men say; "If women want to vote, it is all right. We have no objection. We do not give them the ballot because they do not seem to desire it. Just as soon as they demand it, they will get it."[17]

The leaders of the Southern suffrage movement emphatically denied the charges that they were being untrue to their heritage in seeking the vote. Indeed, they reminded the men of their class, then engaged in a campaign to "restore the reigns of government" to the "better element" in Southern society, of the legendary virtue of Southern womanhood, and suggested the enfranchisement of Southern women as a counterweight to the influence of "undesirables" (see Chapter Four). Mary Johnston insisted that the men of the South would come to see that

> the woman struggling for her political independence is just the pioneer woman, the Revolutionary woman, the woman, unselfish and brave of the War between the States—just the Southern woman working out her destiny now as then. He honoured her under the earlier aspects; he will honour her under this. . . . Justice, fair-play, self government, development, realization—these have been his ideals, and he will come to recognize their value in his sister and his mate. The best of Southern men may, I think, be depended upon to give their voice for the enfranchisement of the women of the South.[18]

II

Despite all of these attempts to avoid the label, Southern suffragists were indeed radical for their culture in their views on woman's role in society, and they advocated a wide variety of feminist reforms. As woman suffrage organizations formed across the South in the 1890s, they affiliated with the NAWSA and adopted its goal of "advancing the industrial, educational, and legal rights of woman as well as securing the right of suffrage." Indeed, in the South of the 1890s, as in the Northeast in 1848, suffrage was considered to be a far more radical and unattainable goal than any number of other changes in women's status. Laura Clay changed the name of the Lexington Suffrage Society to the Fayette County Equal Rights Association to enable the members to work for more than the "far distant" and "abstract" object of suffrage and to appease those who considered the demand for suffrage too radical.[19]

Women's rights and privileges varied considerably within the region. Mississippi, for example, had been the first state in the union to pass a married women's property act, in 1839; and the first to have a state industrial college for girls, a record of which Kearney and Somerville were proud. Most Southern states had made some improvements in the legal status of married women in their Reconstruction-era constitutions (though lawmakers enacted these reforms in order to protect property against seizure for debt rather than to empower women). But in Mississippi as well as in the other Southern states, suffragists considered themselves behind women of the rest of the nation and endeavored to catch up as quickly as possible.[20]

Where women did not already have them, suffragists sought basic legal rights: the right of married women to own and dispose of property; to conduct business transactions with all the privileges of single women; and to claim their own wages. One of Somerville's first acts as president of the Mississippi Woman Suffrage Association was to launch an investigation into the legal status of Mississippi women, and to distribute the results in pamphlet form. Somerville and other Mississippi suffragists were particularly distressed over the fact that Mississippi law failed to protect a mother's right to custody of her children in the event of the father's death, and they sought—unsuccessfully—a "Mother's Rights" law. In 1912, Birmingham suffragists sponsored a year-long series of public lectures, many of them given by members, on the legal statutes affecting women in their state. The Era Club of New Orleans boasted of having legalized the signatures of women. Each of the three hundred votes by proxy collected by Kate Gordon from women in the 1898 water and sewerage referendum had to be witnessed by a man.[21]

Tennessee suffragists in 1895 listed among their reasons for wanting the vote that married women wanted to own their own clothes and their own earnings and to have equal partnership in their children. Virginia suffragists also worked for a mother's rights bill, permission for women to serve on school boards, and the admission of women to the state bar. The Kentucky Equal Rights Association achieved a remarkable record of improvements in woman's legal status. These included: an 1890 law making the wife's wages payable to her instead of her husband; an 1893 law granting women the right to make wills and control real estate; an 1894 law allowing women to make contracts and sue as a single person, to enter business, and to be free of liability for their husbands' debts; and a 1910 co-guardianship or "mother's rights" bill, a goal that suffragists in many Southern states failed to realize. In all of the Southern states, suffragists worked for legal changes that would permit women to serve on school boards, boards of trustees of colleges and universities, as factory inspectors, etc.[22]

Many of the South's universities were already open to women, but suffrage organizations launched vigorous campaigns to remove the remaining restrictions barring women from institutions of higher learning, including schools of law and medicine. In Louisiana, for example, women's rights advocates succeeded in 1894 in getting the legislature to authorize all colleges in the state to confer upon women degrees in law, pharmacy, and medicine. But despite constant and vigorous agitation led by Kate Gordon, Tulane University refused to permit women to study law until 1897 and medicine until 1915. The admission of women to Tulane's medical school was the achievement of which Gordon was most proud.[23]

Virginia suffragists were enthusiastic supporters of their friend Mary Branch Munford's fight, ultimately unsuccessful, for a Co-ordinate College for women at the University of Virginia. Mary Johnston said the fact that Virginia was one of "five states of the United States without any provision for the higher education of women" was a "disgrace to the state of Jefferson, Marshall, and Madison." The provision of two normal schools that offered "a limited number" of Virginia's daughters education for "a limited purpose" was not good enough. Johnston spoke of the poor and middle-class girls of the state who could afford neither the state's elite private schools for girls nor the cost of attending a "real college" outside of Virginia as "Cinderellas," who, if given a chance, might "reflect lustre on the state."[24]

Rebecca Latimer Felton and Georgia suffragists faced similar difficulties in securing additional educational opportunities for the women of Georgia. In 1889, the Georgia legislature declared that all branches of the University of Georgia were to be open to women "under such rules and regulations as shall be prescribed by trustees of the University"; but despite repeated demands for action by Felton and (after 1899) the Georgia Woman Suffrage Association, university officials did not see fit to "prescribe" the terms for female admission until 1921. Felton ridiculed the theory, developed by Harvard Medical School Professor Dr. E. H. Clarke and widely accepted in the late nineteenth century, that coeducation was unhealthy for women, and insisted that the university needed "the presence of women to better it, to refine it, and fulfill its mission of free education."[25]

Felton's personal crusade was to make vocational education available to the poor white girls of her state: "I would like to know," said Felton, "why there is such a constant hurrah and hullabaloo over the crying need for textile education for the boys who are to be educated to manage textile industries and no mention whatever of an opportunity to be offered to the hundreds of girls who have made Georgia cotton mills a magnificent success in years just past and gone." Felton's efforts were rewarded in 1889 in the form of the Georgia Normal and Industrial School in Milledgeville, and in 1915 with the establishment of the Georgia Training School for Girls.[26]

Kentucky suffragists were responsible for the adoption of coeducation at Kentucky University (now Transylvania University) in 1889 and Central University in Richmond, Kentucky, in 1893. Clay fought hard for equal admission of women to that bastion of "the Lost Cause," the University of the South at Sewanee; but that goal was not achieved until 1969.[27]

As for the "industrial rights" of Southern women, Southern suffragists supported a variety of reforms, including equal pay for equal work (focusing particularly on teachers) and improved conditions for women who worked in department stores, as well as the establishment of "industrial schools" that would teach new skills to the young girls of the South. As was mentioned above, Southern suffragists showed a special interest in the plight of the women and children who toiled in the South's burgeoning industries. Despite their economically privileged positions, the suffragists seemed to have a strong sense of gender solidarity and a genuine concern for the women "beneath the pedestal." Madeline McDowell Breckinridge, who traveled to Georgia to witness at first hand the conditions in the cotton mills, observed in an address to a group of Southern reformers:

> I consider another hopeful sign of the times to be the growing consciousness of solidarity on the part of women, the growing sense of responsibility of women fortunately placed for the conditions under which other women are living and working and suffering. I believe there are many comfortable women today who cannot remain long so comfortable because they are beginning to realize that the leisure they have, the freedom from the household drudgery of their grandmothers is bought at the price of the work of little children and of other women working long and exhausting hours in unsanitary conditions, and for a mere pittance of wage.

Most suffrage organizations endorsed compulsory education laws, child labor laws, occupational safety laws, and minimum-wage and maximum-hour legislation for women and children, though it should be noted that Breckinridge was ahead of her time in supporting minimum-wage and maximum-hour legislation for both sexes; saying to exclude men would be "sex discrimination."[28]

Birmingham suffragists took a strong interest in the "working girls" of the city, and converted the suffrage headquarters at lunchtime into a resting spot for working women where they could eat their lunches and drink complimentary tea. An "early closing time committee" secured an arrangement from merchants to close earlier than 10:00 P.M. on Saturdays so that the "girls" would not have to be walking home at such a dangerous hour. The Birmingham suffragists also offered free classes in stenography and ran an employment bureau to help place women in jobs vacated by men. Nashville suffragists kept a sewing room open in winter months for the benefit of unemployed women.[29]

Southern suffragists were also concerned about the "moral" status of women beneath the pedestal, and across the region suffrage clubs crusaded against the shamefully low age of consent laws (the age of protection ranged from twelve to sixteen in the South). They demanded (and often secured) the appointment of police matrons or female physicians to care for female inmates of prisons and insane asylums, indicating that they considered even the fallen or deranged woman entitled to privacy and freedom from exploitation.[30]

III

This record of reforms championed by Southern suffragists on behalf of women clearly indicates that they sought far more change in the status of Southern women than simply enfranchisement. But the private papers of the movement's leaders, including their personal correspondence, diaries, speeches to supporters, and even their more candid utterances directed at editors or politicians, reveal still more about their attitudes on woman's role and the traditional relations between the men and women of the South. Clearly these women regarded existing injustices as more than historic relics that men merely failed to notice—"details that slipped through the fingers" of Southern legislators. These documents reveal the depths of the suffragists' discontent, making it clear that the leaders of the woman suffrage movement in the South were sharply critical of the traditional relations between the sexes in the region. These women were convinced that woman's role within the patriarchical, chivalric society of the South, where women were rhetorically placed on a pedestal but actually required by law and custom to remain dependent and subordinate, needed to be changed drastically.[31]

The women who led the Southern suffrage movement harbored deep-seated feelings of resentment at the restraints Southern society imposed on women and at the unjust treatment that resulted from traditional ideas about woman's nature. Nellie Nugent Somerville wrote in her notebook, "We have been taught that pain is woman's curse and heritage, endurance and submission her highest virtues. . . . It is not so. If in Adam all died so in Christ all are made alive. The suffering of women is due [not to the will of God but] to the sins of civilization." She accused men of discouraging learning in women and encouraging ignorance and a reliance on beauty. Somerville railed against the false modesty and helplessness that Southern society encouraged in women. She was outraged when a doctor's daughter who was pregnant fled from a lecture on prenatal care; she believed that the girl's father "should have taught her false modesty is to be feared. Knowledge is power." She continued: "A century ago, the typical heroine of polite fiction was Lady Arabella Featherbrain who fainted seventeen times in between the church door and the altar. . . . It may gratify a man's vanity to have a helpless, dependent wife, but it will hamper him in his life work if it does not send him to the lunatic asylum."[32]

Laura Clay attributed woman's downtrodden state to the "selfishness" of men, their desire "to retain in their hands the reins of government," and the fact that "women have been loath to engage in any movement which might displease men." Like Somerville, she spoke to women of their Christian duty to self-development as well as to the improvement of society. Rebecca Latimer Felton and Mary Johnston also urged women to stop putting the needs of others ahead of their own and to concentrate on helping themselves.[33]

Though religion was a great source of strength for many of these women, a motivating force as well as a personal comfort to them as they fought for women's rights, they were all too aware of the fact that religious arguments were among those most frequently used by Southerners to justify a subordinate position for women. Answers to St. Paul, such as this passage from one of Johnston's speeches, were a standard part of the repertoire of Southern suffragists.

> Saint Paul told women to be domestic and submissive, to keep their heads covered and if they wanted to know anything to ask their husbands. . . . We hear Paul quoted very often. Those who do so, apparently never notice how they have wrenched his words from context—never realize that they were spoken under certain peculiar circumstances and to fit certain local conditions, and . . . when dragged across two thousand years, from . . . a corrupt and enslaved Asiatic people to a free America—they no longer fit.[34]

Southern suffragists were strong supporters of the campaigns, going on concurrently with the suffrage movement, for increased rights and privileges for women in several Southern denominations. They resented woman's second-class status in the church as in society at large and almost unanimously regarded Southern clergymen as the greatest opponents of woman's emancipation in the South. In *Our Homes*, the organ of the Women's Foreign Missionary Society of the Methodist Episcopal Church, South, Somerville wrote, "What long-suffering creatures women are anyway. They consent to hold office in a sort of sub rosa way, doing all the hard work; but as soon as some immature stripling or reformed drunkard joins the Church he gets the office, while the women keep on doing the work." Laura Clay's demands for laity rights for women within the Episcopal Church were not always supported by the other women of her local church, prompting her to lament, "how little trust women (sometimes) have in their own sex?" But she nevertheless persevered with her demands that "the miserable spectacle of severing labor and responsibility from honor and authority in churches should end." Sue Shelton White, writing to Molly Dewson in the 1920s, recalled how "the poor discredited feminists" of the South had often been shunted aside; instead, Southern women followed women "artificially reared up" and "paraded around" by Southern preachers who told them what to do and thus "became the [real] leaders of the women."[35]

All of the leading Southern suffragists protested against the taboo that precluded a "respectable" woman's working for wages as well as the lack of education and training that kept most Southern women in a dependent state. Belle Kearney recalled that the post-bellum poverty of her family had prevented her from receiving the education she desired; as they would not allow her to work to pay for an education, she was "bound to the rock of hopelessness by the cankered chains of a false conventionality." Sue White recalled the "almost clannish effort" of Southern families in economic distress to "regain

economic power without sacrificing pride or prestige in the struggle," and the renewed emphasis on women's remaining in the home
as economic conditions improved in the postwar South: "Women
had their part to play in the scheme. 'Ladies' went to work—at
home if they could, or at 'genteel' work on the outside. One might
be pitied, but if one 'belonged' one could join the ranks of genteel
workers temporarily without suffering social stigma. As time went
on and the straitened ones got back on their economic feet, there
was a change. . . . Lines were again drawn taut."[36]

Both Kearney and White (who were self-supporting) were bitter
that they had been discouraged from pursuing careers in law, one of
the commonest occupations of Southern men of their class. Kearney
recalled how her father had "utterly discouraged" her youthful desire
to study law, "arguing that if there were in my possession the legal
lore of Blackstone and the ability of a Portia it would not guarantee
me the opportunity of practising in the South. No woman had ever
attempted such an absurdity, and any effort on my part, in that line
would subject me to ridicule and ostracism." After this she thought,
"If my life has to be spent on the plantation, and if living meant no
more for me than it meant for the women around me, what was the
use of reading, of trying to cultivate my mind when it would have the
effect of making me more miserable?"[37]

White found a job as a court reporter, but when she confided her
dreams of becoming a lawyer to the men for whom she worked, they
called her "impractical" and "a visionary." They told her, "It was about
time I was getting married, anyhow. I observed that young men were
encouraged to 'read.' They were taken into offices, into the trial of
cases, sponsored, even fed, sometimes, by the older members of the
bar; and the banks would extend them credit while they were struggling. . . ." White finally attended law school in her mid-thirties,
taking classes at night after work, and received her degree in 1923.[38]

The profound dismay of these suffrage leaders at the dependent
state of Southern women was traceable to their awareness, as Laura
Clay put it, that "there is no true liberty when one is dependent upon
the will of others for the means of subsistence." Clay deplored the fact
that young girls were not educated to earn a living, and that so many
entered loveless marriages solely for support. Kate Gordon was convinced that men consciously conspired to keep women from attaining
financial independence. After her brother's death, she and Jean were
pressured into selling their interests in the family company, a decision
she later regretted. Accordingly, the three Gordon sisters and their
brother's widow started their own business under the name "Jean M.
Gordon and Company, Manufacturers' Agents," and were quite successful, at least initially. In a letter to Clay, Kate Gordon boasted that
the women had done quite "well on our own," and observed: "one of

the deep laid schemes of men to keep women in subjection has been the great fallacy foisted on the uninitiated as to the mysteries and difficulties of business."[39]

Several of the "second-generation" suffragists of the South, including Madeline McDowell Breckinridge, Lila Meade Valentine, and Mary Johnston, were admirers of Charlotte Perkins Gilman—a radical feminist by the standards of any section of the nation—who emphasized that economic independence was essential for a woman's liberty and dignity. In her book *Women and Economics* (1898), Gilman stressed that woman's economic dependence had weakened and debased her over the centuries, and she likened the role of a wife to that of a prostitute—each dependent for her support on her ability to please men. Gilman and Mary Johnston were close friends, and Johnston's suffrage speeches clearly reflected Gilman's influence: Johnston heralded woman suffrage as a crucial first step toward the economic autonomy of women, predicting that the women of the Western world would be enfranchised by 1925 and economically independent by the end of the twentieth century.[40]

That Johnston shared Clay's view that "there is no true liberty" when one is financially dependent is clearly demonstrated in Johnston's suffrage novel *Hagar* (1913), based largely on Johnston's own experiences. Certainly Johnston recognized that she and many other Southern women might not have felt so free to flout convention had they not possessed independent means. In the novel, a young Southern woman raised by her aristocratic grandparents, "Colonel Ashendyne" and "Old Miss" of "Gilead Balm," struggles for "intellectual and spiritual freedom" and to "think away from creeds and dogmas and affirmations" made for her by her ancestors. Hagar gradually frees herself from "the idea of a sacrosanct Past and the virtue of Immobility," and "from a concept of woman that the future can surely only sadly laugh at."[41]

Essential to Hagar's success is her discovery that she could write and could support herself by writing. Hagar's grandfather is accustomed to commanding the obedience of the women in his family. He opposed the Married Women's Property Act in his state, believing that money only encourages independence in women, an attitude he found "the most intolerable feature of this intolerable latter age!" Hagar's father is also frustrated by her willfulness: "If you couldn't write—couldn't earn," he said, "you'd trot along quietly enough! The pivotal mistake was letting women learn the alphabet." A showdown occurs when the Ashendyne family learns of Hagar's involvement with the woman suffrage movement. Angrily and unanimously the family denounces the movement as vulgar and an affront to the Bible and "the chivalry of our Southern men," and demands that Hagar renounce the cause. For a moment Hagar reels from the sting of the familial wrath, feeling "trapped." But "then she realized that she was not trapped, and she smiled." Unlike the other women of her family, and the vast majority of women of the South, Hagar had a "Fourth Dimension," an alternative life, "an inner freedom"—all derived from her "ability to work." "The Hagar Ashendyne appearing to others upon this porch was not chained there," wrote Johnston, "was not riveted to Gilead Balm. Next week, indeed, she would be gone."[42]

A few, but only a few, of the leading Southern suffragists were troubled by the institution of marriage in that it limited a woman's independent development. Sue Shelton White, a single woman, once observed, "marriage is too much of a compromise; it lops off a woman's life as an individual." But she also believed a woman had much to lose by choosing to remain single. "Yet the renunciation too is a lopping off. We choose between the frying-pan and the fire—both uncomfortable."[43]

Jacobs believed "that a woman is never complete, her character formed until she is wife and mother." Yet as a young girl she was troubled by the marriages she witnessed, including several failed unions within her own family. She wrote in her diary that marriage "is certainly meant by God to be a blessed thing, but so few people are really mated and united. They marry often because it is to their interest pecuniarily or because of sensuous desire." And so often, she said, "we see a husband living in a sphere outside and above his wife, a drudge whose life and circumstances are more narrowed and the gulf widens til they are separated in thought, aims, hopes and ambitions."[44]

The suffragists denied that being a wife and mother was woman's *only* path to fulfillment, and vigorously defended the single woman. For example, in 1905, suffragists were outraged when Senator Albert J. Beveridge, unveiling a statue of Frances Willard, praised her for "sacrificing her own life to the happiness of her sisters." They particularly objected to his statement, "For after all, she knew that with all her gifts and all the halo of her God-sent mission, the humblest mother was yet greater far than she." Laura Clay fired off dozens of letters of protest to newspapers across the nation insisting that Willard knew no such thing. Breckinridge, who believed that all women had a "sex duty" to see that the next generation would go forward "in the slow struggle toward civilization" believed that this duty fell most heavily upon single women as well as childless married women like herself, as mothers were busy "paying much of their obligation by the nurture and rearing of children."[45]

Though they all considered marriage and motherhood to be wonderful opportunities, these women were all very critical of certain traditions and laws affecting Southern wives and mothers. In Felton's columns she denied that the wife alone was responsible for the comfort and operation of a home and urged husbands to assist their wives.

She criticized popular columnist Dorothy Dix of New Orleans for her "extended" and "tiresome" advice that a woman should keep a smiling face before her husband "even when she is greatly worried over the baby, or tired to death over a hot stove." Felton was incensed at Southern farmers' failure to recognize and reward their wives' tireless labor on the farm. Women, she said, wore themselves down to "a leather string" for their farms and families without getting so much as "a good pair of shoes or decent clothes at the end of the year" as slaves had, and were routinely left behind on Saturday afternoons as husbands went to town to hold forth with other farmers about the state of "my crop" and "my farm." "I wish I had the power," said Felton, "to put them over the cook stove and wash pot, until they would be willing to say 'our crop,' 'our farm,' and 'our' everything else." Felton denied that men were truly protective of women. In her observation, Southern chivalry was largely expended during courtship, and that after marriage men expected women to stay at home, do all the domestic drudgery, and raise children. In her opinion marriage was a contract, and a husband ought to live up to his part in it.[46]

The suffragists did not go so far as to suggest liberalization of the strict codes regarding divorce in the South; to do so would have significantly undermined their efforts, such was the taboo concerning divorce in the region. Those who discussed the problem of failed marriages at all proposed greater caution in the commencement of marriages rather than greater ease in ending them. Felton objected to the custom of pushing young girls "out of the nest" and into early marriages. She blamed the increase in divorces on hasty and loveless marriages; she urged a girl to carefully examine the history of a suitor, but not to marry for social position or money. Mary Johnston wrote, "the remedy for divorce lies in education and in more careful marriage laws." In many Southern states the only grounds for divorce was adultery by the woman, and consequently the prevailing attitude **toward the divorced woman was little better than toward** "the fallen woman." Thus Johnston defended divorcées, saying that the majority of them were "quite guiltless of wrong-doing." She suggested that philandering men were the cause of most divorces, and said that there might be fewer divorces if regulations were passed "requiring a Board of Health Certificate be attached to every marriage license."[47]

Breckinridge spoke out courageously to Southern audiences against the so-called unwritten law, the tacit assumption within the region that a cuckolded husband had the right to kill his wife's lover and escape prosecution. According to her sister-in-law, Breckinridge resented the "archaic attitude toward the position of women in the family group underlying the whole idea of the 'unwritten law.'" Though the right was described in terms of "protection and affection and chivalric intent," this only concealed the "real relation of the woman to the situation"; namely, that the violation of the husband's claim to "exclusive control and enjoyment of his wife's person" supposedly gave him the right to avenge the wrong.[48]

Among these women only Felton expressed "appreciation" of the Southern male tradition of extralegal violence in defense of Southern womanhood, including dueling and lynching. Felton touched off a storm of controversy in 1897 by publicly advocating lynching as a means of deterring black rapists. But other suffragists, from both ends of the ideological scale in regard to race, denounced lynching, believing with Kearney that it was the work of the "lawless and ruffianly element" and an outrage to "the better element throughout the South."[49]

The suffragists were unanimous in their advocacy of a single standard of morality for men and women and found the prevailing attitude of Southern men toward the relative conduct of the two sexes ironic. In Somerville's words, "any reputable man will defend with his life the moral character of the women of his family while he rarely expects those women to inquire into his moral character." Kearney told a Jackson audience that "the world would be no better 'til purity in man was considered just as necessary as in woman, and the women had it in their power to make it so." And Breckinridge, as usual invoking science in support of reform, offered this intriguing if ambiguous statement: "We now have the wonderful knowledge that physicians have never given to any other generation, that prostitution is not necessary for one half the race, as was formerly believed to be the case."[50]

Southern suffragists launched campaigns against the existence of "segregated districts" (red-light zones) in their communities; during World War I, Somerville led a group of one hundred women before Greenville's city fathers demanding the abolition of the segregated districts and "houses of vice." Southern suffrage organizations also demanded the creation of vice commissions and action against the "white-slave traffic."[51]

The suffragists' feelings of gender solidarity extended even unto the prostitute: they sought to rehabilitate rather than imprison or ostracize the "fallen woman," and to punish the men who kept brothels in business at least as heavily as the prostitutes. As Mary Johnston said: "to the making of one harlot there goes, as a minimum, two rakehells." Felton, who served on the board of a home for delinquent girls in Atlanta, told a women's missionary society:

> When the merciful Jesus could speak kindly to the woman, who had wrecked her life, in defiance of moral law, and womanly purity, then we are taught to be helpful and forgiving in word and in thought to the wretched girls who have outlawed themselves from home and all that a virtuous home stands for in this world of ours—led to ruin by delusions

and snares—and because the fall has been so deep the injury has been so great. God help us to see our duty to ourselves and to each other.[52]

Breckinridge disagreed with those who explained prostitution as the result of the "low mentality" or poor upbringing of the women involved; she emphasized instead their acute economic distress, and cited this as yet another compelling reason for minimum-wage legislation. She supported the establishment of a state "farm colony" for treating women taken from prostitution, and a stricter state law defining and punishing moral offenses by both men and women.[53]

Somerville supported a bill that would prevent the trial of delinquent girls in open court, reasoning that, while a boy can live down his sins, a girl would never be able to do so under "current social conditions." She also organized a group of prominent ladies in a "court watching" venture to assure fair and sensitive treatment of a rape victim in a Greenville trial.[54]

Many of the leading suffragists spoke out publicly on venereal disease—a subject hardly proper for Southern ladies—and condemned roving husbands who brought disease home to innocent wives, contaminating them and their unborn children. In "The Woman's War," Johnston graphically depicted women tied to such men by marriage, saying "on the whole it would be both more moral and more pleasant to be tied, Roman fashion, to a corpse, and so die quickly, than modern fashion, to a [philandering] drunkard and so die slowly. . . ."[55]

Johnston, Kearney, Felton, and Breckinridge were outspoken advocates of sex education. In *Hagar*, Johnston describes a young debutante whose family married her off at eighteen to a wealthy and profligate man without even telling her about sex; after being used "like a slave" and contracting a venereal disease that left one of her children blind, "Rachel Bolt" left her husband and became an advocate of "the Movement to tell the young girl." In 1907, Kearney traveled as a lecturer for the World's Purity Federation, an organization devoted to combatting the white slave traffic but also to promoting higher moral standards through social hygiene programs in schools and for the public. In 1921, Kearney published a novel depicting and thus warning against the "vice-ridden life," a novel with an incredible title for a book by a respectable "maiden lady":

Conqueror or Conquered: or the Sex Challenge Answered; A Revel of Scientific Facts From Highest Medical Authorities, Based Upon the Relations of Sex Life To the Mental, Moral and Physical Welfare of Both Sexes—Young and Old. A Dramatic Story of Real Life, Written In a Fascinating and Entertaining Style, Describing the Tragic Results of Ignorance Surrounding the Mysteries of Sex, Together With Scientific Instruction for Fathers, Mothers, Husbands, Wives, Young Men, and Young Women, and a Thrilling Appeal to the Promotion of Happiness,

Success and Honor for Boys and Girls of the Present Generation and the Unborn Millions, Depicting the Impending Disaster to Health and Character From Lack of Knowledge Essential to Safety.

Mississippi suffragists under Somerville's leadership successfully petitioned their state for a law requiring that argyrol drops be placed in the eyes of newborns (to prevent blindness from syphilis) at a time when only five states in the nation required this precaution.[56]

These Southern suffragists did not believe that women were so well protected in Southern society. Their opinions of the laws regarding married women are evident from the campaigns they led to change them. They found it odd that a society allegedly intent on protecting women clung to antiquated property and inheritance laws that left a married woman totally dependent on her husband's decency *and* his survival. Breckinridge, celebrating the demise of Kentucky's old inheritance laws, observed, "it was one of the anomalies of the old Common law that it seemed to feel that a man left with children to support and without a wife, needed three times as much as a wife left with children and no husband. It was felt evidently that the bereft father belonged to the weaker sex."[57]

Clay's determination to improve woman's legal standing, as well as her intense feminism, can be directly traced to her parent's divorce, in which her mother lost the plantation and the home she had tended so skillfully in her husband's absence. Clay wrote in her diary, "our own unhappy domestic life has left my eyes unblinded to the unjust relations between men and women and the unworthy position of women." Suffragists also condemned the hypocrisy of legislators who celebrated the influence of the mother while refusing to change the laws that gave the father full legal rights to their children, even the power to appoint a guardian for his unborn child.[58]

Indeed, these women had no illusions about the status of women in Southern society, and they clearly recognized the contrast between rhetoric and reality. In truth, suffragists' appeals to the chivalry of Southern legislators were less indicative of admiration for that institution than of the fact that women as yet could still seek "direct influence" only through "indirect influence." Most leading suffragists were known to drop all pretense on occasion and speak their minds, as Breckinridge did when she told the 1911 NAWSA convention in Louisville that Kentucky men "class women oratorically with whiskey and horses, and legally with criminals and idiots."[59]

Among the suffragists, Somerville was perhaps the most direct, as in this article entitled "Are Women Too Good to Vote?":

It is quite common for men to say . . . that women should not vote because they are too good and must not be degraded to the level of men. . . . Now the facts in the case are that there is not a word of truth in this proposition. It is exasperating because it is short-sighted, unreasonably and historically false. . . . Exclusion from the right to vote is a degradation—always has been, always will be, never was intended as anything else, can not be sugarcoated into anything else. The age-long cause of all these things [discrimination against women in education, in industry, in property rights and political rights] has been the theory that women were too bad and too incompetent.[60]

Somerville and the other suffragists were keenly interested in women's history, and they understood that the image of women in Western society had gradually changed for the better, from "weak, vicious, and a necessary evil" to "the conservators of morality." But women, Somerville continued, should not be asked "to believe that political disability is a tribute to their goodness when in fact it is the last mark of worn-out theories." Mary Johnston, tracing the evolution of the relations between the sexes, conceded that the development during the Middle Ages of "chivalry" and "romance" eased woman's lot; however, the idea of man's superiority did not go away, and "justice was considered to be no more appropriate to her then than it had been in more savage ages." She found the same combination of chivalric rhetoric and injustice in her own time: "Last year at the Capitol I heard more talk in one day about chivalry from the lawyer in the pay of the knitting mills who were under indictment from overworking women and children than you could perhaps have heard from Bayard or Sir Phillip Sidney in a year."[61]

To a certain extent these women, particularly the oldest ones, Clay and Felton, were rather disdainful of men and believed that women were superior to men—more pious, peaceable, righteous, and humane. Clay's belief in female superiority is perhaps understandable, considering her father's violent, licentious behavior and his mistreatment of her mother. In 1874, Laura Clay observed: "When I consider the unspotted chastity, the temperance, the unselfishness, the daily ruling of life by duty of women, and compare it to the sensual and selfish lives of men, it seems to me marvelous that their virtue should be overlooked by the world and all the great revolutions in the moral world should be imputed to men."[62]

There were inconsistencies, even within the writings of individual suffragists, on the issue of the nature and causes of the differences between men and women. For example, Mary Johnston wrote in a speech in support of female education to a mothers' club: "All over the thinking world there is recognition today that the human mind is neither male nor female. It is simply human." She demanded equal (and co-educational) educational opportunity for women, and access to all professions. But in her widely circulated pro-suffrage tract, "The Woman's War," published in the *Atlantic Monthly* in 1910, she described men as "dynamic" and women as "static" and said men were better than women at poetry, art, music, science, and philosophy, while women made better administrators.[63]

Such inconsistency was common among feminists of the late nineteenth and early twentieth centuries, the Golden Age of biological determinism. Feminist leaders were understandably confused. They knew from experience that many women were highly capable and intelligent and were discouraged from developing their potential; yet the biological determinists insisted that woman's failure to achieve greatness resulted from innate, sex-linked characteristics that fitted them to be wives and mothers and made them unfit for participation in the world beyond the home. In the period from 1890 to 1920, only a handful of academic scientists in institutions such as the University of Chicago and Columbia University had begun to challenge accepted theories concerning the differences in the sexes and to suggest that environmental conditioning had much to do with personality development and differing rates of achievement between the sexes.[64]

Antebellum feminists had begun to emphasize the similarity of the sexes and to offer proto-environmentalist explanations for the lesser achievements of women relative to men. After 1870, however, the full weight of scientific authority came down on the side of innate female inferiority, just as science became the foremost authority for resolving social issues. The theories of Charles Darwin and Herbert Spencer were adapted by antifeminists such as Harvard's Dr. E. H. Clarke, a disciple of Spencer and author of the influential best-seller *No Sex in Education: A Fair Chance for the Girls* (1875). Clarke argued that though women had evolved separate and desirable characteristics, nature had made them too weak to bear the strain of full competition with men in the world beyond their sphere. As women pressed for admission to Harvard, Clarke lent his authority to the premise that co-education could easily lead to sterility.[65]

Led by Antoinette Brown Blackwell and other writers in the *Woman's Journal*, late nineteenth-century feminists developed an ideology that supported their goals without directly challenging prevailing scientific opinion. They insisted that human nature was twofold, with male and female characteristics that were complementary and equally essential. They conceded innate physical and mental differences between the sexes, but denied that woman's unique characteristics were useful only in the home. They suggested first that the world of business and politics needed woman's instinctive morality and nurturing skills at least as much as the home, that social progress depended on the full development and exercise of the natural attributes of both sexes; and second, that given new opportunities to develop untapped potential, women might surprise the world with new levels of achievement.[66]

Johnston was an avid reader of both evolutionary theory and the *Woman's Journal*. Like Blackwell, she insisted that the full development of the distinctive and positive characteristics evolved by women was essential to human progress: "the sexes are but the two arms of Life, and Life is ambidextrous. And unless the two hands work together, the potter will have an ill-shaped vessel." "Differentiation is unity multiplied by division to the end that unity's work may be better done. The sexes are two halves of one whole." Johnston was convinced that the evolution of women had taken place under unfair conditions, and like her friend Charlotte Perkins Gilman, predicted that "with freedom and education" women would begin to excel in fields usually dominated by men.[67]

Clay echoed this philosophy in many speeches. In 1913, she declared, "I hold that human nature is dual in all its elements and requires the influence of both sexes for the best development. It is this dual element, this mixture of the man and woman, this establishment of checks and balances that we need in politics at present, and woman suffrage offers it." And speaking at a 1917 NAWSA conference called to decide what role women should play in the war, Clay insisted that the ubiquitous comparison of the family to the state "expresses clearly one form of basic truth that our humanity is dual, never wholly revealed either in man or in woman, and can never be wholly expressed in its powers and possibilities except in two terms, the masculine and the feminine, forever co-equal and forever complementary to each other." She urged women to be proud of their special abilities, whose potential importance in the affairs of nations had been exhibited throughout history by women like Florence Nightingale, Clara Barton, and all the women who rose to the aid of their governments during the Civil War. "Let women understand," Clay said, "that they are not an adjunct of men but a co-equal force, and that the best hopes of the nation depend upon the co-ordination of the efforts of both."[68]

Felton, who believed that men badly needed the help of women in government, just as women needed the help of understanding men, described the "woman's movement" as "a great movement of the sexes toward each other." She gave men credit for evolutionary progress since the days when the "hard-drinking, fox-hunting, high-playing, country squire was excused because of his generosity and hospitality" even though he was "not the equal of his sober mate." And she celebrated the advent of the "New Man," who understood that "the call of the age is for partnership in the family, in the church, in the State and national affairs between man and women." "The brothel, the gaming table, the race course and habits of physical excess are still with us," she said, "but the hope of this Nation lies in the broad-minded men, who gladly acclaim woman's success in every field of literature, sci-

ence, music, art, in the organized professions, and great national phil-
anthropies. These are the men to whom we look for the early recognition of women. . . . The call of the age is for wise and capable
women, and the New Man understands that his mate must be his com-
rade and likewise his friend in every emergency."[69]

Like Johnston, Clay, and Felton, all of the Southern suffrage leaders agreed that women's special characteristics were badly needed in
the world of politics, particularly their instinctive morality and their
nurturing tendency. The ideology based on innate differences
between the sexes blended nicely with the political realities of the
Progressive era, when male politicians sought support for good government campaigns, public health and safety legislation, and protective legislation for women and children. Of equal importance, however, they insisted that the innate differences in the sexes made it
impossible even for well-meaning men to adequately represent
women. The suffragists stressed that women had interests and needs
men either did not understand or could not be trusted to represent in
politics.

Perhaps they were trying to be diplomatic, or perhaps they just
assumed that few poor women would qualify to vote; but these leaders of the Southern suffrage movement often suggested that men
needed to enfranchise *them* because *other* women and their children
were not being adequately taken care of and needed the protection of
women voters. As Laura Clay said: "These women are the daughters
of the nation: what man would undertake the care of a family of
daughters with-out the aid of their mother? So these daughters of the
nation need the ballot in the hands of the mother sex so that the
mother care may be exercised in forming and executing the laws
which must now in such large part replace that personal care which
the mothers once threw around them."[70]

There were, as the suffragists reminded Southern legislators,
women who did not enjoy the personal protection of a Southern gentleman. Somerville issued a pamphlet entitled "Who Takes Care of
Mississippi Women," saying that "opposition to woman suffrage in the
South seems to be based upon the theory that men are the real burden bearers, that women are a highly privileged supported class, and
because of special and peculiar exemptions from work they should be
willing to leave the government in the hands of men." But, she asked,
"To what extent is this theory correct?" and she answered it with statistics from the 1910 census showing that one fifth of the state's white
women were working for wages, and the number was increasing all
the time.[71]

Madeline McDowell Breckinridge accused the Southern gentleman, like the knight of the Middle Ages, of failing to protect a large
segment of the female population. "I have noticed," she wrote, "in the

tales of chivalry . . . that the lady for whom the Knight fought was always noble, young and beautiful, never plebian, old or ugly. Who protected the plain, old and ugly woman, I wonder? Who, I have often wondered, protected the peasant woman and the women who did not rank as 'ladies' in those times, climes, and social strata?" Indeed, Breckinridge insisted, "the South has done less for the general protection of women and children than any other part of America." Pointing to the fact that the "age of protection" in the states where women were already enfranchised ranged from eighteen to twenty-one, while in the South the age of consent ranged from ten to sixteen (with only Kentucky having it as high as sixteen), Breckinridge asked: "Do Southern men protect Southern women at all comparably to the way Western women, granted the right to do it, protect their own sex?"[72]

Southern suffragists found having to plead with Southern legislators, with whom they grew increasingly impatient, to be not only inefficient but highly degrading. Mary Johnston stated that the "gravest fault" of women was still the "sinuous, indirect way of approaching and of obtaining the object or the end which they desire," but blamed it on the fact that "from half the pulpits of the land, by the press, by whom not, she is told 'Continue as you are! Pursue the methods you were forced to use when you were the cowering mate of a savage half as strong again as you! . . . Beg: and if you are refused manoeuvre!'" She predicted that the phrase "indirect influence" would become in the near future "most distasteful to a naturally self-respecting and straightforward woman. . . . It means, *make me comfortable, and I will see what I can do about it.*"[73]

The ballot was important to these women as a symbol as well as a tool. From the 1890s until the ratification of the Nineteenth Amendment in 1920, their prime objective was the recognition of the woman's status as an individual with full rights and privileges under the law. Southern suffragists used what Aileen Kraditor has called "the argument from expediency" as much as or more than any; but like suffragists all over the nation they used it simultaneously with "the argument from justice."[74]

Nellie Nugent Somerville made it clear which argument she considered preeminent when she attacked an editor who said that the chief argument of the suffrage movement was that enfranchised womanhood would "bring about great reforms." "The orthodox suffragists," she wrote, "do not base their claims on any such argument. We stand upon the Declaration of Independence, 'governments derive their just powers from the consent of the governed.' Any argument based on results is merely incidental and not fundamental." Laura Clay wrote a pamphlet issued by the KERA in which she listed the accomplishments and goals of the organization, but concluded, "Yet all of these are but steps to the crowning right of citizenship and we shall not abate our efforts until the women of Kentucky possess the ballot, whereby they through the established channels of representation may have a voice in making the laws they are compelled to obey. We appeal to all men and women, who are lovers of justice, to join this Association, and become co-laborers in the establishment of justice and equality."[75]

Despite their acquiescence in and sometime advocacy of the disfranchisement of blacks (see Chapter Four), the leaders of the Southern suffrage movement insisted that they, as American citizens, had the right to self-government. Rebecca Latimer Felton declared in one of her suffrage speeches, "You may grant the women of Georgia a chance to help you—or you may assume to deny it, but I pay taxes and obey the laws, and I know the right belongs to me to assist in selecting those who rule over me."[76]

Above all, the suffragists wanted public affirmation of woman as man's equal under the law; they wanted formal recognition of woman's ability and of her individuality. Living in a society where, as Pattie Ruffner Jacobs said, the right to vote "is restricted and professedly based upon virtue and intelligence," they "understood the symbolism of the ballot." And, they agreed with Mary Johnston that a "chief reason [women should vote] is because to give women the ballot will be the acknowledgement of a common humanity. Women have been too long thought of only in terms of relationships—as some one's wife or daughter." To her, the expediency and justice arguments went hand in hand:

> All over the land . . . women are doing the work of an enlightened citizenship—doing it with the position of aliens—doing it with their hands tied. . . . We want that rope cut. Doing the work of citizens, we want the *dignity* of citizenship. Being people and intelligent, we want a voice in the councils of the people. Being Americans, we want that boon of self-government and equal opportunity which is said to be in the gift of America! We believe in the ideals of democracy, and we refuse to be excluded from the workings of that law. We say, and we say with perfect truth, you cannot have a democracy until you enfranchise women.[77]

The leaders of the woman suffrage movement in the South realized that as suffragists they were most definitely in a minority. Kearney believed Southern men were greater supporters of woman suffrage than Southern women. They sometimes grew discouraged at the failure of white women across the South to respond to their call. Jacobs wrote to Breckinridge in 1914, "If we could only awaken these fine women of the South of ours to feel their own responsibilities." They understood, however, that indifference to the ballot was not at all surprising given the cultural atmosphere in which Southern women were reared. In response to one of the multitude of critics who asked why woman suffrage should be adopted if most women did not want it, Laura Clay responded: "The indifference of many women to the right seems to come from the immense difficulties in attaining it rather than to any indisposition to using it." And they were quick to point out that indifference was not the same as opposition.[78]

These suffragists considered it their duty to awaken other women to new ambition, to an awareness of the opportunities that were being opened up to them in Southern society, and to a sense of responsibility for a world beyond home and family. Both Breckinridge and Felton included a healthy dose of reform and women's rights in their newspaper columns. Felton did not "pet poodles and paint china like certain other women columnists," but offered information and advice on a wide variety of subjects. In 1905, Breckinridge took charge of a weekly page in the Sunday edition of the *Herald* which she called the "Woman's Sphere." She defined that term broadly: "It was not to be given up wholly to discussions of fashion and to ways of making Christmas presents out of old duck skirts—to 'squaw talk' in short," she recalled. She believed "that it would be as unjust to consider such matters the sole interest of the average woman as to believe that the page containing news of the prize ring and the race track bounded the interests of the average man." Believing that "the average woman needs some stimulus to broader interests than she now has," Breckinridge included information on education, industry, art, religion, civic work, and women's rights, with constant comment on measures before the state legislature affecting women and children, such as the equal guardianship bill and raising the age of consent. The page, she said, would have "a 'new woman' flavor." She aimed to ". . . encourage those women already given to such lines of thought . . . and entice other women into an interest which they do not now feel."[79]

Somerville urged on the reform work of the women of the Methodist Episcopal Church, South. She rejoiced that "the sympathies and activities of a woman no longer had to be limited by the walls of her own home," saying "let your sympathies widen, thank God for your freedom, accept the opportunity and help in this work."[80]

The leaders of the Southern suffrage movement called upon other Southern women to look to the future, rather than to the past. They challenged others to become a part of this controversial movement, offering assurance that it would one day be seen in a different light. Mary Johnston spoke to a group of potential converts, saying, "I have heard that certain foolish women are ashamed of our company. You may be sure that Patrick Henry would not have been ashamed of it. Fifty years from now when the history books glorify this period as they will glorify it, when the statues are raised, when the pictures are painted, when music and art and literature hymn the coming of

Henry Blackwell (1825–1909) was a devoted suffragist, a Northerner who played a key role in the Southern suffrage movement. A member of the extraordinary Blackwell family (his sister Elizabeth was America's "first woman doctor"), he married the celebrated women's rights leader Lucy Stone and with her founded the American Woman Suffrage Association and the Boston-based *Woman's Journal.* Though he had been a dedicated abolitionist, Blackwell was the author and active promoter of the Southern strategy of advocating woman suffrage as the key to solving the South's "negro problem." *Blackwell Family Papers, Manuscript Division, Library of Congress*

Carrie Chapman Catt (1859–1947) was the president of the National American Woman Suffrage Association from 1900 to 1904 and 1915 to 1920. In the 1890s, as a NAWSA officer, she worked closely with Henry Blackwell and Laura Clay to promote woman suffrage in the South, believing that the desire to counter black influence in the polls might lead the South to adopt qualified woman suffrage. In her second term she disappointed Southern suffragists by assigning the South a minor role in her successful "Winning Plan" for enfranchising American women. *The Carrie (Lane) Chapman Catt Papers, Manuscript Division, Library of Congress*

COMING—MISS LAURA CLAY

of the famous Clay family of Kentucky, will speak for Equal Suffrage in Iowa

At

1916

Laura Clay (1849–1941) of Kentucky served as the crucial intermediary between Northern and Southern suffragists, convincing Northern leaders of the importance of "bringing in" the South and recruiting Southern women to work with them. She served as an officer in the National American Woman Suffrage Association from 1895 until 1911. After 1911, Clay spoke for state suffrage amendments all over the nation; this poster was used to promote her tour of Iowa in 1916. Her primary interest, however, was always the Southern suffrage movement. *Photograph courtesy of Paul E. Fuller, Lexington, Kentucky*

Kate Gordon (1861–1932), *left*, and Jean Gordon (1865–1931), *right*, shown here as young women, were New Orleans reformers who convinced many Southern women of the importance of gaining direct influence for women in politics. Kate Gordon was an influential officer in the National American Woman Suffrage Association before 1910. As the NAWSA shifted its emphasis to enfranchisement by federal amendment, however, she tried to unite all Southern suffragists under her leadership in the Southern States Woman Suffrage Conference, calling for woman suffrage by state legislation only.
Louisiana Collection, Tulane University Library, New Orleans, Louisiana

NEW
SOUTHERN
CITIZEN

OFFICIAL ORGAN OF
SOUTHERN STATES WOMAN'S SUFFRAGE CONFERENCE

Vol. 1. No. 1.   OCTOBER 1914

Votes for Women a Success

The Map Proves It

1913
Alaska

WHITE STATES: Full Suffrage SHADED STATES: Taxation, Bond or School Suffrage
DOTTED STATE: Presidential, Partial County and State, Municipal Suffrage
BLACK STATES: No Suffrage

Make the Southern States White

PRICE 5 Cents   NEW ORLEANS, LA.   50 Cents PER YEAR

Cover of the first issue of the *New Southern Citizen*. Kate Gordon, president
of the Southern States Woman Suffrage Conference, did not hesitate to use
racist rhetoric or imagery to promote woman suffrage in the South.
Reproduced from a copy of the New Southern Citizen *in the Madeline McDowell
Breckinridge Papers, Manuscript Division, Library of Congress*

Miss Kate M. Gordon, President of the Southern States' Woman Suffrage Conference, is not only prominent in her native Southland, but well known throughout the entire nation for her untiring, unremitting labors in suffrage and other lines of reform. Of magnetic personality and large experience, she is a dynamic force, whose impress will be gratefully remembered when the achievements of America's foremost women are recorded by historians of the future. Southern women can have no braver champion or truer warrior for the right than Kate M. Gordon.

Likewise, Kate Gordon did not shrink from using the SSWSC newspaper to promote her own reputation as a leader of the suffrage movement. This photograph and caption were featured in the first edition of the *New Southern Citizen*. *Reproduced from a copy of the* New Southern Citizen *in the Madeline McDowell Breckinridge Papers, Manuscript Division, Library of Congress*

Southern suffragists celebrated the femininity and domestic achievements of their leaders. Nellie Nugent Somerville (1863–1952), president of the Mississippi Woman Suffrage Association, is shown here with her two daughters Lucy (*left*) and Eleanor (*right*). Lucy Somerville Howorth, who recalls helping her mother with suffrage work as a child and accompanying her to NAWSA conventions, became a suffragist, a lawyer, a state legislator, and a judge. *The Schlesinger Library, Radcliffe College*

Belle Kearney (1863–1939) of Mississippi, a renowned orator and protégée of Frances Willard, enlisted support for woman suffrage throughout the South while working as an organizer for the Woman's Christian Temperance Union. Though Kearney was a major proponent of woman suffrage as a solution to the South's "negro problem" during the 1890s, she did not fear the proposed Nineteenth Amendment as a threat to white supremacy and ardently supported it when all efforts to attain state suffrage amendments in the South failed. *From Kearney's autobiography,* A Slaveholder's Daughter, *1900*

Madeline McDowell Breckinridge (1872–1920) of Kentucky had a distinguished record as a Progressive reformer as well as a leader of the woman suffrage movement. She was one of the second-generation suffrage leaders of the South to whom national leaders looked for support as the Gordon sisters and Laura Clay opposed the NAWSA's renewed emphasis on a federal amendment. She refused to join the Southern States Woman Suffrage Conference, became a NAWSA vice-president, and led the successful ratification campaign in Kentucky. *From Sophonisba Breckinridge,* Madeline McDowell Breckinridge: A Leader in the New South, *courtesy of Paul E. Fuller*

FACING PAGE BOTTOM: Lila Hardaway Meade Valentine (1865–1921), like Madeline McDowell Breckinridge, was among the best known and most successful of Southern Progressives. She was unsuccessful, however, as the leader of the Virginia suffrage movement, which failed to win either a state suffrage amendment or ratification of the Nineteenth Amendment. While loyal to the NAWSA and disapproving of Kate Gordon's extreme views on race and states' rights, Valentine supported the Southern States Woman Suffrage Conference, believing regional cooperation was crucial to the Southern movement. She publicly denounced the National Woman's Party, however, for its "spectacular tactics"— such as picketing the White House—tactics she insisted were "unwise, unpatriotic and injurious to the cause of woman suffrage." *Courtesy of the Virginia Historical Society*

ABOVE: Mary Johnston (1870–1936), whose historical romances were extremely popular at the turn of the century, was a valuable convert to the suffrage movement. Though many causes, including pacifism and socialism, were important to her, woman suffrage was the only one for which she was willing to campaign openly; indeed, she downplayed her radicalism on these other causes to avoid potential damage to the suffrage movement. Johnston's objections to Kate Gordon's racist tactics led her to resign from the Southern States Woman Suffrage Conference: she believed that white suffragists must not betray women of color or poor women in seeking their own enfranchisement. In 1913, Johnston published a somewhat autobiographical novel, *Hagar*, describing the conversion of an aristocratic young Southern woman to the suffrage movement. *Manuscripts Print Collection, Special Collections Department, University of Virginia Library*

ABOVE AND FACING PAGE: Pattie Ruffner Jacobs (1875–1935) of Alabama rose rapidly to national prominence after reviving the suffrage movement in Alabama in 1911. She also rejected a narrow states' rights approach to winning enfranchisement and testified before Congress that a federal suffrage amendment would not create racial problems or violate state sovereignty. Jacobs recognized and defended the prominent role of "women of the leisure class" in the Southern suffrage movement, saying the movement gave them an opportunity to do much for their less fortunate sisters. She is shown (*left*) as a young "belle" and (*above*) as she appeared during her years as a state and national suffrage leader. *Photographs courtesy of the Birmingham Public Library*

Rebecca Latimer Felton (1835–1930) with her husband, William H. Felton.
From the Hargrett Rare Book and Manuscript Library, University of Georgia Libraries

Rebecca Latimer Felton became an important voice for woman suffrage in Georgia and the South in the early 1900s after being active in politics for decades as campaign manager and press secretary for her husband (who served as an Independent in Congress in the 1870s and in the Georgia legislature in the 1880s). Felton was also well known as an outspoken columnist for the *Atlanta Journal,* with a tremendous following among white farm families. Unlike other prominent Southern suffrage leaders, she defended mill owners charged with mistreating women workers and defended lynching as necessary to defend white women. But she joined them in demanding greater educational opportunities for women as well as an equal voice in politics—where she believed woman's moral influence was badly needed. *Hargrett Rare Book and Manuscript Library, University of Georgia Libraries*

Sue Shelton White (1887–1943) was the most prominent Southern woman among the leaders of the National Woman's Party, an organization shunned by most Southern suffragists for its relatively militant tactics and its opposition to the Democratic Party. Unhappy with Carrie Chapman Catt's decision not to support state suffrage campaigns in Southern states and offered influential roles in the NWP, White accepted positions as chair of the Tennessee NWP and then editor of the NWP organ, the *Suffragist*. She played an important role in the successful ratification campaign in Tennessee. After the victory for woman suffrage in 1920, White earned a law degree and played another key role in history as one of the authors of the Equal Rights Amendment—introduced by the NWP in 1923. *The Schlesinger Library, Radcliffe College*

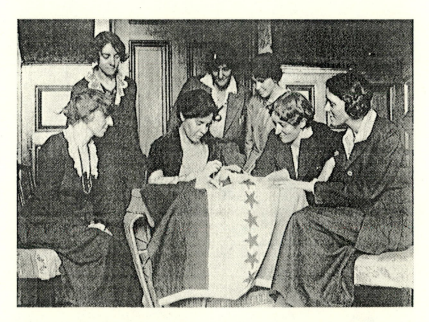

Sue White and other NWP leaders watch Alice Paul sew a "ratification star" on a flag. From left to right, Mabel Vernon, Elizabeth Kolb, Alice Paul, Florence Brewer Boeckel, Anita Politzer, Sue Shelton White, and Vivian Pearce. *The Schlesinger Library, Radcliffe College*

woman into her own, which would you rather be?—would you rather be the woman who can say to her children and grandchildren, to the youth of that time 'Yes I was there! I was a soldier in the War of Independence!' Or would you rather be the woman who must say—and say to free women—'No, the liberty nerve must have been dead in me. I can see now that it was all glorious, but I couldn't see it then.'" She concluded, "The Southern woman has pride,—oh she has pride! . . . When it comes really to her aid, she will become a suffragist."[81]

Like Johnston, the leaders of the Southern suffrage movement saw themselves as part of a great historic movement—part of an awakening of women all over the world—that would have profound consequences for society. Belle Kearney, in her usual extravagant prose, described Southern women as she saw them in 1900:

> Exactly as there are opponents among men, so are there thousands of women in the South who have arrayed themselves in a belligerent attitude toward the movement that was instituted especially for their well-being. There are multitudes of others who are still in a deep sleep regarding the necessity of having the ballot, and are continuing to drone the old song in their slumbers: "I have all the rights I want"; but there are many of their sisters who are beginning to rub their eyes and look up with a glad surprise upon the new day that is breaking, while scores of others have shattered every shackle that bound them to the old conditions and have walked out boldly into the floodtide of the most benignant evolution that the centuries have brought to them, and are working with heart and brain on fire to materialize into legislation the most potent gift that civilization can bestow.[82]

The so-called woman suffrage movement in the South was a full-fledged women's rights movement seeking, in the words of Laura Clay, "absolute equality with men in the right to free enjoyment of every opportunity that . . . civilization, the joint work of both sexes, offers for the development of individual capacity." The goal of the suffragists was to forge a new role for women in the region, with greater legal, educational, and economic opportunities and fewer social constraints. For protection of their interests they wanted to be able to rely on laws that they helped devise, not on the chivalrous impulses of men. But, in seeking the vote—however nicely they tried to put it—the suffragists were repudiating male "protection" and dominance, a fact Southern men understood but for the most part did not appreciate. Southern politicians between 1890 and 1920 acceded to a number of the reforms sought by women's rights advocates. But in rejecting woman suffrage, they made it clear that they still found much about the old pattern of relations between the sexes quite attractive. After 1920, Southern feminists would still have far to go in their quest for equal opportunity in the South.[83]

4

Southern Suffragists and "the Negro Problem"

The southern white women who are one of the most repressed and enslaved groups of modern, civilized women will help willingly to disfranchise Negroes.

> —W. E. B. Du Bois
> "Votes for Women," The *Crisis*
> August 1914[1]

Freedom belongs to the white woman as her inherent right. Whatever belongs to the freeman of these United States belongs to the white woman. Her Anglo-Saxon forefathers, fleeing from English tyranny won this country from savage tribes and again from English bayonets, by the expenditure of blood and treasure. Whatever was won by these noble men of the Revolution was inherited alike by sons and daughters. Fifty years from now this country will hold up hands in holy horror that . . . any man or set of men in America should assume to themselves the authority to deny to free-born white women of America the ballot which is the badge and synonym of freedom.

> —Rebecca Latimer Felton
> "The Subjection of Woman and the
> Enfranchisement of Women"
> May 15, 1915[2]

We know, after our experience in Mississippi, that there are many politicians who, while they would fight to the death the idea of women voting purely on the merits of the question, would gladly welcome us as a measure to insure white supremacy. My old point of choice between nigger or woman, and glad to take the woman, has more truth than poetry in it.

> —Kate Gordon to Laura Clay
> December 5, 1907[3]

100

Southern suffragists were radical for their culture on the subject of woman's rights, including her right to the franchise; however, on the subject of black suffrage, which dominated Southern politics at the turn of the century, radical they were not. Women who spoke eloquently of the inalienable right of women as citizens to self-government advocated or at least acquiesced in the restoration of white supremacy that took place contemporaneously with the Southern woman suffrage movement.[4]

Products of the South's socioeconomic and political elite, most leading suffragists shared the idea characteristic of their race and class and then gaining currency throughout the nation that suffrage was not a right of all citizens but the privilege and duty of those best qualified to exercise it. Indeed, the contemporary meaning of the phrase "the negro problem" to white Southern suffragists was not the use of the race issue against their cause—though this concerned them greatly—but the enfranchisement after the Civil War of several million African-Americans considered by whites to be ignorant, purchasable, and unfit for political participation.

White Southern suffragists generally saw their movement as a drive to clean up Southern politics by improving the quality of the electorate. They believed they were better qualified to participate in politics than most white men; without question, they considered themselves and other white women to be more desirable as voters than the black men who had been enfranchised by the Fifteenth Amendment. Indeed, they were highly indignant that these men had become the political superiors of "the best white women of the South." Thus, most were willing to use racist arguments to promote woman suffrage, some aggressively and enthusiastically and others defensively and reluctantly.

One of the most fascinating aspects about the relationship between the Southern suffrage movement and the South's "negro problem" is the crucial role of the latter in determining the strategy, the rhetoric, and even the timing of the woman suffrage movement in the South. Though historians usually focus on the race issue as a prime obstacle to the suffragists' success, there is considerable evidence to indicate that the race issue was, in fact, a major causative factor in the emergence in the 1890s of the woman suffrage movement in the South. An organized regional movement with strong national support came into existence in that decade because many leading suffragists—both Southern and Northern—believed the South's "negro problem" might be the key to female enfranchisement. Indeed, many Southern suffragists believed that as the men of their class cast about for a means of countering the effects of black suffrage, they might resort to enfranchising white women—just as conservatives in the West had made use of woman suffrage to consolidate their political position.[5]

The existence of this so-called reform movement, like the Progressive movement that came after it, gave white Southern suffragists grounds to argue that the enfranchisement of women was expedient to society. But unlike the Progressive movement, which inspired no great hopes among national suffrage leaders for success in the South, the zealous campaign of the self-proclaimed "best classes" of whites to regain hegemony in Southern society encouraged Southern suffragists and their Northern co-conspirators to believe the South would actually lead the nation in the adoption of woman suffrage.

By 1910 it was clear, however, that the dominant Southern politicians had managed to solve "the negro problem" without resorting to woman suffrage. In the second stage of the suffrage movement in the South, Southern suffragists were almost exclusively on the defensive in regard to the race issue against opponents who claimed that state or federal woman suffrage amendments would endanger the newly reestablished white dominance in politics.

I

There was a range of opinion, albeit a narrow one, among these Southern suffrage leaders on the nature and potential of blacks. The spectrum extended from the negrophobic Kate Gordon of New Orleans, to the relatively liberal Mary Johnston of Virginia. While Gordon used phrases including "fool niggers," "cornfield darkies," and "coon nature" in suffrage speeches and went as far as to advocate a state suffrage amendment explicitly enfranchising white women only, Johnston opposed a suggestion that Virginia suffragists seek woman suffrage with a monetary restriction, saying "I think that as women we should be most prayerfully careful lest, in the future, that women—whether colored women or white women who are merely poor, should be able to say that we had betrayed their interests and excluded them from freedom."[6]

Time and place of birth were significant in determining where these women would fit on this ideological spectrum. It is no surprise that those born before 1865 and reared during Reconstruction in states with large black populations tended to be the most negative in their assessment of blacks: Louisiana's Kate and Jean Gordon (born in 1861 and 1865), Georgia's Rebecca Latimer Felton (born in 1835), and Mississippi's Belle Kearney (born in 1863) and Nellie Nugent Somerville (born in 1863). In their eyes, Southern blacks, numerous, ignorant, and enfranchised, were a blight on Southern civilization. In her *A Slaveholder's Daughter* (1900), Belle Kearney wrote, "The world is scarcely beginning to realize the enormity of the situation that faces the South in its grapple with the negro problem which was thrust upon it at the close of the civil war when 4,500,000 ex-slaves, illiterate and semi-barbarous, were enfranchised. Such a situation has no parallel in history. . . . The South has struggled under its death-weight for over thirty years bravely and magnanimously."[7]

Kearney described blacks as pitiable and childlike, despondent and hapless after emancipation, dependent upon and often devoted to former masters. She described their tastes and habits as those of another, lesser species: a love of "gawdy" clothes and wildly emotional religious rituals. Particularly critical of black men, she wrote, "In negro life, as among all lower races, the woman is the slavish subject of the man." She claimed that black women frequently sought the protection of former masters against the brutality of their husbands. The appalling death rate among Southern blacks Kearney attributed to their "disregard of the laws of health and morality" and concluded "if slavery was an evil for the negro it was infinitely more a curse to the whites who owned the slaves" and were now destined to live among them. For blacks "leave their deadly, immoral trail wherever massed in large numbers."[8]

Rebecca Latimer Felton likewise spoke of African-Americans as inferior to the Anglo-Saxon and Celtic races, even comparing blacks unfavorably to Indians, "who refused to become the white man's slave, while Africa made no resistance." Like Kearney, she spoke of slavery as an evil to the white man, an offense against Anglo-Saxon blood because "unbridled lust placed the children of bad white men in slave pens, on auction blocks," while "no regard was shown to parentage or parental responsibilities in such matters." In her columns she insisted white superiority was innate and permanent, a fact she claimed was recognized by the Negro himself. Felton was notorious as an advocate of lynching: "if it needs lynching to protect woman's dearest possession from the raving human beasts—then I say lynch: a thousand times a week if necessary."[9]

These women were alarmed at evidence that racial barriers might be breaking down. Felton believed Yankees were "pampering and petting the negro," giving him a degree of education and social equality that made him unable to live contentedly among his own race or among the whites who so foolishly advanced him. Jean Gordon, refusing an invitation from Theodore Roosevelt to a White House conference because Booker T. Washington had also been invited, stated: "I declined . . . to attend any function where I would be placed on equal terms with negroes." Kate Gordon was obsessed by fear of amalgamation, a danger she believed to be growing since "the latin immigrants now flooding the ports of entry in the south have no race antagonisms." "If something is not done," she wrote to Laura Clay, "we will be as mongrelized as Cuba."[10]

Somerville and Kearney saw blacks as lacking even in their age-old capacity as agricultural laborers. And like many other wishful thinkers of the New South, they hoped the region could attract "industrious" white immigrants to displace the black laborers, who, in Somerville's words, had a tendency to "silently tie up their bundles of clothes and disappear regardless of crop conditions and their obligations to their employers." Kearney went as far as to predict the eventual solution of "the negro problem" via their extinction, should the South succeed in attracting European immigrants. "Place them in direct competition with the negro in the struggle for existence and let the fittest survive. The victory must ultimately lie with the Caucasian."[11]

The other two leading Southern suffragists born before the end of the Civil War, Laura Clay (born in 1849) and Lila Meade Valentine (born in 1865), reared in Kentucky and Virginia, were more moderate in their ideas on the race issue. They considered the racial views of Gordon and Kearney extreme and unfortunate. Unlike these slave-holders' daughters of the Deep South, Clay was the daughter of a pair of abolitionists. Proud of that heritage, she credited it with teaching her "to hate oppression and injustice." Clay was a life-long supporter of black churches in Lexington. Yet neither she nor her parents were advocates of racial equality. Writing to her mother, Laura Clay said, "Whether the fact suits us or not, observation gives some of the best of reasons for believing that racial differences are not 'matters of com-plexion' but run through the whole mental and physical constitution." Clay believed Kentucky had "no negro problem," but she was very sympathetic to whites in the Deep South where "negroes have a repre-sentation out of all proportion to the intelligence and virtue" they brought to government. At times Clay attempted to temper the racist expressions of her good friend Kate Gordon; however, over time, Gor-don's influence, Clay's own racism, and her passionate determination to win a suffrage victory in a region equally determined not to enfran-chise blacks led her to use explicitly racist tactics.[12]

Like Clay, Valentine thought "Miss Gordon errs on the extreme side" regarding the race issue but that the women of the "black belt states have good reason to be cautious." Valentine believed whites were superior at present but considered blacks quite capable of improvement: indeed, she is a classic example of the type of Southern Progressive Dewey Grantham described, who believed that though blacks were currently inferior, with white guidance and protection they would advance. She firmly believed in the duty of whites to guide and direct black development, and was well known as an advo-cate for the health, welfare, and education of blacks as well as poor whites. In 1903 she was responsible for bringing to Richmond a con-ference on the educational problems of blacks and poor whites. Hosted by the Southern Education Board, this conference was described by the *Times-Dispatch* as the first integrated gathering in the city's post-bellum history.[13]

Mary Johnston (born in 1870), Madeline McDowell Breckinridge (born in 1872), Pattie Ruffner Jacobs (born in 1875), and Sue Shelton White (born in 1887) expressed none of the animus against African-Americans of the older suffrage leaders who had grown up in the Deep South during Reconstruction. Like Clay and Valentine, Johnston, Breckinridge, and White were from states where there were fewer blacks. And Jacobs and White reached social and political consciousness at the time when the South's "negro problem" had been largely resolved. Like Valentine, these women spoke of blacks in positive, though patronizing and stereotypical, terms. They interpreted the current distressed condition of Southern blacks as the temporary result of their historic circumstances. More critical of existing patterns of race relations in the South, they realized the need for new approaches. These suffragists recognized the individual accomplishments of blacks, and expected the race as a whole to progress. To them, Southern blacks, ignorant, good, but hapless people in need of the assistance of enlightened whites, were less to be feared than pitied.[14]

Indeed, Breckinridge, White, and Johnston considered themselves or were considered by their friends to be liberal on the race issue. Like Valentine, Breckinridge was well known for her work on behalf of blacks and regarded by the Lexington black community as a champion whose "liberality and magnanimity" led to the "sharing with the colored people every advance that was adopted for the general good." She was largely responsible for the establishment of new and better school facilities for the city's blacks and community singing activities in which the black residents of Lexington could develop their "beautiful social instinct" and tendency to be "music-loving."[15]

Breckinridge opposed racist schemes such as the exclusive allocation of taxes paid by each race for the education of children of that race, calling this idea "a reactionary step advocated by Vardaman and such Southern leaders." "When the South was able after the war and the period of reconstruction to deal justly and fairly with the negro," she insisted, "there can be no excuse for her adopting now this retrogressive policy." Breckinridge believed that poor housing and theft were so common in the black community because whites charged such high rent for substandard housing and paid such low wages. Both she and her husband strenuously objected to the movie *The Birth of a Nation*, saying it stirred racial passions and discouraged tolerance and justice for blacks.[16]

Sue Shelton White and Mary Johnston were the most critical of Southern race relations and institutions. Defensive about the South, yet clearly troubled by racial injustice, White wrote an anonymous letter to the editor of *Harper's* magazine expressing dismay over the squalid conditions in which African-Americans were forced to live and over the closing of restaurants, Pullman cars, and theaters to blacks. White's ambivalence surfaced when she described her distress over the harassment of an elderly black woman attempting to vote and her own failure to assist her, though she presumed the woman "probably would not have marked her ballot properly anyway." Like Valentine, White stressed the debt owed to Southern blacks for their loyalty during the Civil War. She belittled the threat to white women of rape by black men and lamented the lack of protection black women received against exploitation by white men. Significantly, she deplored the prejudice of white clubwomen toward their black counterparts and spoke highly of the black clubwomen she had known.[17]

Mary Johnston's novels described blacks as "naturally cheerful," religious, passionate, loyal, "wise in their fashion," and "music-loving." When writing about her black servants, her tone was one of patience, indulgence, amusement. A letter to Valentine describing a woman suffrage debate among Johnston's black servants is revealing. The gardener "was intensely interested," but (she was sorry to say) opposed. He was exceedingly anxious "over the 'fearful dangers' the country will suffer if we vote. The debate was killing. Most of the village was there."[18]

Yet according to Johnston's sister Elizabeth, Mary was "always for the Minority, especially if it was a persecuted minority." Mary felt that white Southerners "owed the negro race a debt—both for having brought them here as slaves, and in return for their loyalty to their 'white folks' during the four years of the Civil War." According to Elizabeth, "Mary was attached to the old-time ones, and sympathetic to the strivings of their more ambitious sons and daughters. . . . She thought that the race should have every opportunity to develop itself. She was glad to see them become doctors and lawyers and educators so that they might help the less fortunate of their people."[19]

To a certain extent, Johnston tried to promote racial justice through her writing. In *The Slave Ship*, published in 1924, she took as her theme the common humanity of blacks and whites and the sin and evil of slavery. Indeed, Johnston presented as heroic the choice of an African woman, commandeered as a mistress by the protagonist, to turn against him and ally herself with her people in a bloody revolt during the Middle Passage. In "Nemesis," a short story published in *Century* magazine in 1923, Johnston wrote about a lynching in a small Southern town in order to influence public opinion against the wave of lynchings then sweeping the nation. The story won her the gratitude of NAACP officials Walter White and Albert Spingarn. Said White, "I have never read any story on this great national disgrace of ours which moved me as yours did." Spingarn sent out press releases to all black papers in the nation, and told the author, "It will mean much to them to know that there are white women like Mary Johnston in Virginia."[20]

   This maternalistic concern about the welfare of Southern blacks was not limited to the relatively "liberal" suffragists. Even the older suffragists from the Deep South were at times advocates for African-Americans, though their goals and expectations for black development were quite limited. Like Johnston, they had special feelings for the "old-time ones." Even the negrophobic Kearney spoke of herself as having the "old time affection which is a redeeming legacy of the days of master and slave, which was a tie of love often stronger than blood, whose power a stranger cannot understand and which alas! will be known no more when the remnants of ante-bellum days are gathered to their fathers." Felton's 1901 speech to a United Daughters of the Confederacy convention, "Southern Women in the Civil War," contained far more on the heroics of black women than of white, and concluded, "As I stand in this presence and measure my words in sight of Heaven, I believe we owe the security of Confederate homes to the affection that prevailed between those [black and white women] who had lived together so long and the confidence that both had for each other."[21]

   Somerville was well known in her community for her work to improve health and sanitary conditions in Greenville's black community. She worked alongside black leaders in public health campaigns, including an anti-tuberculosis drive, and insisted that the public health nurse she secured for the city serve the black population as well as the white. She deplored the tendency of Mississippians and their legislators to oppose "progressive and humane" legislation such as compulsory education because of the expense of extending these benefits to the state's black population. The Gordons worked for the establishment of a New Orleans tuberculosis hospital that would treat both races. Even Kearney supported larger appropriations for black schools and aid to black churches, though she warned that advocates for the Negro must temper their expectations by considering "the thickness of [the African's] skull and the length of his under jaw, and the relative smoothness of his brain" and suggested it might be a century before the extent of black potential could be known.[22]

   Felton resented any efforts on behalf of African-Americans that might make them competitive with her beloved "Crackers." She spoke angrily of seeing on a train a young "Negress" studying Greek while at the same time seeing through the window poor white girls chopping cotton in the fields. But even she was moved to launch her successful campaign against the convict lease system after hearing of the exploitation of a young black female prisoner in a convict lease camp. She wanted to see better treatment of blacks so that they would be "more comfortable" and "better satisfied" to remain in the South, though never should they be offered "freedoms said to be available in the North."[23]

Felton excepted, these older suffragists considered themselves champions of blacks against abuse by lower-class whites. Even Kate Gordon lamented the formation in her area of "the Ku Klux." Somerville "abhorred the indignities and mistreatment of the Negroes," and both she and Kearney spoke out publicly against lynching—the work of the "ruffianly classes," deplored by "people representative of the best element throughout the South." Kearney insisted the "outrages" committed since the Civil War were not "the deeds of the old slave, nor is the 'vengeance' that of the old master and rarely that of his sons." "It is the new element of both races that wars one on the other."[24]

It is difficult to ascertain the extent to which the suffragists' advocacy on behalf of African-Americans was undertaken in the interests of blacks or in white self-interest. Pragmatists, these women sometimes used to great effect arguments such as that blacks cooked the whites' food, cleaned their houses, and cared for their children, and could easily bring disease to the families of their employers. Certainly Kearney's concern about lynching seemed rooted more in her desire to protect the image of her region than in any concern that an injustice might be committed. She did not question the assumption that white women needed protection from rapacious blacks; she merely suggested that "prompt enforcement of law" would serve equally well as a deterrent without blemishing the image of the South with lawlessness.[25]

Whatever these suffragists' views on the nature and potential of African-Americans or whatever the degree of their concern over blacks' welfare, none of them was moved to come forward as a champion of the political rights of Southern blacks. Whether they believed that the inferiority of blacks was innate or a temporary, culturally determined condition that would abate gradually under white guidance and protection, these leading suffragists believed that in their time white political supremacy was a necessity. Among the white leaders of the suffrage movement in the South, the prevailing view was that whatever blacks might become, they were not presently capable of governing themselves and certainly not qualified to govern their superiors. Whereas African-American suffragists, including Adella Hunt Logan of the Tuskegee faculty, insisted that blacks needed the vote to obtain for their children adequate school facilities, a fair "share of public-school funds," and just and humane treatment under the law, white suffragists believed that blacks were best served by deferring to the leadership of the best classes of Southern whites, who would represent their interests and protect them from the abuse of less enlightened whites.[26]

All of these suffrage leaders accepted the view, nearly universal among Southern and Northern whites of the late nineteenth and early twentieth century, that black suffrage had led to disaster and that Reconstruction was a period characterized by graft, corruption, and political ineptitude on the part of ignorant and gullible Southern blacks. Consequently, they were grateful for the return of white supremacy. Nellie Nugent Somerville (who, like Felton and Kearney, was a member of the United Daughters of the Confederacy) was abundantly proud of her father's prominent role in "the campaign to free Mississippi from the debauchery of reconstruction politics." Kearney also applauded the 1877 victory of the white Democrats of Mississippi, saying "every man felt that he who would longer submit to the rule of an inferior race deserved to be a slave." But even Johnston spoke of Reconstruction as a "dreadful period" in which the white man was disfranchised for ten years, "the carpetbagger and his kind" dominated, and "misery, privation, and suffering" were the norm. And Lila Meade Valentine viewed Reconstruction as a period in which "harpies" descended upon the South and misled the ignorant blacks.[27]

The development of the post-bellum, patron-client relationship between upper-class whites and blacks and the return of white political supremacy was, according to Lila Valentine and her husband Benjamin, a natural and fortuitous development. In a remarkable poem, "A Southern Symphony," written by Ben Valentine but based on both Valentines' interpretation of the history of Southern race relations, white Virginians magnanimously accepted the responsibility of civilizing "this lowest race known to man" only after slavery was inflicted upon the colony by greedy English sponsors. After emancipation, the right of blacks to the continued protection of the white aristocracy was assured by the loyalty blacks had shown to their masters in wartime and by their aid to the Confederacy. Though they had been temporarily misled by the "harpies," the black race now gladly "bids the white guide and lead him on." And whites, with a sense of justice and mercy inherited from their forefathers and mothers, cannot refuse, but "must use their inherited gifts, *Noblesse Oblige*."[28]

To these suffragists, the failure of the "experiment" in black suffrage fully justified a return to government by the elite. As Breckinridge put it, "the experience of the South with a great body of illiterate and controllable voters has effectively taught the lesson that the value of Democratic government depends on the intelligence and character of the individual voter."[29]

Belief in unrestricted, universal suffrage was waning all over the United States in the late nineteenth century, and it had never caught on among the upper echelons of white Southerners. Upper-class Southerners of the postwar period inherited an hierarchical concept of social organization, a self-serving theory that a harmonious society free of factional conflict depended on governance by educated, statesman-like patriarchs who could govern in the best interests of all. In the wake of Reconstruction and the Populist revolt of the 1890s, conservative Democrats led by affluent whites of the black-belt counties engaged in a concerted effort to re-establish their hegemony. And in this effort they enjoyed the support of the woman suffrage leaders who agreed that political participation was the right and duty of those most "fit" to exercise it. In the struggle for woman suffrage in the South, these privileged white women promoted a revised version of natural rights philosophy that upheld, as Laura Clay phrased it, "the principle of the right of every fit person to have a voice in government."[30]

For Felton, whose husband's former constituency and whose own following consisted largely of poor whites, the definition of "fit" was racial: "Freedom belongs to the white woman as her inherent right. Whatever belongs to the freeman of these United States belongs to the white woman. . . ." The leaders of the Southern suffrage movement, however, generally supported voting restrictions that barred the "unfit" of both races. Indeed, many were outraged that a number of states adopted loopholes, such as the "grandfather clause" or "fighting grandfather clause," which would, at least temporarily, allow illiterate whites to register despite educational restrictions on registration. Gordon denounced the grandfather clause as an invitation to rule by the ignorant. And from Gordon to Johnston the suffrage leaders opposed the discriminatory application of the "understanding" clause by white registration officials who allowed illiterate whites to register while disqualifying all blacks. Ironically, Gordon and Kearney publicly denounced this practice as harmful to the white race. Gordon wrote, "we have such an awful boomerang in the understanding and grandfather clauses. . . . It has been a veritable goal for literacy among the negroes and goal for illiteracy on the part of the white."[31]

Gordon, of course, had no quarrel with the fact that discriminatory application of registration laws resulted in the "virtual disfranchisement" of Southern blacks. But moderate and relatively liberal suffragists were disturbed that qualified African-American applicants were being denied the vote. Though convinced of the importance of disfranchising the vast majority of blacks (and whites), they considered it unnecessary and unjust to exclude the minority of blacks who could meet the qualifications for registration. Clay believed the South must "restore a due supremacy of the more highly developed race" but "without corrupting the ballot box," and for most of her career advocated accomplishing this goal through educational qualifications applied equally to the two races. According to Jacobs, "qualified Negro men and women should be allowed to express their choice of candidates and their opinions on public questions in the ballot box; and exactly the same test should be applied to them as is applied to other citizens, no more, or less." Breckinridge favored the adoption of "a thorough Australian ballot with no party emblems" as an effective mechanism to screen out the illiterate rather than "inserting being able to read and write or read the constitution because that allows a corrupt elections officer to manipulate a more or less helpless class of voters." And she believed that "qualified" blacks deserved the "same protection of their political rights" as "qualified" whites.[32]

These women argued that restricting the suffrage to the educated meant guaranteeing good government while furnishing incentive to the lower classes to take advantage of the increased opportunities for education available in the New South. Breckinridge thought educational qualifications should be temporary: "When the masses of voters are able to read and write . . . I believe in pure democracy. I believe the only way we can get rid of the undesirable element is to make them desirable."[33]

These elite white suffragists, however, were no more the champions of educated blacks than of the uneducated masses. Their quarrel with Southern politicians was over the ability of men to represent women, not of whites to represent blacks. Well aware of the historic association in the minds of white Southerners between advocacy of the rights of blacks and feminism, and of white Southerners' fears of enfranchising black women—both issues skillfully manipulated by the antis—Southern suffragists tried to avoid any semblance of radicalism on the race issue. Breckinridge, for example, claimed to have "respect for colored women" and believed they could "be made excellent citizens." But she did not bring them into the suffrage campaigns, and in fact discouraged any such efforts because, as she said, "one war was enough at a time." African-American suffragists, including Adella Hunt Logan, who was as articulate as and more educated than any of these white suffrage leaders, were deliberately excluded from the Southern suffrage movement; though Logan was a life member of the NAWSA and published articles on woman suffrage in the *Woman's Journal* as well as in the *Crisis*, she was not allowed to attend suffrage conventions in the South. Jacobs' statement about the importance of allowing qualified blacks to vote, and even Mary Johnston's publication of "Nemesis," came shortly after the victory of the Nineteenth Amendment in 1920. White's letter to the editor of *Harper's*, also written in the 1920s, was anonymous.[34]

Intent on victory, the Southern suffragists tried to present their cause as consistent with widely shared values and goals of their society, including white racism. They lost no opportunity to drive home the point that black men, to whom they felt infinitely superior, had higher legal standing than white women. For example, during the 1898 referendum in which Kate Gordon drove around New Orleans collecting the proxies of 300 upper-class women unwilling to vote in public, she took the opportunity to demonstrate that no woman, but a black man, could serve as a witness to the signing of a legal document. "Sam," her long-suffering coachman, was repeatedly called in to act as a witness when, as was frequently the case, no man was at home. These Southern ladies were highly indignant, even after disfranchisement had been accomplished, that black men had been enfranchised ahead of white women. The stationery of the Southern States Woman Suffrage Conference proclaimed: "A government is not yet complete that withholds from its most enlightened women what it freely gives to it most benighted men." And Jacobs, speaking in 1917, predicted that after enfranchising their (white) women, the Southern states "would glory in the fact that they had raised the noble women of the South above the level of the negro."[35]

Even more bitterly, the suffragists resented the fact that the South's "negro problem" compounded their own difficulties in seeking enfranchisement. Kate Gordon believed the black vote (if allowed expression) would constitute "a large vote against us whenever the question of votes for women is before the people." Furthermore, Southern politicians frequently told suffragists that they would be happy to enfranchise women if only a way could be found to avoid enfranchising black women along with white, thus increasing the South's racial difficulties. In *A Slaveholder's Daughter*, Kearney wrote, "if the dangers of negro suffrage were settled forever it is scarcely a matter of doubt but that the men of the South would trust the women with the ballot. . . ."[36]

More skeptical than Kearney, Valentine deplored the exploitation of the race issue by politicians determined to block woman suffrage. In her 1917 "Presidential Address" she warned that if this strategy was successful, "because of the presence of the negro race, and because some negro women will be enfranchised, just as negro men are now when able to meet the qualifications . . . therefore white women in the South must forever be deprived of political rights, must be forever inferior, not only to white men but to negro men also, who now have those rights."[37]

The maternalistic, aristocratic concept of the patron-client relationship between the self-proclaimed best classes of white Southerners and Southern blacks and the idea that most African-Americans were (whether now or forever) unqualified to vote intelligently and honestly allowed these suffragists to reconcile advocacy of their own political freedom and the disfranchisement of most blacks. But it was the indignation of these genteel Southern women over the enfranchisement of black men ahead of white women, their frustration with the use of "the negro problem" as justification for denying female enfranchisement, and above all, their burning desire to win their own political rights that led to their firm embrace of racist tactics in their campaign for woman suffrage.

Indeed, the first-generation suffragists proposed that Southern legislators restore white women to their rightful position as superiors to black men while utilizing educated white womanhood as a resource with which to solve the South's "negro problem."

II

Given that the leaders of the Southern suffragists agreed with their white contemporaries that the wholesale enfranchisement of black men had been a grave mistake, and that power rightfully resided in the most intelligent, moral, and educated portions of the population (including themselves), many were enamored of the idea that "the best white women of the South" could secure their own enfranchisement while providing the solution to "the negro problem." Indeed, the search by Southern whites for a permanent and "legal" solution to "the negro problem" offered suffragists that crucial desideratum of all serious reformers: a practical and expedient argument for the reform they sought. It was the desire for power "to right wrongs" and for recognition of female equality and individuality—*not* the desire to disfranchise blacks—that motivated Southern suffragists to seek enfranchisement. And it was the WCTU and other women's religious and civic clubs that led women to make the leap "from pedestal to politics" and provided the constituency for the suffrage movement. It is unlikely, however, that a unified, organized Southern suffrage movement, supported and coordinated by the NAWSA, would have emerged in the 1890s had not suffrage leaders had a reason to believe Southern legislators might consider the enfranchisement of women politically expedient.[38]

Ironically, it was former abolitionist Henry Blackwell who first planted the seeds of the idea that "the negro problem" might be the lever with which to pry woman suffrage from a reluctant South—an idea he would continue to promote for forty years. In January 1867, Blackwell sent a letter, "What the South Can Do: How the Southern States Can Make Themselves Masters of the Situation," to the legislatures of the Southern states, offering statistics showing the numerical preponderance of white women over black in the region. Even before the Fifteenth Amendment was adopted, Blackwell suggested that these "intellectual leaders of the Southern people" enfranchise women as a means of counterbalancing black suffrage, which would inevitably be forced upon them. By 1885 he had modified his proposal to suggest enfranchising educated women only. While on an extended business trip in the South in 1885, Blackwell wrote to his wife, Lucy Stone, and daughter, Alice Stone Blackwell: "I fully believe that in the present state of southern opinion, if the subject of woman suffrage with an educational qualification were properly presented in the legislature and the press, it would get a considerable sympathy and attention. Suffrage on a general basis would not be listened to for a moment. For to add the still greater ignorance of the poor white and black woman to that of the men . . . would seem to them utter insanity. . . ." Enfranchising educated women only would resolve a problem Blackwell initially overlooked: the black population of the South was not evenly distributed state by state. Unqualified enfranchisement of women would actually compound "the negro problem" in states with high percentages of blacks like Mississippi, Louisiana, and South Carolina, and in the black belts of other states.[39]

With renewed enthusiasm over the possibility of winning woman suffrage in the South, Blackwell soon approached Laura Clay, the woman who was to become the key link between Northern and Southern suffragists, asking her opinion about taking this argument before Southern legislatures. Clay clearly found the idea intriguing. Though she did not immediately incorporate "the statistical argument" (as Aileen Kraditor dubbed it) into her arguments before lawmakers, her statement in response to an 1890 article advocating complete disfranchisement of blacks indicated she saw great potential in this strategy. Believing that totally depriving blacks of representation was not only wrong but would not be tolerated by Congress, she saw a solution to the South's race problem by conferring suffrage on literate women regardless of race. Clay and others who would subsequently argue for woman suffrage as the key to solving "the negro problem" saw giving the vote to women, even with qualifications, as a liberalization of the suffrage laws. The South had an opportunity to insure white political supremacy without taking the vote away from those already enfranchised and risking the consequences of violating the Fifteenth Amendment.[40]

As Mississippi was soon to hold a constitutional convention seeking "a legal way to disfranchise the Negro," Blackwell obtained an introduction to the Mississippi delegation in Congress and laid out his plan for their consideration. Impressed, they advised him to send literature on the subject to the convention, and several promised to promote the idea with their political acquaintances. Blackwell sent copies of one of his *Woman's Journal* editorials suggesting enfranchising qualified women as the key to "the negro problem" to each delegate, and many asked for additional literature. Before long Blackwell flooded the assembly with leaflets and copies of the *Woman's Journal*.[41]

It was this consideration of qualified woman suffrage by the 1890 Constitutional Convention of Mississippi—a state with no organized suffrage movement at that time—that suggested Blackwell's scheme might indeed be credible and fired the imaginations of the suffragists. Though the "Mississippi Plan" finally adopted relied upon the understanding clause and a poll tax to disfranchise blacks, the delegates and the Mississippi press gave serious consideration to a proposal to enfranchise all women who owned or whose husbands owned three hundred dollars' worth of real estate. Similar to Blackwell's plan, this proposal was designed to secure a more favorable ratio of white to black voters and solve the problem of black suffrage without resorting to disfranchisement or risking congressional repercussions.[42]

Clay, whose recent plea before the 1889 Kentucky Constitutional Convention on the basis of "justice, and justice only" had fallen on deaf ears, was impressed. And armed with the news from Mississippi, she convinced NAWSA officials they should launch a major offensive in the South. "If there had been an association in Mississippi in 1890," she told them, "it is possible that Mississippi would now be a suffrage state."[43]

NAWSA leaders, eager to expand their base of support geographically, and indignant that woman suffrage had not been included in the Fifteenth Amendment, were quite sympathetic to the views of white Southerners on "the negro problem." Elizabeth Cady Stanton and Susan B. Anthony had opposed the ratification of the Fifteenth Amendment, incensed that women had been excluded. As early as 1867, Stanton had advocated educational qualifications for voting that would eliminate lower-class, uneducated males whom she believed to be unfit to govern and obstacles to woman suffrage.[44]

Younger leaders, including the brilliant organizer Carrie Chapman Catt, shared these sentiments. Writing in 1920, Catt recalled that the late nineteenth-century suffragists "could not believe that the nation would long allow its record of enfranchisement of illiterate men, fresh from slavery, and its denial of the same privilege to intelligent white women to stand unchallenged." The sympathy of the Northern suffragists for the views of Southern suffragists on the race issue stemmed largely from their own fear and resentment of the enfranchisement of new immigrants. Speeches by Catt and others denouncing "the ignorant and corrupt foreign vote . . . manipulated by corrupt politicians to party advantage"; "the foreign menace" that threatened to "reproduce the horrors of the Old World when their numbers are sufficiently increased"; and the unspeakable injustice that had been done to "the loyal women, pioneer women, the descendants of the Pilgrim Fathers" who have been made "the political inferiors of all the riff-raff of Europe that is poured upon our shores" bore a strong resemblance to speeches by Southern suffragists on the South's "negro problem." Indeed, in 1893, the NAWSA adopted a resolution applying Blackwell's statistical argument to the North as well as to the South, advocating the enfranchisement of literate women to "settle the vexed question of rule by illiteracy, whether of home-grown or foreign-born production."[45]

Frustrated in their attempts to win approval of a federal suffrage amendment in Congress (first introduced in 1878), national leaders recognized they must first cultivate support in the states, which, once converted, would put pressure on Congress. Warning that the South "cannot be left out of our calculations" and that a federal amendment could never be won "unless you bring in the South," Clay persuaded the organization's leaders to establish a Southern Committee in 1892. For the next decade, the NAWSA spent considerable time and resources in the region. Much of the flurry of suffrage activity in the South in the 1890s can be attributed to Clay's Southern Committee and to the "outside agitation" of the NAWSA.[46]

Clay brought together the handful of Southern women already identifiable as suffrage sympathizers, including Virginia Durant Young of South Carolina, Clara McDiarmid of Arkansas, Caroline Merrick of Louisiana, and Augusta Howard of Georgia, and recruited many more. They solicited and distributed funds, circulated NAWSA literature, sent forth recruiters, and by 1895 succeeded in organizing (though in some cases, temporarily) every state assigned to the committee except West Virginia. In that year, Clay was disappointed to have the committee absorbed by the NAWSA's "Organization Committee" headed by Catt, but that committee continued to try to develop the South for suffrage.[47]

On Clay's advice, Anthony and Catt "launched their bark in the southern sea" with an extensive speaking tour in 1895. In addition, the NAWSA took the extraordinary step of holding its 1895 convention in Atlanta—the first time in twenty-seven years it had met outside Washington, D.C. Taking care to ingratiate themselves with their Southern hosts, Anthony asked her old friend Frederick Douglass—a champion of woman suffrage since 1848—to stay away; after a speech by the hero of the South Carolina suffragists, General Robert Hemphill, Anthony asked the band to strike up "Dixie." And Henry Blackwell and Carrie Chapman Catt recommended to enthusiastic audiences that the Southern states adopt woman suffrage only with an educational qualification.[48]

Brimming with optimism for the future of suffrage in the South, the Northern and Southern allies announced plans to seek woman suffrage with an educational qualification at the constitutional convention to be held in South Carolina later that year (the first such convention since Mississippi's). Once in South Carolina, Clay recommended the addition of a property qualification when the South Carolina press expressed doubts that a literacy test was sufficient to prevent the enfranchisement of most Negro women. In an address to the assembled convention, Clay deplored the problems confronting the entire nation owing to the "rash prodigality with which the franchise [had] been extended to all classes of men, regardless of their unfitness for such political trust by illiteracy, foreign birth, or other causes." She urged South Carolina to set an example for the entire nation by extending the vote to qualified women and assuring white supremacy through a method that was legal, fair, honest, and unlikely to be struck down by the courts.[49]

The suffragists succeeded in winning the support of many men of their class, including Pitchfork Ben Tillman's estranged brother, George D. Tillman, the leader of the conservative delegates, and both General Robert Hemphill and his brother James, editor of the

Charleston *News and Courier*. But the South Carolina campaign ultimately failed because the convention was controlled by Ben Tillman and his supporters, many of whom were illiterate and poor and understandably reluctant to support a suffrage bill that would disqualify the women of their own class. And like the delegates in Mississippi, many of these men were as eager to keep woman in her traditional role as to restore the black to his: as one Mississippian put it, they refused to "cower behind petticoats and use lovely women as breast-protectors in the future political battles of the state."[50]

Undaunted, the suffragists remained convinced that "the negro problem" would provide the key to victory. Clay predicted that the measures adopted in South Carolina, which like those chosen by Mississippi, unofficially permitted registration officials to register illiterate whites and exclude all blacks, "of necessity can only be temporary," as they promoted fraud as well as ignorance. She applauded General Hemphill, who said that only women's votes "will secure the State from the debasing effects of fraud in elections and the control of ignorance. Woman suffrage is the only way out of the present difficulty." The suffragists fully expected federal intervention that would disallow disfranchisement as a solution to the problem. And with equal confidence, they expected the men of their class to prefer legal action doubling the number of educated voters from the propertied classes to laws that disfranchised black voters while allowing illiterate whites to register. Apparently the suffragists did not comprehend the fact that whatever suffrage restrictions were adopted had to be voted in by the masses; even if most men of their class agreed with them that educating the best women of the South was the most desirable solution to "the negro problem," they lacked the power to carry out the plan.[51]

Yet even Carrie Chapman Catt, later considered to be the movement's most brilliant strategist, was encouraged by the support the suffragists drew among the low-country conservatives and saw in the South Carolina campaign proof "that Miss Clay is right when she demands more work for the South." Catt pledged to collect thousands more to be spent in the Southern states. Five months later, as chair of the NAWSA Organization Committee, she launched a major organizing effort in Mississippi, saying: "In the fall, provided we have money sufficient, we desire to concentrate our forces upon the South. . . . While the South is not yet favorable to woman suffrage, it gives a very cordial hearing to it and I may also say that when interested at all they are invariably the very best people. A year or two of work there will change the sentiment and quite revolutionize." One of Nellie Nugent Somerville's first acts after being recruited to head the Mississippi Woman Suffrage Association in 1897 was to try to make contact with all of the delegates to the 1890 Constitutional Convention who had favored woman suffrage.[52]

Throughout the 1890s and into the 1900s, Southern suffragists and their NAWSA supporters continued their Southern strategy of appealing for enfranchisement at constitutional conventions, in Louisiana in 1898, Alabama in 1901, and Virginia in 1902. During the Alabama convention, the Huntsville *Republican* complained that "No matter how modest a constitutional convention is nowadays some female suffragist will find it out and insist on making a speech." Alabama suffragists won the right to vote for "women taxpayers," only to have this victory overturned the next day. The only permanent victory won was the 1898 Louisiana measure giving taxpaying women the right to vote on tax questions that were submitted to the electorate. The woman responsibile for that victory, Kate Gordon, rose quickly to national prominence and was elected NAWSA Corresponding Secretary in 1901—adding a second strong Southern leader to the national board. As she left for New York to assume her new duties, she told the New Orleans *Daily Picayune*:

> the question of white supremacy is one that will only be decided by giving the right of the ballot to the educated intelligent white women of the South. . . . Their vote will eliminate the question of the negro vote in politics, and it will be a glad, free day for the South when the ballot is placed in the hands of its intelligent, cultured, pure and noble womanhood. . . . The South, true to its traditions will trust its women, and thus placing in their hands the balance of power, the negro as a disturbing element in politics will disappear. . . .[53]

The NAWSA Convention at New Orleans in 1903 was perhaps the high-water mark of the Southern strategy based on exploitation of "the negro problem." Events at the convention demonstrated the full extent of the National's capitulation to Southern racism and the height of Southern influence with national leaders owing to the misplaced optimism about suffrage in the South. Once again, NAWSA leaders, with Anthony the most reluctant, made an effort to appease their Southern hosts. African-American women were excluded from the convention. And at an open lecture, Dr. Anna Howard Shaw publicly chided her audience for "putting the ballot into the hands of your black men, thus making them the political superiors of your white women." "Never before," she insisted, "in the history of the world have men made former slaves the political masters of their former mistresses!" More significantly, the NAWSA capitulated to the desires of the Southern hosts, particularly their new corresponding secretary, with the adoption of a statement officially recognizing "the principle of State rights, and leaving to each State Association to determine the qualification for membership in the Association and the terms upon which the extension of suffrage to women shall be requested of the respective State Legislatures."[54]

Belle Kearney's extraordinary keynote address celebrated and defended the South for its Anglo-Saxon purity and political sagacity and held it up as a model for the rest of the nation. The new state constitutional amendments limiting the right to vote by property and educational qualifications were "pioneer statecraft," she said, the result of a "desperate effort to maintain the political supremacy of Anglo-Saxonism" after having "4,500,000 ex-slaves, illiterate and semi-barbarous" thrust upon them as voters. Had the United States government been wise enough to enact such laws when the Negro was first enfranchised, she insisted, it would have saved "years of bloodshed in the South, and such experiences of suffering and horror among the white people here, as no other were ever subjected to in an enlightened nation."[55]

Kearney recommended, however, the enfranchisement of women of education and property as a better and more permanent solution to "the negro problem." Assuming that the discriminatory application of the new laws would eventually be questioned by Congress, she proferred the argument that they provided only a temporary solution to the problem and worsened race relations by providing incentive to blacks to acquire education and property while providing none to poor whites. Far preferable, she said, was "an education and property qualification for the ballot that would be impartially applied to both sexes and races, and spur the poor white to keep up with the march of progression" while "insuring immediate and durable white supremacy, honestly attained."[56]

Indeed, Kearney insisted there was more suffrage sentiment among the men of Mississippi than of Massachusetts; the best men of her state, she insisted, were eager to extend the vote chivalrously to women whenever the women made it clear that they wanted it. It was, after all, only the "liquor dealers, the wily politicians of the lower stamp, the ultra-conservative ecclesiastics . . . and men who have risen from the humbler walks of life deprived of . . . the refinements of elevated home environment" who were opposed. Citing examples of "generous" treatment of Southern women, including Mississippi's preeminence in awarding property rights to married women (1839), consideration of woman suffrage by the constitutional conventions in Mississippi in 1890 and South Carolina in 1895, and the awarding of partial suffrage to tax-paying women in the Louisiana constitution of 1898, she insisted that the South would yet "astonish the world" by leading the nation in granting woman suffrage.[57]

Obviously the predictions of Clay, Gordon, and Kearney, as well as those of Blackwell, Catt, and other exponents of the statistical argument, failed to materialize, and the South has yet to astonish the world with its precocity in regard to women's rights. As the 1890s progressed and the Republican Party abandoned its championship of

black suffrage, and state after state disfranchised blacks through methods of dubious constitutionality unchallenged by Congress or the
courts, NAWSA leaders other than Clay and Gordon began to recognize what the Southern leaders did not want to believe: the Southern
strategy was a failure. In most Southern states, the fledgling suffrage
societies grew inactive after failing to win the vote at constitutional
conventions or to win substantial support from the politicians of their
states. At the national level, Catt retired temporarily from leadership,
and the National entered a relatively inactive period under the unfo-
cused leadership of Dr. Shaw. What scant resources NAWSA officers
had at their disposal they were increasingly reluctant to allocate for
work in the South.[58]

In 1906, Harriet Taylor Upton, NAWSA Treasurer and in many
respects the central force in the organization during this phase of
Shaw's administration, confessed her doubts about the optimism of
her friends Clay and Gordon: "I have often thought that the southern
women might be enfranchised before the northern women because of
the solution of the colored question, but we meet the indifference of
southerners at every turn." The NAWSA's initiatives in the South
ceased. Except in states such as Kentucky and Louisiana where there
were exceptionally committed leaders, the Southern suffrage movement foundered. Most Southern suffrage clubs dissolved or lay dormant until approximately 1910.[59]

NAWSA leaders now directed their attention to the West, the
scene of the few suffrage victories to date, and the region in which
they would finally achieve the crucial breakthroughs that gave
momentum to the suffrage campaign and led to the passage of the
federal amendment. Regarding Oregon as a promising field, the Executive Board selected Portland as the site for the 1905 national convention. They attempted to gain suffrage in Oregon through the new
processes of initiative and referendum in 1906; in Oklahoma, which
drafted its first state constitution in 1907; and in Arizona, where the
territorial legislature considered a woman suffrage bill in 1909. Clay
and Gordon were both actively involved in the Western campaigns
but always urged work in the South; they insisted that the NAWSA
support suffragists in Oklahoma, a state containing many Southern
emigrants, when a renewed campaign for suffrage via a referendum
was launched in 1909. Clay spent much time and a great deal of her
own money there, again promoting enfranchisement of literate
women as a solution to the race problem. After the defeat of the 1909
referendum, Clay and Gordon were involved in a heated controversy
over continued aid to the state, a policy that Upton and Shaw
opposed.[60]

When Kearney and Blackwell, and later Gordon and Clay, clinging to the strategy of winning woman suffrage by exploiting "the
negro problem," initiated still more blatantly racist campaigns in 1906

and 1907, the NAWSA refused to give its endorsement. In 1906, Belle Kearney (inspired by her silent partner Henry Blackwell, who feared the public would react negatively to his involvement) issued a call to Southern suffragists to meet at Memphis's Peabody Hotel; the stated purpose was to launch a Southern campaign explicitly asking for woman suffrage "as a solution of the race problem." Kearney's belated request for NAWSA endorsement of the meeting received a cold and negative reponse. Wary of the flamboyant and unpredictable Kearney and increasingly skeptical about this strategy, Shaw replied, "as a National Association it would be impossible for us to be allied with any movement which advocated the exclusion of any race or class from the right of suffrage."[61]

Reluctant to discourage work in the South and fearful that Clay and Gordon would take offense at her decision, Shaw apologized to Clay for appearing to neglect the South and pleaded for understanding:

> Now it must appeal to you as to every fairminded woman that such a call could not be sanctioned by the National Suffrage Association. It is contrary to the spirit of our organization and I am very sure would create discord in the body itself if the officers were to sanction such a meeting called in this manner. Whatever our opinion of the effect of woman suffrage in the South and the need of white domination in government, as a National Association we could not make a public call of that sort and expect the co-operation of all the country and it would re-act against ourselves by show-ing that we really don't believe in the justice of suffrage, but simply that certain classes or races should dominate the government.

Shaw encouraged the "level-headed" Clay to attend the conference to prevent the "brilliant" but "erratic" Kearney from embarrassing the NAWSA or forming a separate Southern suffrage organization. But even with Clay as president of the convention, the handful of delegates proclaimed the establishment of the "Southern Woman Suffrage Conference," and issued a statement of purpose endorsing the enfranchisement of literate women and asking for the ballot "as a solution of the race problem."[62]

The following year (1907) a second blatantly racist suffrage initiative, this one advocating an amendment to the Mississippi constitution explicitly enfranchising white women only, also failed to win NAWSA support. This campaign was particularly significant in that it revealed much about the relationship between Northern and Southern leaders, the extent to which Clay and Gordon believed the hopes of Southern suffragists rested in exploitation of the race issue, and the limits to the racist practices that the National would support.

The effort began when Kearney, acting for herself and Blackwell and the titular organization, the Southern Woman Suffrage Conference, announced a campaign to win presidential suffrage in Mississippi for women of education and property—a campaign they hoped would be the first of many throughout the South and West. But when asked for their assistance, Gordon and Clay, who had plans of their own, quickly changed the nature of the campaign. They saw it as an opportunity to test Gordon's theory (which they had discussed at length during Gordon's recent visit to Lexington) that Southern women must reject all "subterfuges" such as literacy or property qualifications and seek explicit enfranchisement of white women only. Gordon was convinced they could yet "make this race question the power to enfranchise the white women of the South by linking it with the question of miscegenation . . . which will never be combatted until the white women of the south are in a position to create public opinion." And rejecting presidential suffrage as totally worthless in the one-party South, Gordon refused to grant her endorsement unless the campaign was for full suffrage for white women only.[63]

Clay's endorsement of Gordon's scheme was in conflict with her stated convictions and a definite departure from her usual strategy of seeking suffrage for qualified women of both races. Apparently, she was influenced by her strong friendship with Gordon, her need for Gordon's support on the NAWSA board, her determination to win a suffrage victory in the South, and her growing conviction that Southern legislatures, "now resting on their oars" after disfranchising black men, would never enfranchise women unless they could be certain they would enfranchise no black women in the process. Convinced that "after all this question of woman suffrage is going to be settled by politicians largely upon party grounds," Clay believed that "if either party can see its gain in granting it . . . the legislators will . . . give [woman suffrage] in spite of what they now choose to call their convictions against it." The enfranchisement of white women offered Southern Democrats the inducement of adding to the white and Democratic voting majorities already achieved through methods such as literacy and understanding tests.[64]

Ironically, Kearney, whom NAWSA officials considered rash and more extreme in her racism than Clay or Gordon, was reluctant to go along with this scheme. In her opinion, it was unnecessary to bar black women explicitly when the Mississippi black vote was "so completely under control," and a whites-only measure would probably be ruled unconstitutional. Blackwell was also opposed, saying he personally did not believe in "white man's government," though he knew Southerners did. He also believed educated black women must be enfranchised to gain for all black women some measure of legal protection against white men. Nellie Nugent Somerville, like Kearney, thought it inappropriate to promote woman suffrage as an antidote to black suffrage in Mississippi, since blacks had been disfranchised since 1890. But all three of these dissenters finally backed the "whites only" scheme when the other Mississippi suffragists involved endorsed Gordon's plan.[65]

A battle royal followed over the issue of NAWSA support, a battle in which the differences of opinion among these Northern and Southern suffragists on black suffrage were more clearly revealed. Gordon demanded in no uncertain terms the National's endorsement, making it clear that if the NAWSA refused because of the race issue, Southern states—including Kentucky and Louisiana, which had been contributing heavily—should not be expected to give money to the national organization. Clay, clearly uncomfortable, though optimistic about the campaign, was willing to work in the campaign and support it financially, but opposed NAWSA involvement: "This ought to be a strictly southern movement, and the National ought to remain the advocate of the abstract principle of the right of every fit person to have a voice in government." She agreed with Henry Blackwell that the National should not be asked to endorse or fund the Mississippi campaign, and voted with the majority on the board against NAWSA support when the question was officially submitted by Gordon.[66]

Not only Henry Blackwell, but also his daughter Alice Stone Blackwell, editor of the *Woman's Journal*, pleaded with Clay and Gordon to call off the whites-only campaign to avoid giving "a black eye to the woman suffrage movement all through the North and West." Though she had previously defended the National's Southern policies, Alice Blackwell now made it clear that in her opinion the Southern women had exceeded the limits of NAWSA tolerance:

> It is generally recognized through the North and West that the governments set up by the ignorant and newly enfranchised slaves were so intolerably bad and corrupt that the white people had to get rid of them and the setting up of qualifications of education, character or property, so far as these are applied impartially to both races, is approved of by almost everybody in our part of the country except by a few ultra theorists who are absolutely wedded to the idea of a literally universal suffrage. But the application of these tests in such a way as to let in every white man, no matter how ignorant or bad in character, and to shut out every colored man, no matter how intelligent or how good, is regarded everywhere outside the Southern States as an unmitigated iniquity.[67]

Only a few months earlier, Gordon had "electrified" the NAWSA convention in Chicago with a "fiery" denunciation of Reconstruction policies that enfranchised "cornfield darkies" and left "intelligent motherhood on a meaningless pedestal." Indeed, according to the Chicago *Defender*, "every woman in the hall clapped wildly, some waving their handkerchiefs and the applause continued for several minutes." But Alice Blackwell believed that non-Southern suffragists (despite their sympathy for Southern white women) would refuse to condone a proposal that would enfranchise the women of only one race, just as they objected to these discriminatory procedures already practiced in the Southern states.[68]

Woman suffrage with an educational qualification could be defended, according to Henry Blackwell, as long as free public education was available, even though literacy tests disfranchised foreigners in the North and illiterate blacks and whites in the South. Literacy tests did not discriminate against "foreigners and negroes as such." To Blackwell and to the majority on the NAWSA Business Committee, however, support for Gordon's proposal would undermine the National's "justice argument"—though advocacy of the disfranchisement of illiterate blacks and whites and the white political supremacy that ensued had not. In her letter announcing the board's decision not to support the Mississippi initiative, Shaw wrote, "I have great sympathy with Miss Gordon and the other Southern women in their struggle and the obstacles which are in their way, and regret that it is impossible for me conscientiously to advocate the measure they suggest."[69]

If Clay and Gordon, believing that the "whites only" measure represented their only hope for victory in the South, wished to proceed with that strategy, it was now clear that they must do so without the endorsement of the national organization. Any victories they might win would be to the National's benefit. Out of principle and expediency, however, the NAWSA was unwilling to make further concessions to racism in order to exploit the South's "negro problem." The NAWSA was looking to the West; the day in which the South was seen as the hope of the movement had passed.

Though Clay understood and basically agreed with the principles of the Blackwells and Shaw, both she and Gordon were indignant at what they felt to be a lack of understanding of the position of Southern women. Clay defended her views, pointing to the absolute intransigence of Southern whites based on "a horror of negro suffrage from painful experience, and from constant observation of what seems to them the incompetence of negroes for the government of a race different, if not superior, to themselves." Furthermore (presenting an opinion directly opposite that of sponsors of the Fifteenth Amendment, who had proclaimed it "the Negro's hour"), she declared it more important for "some" women to have the vote—to represent the interests of all women and to improve the law for both sexes—than for any blacks to vote:

> I believe the condition of women requires the ballot in the hands of some women, at least, far more than the condition of negroes requires the extension of suffrage to negro women; or even that the negro men may vote. . . . I believe it is impossible to show that men any where in our country suffer such unjust laws as those which do not permit a married woman to own her clothes or to collect her wages, or to have any legal right to her children, or a multitude of injustices which are to be found on our statute books. Such laws will not be completely removed till some women have the ballot.

Clay also insisted that if suffragists succeeded in winning the vote for white women alone, "the negro women will participate in the improved laws"; the suffragists "would not be taking anything away from negro women," and they would be improving the laws for both races—possibly even hastening the enfranchisement of blacks.[70]

To Gordon, who discounted as absurd the idea that Southern women might someday be enfranchised by federal amendment, the sentiments of Alice Stone Blackwell and others like her reflected a selfishness and lack of concern for Southern white women: "Alice Blackwell is certainly worked up over any efforts that may keep the black ladies out of their rights," she wrote to Clay. "We white ones can remain forever disfranchised so long as these ladies are not discriminated against." As for their old ally Henry Blackwell, Gordon declared, his "old abolitionist sentiments" were showing: he thought he was being "fair and generous" but "he absolutely cannot be."[71]

At one point during the campaign, when Clay reported receipt of a favorable legal opinion on the whites-only clause from Illinois suffragist and attorney Catharine Waugh McCulloch, Gordon replied: "I nearly died laughing over the way you expressed Mrs. McCulloch's 'swallowing the white supremacy dose with pain,' but as you say, she does swallow it loyally." Clearly, their efforts to persuade the NAWSA to stomach Southern racism had taken on a meaning apart from winning support for a Southern suffrage effort. It had become a moral power struggle, to see to what extent the Northern women would defer to or adopt the values of the Southerners in the fight for woman's enfranchisement, and perhaps in Clay's case, an effort to find reassurance for her own acceptance of blatantly racist tactics.[72]

Eventually the Mississippi campaign came to an end when the suffragists could find no jurists or politicians in the state who believed the measure was constitutional and when Belle Kearney abruptly abandoned it to lead a more promising prohibition campaign. In the process Clay had compromised her values and Gordon had fully displayed hers. The NAWSA had let it be known that there were, after all, limits to the racism in which they would indulge. The campaign also provided evidence of the growing influence of Gordon over Clay and of a widening ideological (if not personal) rift between these two most prominent Southern leaders and other national leaders. It foreshadowed their eventual fall from power and with it the decline of Southern influence in the national organization as the Southern strategy bore no fruit.[73]

III

In the second stage of the Southern suffrage movement, roughly 1910 to 1920, the race issue continued to be important in a different, though still prominent, manner. Generally, Southern suffragists were on the defensive, attempting to convince legislators and the public that the issues of woman suffrage and black suffrage were unrelated, that woman suffrage would not exacerbate the South's "negro problem." There were relatively few attempts by suffragists to exploit the race issue strategically.

The stubborn and indefatigable Gordon took hard the demise of the argument that woman suffrage would guarantee white supremacy. Increasingly alienated from the NAWSA, not only over the race issue, but also over the related issue of states' rights (Gordon resigned temporarily from the NAWSA Board in 1909 protesting a "Great Petition" calling for a federal suffrage amendment), Gordon continued to try to devise a strategy suited for Southern conditions. And she was loath to let go of the strategy for which she had had such high hopes. As president of the Southern States Woman Suffrage Conference (SSWSC), founded in 1913, she threatened to challenge formally the "subterfuges" adopted by the various Southern states as well as to publicize the negative implications of the grandfather clause in Maryland and Louisiana. In 1913, she wrote to the presidents of the Southern state suffrage associations, saying, "what a wealth of opportunity is being lost in not showing up in both of these states how men of the politician type prefer to create an ignorant electorate rather than to enfranchise educated, intelligent women as the balance in preserving white supremacy!" Though no such legal challenge was issued, still, Gordon claimed credit for the SSWSC when the grandfather clause was struck down in 1915.[74]

Gordon also solicited legal opinions on the constitutionality of the understanding clause, saying to her attorney:

> Now do not misunderstand me: if Louisiana employs an understanding clause to preserve white supremacy and will grant woman suffrage, then I will not have a word to say against it. White supremacy is going to be maintained in the South by fair or foul means. The only ammunition I want is to strike at the unconstitutional points in any subterfuge that will not include white women in its protection. I want to make it clear that the fighting of these subterfuges will not be left to defenseless negroes but that the white women of the South will fight them in order that they may be raised to the status of the negro men in the United States.

Gordon abandoned this approach only when instructed that literacy tests were considered constitutional unless applied in a discriminatory fashion and that she could successfully challenge their constitutionality only if she were prepared to prove this was not the case.[75]

Another notable example of the use of the "statistical argument" during this latter stage of the suffrage movement occurred in 1911 at the NAWSA national convention in Louisville. There Madeline McDowell Breckinridge proposed in a keynote address the adoption of woman suffrage with an educational qualification as a first step toward restricting the suffrage to the best-qualified voters in Kentucky—significantly, the one Southern state that had not yet enacted some kind suffrage restriction. To the assembled delegates she said:

> If the literate women of the South were enfranchised it would insure an immense preponderance of the Anglo-Saxon over the African, of the literate over the illiterate, and would make legitimate limitation of the male suffrage to the literate, in the States where this has not been done, easily possible. It would, therefore, not only solve one question, that of extending the cardinal principle of our government, no taxation without representation, to the half of our adult population heretofore excluded from its workings, thereby allaying the growing unrest of the most active minded and public-spirited Southern women; but it would also solve another otherwise unresolvable problem: The intelligent limitation of the present unrestricted suffrage without fraud or violence.

Outside of Kentucky, however, the statistical argument was a moot point. "The negro problem" had been resolved to the satisfaction of conservative Democrats. The suffrage restrictions they put into place would guarantee their domination of Southern politics for another half century.[76]

In this last decade of the suffrage campaign, it was the Progressive Movement rather than the disfranchisement movement that gave hope to the suffragists and shaped their strategy. Southern suffragists still attempted to convince politicians that it would be expedient to give the vote to women, but it was far more common for them to present woman suffrage as a boon to Progressive reform than as a boon to white supremacy. "The negro problem" appeared in suffrage rhetoric almost exclusively in their defense against critics who argued that woman suffrage amendments to state and national constitutions would jeopardize the newly restored white supremacy. Rather than promoting woman suffrage as the key to maintaining white supremacy, most Southern suffragists denied that there was any connection between the race issue and the woman suffrage issue.

Southern suffragists insisted that the race issue was a "non-issue" trumped up by their opponents. "If it wasn't the negro woman (Poor soul!) it would be something else," wrote Mary Johnston. "Anything or everything—far fetchedness wouldn't matter." She and other suffragists denied repeatedly that state suffrage amendments would enfranchise large numbers of African-American women. Only "a few educated, property-owning coloured women will vote, but not the mass of coloured women."[77]

In 1914, Somerville dismissed as hardly deserving of an answer her opponents' claims that a state woman suffrage amendment would endanger white supremacy. Though the 1910 census indicated that 59.2 percent of Mississippi females of voting age were black, the state's black population had been disfranchised since 1890. In an article featuring her answers to the typical arguments of antisuffragists,

Somerville went on at length refuting biblical arguments, the objection that Mississippi women were well cared for and did not need the vote, and the contention that few women wanted the vote. But she brushed aside the question, "How would woman suffrage apply to the American negress?" saying, "I answer, just as it applies to the American negro."[78]

All over the South, suffragists were challenged by those who insisted woman suffrage amendments would call into question the recent settlement of "the negro problem." Valentine and the Virginia suffragists were put on the defensive by antisuffragists, including powerful newspaper editors who accused them of meddling in affairs beyond their understanding. In 1915, the Richmond *Evening Journal* published an editorial, reprinted in leaflet form, proclaiming "twenty-nine counties will go under negro rule" if the wishes of a handful of suffragists were granted. These women, who "are not very practical or very logical or very well informed or disposed to bother their heads with the actual facts of politics," might in their naïveté force the men of Virginia to return to defending white supremacy through fraud and violence, to "return to the slimepit from which we dug ourselves."[79]

Valentine and her lieutenants responded by gathering statistics and conferring with pro-suffrage legal talent on constitutional devices used to disqualify blacks in the Black Belt counties. A bulletin outlining the recommended legal arguments with which to answer the antis was then dispatched to suffragists throughout Virginia; the key measure was Article 2, Section 30, of the 1902 Virginia constitution, an escape clause that would permit counties to impose a property qualification for voting in the event that white supremacy seemed in jeopardy. In a letter to the leader of the Norfolk suffragists, Valentine spelled out the official position:

> Where women are given the right to vote on equal terms with men, if the educational poll tax and residential qualifications prove in any black county insufficient to maintain white supremacy, this additional qualification (Article 2, Section 30 of the state constitution) can be made legal by passing a bill in the Legislature making it applicable to the county so desiring it. Hence, all this talk about negro rule, if women are enfranchised is nonsense, and not only the Attorney General, but other well-known lawyers are of this opinion.

To Virginia suffragists assembled in convention, she said: "The farcical assumption of the antis that if women were given the ballot, the negro women would learn to read and write over night, 'would go hungry to pay their poll tax of $1.50 and immediately obtain absolute control of some twenty counties in Virginia' is not to be considered seriously by any reasonable person."[80]

By mid-decade, as the movement for a federal woman suffrage amendment gathered steam nationwide, the saga of the woman suffrage movement and "the negro problem" entered its final phase. Opponents of the proposed woman suffrage amendment proclaimed it the "sequel" to the Fifteenth Amendment, a new threat to the right of states to determine suffrage requirements within their borders. They insisted the "Susan B. Anthony Amendment" (as supporters in the North and opponents in the South chose to call it) would destroy white supremacy as it took away the power of the states to protect themselves.[81]

All of the prominent Southern suffragists except the Gordons and Clay supported the federal amendment. But the suffragists who opposed ratification, led by Kate Gordon, publicly agreed with anti-suffragists that the federal suffrage amendment would guarantee Negro domination by undermining the sovereignty of the states (see Chapter Six). In a general letter to "Southern Suffragists" urging them to work for state rather than federal suffrage legislation, Gordon insisted:

> There will never be another amendment to the national constitution repeating the error of the 14th and 15th Amendments. These war amendments were only ratified by force legislation and are the blackest pages of our reconstruction history. Granting that submission to the states is achieved, the "solid South" has within its border the requisite number of states to block ratification. Is it reasonable for southerners to suppose that the sentiment that has held intact the "solid South" for over forty years is, presto, to change for the sake of woman suffrage and ratify an amendment which will re-open the blackest and bloodiest pages of our history?[82]

Incredibly, she now began to ridicule Henry Blackwell's original statistical argument, which now surfaced occasionally in the Upper South. When Chief Justice Walter Clark of North Carolina argued for ratification of the Nineteenth Amendment on the basis that the numerical superiority of white women to black in that state would guarantee white supremacy even if the current safeguards were endangered, Gordon dismissed this reasoning as "fool talk" that failed to recognize that the black population was unevenly distributed. She insisted that this very unevenness was what must compel the Southern states to be "solid" in their opposition to the federal amendment. Gordon was thus furious with the Southern suffragists who, in her opinion, turned their backs on heavily black states such as Louisiana and Mississippi by working for the federal amendment.[83]

The Southern suffragists supporting ratification of the amendment vigorously denied that it would imperil white supremacy. Pattie

Ruffner Jacobs, speaking at a United States Senate hearing in 1915, testified that the amendment raised no "new problems" in regard to race, that it would leave intact all suffrage requirements adopted by the Southern states except for the sex qualification:

> It does not inject any new problem into the franchise problems of the State; it does not complicate any existing problem. It is a fallacy to contend that the prohibition of discrimination on account of sex would involve the race problem or any other complication. Both sexes will be obliged to meet all requirements of citizenship imposed by the State and each State can still protect the exercise of that franchise to the fullests [*sic*] extent of its power.

The actual effect of the amendment in the South, she insisted, would be to "enfranchise a very large number of white women" and "the same sort of negro women as there are now negro men permitted to exercise the privilege." To the Birmingham *News* she wrote, "Qualifications that have kept Negro men from voting in the southland can be adjusted to keep Negro women from voting, when the ballot has been made equal for white men and women."[84]

Some suffragists were uneasy about the movement's complicity in racism. In a letter to Valentine, Mary Johnston opposed a Virginia legislator's suggestion that suffragists support a woman suffrage bill with a "monetary" qualification designed to exclude African-American women, saying, "as a Virginia woman, I will have to accept whatever proportion of a loaf the present electorate gives me. But I don't see much use in pointing out to them this woman and that whom they needn't to let vote. I don't believe we'll get the suffrage any earlier by so doing—or any later by not so doing—and there's an inner query. . . ." Women active in the suffrage movement, she believed, should take care not to seek their own enfranchisement in such a way that black or poor white women would one day look back and conclude that the suffragists had "betrayed" them or "excluded them from freedom."[85]

Both Johnston and Valentine were offended by the rabid racism of Kate Gordon, which reflected upon the Southern States Woman Suffrage Conference. After reading one of Gordon's circulars, Johnston wrote to Valentine, "I do personally, honestly object to the assertion that we fear, (hence inferentially will fight) the presence of the negro woman at the polls." Believing it important for views other than Gordon's to be expressed in the SSWSC, Valentine elected to remain in the organization; however, by 1915 Johnston could no longer bear being associated publicly with Gordon and her overt racism. Just prior to her resignation as SSWSC honorary vice-president, Johnston wrote to her friend:

> I, no more than you, like the matter or the tone of Kate Gordon's utterances. In many instances they are so opposed to my own moral and mental convictions, silent and expressed that, standing to the outsider as they

must do for the opinion of the Conference as a whole, I am coming to feel that I cannot much longer leave my name upon its letterheads, even as honourary vice-president. Apparently she sees the universal situation through the window pane of Louisiana politics.[86]

But Johnston made no public announcement of her resignation, or of her dissent from Gordon's views. Nor did she challenge Virginia's poll tax and residency requirement, to which she was opposed. Like Jacobs and White and others who claimed to be concerned about discrimination against "qualified" black voters, Johnston and Valentine kept such thoughts to themselves. The turn-of-the-century South was firmly wedded to Booker T. Washington's "Atlanta Compromise." Advocacy of the health and welfare of Southern blacks was tolerated; advocacy of their political rights was not. White suffrage leaders would not have wished to confirm public suspicions of any links between the advocacy of the political rights of blacks and the woman suffrage movement, even if as individuals they were so inclined.[87]

Explaining her own reluctance to act on her convictions in regard to race, Sue Shelton White observed, "No matter how much of a free thinker one may be, the conditions and traditions of one's environment are restraining." White's experience was a prime illustration of the truth of this statement. The most "militant" of the leading Southern suffragists, this woman had the courage to burn President Wilson's speeches in Lafayette Square and go to prison for it; however, the first time she attempted to speak before a black woman's club, she fainted on the spot.[88]

The "conditions and traditions" that led these Southern suffragists to embrace attitudes about woman's role radical for their region did not lead them to radical views on the race issue. The patronizing but protective attitude toward blacks characteristic of their class was, in fact, enlightened compared to the attitudes of most white Southerners in this period, which is considered to be the nadir of black-white relations in the United States. Furthermore, the Northern and Western feminists, whom Southern antis accused of corrupting the minds of Southern women and who did indeed encourage Southern suffragists in their feminism, also encouraged them in their racism. Caught up in their own xenophobic reaction to the rapid increase of immigration in the late nineteenth century, sympathetic NAWSA leaders not only "allowed" Southern women to use racist arguments as is generally assumed, but worked with Southern suffragists to design and implement a Southern strategy based on exploitation of the South's "negro problem."

Despite their maternalism toward Southern blacks, the leaders of the Southern suffrage movement were determined to improve their own political situation even if others were "excluded from freedom." Their strategy was to exploit the South's "negro problem" if possible, or at least not allow it to defeat them. Southern suffragists assumed their own enfranchisement would accrue benefits for women both white and black—*noblesse oblige*. And believing that the suffrage was the right and duty of the "fit," few perceived any incongruity in pursuing their own emancipation while encouraging or accepting the disfranchisement of the majority of blacks.

5

Women's Rights and States'
Rights: Dissension
in "the Solid South"

*I would rather see my right arm withered in its socket than to raise it in
behalf of vitalizing the Fifteenth Amendment, and above all destroy the
safeguard of our liberty, state sovereignty.*

—Kate Gordon to Ida Porter Boyer
September 16, 1918[1]

*We are utterly weary of sectional feeling and anything which keeps it
alive; we are tired of those people who think in terms of the United States
and that other department of the universe south of the Mason-Dixon line.
We know we have background and an honorable past, but we wish to
occasionally be allowed to forget it, and to live in the present and build for
the future.*

—Pattie Ruffner Jacobs
Speech to the NAWSA Convention
Chicago, February 1920[2]

The leaders of the woman suffrage movement in the South had much
in common: a similar lineage, a heritage of *noblesse oblige*, a high esti-
mate of the nature and potential of women, and a determination to
improve woman's position in society. They differed on the race issue,
but all believed that white supremacy in politics was a necessity in
their time. And they presented a united front to a public much concerned about "the negro problem."

Southern suffragists were also similar in their devotion to their

133

states and region. Mary Johnston called herself a socialist, and, of the leading suffragists, she was one of the most critical of Southern institutions; nevertheless, this descendent of Confederate heroes indulged in the monument-building fetish of her age as if she were a Lost Cause devotee. "In spite of all reason and [owing to] merely an ingrained and hereditary matter," she wrote in 1905, "Virginia (and incidentally the entire South) is my country, and not the stars and stripes but the stars and bars is my flag."[3]

To Johnston and her associates, winning the suffrage battle *at home* was paramount. Even the suffragists with no theoretical objection to a federal amendment longed for suffrage victories on the state level—victories that would proclaim an acceptance of women's equality and the triumph of a new progressive spirit over Southern conservatism. Ellen Glasgow, a founder of the Virginia suffrage movement before fleeing the South for New York City and a freer social climate, admired the determination of her friends Lila Meade Valentine and Mary Johnston to reform their beloved but intransigent South: "You and Mary are wonders," she wrote to Valentine in 1912. "I can look on and admire, but I can't hope to emulate you. I suppose a part of it is that you both have your roots still clinging to Virginia and I haven't. I've been plucked up, root and branch. . . ."[4]

Devotion to their states, however, did not automatically mean devotion to preserving "states' rights," and the leaders of the woman suffrage movement in the South were not united on this issue. All were well aware of the regional reverence for the concept of state sovereignty—particularly in regard to the franchise. And expediency as well as filial attachment led Southern suffragists to concentrate initially on state campaigns. In the last decade of the suffrage movement, however, as the federal suffrage amendment gained momentum elsewhere in the nation, differences of opinion over the state sovereignty issue divided Southern suffragists. Ideological differences led to bitter conflict as the Southern States Woman Suffrage Conference, the National American Woman Suffrage Association, and eventually the National Woman's Party competed for the loyalty of Southern women. The controversy over strategy strained, and in some cases severed, long-existing friendships and added to the difficulties the woman suffrage movement faced in the South.

The champion of state sovereignty, Kate Gordon, failed in an effort to enlist all Southern suffragists under a states' rights banner in a regional association eschewing a federal amendment and NAWSA leadership. Most Southern suffragists—like other Southern reformers in the Progressive era—drifted toward seeking federal solutions to problems that Southern legislatures could not or would not resolve through state action. After 1916, when many pleas for state suffrage amendments had been made and rejected and the NAWSA was fully committed to securing enfranchisement through federal action, the majority of Southern suffragists campaigned actively for a federal woman suffrage amendment. Some, including Nellie Nugent Somerville, set aside reservations about federal intervention in the affairs of states and labored to convince fellow Southerners that the federal amendment held "no menace for the institutions of any State or any group of States." Others had no such reservations to overcome. Among the leading suffragists, only Laura Clay and the Gordons were so committed to the concept of state sovereignty that they ultimately refused to support and indeed opposed the federal amendment.[5]

I

Between 1910 and 1913, the federal suffrage amendment, waiting in the wings since the 1890s, re-emerged. This development, together with the departure of Kate Gordon and Laura Clay from the NAWSA executive board, set the stage for the dissension among Southern suffragists over the states' rights issue and the conflict between states' rights advocates and the NAWSA. Dismayed that the National, without its self-appointed Southern "watchdogs," was renewing its emphasis on the federal amendment, Gordon and Clay attempted to lead Southern women through a regional organization designed to exploit rather than mollify the fears of Southerners about federal intervention in the electoral process. This challenge to NAWSA leadership in the South, instigated and primarily guided by Gordon, was essentially over by the time Carrie Chapman Catt took command of the suffrage movement in December 1915—though Gordon never conceded defeat. Southern suffragists understood the need for a suffrage strategy designed particularly for Southern conditions, and many agreed with Gordon and Clay that a coordinated, regional suffrage organization would be valuable indeed. Most agreed with the NAWSA, however, that suffragists should press for victories at both the state and the national levels. And, while preferring enfranchisement by their states, when pressed by Gordon to renounce federal action, most were unwilling to eschew what might well prove to be their only means of enfranchisement.

For the two decades in which Southern women had been actively involved in the national suffrage movement, the National had concentrated its attention on the states. Unlike its abandonment of support for the rights of African-Americans, the NAWSA's temporary shelving of the federal woman suffrage amendment represented, not so much an acceptance of the terms of conservatives, as a recognition that more states must be won before a federal amendment could be achieved.[6]

As long as the National's focus was clearly on the states, however, even the most conservative Southern suffragists felt comfortable in the NAWSA, despite its constitutional goal of securing woman suffrage by "appropriate federal and state legislation." The fledgling Southern suffrage associations organized in the 1890s included this "federal and state legislation" clause in their constitutions, even firing off an occasional resolution of support for a federal amendment to their congressional delegations. While there was no real danger of a federal amendment's being enacted, they considered endorsement of the amendment "a good form of suffrage agitation." The consensus was that threatening to support a federal amendment was good strategy in seeking state suffrage amendments, as long as they made explicit their strong preference for enfranchisement through state action with the restrictions necessary to preclude any threat to white supremacy.[7]

Kate Gordon and Laura Clay generally felt comfortable as NAWSA officers, especially after the National's adoption at the 1903 New Orleans convention of the "states' rights" policy allowing state organizations to set their own strategy. In 1914, Gordon insisted that, as corresponding secretary, she had always opposed the federal amendment, but considered the NAWSA's limited federal suffrage campaign a good idea "as long as the chances for a national amendment were not within the range of possibility." Her staunch states' rights views led to open conflict with fellow officers only once: she resigned in 1908 when the NAWSA embarked on its "Great Petition" campaign (urging congressional action on woman suffrage), but returned to the board a year later when the threat subsided. Clay, secure in her conviction that the South would never allow a federal suffrage amendment to succeed, supported the Great Petition Campaign as "useful agitation."[8]

The NAWSA pattern of inactivity on the federal amendment continued through 1912. When Alice Paul returned from England in 1912, demanding a renewed commitment to securing a federal amendment, the NAWSA's budget for congressional action was only ten dollars, which remained unspent. Between 1910 and 1914, however, a spate of state suffrage victories in the West, together with the demands of Alice Paul and the Congressional Union, rapidly rekindled interest in securing federal resolution of the drawn-out suffrage campaign.[9]

The National vacillated under the leadership of Dr. Anna Howard Shaw (renowned as an orator, not as an organizer) but gradually shifted its emphasis back to the federal amendment. In 1913 and 1914, NAWSA conventions were the scenes of heated debates. The Congressional Union demanded the National end all state campaigns, while states' rights hard-liners insisted that a federal amendment campaign could never be won and should not be attempted. States' rights advocates were thrilled in 1914 when the NAWSA expelled the Congressional Union for its campaign against the Democrats in violation of the National's nonpartisan policy. The states' rights suffragists were less pleased with the proposed Shafroth-Palmer Amendment, which was designed in part to placate them. This short-lived NAWSA initiative called for federal legislation to facilitate state suffrage victories, but it pleased no one and nearly split the organization. States' rights suffragists were alarmed when the National reactivated its Congressional Committee in hopes of winning back the members lured away by the Congressional Union, and the committee immediately began to press the House of Representatives for a standing committee on woman suffrage.[10]

The National rejected a motion by Carrie Chapman Catt (then head of the suffrage movement in New York State) urging the NAWSA to adopt a new constitution giving the National board power to assign work to state associations and oversee its execution. Though it failed, Catt's motion signified the growing dissatisfaction with the disjointed policies of the NAWSA under Anna Howard Shaw and foreshadowed a shift within the national organization toward a coherent national policy centered on the federal amendment.[11]

Meanwhile, Laura Clay and Kate Gordon, who as NAWSA officers were largely responsible for bringing the South into the National and who had served as self-appointed representatives for Southern interests on the NAWSA board, were removed from or left the board. Clay and Gordon had been at odds with Anna Howard Shaw for several years prior to their 1911 fall from grace as differences of opinion over policies to be followed in the South strained their relationships with Shaw. But their downfall seems to have been primarily the result of a dispute over changes in the NAWSA's administrative policies, particularly after the transfer of the national headquarters from Warren, Ohio, to New York in 1909. Many of Shaw's changes were part of an attempt to increase NAWSA efficiency. But as Clay discerned, the effect was to make it difficult, if not impossible, for women outside "a restricted circle extending from New York to Boston and Philadelphia" to serve as officers. By June 1911, Clay had become known as the leader of a group of Southern and Western "Insurgents" on the NAWSA board. And Gordon, with characteristic directness, offended Shaw by suggesting that she resign.[12]

At the 1911 NAWSA convention in Louisville, Kentucky (despite the fact that Clay and her sister, assuming the role of host, paid for the hotel rooms of all members of the Official Board), Clay was defeated in four separate contests for NAWSA offices. Shaw's supporters, led by M. Carey Thomas, president of Bryn Mawr College, engineered Clay's defeats, using a new set of rules that gave an advantage to the delegates from the East despite their numerical inferiority. Gordon and the other "Insurgents," who would certainly have been defeated had they stood for re-election, chose not to run.[13]

These developments left Kate Gordon with a deep-seated bitterness toward Shaw and the NAWSA that would influence her behavior for the rest of the decade. Never, she said to Clay, would she forget Shaw's treatment of them during their last year on the NAWSA board. Gordon resented Shaw's "humiliation" of Clay at Louisville "with every honest bone in my body." Characteristically, Gordon regarded Shaw's affront to Clay as sectional as well as personal. When the National "slapped at Clay," said Gordon, "it sounded like memories of the Grand Army of the Republic."[14]

Gordon wanted to form a Southern suffrage organization at once. Within two months after the Louisville convention she met with Nellie Nugent Somerville, also offended by the treatment of the heroine of Southern suffragists, and discussed plans for a Southern suffrage federation that would affiliate with the NAWSA while following a strategy of its own design. But Clay was hesitant about such a venture and eager to avoid a schism in the national suffrage movement. She tried to soothe her indignant supporters, urging against "secession" and insisting that a breach "between the East and the rest of the country" must be avoided. She refused to consider the presidency of such an organization. Gordon wanted Clay, who had "pre-eminently stood for suffrage among Southern women," to serve as president of any regional organization that might be formed, but this Clay was never willing to do.[15]

Convinced that the most important suffrage work to be done was at the state level, Clay believed the apparent "disintegration of the N.A.W.S.A. would not seriously check the suffrage movement." She continued to be active in the NAWSA as chair of the Membership Committee but devoted her efforts to supporting state campaigns throughout the country, particularly in Kentucky, where she worked closely with her handpicked successor, Madeline McDowell Breckinridge. Throughout the decade, Clay clung to the hope that she could persuade the NAWSA to support an alternative to the federal amendment, specifically her own compromise "United States Elections Bill," which would permit women to vote in federal elections only and leave the qualifications for voters to the states.[16]

By 1913, however, both Clay and Gordon were alarmed at the direction in which the National seemed to be headed without their guidance. The only Southerner elected in Louisville to the NAWSA's Official Board was Sophonisba Breckinridge, Madeline's sister-in-law, who had not lived in the South since 1895 and was an active member of the newly created National Association for the Advancement of Colored People. Though Clay was personally fond of Sophonisba and appreciative of the latter's offer to represent Southern interests on the board, Clay was clearly concerned about a perceived lack of understanding by national suffrage leaders of Southern sentiments. In 1912 she complained to her friend Alice Stone Blackwell, editor of the *Woman's Journal*, that articles on the South were often inaccurate and written with no regard "to the effect such articles will have upon the spirit of the Southern people towards the reform for which the *Journal* stands." And Gordon urged the NAWSA to continue its policy of consulting Southern women when planning programs in the South "as to whether or not the speakers are persona non grata to the people." To Clay, Gordon insisted that Anna Howard Shaw possessed "as much of a National grasp of affairs as my cat." Aided by the NAWSA's new corresponding secretary Mary Ware Dennett "with her view point bound north, east, south, and west by New England," Shaw would "yet get the whole country in genuine row." By September 1913, Gordon concluded that "a 'flank movement' in the South led by women in tune with southern sentiments was absolutely essential."[17]

Of course it was the resurgence of the National's interest in the federal amendment, perceived as directly related to NAWSA's insensitivity to Southern concerns, that so alarmed these two Southern leaders. The profoundly negrophobic Gordon was convinced that such an amendment would lead to black rule in the South, that the South would yet lose its struggle to regain control of the suffrage, that state sovereignty and white supremacy were inextricably connected. She agreed with the antis that acceptance of "another" federal suffrage amendment would signify national approval of the "mistake" that had been the Fifteenth Amendment and could not understand how anyone could fail to recognize this fact. Indeed, said Gordon, she "would rather see my right arm withered in its socket than to raise it in behalf of vitalizing the Fifteenth Amendment, and above all destroy the safeguard of our liberty, state sovereignty."[18]

Clay publicly denied charges that her opposition to the federal amendment was based on race. Rather, "like the founding fathers," she believed the national well-being depended on widespread distribution of power and local control over local matters. During World War I, Clay would stress the danger to liberty of highly centralized, autocratic states like Germany and insist that local autonomy was essential. It is also interesting to note that Clay once told Gordon she was opposed to a Southern suffrage organization avowedly for states' rights for fear of antagonizing the black vote in Kentucky. But Clay's statements on race and suffrage, including the statement that in predominantly black areas of the South, unrestricted suffrage would mean "an abandonment of civilization as white Americans have lived it, and a decline to a state of society suited to the mental and moral development of negroes," suggested that racism had a great deal to do with her defense of state sovereignty.[19]

Clay was convinced that a national suffrage campaign centered on the federal amendment would not only be fruitless, diverting resources away from the true hope of the suffragists—i.e., state suffrage campaigns—but would also awaken insurmountable obstacles for suffragists working for state victories in the South. Following the series of suffrage victories in the West in 1910, 1911, and 1912, she concluded that "the time is come or will soon come, when the interests of the [Southern] suffrage cause will need more direct and energetic consideration than it is apt to get from the divided efforts of the National Association," which was "becoming more and more a sectional organization." Southern suffragists would soon have to confer on a suffrage strategy harmonious with their "sectional interests." In July 1913, Clay finally gave her consent to Gordon's plans to issue a "call" for a major conference of Southerners to determine just what that suffrage strategy would be.[20]

Kate Gordon's idea for the conference was, as always, ambitious: a conference of all Southern suffragists with the governors of all Southern states. At the conference these loyal Southerners would together devise a plan to see that each group would get what it wanted—suffrage for the women and preservation of states' rights and Democratic hegemony for the governors.

Gordon's "Letter to the Governors of the Southern States" was signed by twenty-one prominent Southern suffragists, including the presidents of ten Southern state suffrage organizations. Among the signers were Laura Clay and her sisters Sallie Bennett and Mary Clay, Nellie Nugent Somerville, Pattie Ruffner Jacobs, Lila Meade Valentine, Madeline McDowell Breckinridge, Rebecca Latimer Felton's sister Mary Latimer McLendon, and Jean and Kate Gordon. Indeed, the call represented the high-water mark of unity among Southern suffragists. It read, in part:

> We are united in the belief that suffrage is a State right, and that the power to define a State's electorate should remain the exclusive right of the State. However, we recognize that woman suffrage is no longer a theory to be debated but a condition to be met. The inevitable "votes for women" is a world movement, and unless the South squarely faces the issue and takes steps to preserve the State right, the force of public opinion will make it mandatory through a National Constitutional Amendment. . . .
>
> While as Southerners, we wish to see the power of the State retained, yet as women we are equally determined to secure, as of paramount importance, the right which is the birthright of an American citizen. We, therefore, appeal to you gentlemen vested with the power to so largely shape conditions, to confer with us and influence public opinion to adopt woman suffrage through State action. Failing to accomplish this,

the onus of responsibility will rest upon the men of the South, if Southern women are forced to support a National Amendment, weighted with the same objections as the Fifteenth Amendment.[21]

Most governors ignored the letter. The governors of North Carolina and Arkansas sent women to represent them. No governor accepted the invitation. But a large number of Southern suffragists, representing eleven states and the District of Columbia, attended the conference held in New Orleans, November 10 to 12, 1913.[22]

As Gordon had hoped, the delegates voted to establish a permanent organization. They adopted the title "Southern States Woman Suffrage Conference," and elected Kate Gordon president, and Laura Clay (not present owing to the Kentucky state convention) vice-president.[23]

Despite the governors' weak response, President Gordon had great plans for the SSWSC: through the Southern Conference, the South was going to lead the nation to the realization of woman suffrage. Gordon was convinced that the South's devotion to preserving state sovereignty—similar to its commitment to maintaining white supremacy—gave Southern suffragists a unique strategic advantage: she now had a new Southern strategy to replace the one that had failed.

As the call suggested, Southern suffragists would bid for the support of Southern legislators by proclaiming their steadfast loyalty to states' rights while holding the threat of the federal amendment over the heads of the politicians. It was ironic, considering Gordon's assumption that Southern politicians had the power to block congressional approval and, if necessary, ratification, of the federal amendment, that her entire strategy presumed Southern politicians were so frightened of the federal amendment that they would embrace woman suffrage through state action. Nevertheless, Gordon was convinced that this fear of the federal amendment, combined with the Democratic Party's stranglehold on Southern politics, rendered the South "the strategic area" for suffrage agitation, since the party that was dead set on avoiding another federal suffrage amendment was firmly in control and could easily award suffrage to women on a state-by-state basis if it so desired.

Under the guidance of the Southern Conference, Southern suffragists would eschew such heresies as direct advocacy of a federal suffrage amendment. Already Gordon was alarmed by the formation in New Orleans of a new suffrage association by a group of maverick suffragists who planned to actively support the federal amendment. Gordon had strenuously opposed the National's recognition of the new club, and was furious when the NAWSA welcomed her rivals despite her open opposition—a blow to her prestige within the area. Gordon hoped that a Southern suffrage federation publicly identified with opposition to the federal amendment could make up for such NAWSA blunders and save politically naïve suffrage converts from further error.[24]

Also fundamental to Gordon's strategy was the idea that suffrage work in the South must be the exclusive province of Southern white women. Writing to Clay in 1914 after a trip to Mississippi, Gordon said, "the attitude of Mississippi men [legislators] makes it positive that none but Southern women can handle this suffrage situation in the South. I went through a whole catechism to see that I was the genuine article, and woe would have been my fate if any Yankee blood in my makeup had accounted for my suffrage tendencies." In a letter to officers of the SSWSC, she insisted that "the National Amendment agitation" had stirred up "intense sectional feeling." "The ghost of reconstruction stalked boldly. It will take we Southern women to rebury him."[25]

The main political objective of the SSWSC was an endorsement of woman suffrage through state suffrage amendments in the 1916 platform of the National Democratic Party. Gordon envisioned an intensive three-year campaign toward this end, assuming that after the endorsement, the Southern states would then immediately comply with the judgement of the party. The rest of the nation, she presumed, would follow suit, and Gordon, Southern suffragists, the Democratic Party, and "the Solid South" would have the credit for the victory. The Democratic South, she reasoned, must recognize that it had before it the opportunity not only to avoid the dreaded federal amendment but to strengthen the Democratic Party nationally by earning the gratitude and loyalty of a massive number of new voters.[26]

Kate Gordon's dream of Southern suffragists united under a states' rights banner and her leadership would not be realized. Even at the organizational conference, the majority of suffragists were unwilling to declare the new association a "states' rights" suffrage association, supporting the enfranchisement of women by state action only. Kate Gordon had many supporters, including her sister Jean (who believed Southern suffragists should also exact concessions from Southern Democrats by joining or threatening to join the Progressive Party as she did). And Nellie Nugent Somerville, whose states' rights sentiments led her to vote against ratification of the child-labor amendment while serving in the Mississippi legislature in the 1920s, led the suffragists supporting Gordon on the use of states' rights in the organization's title.[27]

The delegates to the 1913 conference were not averse to using states' rights rhetoric, as was evident in the "call" in which they had declared themselves "united in the belief that suffrage is a State right, and that the power to define a State's electorate should remain the exclusive right of the State." They agreed that the state suffrage method was the one that should be promoted in the South and even adopted a resolution stating that the right to confer suffrage was reserved by the founding fathers to the states. And none questioned the idea that Southern suffragists should exploit legislators' fear of a federal amendment.[28]

But few considered the federal amendment to be the dire threat that Kate Gordon envisioned. Though agreeing that white supremacy must be maintained, most suffragists believed the disfranchisement movement had successfully resolved "the negro problem" and that the South did not need to fear further Northern intervention on behalf of Southern blacks.

Even Belle Kearney, as negrophobic as Gordon, rejected Gordon's exclusively states' rights position, and indeed led those who opposed the inclusion of "States' Rights" in the title. Kearney clearly did not share Gordon's passionate distrust of the North. In fact, she was convinced that Northerners were deeply sympathetic with the South on "the negro problem" and there was no need for continued insistence on state sovereignty. For much of her career, Kearney had been a "Chautauqua circuit" lecturer, giving lectures throughout the North that she believed went far toward "enlightening the people of the North relative to Southern conditions and cementing more closely the bond of re-union between the two sections." Furthermore, as a WCTU organizer and an advocate of a national prohibition amendment, she had become accustomed to searching for solutions to problems through federal action. Stubborn insistence on preserving states' rights, she believed, was a part of the Old South that had passed into history; the New South, "strong and beautiful, full of majesty and power" had a destiny of full merger with the Republic. "Our sectionalism," said Kearney, "must broaden into nationalism without reservation."[29]

Furthermore, Kearney and her supporters feared that the use of the words "States' Rights" in the title would undermine their strategy by implying a refusal to support a federal amendment should such support become necessary. They also wished to avoid arming potential opponents by suggesting that a federal amendment was a violation of state's rights. And most delegates were eager to avoid any suggestion of disloyalty to the NAWSA. A former member of the NAWSA's Congressional Committee (1911), Kearney insisted that the creation of an avowedly states' rights organization would "stir up old prejudices." "In some sections," she told the delegates, "the mention of 'States' rights' is like waving a red flag." Suffragists must not "give unnecessary alarm or take any action that would prove an obstacle in the way of a national amendment."[30]

Gordon did not give up easily on this or any other issue. Likening herself to other champions of "the Lost Cause," who refused to concede defeat, Kate Gordon raised the issue of including "states' rights" in the Southern organization's title yet again at the 1914 SSWSC convention in Chattanooga. She challenged the signers of the "call" to live up to its "unequivocal" assertion about the rights of the states to control the suffrage. But even Clay refused to support Gordon on this issue, believing that putting the organization on record as exclusively for suffrage by state action would "limit our usefulness . . . as many who do not agree with this opinion are in sympathy with our immediate objective, to make the Democratic Party declare itself for votes for women." And Clay sought and gained SSWSC endorsement of her U.S. Elections Bill, which she insisted was an amendment that the Democratic Party could support and take credit for and that Southern women could advocate without opposing their sectional interests.[31]

Failing again to persuade SSWSC members to include "states' rights" in the organization's title, President Gordon finally dropped the issue. But she continued to make statements in the name of the organization as though all members were as hostile as she to the federal amendment—a policy that vastly complicated SSWSC relations with the NAWSA and one that would ultimately cripple Gordon's efforts to command the allegiance of Southern suffragists.[32]

The formation of the Southern Conference created considerable anxiety within the ranks of the NAWSA. The 1913 NAWSA convention in New York was rife with rumors that the new Southern organization meant to secede from the national organization, rumors Gordon claimed were spread by her rival suffrage group from New Orleans. Yet the audacious Gordon, who was counting on the National to give her funds sufficient to open a SSWSC headquarters, pay a press secretary, publish a newspaper, and "suggest to all the [Southern] suffrage organizations to line up with the Southern Conference," nevertheless denied any disloyalty to the NAWSA, while publicly and emphatically denouncing its ultimate goal, the federal amendment.[33]

In an "Open Letter to the Members of the National Woman Suffrage Association" issued in January 1914 and published in the *Woman's Journal,* Gordon announced that the SSWSC "heartily concurs" with the congressmen of the South in their insistence on preserving the rights of the states and their opposition to the federal amendment. Furthermore, Gordon demanded that NAWSA members recognize that the strategy the Southern Conference meant to pursue was "logical," and insisted that if the SSWSC, a "flank movement" within the NAWSA, received sufficient support, it would "make unnecessary a national amendment."[34]

The Southern Conference, she explained, was designed "to educate the Democratic Party" that they must grant woman suffrage by state action, or the "Southern women, to whom the suffrage is greater than even the State right principle, will be placed in a position to appeal to the other States to force the suffrage nationally, our own men having failed to protect us from whatever disadvantage a national amendment may incur." Since the federal amendment was and would continue to be blocked by the "solid Southern delegation," Gordon believed the NAWSA should be thrilled to support the SSWSC. Indeed, she believed that the value of the Southern Conference ought to "be apparent to every suffragist not afflicted with mental myopia of an aggravated type."[35]

The NAWSA's initial response was more positive than Gordon had any right to expect, or indeed expected. For all her protestations to Clay and others that there was no reason the SSWSC should be perceived as antagonistic to the National, she admitted to being "struck silly" by the cooperative attitude NAWSA officials initially adopted. Medill McCormick, head of the NAWSA's Congressional Committee, wrote Gordon as SSWSC president "asking for advice and cooperation," and both McCormick and Dennett made extensive use of Gordon's "Letter to the Governors" with its impressive list of signatures as evidence of the strength of suffrage sentiment in the South. Early in 1914, Shaw called upon Gordon to represent her at numerous engagements in Southern cities and invited her to meet with the NAWSA Board in Birmingham in April 1914 to "confer with them on the Southern situation."[36]

SSWSC relations with the NAWSA, however, rapidly deteriorated. The National was eager to keep Southern suffragists in the organization and to prevent further fragmentation of the organization (after the expulsion of the CU), and NAWSA officials believed the SSWSC might well help the cause with Southern Democrats. But they were not about to turn all activity in the South over to one who opposed their organization's oldest and ultimate goal, at least not when they had such attractive alternatives.

II

Even as Kate Gordon launched her rival organization, the National was discovering younger, more cooperative Southern suffrage leaders, products of the second stage of suffrage activity in the South, who did not share Gordon's and Clay's fervent opposition to the federal amendment. Foremost among these were Madeline McDowell Breckinridge and Pattie Ruffner Jacobs, who rose to prominence in the NAWSA between 1912 and 1915.

By 1913, NAWSA officials regularly consulted Breckinridge, well known to them through Laura Clay and Sophonisba Breckinridge and her own prominent participation in national Progressive organizations. In 1914, Madeline Breckinridge was elected to the NAWSA board, the only Southerner serving at that time. So well respected was she that Sophonisba Breckinridge and Jane Addams urged her to run against Shaw (in whom most suffragists now had little confidence) in the period before Catt rose to that task. Breckinridge decided not to run for NAWSA president. But Shaw's weak leadership and her refusal to step down were key factors in Breckinridge's resignation from the national board after only one and a half terms.[37]

Jacobs was a protégée of Shaw's, who credited this charismatic younger woman with "the almost meteoric development of suffrage sentiment in Alabama." At her first appearance at a NAWSA convention in 1912, said Shaw, Jacobs "was instantly recognized as a power." Invited to give a major address at the 1913 NAWSA convention, she made headlines nationally by proclaiming that southern women *did* want the vote, that it was insulting to their intelligence to suggest that they did not, or to say that suffrage sentiment was weak in the South. As the convention buzzed with the rumors of the impending secession of Southern suffragists, the New York *Tribune* reported that "unlike many of the Southern women [Jacobs] stands with the 'National' in its demands for a federal amendment."[38]

Both Breckinridge and Jacobs served on the National's Congressional Committee and testified before Congress for the federal amendment. They also offered testimony before the House Rules Committee in support of the NAWSA's bid for a special congressional committee on woman suffrage. Breckinridge was part of several delegations that met with President Wilson. And they each represented the National on countless speaking tours, building support for the organization in the South and giving evidence outside the region of Southern support for the NAWSA and its goals.[39]

Both Breckinridge and Jacobs were especially eager to win support for suffrage in their home states and region, and both signed Gordon's "call" for the conference with Southern governors. But they could not support the states' rights strategy she devised, nor were they interested in being part of an organization they perceived as antagonistic to the NAWSA and its policies.

Breckinridge, as Clay warned Gordon in 1913, was "not a States' Rights Woman." She signed the "call" to the 1913 conference only at Clay's request, and did not attend the New Orleans conference. When informed afterwards that the presidents of the state suffrage associations had been named vice-presidents of the SSWSC, she politely declined. She maintained cordial relations with Gordon, to whom she felt a "sense of general indebtedness . . . for suffrage sentiment in the South," but, despite Gordon's frequent overtures, Breckinridge never affiliated with the SSWSC.[40]

Actually, state suffrage work was *more* important to Breckinridge than congressional work; indeed Sophonisba Breckinridge said that to Madeline state work was "first, last, and always." Breckinridge not only longed for recognition of women's equality in her beloved Kentucky but was always acutely aware that the legislatures of the states as

well as the United States Congress had to approve a federal amendment. She agreed with Gordon that Southern politicians' fears of a federal amendment must be exploited but thought that Gordon was going
about it all wrong. Explaining to Gordon her refusal to join the
SSWSC, Breckinridge wrote: "I believe firmly in pressing Southern
Democrats both at home and at Washington. I still consider that the
Washington end is more for purposes of agitation than with the hope
of results; but I believe that if some of us press hard enough at Washington, there is much more hope of results at home." Whereas Gordon
wanted only to *threaten* to support a federal amendment if Southern
legislators made it necessary, Breckinridge believed the time of necessity had already arrived, and she not only threatened but actively supported the federal amendment. In 1914, she informed members of the
Kentucky congressional delegation that the day had come when the
women of their state were forced to seek a federal solution to the suffrage problem, to end the "tread-mill work" of the state suffrage campaigns and free suffragists—"the most progressive, intelligent and willing to serve" people in most communities—so that they might pursue
the "purposes for which they really want the ballot."[41]

Jacobs had been pleased to sign Gordon's letter calling for a conference of suffragists and governors. In fact, at the time she wrote
Gordon regretting her inability to attend the conference and com-
mending Gordon for "taking the initiative" in trying to speak to the
Southern legislators in terms they would understand. "Such an obviously simple political expedient as enfranchising the white woman of
the South ought to appeal, if no higher motive moves them, to consider the woman suffrage question seriously," she wrote. Jacobs freely
indulged in the use of states' rights rhetoric, and as she sought suffrage by state action in 1914 and 1915 she sounded much like the
Gordons, who had converted her to the suffrage cause. "Alabama suffragists do not seek any interference of Congress with our State
rights," she insisted, but wanted to have the franchise "chivalrously"
extended to them by the men of their own state rather than suffer the
"humiliation of taking their statehood from men outside their own
state." She appealed for state suffrage as in keeping with the great traditions of the Democratic Party, saying suffrage by state action had
been endorsed by such "great leaders" as Champ Clark, William Jennings Bryan, and Alabama's favorite son Oscar Underwood.[42]

But Jacobs did not fear a federal suffrage amendment and had no
wish to be a part of an exclusively states' rights organization at odds
with the NAWSA, in which she was already seen as a rising star. She
actively and successfully opposed the Southern Conference in
Alabama, where Gordon had many supporters. When Birmingham
suffragists met to discuss the SSWSC, she declared, "personally I do
not think much of the states' rights idea" as a suffrage strategy,

explaining that the federal amendment was "no threat to white dominance in politics as qualifications that have kept the negro men from voting can be adjusted for women."[43]

Working with Jacobs and Breckinridge, NAWSA officials proceeded to develop their own plans for suffrage activity in the South. The formation of the SSWSC and the defeat of a proposed standing committee on woman suffrage in the House of Representatives, engineered by Southern Democrats led by Oscar Underwood of Alabama, clearly demonstrated both the need for suffrage work in the South and the need for a thorough consideration of methods. Thus NAWSA leaders called the March 1914 Birmingham conference where the NAWSA board could confer with regional suffrage leaders. Ecstatic at the prospect of hosting a conference of such importance, Pattie Ruffner Jacobs invited the presidents of all of the Southern state suffrage organizations, declaring that "this conference is not confined to the Birmingham suffragists or even to Alabama, but is intended to arouse and benefit the entire South."[44]

After the conference it was clear that the National did not intend to back down from advocacy of the federal amendment in the South, nor to defer to the leadership of the SSWSC. The NAWSA would support state campaigns in the South and elsewhere, but as part of its larger strategy of gaining a sufficient number of states to secure the amendment's adoption. NAWSA leaders recognized, as they informed the presidents of the Southern state organizations, that "it will be necessary to carry fifteen or twenty more states before ANY Federal Amendment is possible," and thus they were "particularly interested in aiding the Southern States to secure suffrage." During the conference and shortly thereafter, the National announced plans to curry favor with Southerners through new promotional literature designed especially for Southern conditions and such symbolic gestures as a "Buy A Bale" of cotton campaign planned by Shaw. Believing that it was best to concentrate the resources of the national organization and those of its Southern supporters on carrying one Southern state at a time, they asked Southern delegates to the 1914 NAWSA convention to select the state. Southern suffragists voted to begin with Alabama, where suffragists had already adopted as their slogan "We Mean to Make Alabama Lead the South for Woman Suffrage."[45]

When at Shaw's invitation Kate Gordon arrived at the Birmingham conference, she apparently expected to receive the endorsement of the NAWSA and the mantle of leadership for the South. Instead, she encountered considerable hostility as she denounced the federal amendment and the newly proposed Shafroth-Palmer Amendment the National had hoped would placate her and her supporters. After the conference, Gordon reported to SSWSC officers, "I found a spirit of opposition in Alabama that was incomprehensible." Indeed, the

very day after the conference, the Alabama Equal Suffrage Association adopted a statement saying it would not "join any permanent
organization separate from and not affiliated with or auxiliary to the
NAWSA . . . such as the Southern Conference."[46]

Outraged, Gordon wrote to the NAWSA complaining about
Jacobs' change of heart since signing the "call," and claiming that the
NAWSA board apparently "has no grasp of the purposes" of the
SSWSC; i.e., to be a "flank movement" necessary for "the development of suffrage work in the South particularly and the United States
in general." Again Gordon blamed her rival faction in New Orleans
rather than her own inflammatory rhetoric for the "misunderstand-
ing" concerning the SSWSC's relationship to the NAWSA. She
demanded that the National send her at once "an unequivocal
endorsement, or rejection, of this movement."[47]

The conference, however, apparently convinced the NAWSA they
should keep their involvement with the SSWSC to a minimum:
within days after the Birmingham conference, the board voted not to
fund the SSWSC headquarters or pay for a full-time press secretary
for the organization. Mary Ware Dennett instructed Gordon to forward her ideas to the National's Washington, D.C., headquarters to be
employed by their "experienced newspaper man," who, though
working primarily on the federal amendment, should also be able to
manage "the right kind of press work in the South."[48]

In May, Gordon finally received a mild statement from the
NAWSA board expressing confidence "in the general idea of the
Southern Conference" and saying that the NAWSA did "not consider
the movement antagonistic to the National Association." But the
statement was far short of the "unequivocal endorsement" Gordon
had hoped for.[49]

At that moment, however, a handsome, secret, and totally unexpected contribution ($10,000) from Alva Vanderbilt Belmont revived
the hopes of Gordon and Clay that suffragists would rally in support
of the SSWSC and its superior strategy, and made it possible for Gordon to proceed with her plans. Jubilant at this stroke of good fortune,
Laura Clay played a "little jig" on her piano and sat down to write
Gordon. "I thought from the first that you could get money quite as
readily as the National," she said. "The South is the strategic section
and States Rights the great obstacle now to the U.S. Congressional
help. So naturally, the eyes of suffragists are turned to the South."
Ironically, Belmont was also a major backer of the Congressional
Union, but as a native of Mobile, Alabama, she had considerable
knowledge of the South and "its peculiar conditions" and said that she
"realized the value of the methods of the SSWSC for that section."[50]

Belmont's money enabled Gordon to launch the Southern States
Woman Suffrage Conference in grand style; indeed, to make the
SSWSC a factor in the Southern suffrage movement whose impact

belied their actual numbers. Gordon and her supporters opened an impressive headquarters on Camp Street in New Orleans. In September 1914, she informed SSWSC officers of the "splendid progress" that was being made. "Our press service is reaching out to a thousand newspapers weekly, and our membership is growing. . . . Through the generosity of a friend I am able to furnish every legislator in the South the *Woman's Journal*."[51]

Gordon was able to retain Ida Porter Boyer, the experienced press secretary with whom Gordon had worked in the Oklahoma campaign. In October the SSWSC announced the "debut" of its new official organ, the *New Southern Citizen*, anticipating making many "conquests" and having "a prosperous reign in Southern society." The *Times-Picayune* described the SSWSC's Camp Street office as "the most up-to-date suffrage headquarters in existence," with sophisticated office equipment, ample personnel capable of getting out between 500 and 600 letters an hour, and an elaborate clipping bureau that sorted more than 600 papers and periodicals weekly to create an impressive "suffrage encyclopedia."[52]

Belmont's money also enabled Kate Gordon to continue her propensity for ignoring the opposing views of others, including the NAWSA and the SSWSC's own members, as Belmont specifically granted Gordon a free hand with the money. Gordon's own views permeated every issue of the *New Southern Citizen*. Though she consulted with Clay about almost every action and relied heavily on her for moral and financial support, Gordon ignored even Clay's advice if it conflicted with her own preferences. She never gave more than token support to Clay's U.S. Elections bill, though Clay was constantly pleading for support for the measure as a way to channel the congressional work of Southern women into federal agitation not damaging to the South.[53]

Now free of the need for the NAWSA's financial assistance, Gordon seemed to relish conflict with the organization and its representatives and constantly picked fights with the National despite Clay's warnings. When the hard-fought Alabama suffrage campaign failed, Gordon gloated, laying the entire failure at the foot of the National and Alabama suffragists who had followed NAWSA's advice while spurning the SSWSC. She attacked the NAWSA leaders for their insensitivity to Southern conditions, their readily apparent involvement in the campaign, and blunders such as the infamous "blacklist" episode. The National had embarrassed Alabama suffragists by issuing a blacklist of congressmen who consistently opposed the federal amendment and asking local suffragists to campaign against them. Issued in the midst of the campaign, the list included the powerful Oscar Underwood, who had committed to woman suffrage by state action back in 1913, but would never again openly support woman suffrage of any kind. Gordon insisted that the Alabama campaign confirmed her theory that suffrage work in the South must be conducted by Southern women alone. Indeed, she said there was some truth in the legislators' claims that suffrage activities in the South by non-Southerners constituted outside interference, attacks on the prerogatives of the states, attempts to enfranchise the Negro, and threats to Democratic supremacy.[54]

Given the passionate opposition among Southern politicians to the federal amendment, the question of appropriate suffrage strategy was indeed a difficult one for Southern suffragists who received such conflicting advice from the SSWSC and the NAWSA. And, beginning in 1915, the efforts of the Congressional Union, or CU (precursor to the National Woman's Party) to begin operations in the South further complicated the lives of suffrage leaders in some states. The SSWSC and the NAWSA differed over whether Southern suffragists ought to support the federal amendment, or oppose it while threatening to support it if Southern legislators failed to enfranchise women by state amendment; the CU advised plunging directly into the fight for the federal amendment. Few Southern suffragists had any use for the CU, with its campaign against the Democratic Party and its exclusive focus on the federal amendment. Most Southern suffragists, trying hard to win support for state suffrage amendments, tried to sidestep the issue of the federal amendment altogether. Yet, unlike Madeline McDowell Breckinridge and Pattie Ruffner Jacobs, who chose not to affiliate with the SSWSC, many other prominent Southern leaders tried to work with both the NAWSA and the Southern Conference.[55]

Mississippi's Nellie Nugent Somerville was one of these suffragists trying to work with—and retain the support of—both the SSWSC and the NAWSA. Kate Gordon assisted Mississippi suffragists in their first attempt to win a state constitutional amendment in 1914, even addressing the Mississippi House of Representatives at Somerville's "urgent request" when the suffragists received an unexpected opportunity to appear before the legislators. Mississippi suffragists participated in the 1914 national "May Day" celebrations sponsored by the NAWSA, but made state rather than federal action the focus of their demands. In April 1915, Dr. Anna Howard Shaw spoke in the Mississippi House of Representatives for suffrage, though Gordon was strongly opposed to Shaw's venture into the South, fearing that Shaw's oratorical magic would lead Southern suffragists to "lose their heads" and "come out pro federal amendment." Somerville and her associates kept theirs and issued a statement at their annual convention saying they did not "oppose other methods" but preferred "to obtain the ballot at the hands of Mississippi men."[56]

Valentine of Virginia had to deal with the SSWSC, the NAWSA, and the CU. She was active in the SSWSC but did not publicly oppose the federal amendment. Indeed, she neither renounced nor endorsed the federal amendment, but hoped to avoid the issue until all chances of winning enfranchisement at the state level were exhausted. Valentine was not only fearful of raising opposition among Virginia politicians but afraid an endorsement of the federal amendment would alienate potential supporters among the state's women as well. When the Congressional Union began organizing in Virginia in 1915, she was alarmed that their support of the federal route to suffrage would undermine the campaign for a woman suffrage amendment in Virginia and that the general population would not distinguish between the moderate and the "radical" suffagists. There would be constant tension through 1920 between Valentine and the Equal Suffrage League of Virginia and the Virginia suffragists who split off from the League to affiliate with the CU.[57]

Mary Johnston, believing that all suffrage agitation helped the cause, tried to cooperate with all three groups. She was never at ease with Gordon's overt racism, but, wishing as she did to promote suffrage all over the region, was "persuaded against her convictions" (in Gordon's words) to accept an honorary vice-presidency in the SSWSC. She attempted to promote harmony between the NAWSA and the CU and was once summoned to Boston by Alice Stone Blackwell for a "peace conference" between the two organizations. She tried to soothe Valentine's fears about the CU's raising of the federal amendment specter in Virginia: "I do feel that having weathered so much we may weather some insistence upon the Federal Amendment. It will alienate some, but it will not all. A certain number will take it for the cover behind which they will fight. But if they had not that they would find other cover. They are going to fight you anyhow. What I do hope is that the two associations may be able to preserve the courtesies and amenities toward each other." But Johnston, who by 1915 had withdrawn from active involvement in the suffrage movement, discounted her own advice, saying to Valentine, "I know it is easier to be philosophical over unidentical ways here on the hill top, than where you are in the heat of the battle."[58]

As 1916 and the Democratic National Convention approached, the battle over woman suffrage in the South was heated indeed, not only between suffragists and antis, but within the suffrage movement itself. Kate Gordon's strategy for winning the support of the Democrats called for Southern suffragists to present a united front for state suffrage and against the federal amendment, and to make it clear to all that theirs was truly an indigenous movement. She believed Southern suffragists must not publicly align themselves with organizations led by outsiders promoting the federal amendment. She became increasingly radical, increasingly hostile to the National, and ever more demanding of the loyalty of Southern suffragists.

Gordon was furious with Medill Hanna McCormick, the chair of the NAWSA's Congressional Committee, for trying to enlist Southern suffragists in support of the federal amendment. Indeed, she adopted McCormick (the daughter of the late Republican leader Mark Hanna of Ohio) as her personal enemy, charging that McCormick was more interested in promoting the Republican Party than in woman suffrage. Gordon urged Valentine to join her in "heading off McCormick" before the idea of Mark Hanna's daughter promoting suffrage in the South "would spike our guns for all time and eternity." When McCormick tried to organize Southern women for a demonstration supporting NAWSA goals at the Democratic convention, Gordon accused her of "stealing" her ideas, trying to duplicate her program, and generally ignoring the SSWSC's "priority of right" in the region.[59]

Gordon repeatedly warned Southern suffragists that the errors being made by the NAWSA and the Congressional Union were offending the Democratic Party and threatening the success of Southern suffragists. The *New Southern Citizen* cheered the February 1915 defeat of the "Anthony Amendment" in the House of Representatives, celebrating the fact that of the 174 opposed, 171 were Democrats. The CU's opposition-to-the-party-in-power strategy, she charged (quite accurately) was "a joke in our part of the country where only one party exists." As for the National, it was absurd to blacklist opponents of the federal amendment and to urge Southern suffragists to oppose them—to offend the very party from which Southern women must get the vote.[60]

Gordon's attacks on the NAWSA became increasingly vicious, inspired by her hatred of Shaw. The National, Gordon charged, had become "nothing else but an association to attack the Congressional Union and certainly senile debility and impotence are their only characteristics." That Gordon's feud with the NAWSA was motivated to a certain extent by personal rather than political differences was demonstrated by the fact that her hatred was reserved for Shaw and the National rather than Alice Paul and the CU, whose suffrage strategy was diametrically opposed to her own. Indeed, while NAWSA loyalists and even Clay reviled the militants, Gordon had a good deal of respect for Paul, with whom she had much in common, including a bold political strategy, incredible self-confidence, a common benefactress, and dislike for Anna Howard Shaw, whose administration had rejected them both. Paul, said Gordon to Clay, "will at least always give you a respectful hearing," and her organization had "nearly all the women worth while."[61]

Throughout 1915, Gordon ignored Clay's admonitions to proceed cautiously and avoid open battle with the NAWSA, which, said Clay, was in a weakened state, unable to reconcile factions, and "no threat" to the SSWSC. But instead, Gordon's charges became more extreme and her strategy more radical and unrealistic. On June 23, 1915, when the United States Supreme Court struck down the Grandfather Clause, Gordon sent her most incredible letter to the NAWSA Executive Board, claiming that if the Southern suffragists would only follow her lead, the South now had a better chance than ever to win woman suffrage as a solution to "the negro problem." Ironically, she blasted the National for wasting a precious opportunity, for "not being awake to the situation in the South in the 1890s and thus getting suffrage years earlier." She demanded that the NAWSA Board announce that in Southern territory they would now absolutely leave all policy matters to Southern suffragists, a statement Gordon claimed would "spike the guns of the antisuffragist organizations that [were] now bobbing their heads."[62]

Gordon then wrote to all members of the Southern Conference, claiming credit for the SSWSC for the Supreme Court's decision against the Grandfather Clause and outlining plans for capitalizing on this new situation. She announced that she had called a meeting of the governors of thirteen Southern states to be held immediately following the SSWSC convention in Richmond, a meeting at which Southern suffragists would discuss with the governors "the preservation of white supremacy." Gordon also called for a delegation from the SSWSC convention to testify before the governors that "our women will protest any subterfuge employed to protect white men which does not include white women." She enclosed a proposed resolution containing a pledge to boycott goods not made in suffrage states, and concluded, "I believe that if the Southern States' organizations and individuals make a united stand before the next Democratic Convention for a 'votes for women' plank, the Southern suffrage landslide will be a question of the near future."[63]

By the December 1915 SSWSC Convention in Richmond, Gordon's radical tactics and her attacks on the NAWSA and its officers had alienated most Southern suffragists, including many former supporters. As Nellie Nugent Somerville put it, "the fact is many southern women have come to consider Miss Gordon as too radical and have quietly declined to follow her any longer." It was at this point— November 1915—that Mary Johnston resigned, unable to bear further public association with Gordon and her racist pronouncements.[64]

Gordon also achieved the notoriety of being formally reprimanded by two state suffrage organizations. Led by Sue Shelton White and Pattie Ruffner Jacobs, respectively, the state suffrage associations of Tennessee and Alabama rebuked Kate Gordon and her presumptuous claim to speak for Southern suffragists. When Shaw informed Tennessee suffragists of Gordon's assault on McCormick, the state suffrage organization adopted the following resolution, offered by White, that the Convention of the Tennessee Equal Suffrage Association go on record as disapproving the action of Miss Kate M. Gordon in undertaking to dictate to the NAWSA or its Congressional Committee in regard to its policy, methods, or plans toward securing a suffrage plank from the Democratic party; and in her presuming to speak for the women of the South; and that the Recording Secretary of this convention be instructed to immediately notify the National officers and the Chairman of the Congressional Committee of such action.[65]

A similar resolution was adopted unanimously by the Executive Committee of the Alabama suffrage association:

> Whereas, the President of the Southern States Woman Suffrage Conference (of which organization the Alabama Equal Suffrage Association is not a member) has made repeated public utterances in derogation of the National Amendment, holding up Alabama's recent legislative experience as a warning to Southern Suffragists not to support it, assuming in so doing to speak for Alabama Suffragists; therefore be it Resolved by the Executive Committee of the Alabama Equal Suffrage Association that it hereby reasserts its allegiance to the National American Suffrage Association and protests against the attitude of the President of the Southern States Women Suffrage Conference in assuming to speak for Alabama Suffragists in her denunciation of national suffrage legislation.[66]

Perhaps the most dramatic evidence that Gordon had lost the fight for command of the Southern suffrage movement was the resignation from the SSWSC of Nellie Nugent Somerville, who had been one of Gordon's earliest and strongest supporters. A friend of the Gordon sisters for more than a decade, Somerville was forever grateful to them for their assistance in developing the suffrage movement in Mississippi. She had been involved in the decision to issue the call that led to the SSWSC, had served on the committee that devised the organization's constitution, and had backed Gordon on the issue of including the words "states' rights" in the Conference's title. She had served the SSWSC as auditor in 1913 and corresponding secretary in 1914. By the summer of 1915, however, Somerville had become increasingly alarmed at Gordon's behavior and indignant at Gordon's tendency to "confuse her own personal feeling . . . with the deliberate action of the Conference" despite Somerville's own protests and those of other Southern suffragists. In a letter marked "read and return" that she sent to "only a few prominent southern suffragists," Somerville seemed to be looking for allies in coping with a situation that had gotten out of hand.[67]

In particular, Somerville was outraged and embarrassed by Gordon's June 23, 1915, "Letter to the Members of the National Board" claiming the SSWSC had influenced the Supreme Court in its decision

on the Grandfather Clause and that the SSWSC would attack the constitutions of the South if the Democratic Party refused to go on record
in favor of votes for women. She found it "incomprehensible" that "at
this critical juncture of our suffrage history" Gordon would demand
that the NAWSA acknowledge that "'the line of least resistance will be
found in the states rights activity'" and withdraw from the South, giving Southern suffragists "over bodily to Miss Gordon's leadership
through the Southern Conference."[68]

Somerville was appalled to learn from the National's Congressional Committee that representatives of the SSWSC were lobbying
congressmen against the federal amendment. "My own idea of the
object of the Southern Conference was the promotion of suffrage
work in the South, and that no part of its work should be or was ever
intended to be in direct opposition to any national work being carried
on by the National Association."[69]

Finally, Somerville accused Gordon of blaming the National for
the South's failure to embrace woman suffrage, and thus excusing
herself and the South from responsibility:

> In my judgement, progress of the work in the southern states depends
> not upon any resolutions which the National Board could pass, nor upon
> any action of the Supreme Court of the United States, but upon the orga-
> nizing which suffragists in the different states are able to do for them-
> selves. Nothing is more common than to attribute to some outside
> influence weakness which is due solely to internal conditions. The policy
> of the different southern states should be to bring the suffrage question
> before their own people in their own way and to enlist as rapidly as pos-
> sible those who are in sympathy with this cause.[70]

After so many years of trying "to bring the suffrage question
before the people in their own way" in Mississippi without success,
Somerville then embraced the federal amendment as the only means
of gaining enfranchisement in her lifetime.

While both Kate Gordon and Laura Clay occasionally made the
rhetorical statement that if they could obtain the vote only through a
federal amendment, then they would embrace it willingly, they never
could bring themselves to do so. Somerville could. In December 1915,
after seventeen fruitless years of promoting woman suffrage in Mississippi, she accepted a position as a vice-president of the NAWSA and
began active promotion of the federal suffrage amendment.[71]

Gordon was furious. The NAWSA, she told Clay, was trying to
undermine the SSWSC in "an intriguing, insidious way," spreading
rumors of SSWSC disloyalty and of SSWSC members' working against
the federal amendment. "I am sorry to say," she concluded, that "Nellie Somerville is their agent."[72]

In the unenviable position of hosting the Richmond SSWSC convention, Valentine desperately sought to make peace within the organization. Johnston loyally attended, even giving a major address, but

her resignation stood. Of the most prominent Southern suffragists, only Valentine, Clay, and, of course, the Gordons remained within the Southern Conference. Valentine pleaded with Somerville to reconsider and to attend the convention and also tried to persuade Jacobs to support the SSWSC. She begged Gordon to "play the part of 'conciliator' to the disaffected and get them all to come. They need coaxing and a denial of the rumor of disloyalty." "If we allow the idea to get abroad that membership in the Southern Conference is disloyalty to the National, we might as well give up the idea of a Conference." We must preserve unity, said Valentine, allowing no Southern state to go unrepresented in the SSWSC. "Our only strength lies in solidarity in our appeal to the Democratic Party."[73]

But there was and would be no solidarity among suffragists in "the Solid South" on the issue of states' rights. And no amount of bullying by Kate Gordon would persuade the majority of Southern suffragists to adhere to her strategy. As relations between Gordon and the NAWSA deteriorated, Southern suffragists could no longer sit on the fence but had to choose between supporting Kate Gordon, the SSWSC, and states' rights, or supporting the NAWSA and the federal amendment. Most chose the latter.[74]

As Catt came into office, relations between the Southern Conference and the National improved temporarily. At that point, Gordon had as much respect for Catt's political judgement as she had contempt for Shaw's. Gordon and Catt had worked together during the initial period of Southern suffrage activity in the late 1890s and early 1900s, in which Catt had been quite willing to use Gordon's favorite tactic, the promotion of woman suffrage as a solution to "the negro problem." Both were interested in renewing their old friendship: Gordon longed to be restored to her influential position among national leaders and to be recognized as the leader of the Southern suffragists; and Catt did not seem to realize that Gordon was no longer the power in the South she had once been. A mutual courtship began at the 1915 NAWSA Convention, at which Catt was elected. Gordon, reported Somerville, "made every effort to take up her old friendly relations with Mrs. Catt; had Mrs. Catt take meals with her, impressed Mrs. Catt with the idea that the Southern Conference leads and controls the entire South." The two women appeared to be on such good terms that Somerville feared Catt was going to "turn us [Southern suffragists] over bodily to Miss Gordon." Indeed, Somerville feared that, having openly opposed Kate Gordon while members of the NAWSA board, "neither Mrs. Jacobs or myself has any influence with Mrs. Catt." In one of her earliest letters to Southern state presidents, Catt praised Gordon; said she was well aware of "the difference in the position of the Southern states and those of the Northern states owing to the State Rights Doctrine"; praised the SSWSC as "based on an excellent idea"; and said, "I do not want to do anything offensive to the South nor anything which will alienate our workers in that section of the country who I am sure have troubles enough as it is."[75]

Nevertheless, the amicable relations between the two suffrage leaders quickly evaporated as Gordon and Catt clashed over plans for the Democratic Convention and openly competed for the allegiance of Southern suffragists. Catt had hoped to persuade her old friend to be less antagonistic to the NAWSA and to the federal amendment. Specifically, she hoped to persuade Gordon not to carry out her plan to seek a state-action-only suffrage plank from the Democratic National Convention of 1916. As the state suffrage plank had been the desideratum of the SSWSC from its inception and the key feature of Gordon's strategy, however, Gordon was not about to back down. While Catt told Gordon she believed that "the Democratic Party going on record for a states' rights form of suffrage is another form of opposition," Gordon insisted such a plank would be "the cornerstone of practical suffrage work in the South . . . and the only form of suffrage we can reasonably expect the Democratic Party to endorse."[76]

In a battle of letters, Gordon and Catt competed for the support of Southern suffrage leaders. To officers of the SSWSC, Gordon declared her intent to proceed with this plan despite Catt's opposition. (The intention to demand the state suffrage plank had been reaffirmed by the majority at the Richmond SSWSC convention.) A week later, Catt wrote directly to the presidents of Southern state suffrage organizations, asking them to support instead a plank endorsing the principle of suffrage without specifying the method, saying, "division of our appeal at St. Louis will lessen our strength and jeopardize our success." A letter from Gordon to the same group soon followed, denying Catt's charges and saying, this is not an academic issue, we should ask for what we can get. "It certainly cannot be politically unwise to make it difficult for the party to refuse us by asking for an endorsement of woman suffrage along the lines of the party's traditions and prejudices." Gordon insisted that, whatever Catt's opinion, the Southern Conference was doing a great service to the cause. Sending Catt a copy of this letter to the Southern presidents, Gordon expressed regret that Catt had stressed divisiveness. To suggest her own magnanimity, Gordon reported that Louisiana suffragists, as part of the NAWSA, would endorse the request for a Democratic endorsement of suffrage as an abstract principle. "But I think it highly important," she wrote, "that the Democratic Party be made to realize that the distinctly southern women are going to make their demand along the line of party fealty. I therefore regret your stand. We could have made the two appeals without any endangering of feeling."[77]

As their relationship deteriorated, Catt confronted Gordon with rumors that had come to Catt from "three women in three different states," charging Gordon with being "in conspiracy with the CU to smash the National" by the states' rights plank. In reply Gordon wrote, "I give you credit for integrity of purpose, and I demand for myself a like recognition." And Gordon resolved to "never voluntarily initiate any [further] correspondence" with Catt, a vow she upheld for over two years.[78]

When the Democratic Convention adopted the plank endorsing the "extension of the franchise to the women of the country, State by State, on the same terms as to the men," Gordon was ecstatic, congratulating herself and the SSWSC on the achievement of their goal. But despite its great "victory," the Southern Conference was in disarray. In St. Louis, most Southern presidents had cooperated with Catt and the National. Belmont's funds were virtually gone, and few new contributions came in. The SSWSC was quietly dying.[79]

Gordon tried hard to keep the Southern Conference alive, that it might "compel" the Democratic Party to make good its promise. To SSWSC officers, she outlined her plans: to urge Western Democrats to demand that Southern Democrats "fall en bloc for woman suffrage"; to secure President Wilson's aid in getting Southern states to call constitutional conventions and enfranchise women by state action. She also wrote to all Southern governors summoning them to yet another conference, this time to plan regional bloc action to enfranchise Southern women, live up to the Democratic platform, and avoid a federal amendment.[80]

Bitter over the lack of support, Gordon wrote to SSWSC loyalists: "our press service is beyond compare, the best of its kind in the United States. If we had money enough to do for southern suffragists what the southern presidents hope National will do for them, there is no doubt we could make the Southern Conference a tower of strength, for I realize that if our women have any political sense whatever, they cannot run in the face of party traditions."[81]

Though Clay agreed with her friend that the Southern Conference was "of more importance now than ever it has been before," few others concurred The financial difficulties that had first become acute in August 1916 worsened steadily. By April 1917, the SSWSC was forced to close its headquarters, let Ida Boyer go, and cease publication of its press bulletins and the *New Woman Citizen*. By January of 1918, the SSWSC existed in name only, with Gordon and Clay making all decisions and pretending that the SSWSC was still a viable organization.[82]

III

While Kate Gordon celebrated the Democratic endorsement of woman suffrage by state action, Catt moved quickly to commit the National to an overarching national strategy to win congressional approval of the federal amendment. As the NAWSA worked toward that goal, most Southern suffrage leaders gave Catt their full support, though disappointed at the minor role the South was assigned in Catt's "Winning Plan." Gordon and Clay were appalled to see Catt take such firm control of the NAWSA and focus its efforts even more directly on the federal amendment. They continued to press for state instead of federal resolution of the suffrage question, even as the federal amendment gained momentum. Meanwhile, Catt learned that her lack of support for suffrage campaigns in the South could drive even pro-amendment Southern suffragists into the arms of a rival suffrage organization.

Kate Gordon considered the adoption of the plank endorsing woman suffrage "state by state" a great victory and assurance that the solidly Democratic South as "an organic body" would now lead the nation for woman suffrage. But Carrie Chapman Catt feared that the Democrats' decision would strengthen the resolve of states' rights advocates—including President Wilson—and make it far more difficult for her to lead the NAWSA to the end of its sixty-six-year quest. Gordon recalled that Catt, "bumping into" Gordon in the corridor immediately after the platform committee's decision, was furious with Gordon for her role in this setback and called the Democratic plank an "insult to womanhood." Inasmuch as the Republican Convention had also endorsed the enfranchisement of women through state action without Catt's taking offense, Gordon interpreted Catt's reaction as yet another indication of NAWSA partisanship. The truth was that Catt had fought hard to secure from each party endorsements of suffrage without mention of method, but preferred the planks endorsing state suffrage to no endorsement at all. Gordon believed the support of both parties for woman suffrage by state action ought to make clear the proper direction for future suffrage agitation.[83]

In light of these developments, Catt immediately called for an emergency convention at Atlantic City to determine the NAWSA's future course. She set Clay and Gordon up as key figures in a "Three-cornered Debate," which was supposed to help NAWSA members decide between dropping the federal amendment and working for state action only; dropping state work and seeking a federal amendment only; or continuing to promote suffrage by both methods.[84]

With Gordon as her second, Clay argued the first position, insisting that the proposed amendment was not a short cut to victory; that the national experience with the Civil War amendments (which gave women "nearly a million new political masters in the persons of the emancipated negro men") was far from conclusive proof of the wisdom of taking decisions about enfranchisement away from the states; and that all over the world the principle of limitation of centralized power, whether "state sovereignty" in the United States or "home rule" in the British Empire, was growing stronger. She also claimed that the "Anthony Amendment" was but "a repetition of the Fifteenth Amendment" and that the Southern states "will hardly subscribe voluntarily to a principle they rejected formerly." Furthermore, advocacy of the "Anthony Amendment," she concluded, must involve the NAWSA in the partisan politics they had vowed to avoid, since Democrats were insistent upon protecting state sovereignty. And she offered once again her U.S. Elections Bill, saying she favored working only for legislation (such as state amendments or the U.S. Elections Bill) that did not require the states to surrender any portion of the rights reserved to them by the Constitution.[85]

By the end of the emergency convention, the National had officially committed itself to continuing both state and federal work. Clay and Gordon regarded this decision as a victory, believing that Catt and her lieutenants had determined before the convention to commit the NAWSA exclusively to the federal amendment. Clay was also pleased when Catt, as a gesture to the suffrage pioneer, had the convention endorse Clay's U.S. Elections Bill, which Catt privately regarded as "an utterly impossible measure."[86]

Clay and Gordon soon discovered, however, that all was proceeding exactly in accordance with Catt's plans: Catt intended to continue state work only selectively, subordinating it to the overall goal of winning a national victory. She was convinced that a federal amendment was within reach, that the states' rights position was losing ground. Even President Wilson, the hero of the states' rights suffragists, hinted in his speech to the Atlantic City convention that he might support a federal amendment. Suffrage was coming, he said, and "we won't quarrel about the method."[87]

Two aspects of Catt's "Winning Plan," which she outlined in a closed meeting of the executive council following the convention, were of crucial significance for the suffrage movement in the South. First, campaigns for state suffrage amendments were to be undertaken only where the NAWSA believed victories were extremely likely. Secondly, the loose "states' rights" relationship between the National and its affiliates adopted officially in 1903 was discarded. There would now be a national policy in which state associations were expected to subordinate their own goals to winning a nationwide victory through the federal amendment.[88]

The Southern states would play only a minor role in Catt's grand strategy for winning congressional approval of the amendment, a strategy that called for piling up state victories until the cumulative effect would be irresistible. The National's attention was focused on key states like New York (in which Catt had headed the state suffrage campaign since 1912) and more or less conceded the South for the present. Catt did not expect any victories for state suffrage amendments in the South, and she wanted no defeats. Southern suffragists were instructed not to to launch campaigns for state amendments without NAWSA approval, but to seek only partial enfranchisement—primary or presidential suffrage—which state legislators could grant without holding referenda. Accordingly, suffragists in Arkansas (1917) and Texas (1918) secured the enactment of primary suffrage—the first breakthroughs for the cause in the South—and Tennessee suffragists won presidential suffrage in 1919. Southern suffragists were also encouraged to hold "Congressional Conferences" to learn how to lobby Congress more effectively.[89]

NAWSA loyalists in the South welcomed Catt's bold leadership as a breath of fresh air after Shaw's vacillation and supported Catt's policies. After Catt presided over a Congressional Conference in Kentucky (where Breckinridge spoke on state work as "incidental to congressional success"), Breckinridge wrote, "Mrs. Catt is splendid. I wish that we could have her for National President always." Mary Johnston, discussing the new state of affairs with Valentine, thought Catt was "wise in thinking it would be a tactical mistake to bring a state bill this year [1916]. It seems to me that the federal amendment is coming, and coming before very long." Thus suffragists should "work for a favorable state of the public mind toward the whole objective" rather than engage in "a bitter local fight."[90]

Having tried and failed to win suffrage by state action, Jacobs, Valentine, Somerville, Kearney, Felton, and their followers now had nothing to lose by lobbying for congressional action on the federal amendment. At the close of its unsuccessful campaign in 1915, the Alabama Equal Suffrage Association had announced its intention to work for the passage and adoption of the federal amendment. Pattie Ruffner Jacobs served from 1916 through 1918 as second auditor of the NAWSA and as a member of its Congressional Committee testified before Congress that the federal amendment did not involve states' rights or the race issue. Lila Meade Valentine, having watched for six years as the Virginia legislature gave a state suffrage amendment a "cursory hearing followed by a dismissal," also came out in support of the Anthony Amendment. In January 1918, Virginia suffragists asked the legislature to urge the state's senators to support the federal amendment, pointing out that the Democrats must not let the Republicans "outdo" them in the Senate as they had in the House and get credit for enfranchising the women of the country.[91]

Nellie Nugent Somerville and Belle Kearney likewise supported the new NAWSA policy and the federal amendment. At its April 1917 state convention, the Mississippi Woman Suffrage Association adopted a resolution asking Congress to submit the federal amendment to the states. They did not launch further state suffrage campaigns. But, when a state bill was introduced in 1918 without being initiated by the MWSA—possibly by opponents who wished to raise the issue and vote it down—Somerville and Kearney gave the bill all the support they could.[92]

The NAWSA loyalists tried to combat the states' rights argument against the federal amendment by insisting it was not a threat to the South, that it did not undermine state sovereignty and the interrelated institution of white supremacy or the Democratic Party. Said Somerville, optimistically, "We all believe in [the federal amendment] and we are gradually convincing thoughtful men and women in the South that it holds no menace for the institutions of any State or any group of States."[93]

Breckinridge and Valentine stressed that Southern heroes including Jefferson and Madison had favored the amendment process as a way of keeping the government in touch with the times, and that Madison was the father of Article V of the Constitution, which provided for amendment. Furthermore, Breckinridge insisted, the amendment process actually protected the rights of the states. "In fact," she said, "the method of amendment is a distinct acknowledgment of the principle of States' Rights, since the amendment is referred for ratification to the representatives of the states, the legislatures." A federal amendment could only be construed as a denial of states' rights when the consent of the states was the result of coercion: this, she said, was as the difference between the proposed federal suffrage amendment and the Fourteenth and Fifteenth Amendments. The "so-called 'crime of the Fourteenth Amendment,'" she said, "consisted in forcing ratification by blood and iron through the carpetbag legislatures of unwilling southern states." Indeed, "the real violation of the States Rights principle," she argued, would be "not to allow the states to pass upon" the amendment.[94]

The suffragists accused their opponents of hiding behind the states' rights idea to conceal their opposition to woman suffrage by any method. In her President's Address of 1917, Valentine said: "To those who may yet cling to the old tradition of State Rights and who object to a Federal Amendment in dealing with this fundamental right of self government, I would say that this objection, reduced to its final analysis, usually means an objection to giving the vote to Southern women by any means, state or federal." That this is the case, Valentine continued, "is abundantly proved by the fact that objectors cheerfully submitted to Federal control of child labor, interstate commerce, the liquor traffic, food and fuel, but balk at the prospects of dealing federally with the question of woman." Valentine also accused opponents of "conjuring up the negro bogey," of denying white women the vote because of their fear of the votes of black women, a fear she insisted was ridiculous in the extreme. And she endeavored to demonstrate that the laws of the state could prevent a black majority in any county.[95]

The National's supporters rejected Gordon's and Clay's theory concerning NAWSA partisanship in supporting the federal amendment. The loyalists believed the amendment's success would only be a threat to the South if the Democratic Party drove women into the arms of the Republicans through its own intransigence, by refusing to grant suffrage in the Southern states and then opposing the federal amendment. Sue Shelton White, speaking for the Tennessee Equal Suffrage Association, warned that even "Southern suffragists with a predeliction toward the Democratic Party" were growing impatient and would "plant themselves uncompromisingly upon the Federal Suffrage Amendment . . .": "Moss-backed traditions of political parties will no longer be accepted as an excuse for withholding democracy from women. There are suffragists born Democrats who have hoped to live and die in the political faith of their fathers who can no longer accept such an excuse. The Mountain will cast off its moss and come to Mohammed, and America will be made safe for democracy— and perhaps for a more democratic Democracy."[96]

Though the National's Southern supporters dutifully lobbied for the federal amendment, and were pleased that the NAWSA was now in such capable hands, they regretted Catt's refusal to sanction full-suffrage campaigns in Southern states. Southern leaders who retained hopes of victory—or at least winning many converts through campaigns for suffrage amendments in their states—were extremely unhappy when their own states were classified by the National among the "unwinnable." They complied with the new NAWSA policy only with regret and a strong sense of sacrifice. At the May 1918 convention in Alabama, Jacobs sadly reported that Alabama had been "unfairly classed" as a "Hopeless State" by the National and that it could count on no assistance. And Breckinridge's loyalty was sorely tested in 1918 when Catt deemed Kentucky one of the states in which a state effort would be fruitless (because Kentucky was a "whiskey state"), even though such intelligent and experienced leaders as Breckinridge and Clay were convinced they could win. As the KERA complied with the NAWSA's request to cancel their campaign, Breckinridge wrote to KERA president Christine Bradley South, "It seems too bad for I think we probably have the only chance to win that we have had in my life time, or that we will have again. . . ." Breckinridge "believed in a national policy," but feared that "the Federal route" was not going to be so quick as some suffragists thought. And as more states would be needed before a federal amendment could be approved, "one or two southern ones would help." "The National will never know what they ask us to give up."[97]

Clay and the Gordon sisters, of course, opposed Catt's "Winning Plan." Still convinced that a federal amendment could not be won, they considered Catt's plan "idiotic" and unconstitutional, a violation of the states' rights agreement under which Southern suffragists had entered the organization as well as of the NAWSA constitution, which called for both state and federal action. Kate Gordon called on Clay to join her in defying the new policy: "Not to allow a state to vote on its own initiative to enfranchise its women is a form of kaiserism I hope you will not be a party to." Clay agreed. The NAWSA board's attempts to discourage some state campaigns, she believed, were contrary to the decisions made at Atlantic City, and unwise. Even unsuccessful state campaigns would help the cause. Most important, state workers must be the judge of their own conditions.[98]

Characteristically, Clay tried to stay on good terms with Catt and the National and to convince them of the error of their ways, while Gordon denounced Catt, Dennett, and all of the top NAWSA leaders as, first and foremost, Republicans who were eager to prevent state suffrage campaigns in the Southern—and Democratic—states, and who wanted the federal amendment as a chance to "reopen the negro question." "The reason Mrs. Catt is afraid of submission [of proposals for Southern state amendments] is that she fears if the South does give woman suffrage there will be no earthly chance to put over a Federal Amendment on us and incidentally pin the standard for woman suffrage to the Republican banner. Certainly if the South which she is always insulting on the score of suffrage gives the suffrage to its women what right will there be for the North and the West to reopen the negro question."[99]

President Wilson's endorsement of the federal amendment on the eve of its first victory in the House of Representatives stunned Clay and Gordon and "threw their forces all into confusion." For a few months Clay abandoned her opposition to the amendment. Writing to her sister Sally, Clay observed, "Of course this has changed my attitude towards [the amendment], for it is futile for me to hold out opposition on account of states' rights when a great statesman and leader of the Democratic Party contends that it is not an infringement of states' rights. I shall not oppose the Federal Amendment any longer." On January 16, she announced her change of mind to Carrie Chapman Catt:

> I have changed my attitude to the S.B. Anthony Amend. since Pres. Wilson has expressed a view of it which I never expected from him. I am indeed strongly attached to the states' rights doctrine but I think an individual's support of an aspect of a governmental doctrine is of no service when it is not supported by dominant political opinion. Therefore, when a great statesman, as Pres. Wilson is conceded to be, and one weighted with responsibility in the world-war, declares that he thinks the Amendment does not impair states' rights and that it is expedient in the exigencies of this war, I am unwilling to jeopardize any chance for my enfranchisement by opposition to it.[100]

Equally astounded by Wilson's endorsement of the federal amendment, Gordon called it "the surprise of my life." Immediately she wrote to Clay, asking her friend to come and spend the rest of the winter with her and Jean and "reconnoiter" in the wake of this astonishing development. Clay was unable to accept, but the pair debated the significance of Wilson's action in a flurry of letters between Lexington and New Orleans.[101]

As might be expected, Gordon did not question her own position but concluded that the great champion of state sovereignty had endorsed the amendment only to placate the National Woman's Party, which "got on his nerves" and embarrassed him as he was "trying to make the world safe for democracy." Though distressed that her hero would collapse under the pressure of the NWP (she gave no credit at all to the NAWSA), Gordon finally concluded that Wilson still opposed the amendment and secretly "had the Senate fixed so that it will not be submitted." Under the influence of her friend and a bit of wishful thinking, Clay also began to doubt that Wilson was truly behind the amendment.[102]

The Senate's delay in acting on the amendment renewed the hopes of Clay and Gordon that woman suffrage might yet be won without sacrificing states' rights. "Every day that I think of [the federal amendment] seems to increase my antipathy to it," Clay wrote to Gordon. "I believe in States' Rights: and in these war times, when so much extraordinary power is being given to the Administration, it may well turn out that undiminished states' rights may be the anchor of our government. I shall not give up hope that another way than the Federal Amendment may be found until it is taken from me by the accomplishment of that amendment, both in Congress and by the ratification of 36 state legislatures." Gordon remained convinced that congressional approval of the amendment would be a devastating blow to the suffrage movement, as it would "rouse the sleeping dogs of negro suffrage," unleash on woman suffrage in the South "an almost insurmountable opposition," and "the Antis will certainly have things their way."[103]

The hopes of Gordon and Clay soared to new heights in April 1918, when Louisiana's Governor Pleasant personally called for the adoption of a state suffrage amendment and asked Gordon to frame a memorial to the state legislature recommending the Southern states preclude the federal amendment by taking similar action. "This means," wrote Clay, that "the Democratic party is really going to bid for women's votes by carrying out the promises of their St. Louis platform." Firmly convinced that it was now more important than ever for the "states' rights women" to show support for alternatives to the federal amendment, Clay publicly declared her irrevocable opposition to the federal amendment and vowed "to keep up [her] open opposition hereafter."[104]

During the summer, Clay and Gordon were discouraged, as their hero Wilson seemed to be more vigorous in support of the federal amendment than befitted an opponent. Gordon was disgusted with the way Wilson "kept injecting himself" into congressional elections in the states, especially in Louisiana. On September 26, 1918, four days before Wilson's address to the Senate asking for the federal woman suffrage amendment as a war measure, Gordon wrote to Clay: "It may be treason on my part, but I tell you, Miss Clay, I have lost a great deal of respect for Mr. Wilson, for the way that he has played politics with so vital an American principle as the sovereignty of the States. Had he come out and made an appeal in the right way, the States would have passed woman suffrage long ago. The same energy that he has used in getting into the States, exercised upon a direct appeal for woman suffrage to vindicate National honor by action of the States, in conformity with the planks of both dominant parties, would have yielded results worthy of his statesmanship."[105]

But the two were jubilant when, despite Wilson's personal appeal to the Senate, the Democratic South nevertheless blocked the amendment. The two champions of states' rights now were full of hope for a series of victorious state campaigns, beginning with Louisiana. "If several of the states win out on the state suffrage amendments," Clay wrote Gordon on the eve of the Louisiana campaign, "possibly the women all over the country will get tired of waiting on the Fed Amend. any longer, and there may be a rich harvest of state amendments under the pressure Pres. Wilson may put on, if he is in earnest about the need of woman suffrage." Clay also asked Gordon's opinion about resurrecting the "Laura Clay Amendment as it was now being called," as another alternative to the Anthony Amendment.[106]

Though Gordon's rivals, the NAWSA loyalists in New Orleans, tried to prevent the submission of the state suffrage amendment, Gordon now had the backing of the governor and would not be deterred. Breaking her vow not to communicate with Catt, Gordon warned Catt and the National in the strongest terms to stay out of her way: "If you come you will be the ally of the liquor interests," who were using their full measure of influence against the suffrage amendment. In a letter to Clay, Gordon swore that if Catt came to New Orleans, she would personally publicize the fact that Catt said at a NAWSA convention in 1912 that, "in the event of the South interfering with the ratification of the Federal Amendment, that the North before had trained its guns on the South and would do it again." Catt replied sarcastically that she would "use my utmost influence to see that no assistance of any kind or description is given to Louisiana," and warned Gordon a defeat was being set up by suffrage opponents, who would "see to it that your state amendment is voted down good and hard."[107]

Absolutely confident of victory, however, Gordon predicted

Louisiana's adoption of a state suffrage amendment would demonstrate the error of NAWSA policy and vindicate her strategy. She and her sister Jean made their theme loyalty to the Democratic Party and resistance to federal intervention in the state's right to regulate the franchise. A "Call" for support issued by the Louisiana State Suffrage Association, with Jean Gordon as president, stated, "The ratification of the State Amendment to enable women to vote in Louisiana will vindicate the spirit and sacrifices of the men who in the dark days of Reconstruction fought and died to maintain white supremacy. A vote against the State Amendment November 5 discredits these patriots. Justifies and Vitalizes the 15th Amendment." They also appealed for loyalty to the 1916 Democratic platform and insisted that the principle of state sovereignty was in jeopardy. "We urge on our people a realization of the issue at stake. State Sovereignty the basic principle upon which our government was ratified will be destroyed in the event of a National Woman Suffrage Amendment being submitted and ratified and Centralization in government substituted. The autocratic ideal of Hamilton supplant the democratic ideal of Jefferson."[108]

The two rival suffrage organizations in Louisiana buried the hatchet temporarily and worked together for the amendment— though Kate Gordon complained of her new associates' drinking cocktails, smoking cigarettes, and hobnobbing with "the liquor interests." Working together, the Louisiana suffragists secured the endorsement of both of the state's senators, all of the congressmen except one, and the backing of the state's Democratic National Committeeman "and his two newspapers." Governor Pleasant gave his full support, though he prudently declined Gordon's suggestion that he call a conference of governors to plan how they could follow the example of Louisiana, suggesting it would be better to wait until a victory was in hand. Writing to Clay and Boyer, Gordon told them to get ready to "take off your hats to me for Louisiana will submit the suffrage bill and the administration is behind it. I believe now if I got down on my knees to them and implored them not to give us suffrage they would administer it with the big stick."[109]

So confident was she of victory, Gordon declared that if the referendum failed, she would withdraw entirely from the suffrage movement and drop her opposition to the federal amendment: "The Federal Amendment people will be vindicated." But, when defeat came, the Gordon sisters did not withdraw. Blaming the failure on the torrential rains and flu epidemic that plagued the campaigners, and above all on the evil influence of New Orleans' Mayor Behrman, they pledged to continue their opposition to the federal amendment.[110]

Jean Gordon wrote immediately to her co-workers, saying that she could not support the federal amendment, and pledging to continue working for suffrage through state action. The rights of the federal government to supervise our state elections, she said, were "so fraught with danger to the future of our government that I refuse to have it on my conscience." More tolerant of disagreement than Kate, she urged the suffragists who wished to support the federal amendment not to be halfway people, but to join the other group of Louisiana suffragists. But the Gordons made it clear that the Louisiana State Suffrage Association and the Era Club would be making a very positive stand on the states' rights principle.[111]

Indeed, Kate informed Clay that the Louisiana State Suffrage Association was seriously thinking of withdrawing from the National, which "is really no longer in sympathy with state work and its whole aim and purpose is to force a Federal Amendment, and as such I do not think that we should be a party to it any longer." And at this point Kate Gordon began to consider new ways to deal with the threat of the federal amendment, including working with her allies in Congress to remove the enforcement provision in the amendment.[112]

NAWSA officials were understandably vexed with Gordon. Earlier in the year they had asked for Gordon's resignation, pointing out that Gordon's "auxiliary was the only one of our affiliated members, in fact the only suffrage organization in the country, which was working at cross purposes with the National Association in its effort to push the Federal Amendment." Now Ida Husted Harper urged the defeated Gordon to accept the inevitable and support the Anthony Amendment; or, if she could not support it, at least to stop impeding the NAWSA's efforts. Harper insisted that the federal amendment's success would not mean the reinstatement of Negro suffrage. Harper seemed to think if Gordon would drop her opposition, the National could get one of Louisiana's senators (Edward J. Gay) to change his vote, one of the two votes yet needed for congressional approval of the federal amendment.[113]

Harper's letter seemed merely to fuel Gordon's resistance. "The trouble with you northern suffragists," she replied,

> is your inability to see that the principle of self government for the state is as great as self government for the individual. . . . As I reread your letter on the negro woman and the question propounded, I realize how far apart we are in the understanding of the question. It is not the negro woman nor the negro man especially but the realizing of the frauds of the 14th and 15th Amendments, and which if applied will mean for the south to accept the ideals of an inferior race or continue to perpetuate upon our people the tyranny of a one party power as a matter of self defense.

She would not change "Eddie Gay's vote" if she could, said Gordon. And, ironically, considering her own career of using threats to persuade politicians to change their votes, Gordon expressed outrage that the Northern suffragists refused to "honor men carrying out the mandates of their constituencies."[114]

There were still other Southern suffragists who were unhappy with the National and its policies but not at all interested in following Gordon's lead. At the other end of the ideological spectrum in regard to the federal amendment, Sue Shelton White and others who affiliated with the National Woman's Party (formerly the CU) also objected to Catt's "Winning Plan." Distressed that the NAWSA was discouraging suffrage campaigns in the South, Sue White embraced the NWP largely because it began a bold new effort to recruit in the South in 1917, just as the NAWSA seemed to be conceding the region to the antis.

The CU had tried with limited success to organize in the South in 1915. Southern suffragists regarded with fear and hostility a suffrage organization that opposed the Democratic Party, criticized the South's favorite son Woodrow Wilson, and belittled the concept of states' rights. Thus NAWSA loyalists did everything possible to distance themselves from the more militant suffragists. Said one discouraged organizer assigned to South Carolina, "I'm sorrier than ever that the South didn't seced [*sic*] successfully." Recognizing the grip that Southerners held on powerful congressional committees, however, the CU, now renamed the National Woman's Party, renewed its efforts to organize the South, and in 1917 dispatched twelve representatives on speaking tours throughout the region.[115]

With the picketing of the White House (begun in January 1917) added to their list of offenses, the NWP was even less welcome in the South. Their organizers were denounced as "pro-German, disloyal, and un-American." Initially, Sue White became involved with the NWP out of outrage at the treatment fellow suffragists of any variety were receiving as they attempted to speak publicly for the cause. White came to the rescue of NWP orator Maude Younger, helping her find halls in which to speak when local bar associations, civic officials, and the so-called Home Defense Leagues tried to prevent Younger from speaking in towns and cities throughout Tennessee. Greatly impressed with White's influence, dedication, and courage, the NWP tried to recruit her, while NAWSA loyalists, appalled that White would associate with these "radicals," reacted so negatively that they practically forced her "into the bosom of the National Woman's Party."[116]

No doubt White, who had contributed her stenographic skills to the suffrage cause since 1912 in the unglamorous position of recording secretary, was flattered by the attentions of the NWP, which quickly moved White into positions of influence—first as chair of the National Woman's Party in Tennessee (June 1918) and later as editor of its national paper *The Suffragist* (1919). She must have been astounded when the issue of her loyalty attracted even the attention of President Catt, who wrote to White criticizing the NWP as "untrust-worthy and extremely disloyal to the old association which made conditions possible for their work." But, as White explained to Catt, her initial sympathy for the NWP organizers turned into serious interest in the organization only "after it developed that the southern states could not expect any assistance from the National." Catt urged the younger woman to try to "take a big view" of the suffrage situation and understand that if the NAWSA could carry the four "fighting states," "ratification in Tennessee will be far more possible than it can be made by a few meetings at this time" in Tennessee. And Catt told White she could not belong to both groups but must "take your stand fair and square, one side or the other." White would always try to cooperate with both organizations, but she "took her stand" with the NWP.[117]

Catt may well have been correct in her assumption that the defeat of state suffrage campaigns in the South would have strengthened the opposition in Congress and made it even more difficult to secure congressional approval of the measure. But it is possible that there would have been some victories: in her history of the Kentucky suffrage movement written for *The History of Woman Suffrage*, Breckinridge said that the 1918 legislature "undoubtedly would have passed the state's rights amendment . . . or would have ratified had the U.S. Senate acted in time. The leaders of both parties in Kentucky were by this time entirely educated on the woman suffrage question." And full suffrage victories may have been possible in the Southern states that secured partial suffrage and later ratified the Nineteenth Amendment. Catt never seemed to understand the degree to which Southern suffragists wanted their states to *contribute* to the suffrage victory rather than simply to be vanquished. Southern suffragists wanted to persuade the men of their states to enfranchise them and thereby formally recognize female equality, individuality, and desirability as voters—a situation they considered infinitely preferable to being enfranchised through federal coercion. Should state suffrage amendment campaigns have failed, many voters would have been converted nonetheless. Breckinridge, Jacobs, White, and others were very disappointed to be denied the advice and consent—and financial resources—of the national organization. They supported the NAWSA, but they wanted the NAWSA's support in return.[118]

6

━━━◁◦▣◦▷━━━

Bitter Fruit: An Incomplete Victory, Courtesy of Uncle Sam

It is an awful thing to feel that a life's work had borne such dead sea fruit.

—Kate Gordon to Alice Stone Blackwell
July 18, 1920[1]

It only remains for the outward and visible sign of our freedom to be put in the hands of Southern women by the generous men of other states, a situation which hurts our pride and to which we submit with deep regret but not apology.

—Pattie Ruffner Jacobs
Speech to 1920 NAWSA "Jubilee"
Convention[2]

When, on June 4, 1919, the Congress of the United States finally submitted the proposed Nineteenth Amendment to the states for ratification, the leaders of the Southern suffrage movement remained divided in their attitudes toward the amendment. At odds about both goals and strategy, Southern suffragists found themselves fighting each other as well as the antis, a situation that did nothing to help their cause. Only in Kentucky, Texas, Arkansas, and Tennessee did suffragists have the satisfaction of seeing their states ratify the amendment—though when Tennessee ratified on August 13, 1920, all Southern supporters of the amendment were heartened "that a Southern State had redeemed the honor of the country," and made partial recompense for the South's dismal record in the suffrage struggle. For most Southern suffragists, whether for or against the federal amendment, the ratification period was a time of disappointment and frustration.[3]

As the end of the long struggle for woman suffrage approached, those who opposed the Nineteenth Amendment were bitter, disappointed in their fellow suffragists, and dismayed that the success of the reform to which they had devoted so many years helped undermine another cherished political ideal—state sovereignty. Most Southern suffragists, however, were jubilant at the ratification, though their celebration was dampened by the fact that so many of them had to be enfranchised by courtesy of Uncle Sam. In the states that refused to ratify, suffragists ruefully acknowledged their failure to win recognition of the political equality of women *at home.* Their experience in the ratification fight further alienated them from the concept of state sovereignty, which Southern politicians were upholding so selectively. Indignant that their bid for recognition as "fit" voters had been rebuffed, they accused the politicians of wanting to withhold from women what the women most desired, the power to promote "justice" in their states and region. Most Southern suffragists were convinced that in its attitude toward women's rights as well as toward states' rights, the South must divest itself of "moss-backed traditions" and look to the future instead of the past.[4]

I

By 1919, most Southern suffragists supported the federal amendment, and they celebrated its victory in Congress, thrilled that the amendment had reached this significant milepost. Eighty-four-year-old Rebecca Latimer Felton traveled all the way to Washington to witness congressional approval of the amendment. Afterwards, she told waiting reporters that a national law was better than a state suffrage amendment after all, as it had more "stickability."[5]

Suffragists had little time to celebrate, however, before the strength of the opposition to ratification in the South was made manifest. Returning to Georgia, Felton was irritated to find Georgia legislators scrambling to beat out Alabama as the first state to pass a "rejection resolution." In vain, Georgia suffragists urged legislators to take no action, rather than reject the amendment. Felton reminded Georgia's political leaders they were acting against the wishes of their beloved Woodrow Wilson and warned them that the women of Georgia would soon be voting and that they had long memories: "Although it is embarrassing to apologize for the ignorance or stupidity of Georgia legislators, the right to vote cannot be long witheld from the women of Georgia. The manifest preference of certain Georgia legislators for giving the franchise to Negro men over intelligent white women will become an incentive in years to come to vote against such misfits whenever they offer for political promotion."[6]

Aware they must win at least a few Southern states to secure ratification, the National sent three organizers to help Alabama suffragists combat the powerful Alabama antisuffrage lobby. Sue White and several delegates from the NWP also went to Alabama where they worked for three months as the legislators prepared to vote on ratification. At that point Jacobs and the NAWSA regulars felt that they had enough problems without the stigma of association with "militants," and refused to work with them, though as Sue White said later, "they never did repudiate us or show a mean spirit." The pro-suffrage Montgomery *Journal* claimed that national Republicans had sent the militants to Alabama to prod the legislature into rejecting the amendment and embarrassing the Democrats.[7]

In Virginia there was open hostility between Valentine and her supporters and the NWP and their Virginia followers. Valentine, trying to follow NAWSA advice to delay introduction of the amendment until the most opportune time and by all means to prevent the adoption of a rejection resolution, hoped to postpone any action on the amendment until 1920. Believing that the amendment would have a better chance of success if considered after many other states had ratified, the Equal Suffrage League quietly secured a pledge from President Wilson and Governor Westmoreland Davis not to ask the Virginia legislature for action until the time was right. NWP members, however, believing that even a defeat would aid their cause morally and strengthen sentiment for the amendment elsewhere, wanted immediate consideration. Having found out about the pledge, they sent a member to Washington to tell Wilson that the Virginia suffragists wanted his endorsement immediately. His ensuing telegram to the General Assembly caught most supporters of the amendment off guard, and, they believed, significantly undercut their chances to win approval for the amendment in their state. Within days, the Virginia House passed the antis' rejection resolution, while amendment supporters in the Senate barely managed to postpone the issue until 1920. The 1920 ratification fight was described by one historian as "the most dramatic, most publicized and most bitterly contested" of the legislative session, featuring bitter denunciations of the "outside interference" of Wilson and of Catt, who was insulted to her face as she appeared before the legislature.[8]

Mississippi suffragists, according to Somerville, had little hope for ratification, but "showed their colors," hoping to "encourage other states in their efforts to secure ratification." "Whatever could be done was done," she observed soberly. Mississippi suffragists endured the bitter experience of sitting in the gallery while Kate Gordon, speaking in Jackson at the invitation of the *Clarion-Ledger*, denounced the federal amendment in the strongest of terms. "That day on which the Susan B. Anthony amendment is ratified, if it is, that day is the constitution of the United States lost," she said. Insisting that within five years every state would give its women the right to vote, she declared,

"If we women have the elements of statesmanship within us surely we will not give up the blessings of the liberty of the States for the transient blessing of the ballot a little earlier." The *Clarion-Ledger* described Gordon as beseeching her audience "not to believe tales that the Federal government would never attempt to regulate elections. . . . She knows that this amendment is not so much to attain woman's suffrage but to attain federal regulation of elections." Gordon urged Mississippians not to "vindicate Thaddeus Stevens and in the same breath repudiate that long dead company of her distinguished and patriotic sons" who had fought for Southern civilization and for Mississippi.[9]

The most amicable contest between pro- and anti-federal amendment suffragists took place in Kentucky, where Clay and Breckinridge respectfully squared off against each other in the ratification fight. Following congressional approval of the federal amendment, Clay and a small group of followers withdrew from the KERA and founded the "Citizens Committee for State Suffrage Amendment" to urge enfranchisement only by state action. Opening a headquarters in Lexington, they called on "the two great parties" to fulfill their pledges of 1916.[10]

Hoping that even at this late date a quick series of state suffrage amendments could prevent ratification of the federal amendment by proving federal action to be unnecessary, Clay pressed this argument in Kentucky and beyond. She exchanged literature and advice with leading Southern antisuffragists, including Judge J. B. Evans of Alabama. But even as they discussed strategy for defeating the Nineteenth Amendment, she lectured them on the self-destructiveness of Southern Democrats in being so absorbed with the region's racial problems that they would not grant woman suffrage by state action and would apparently have to suffer a federal amendment: "Though a Southern woman myself," wrote Clay to Evans, "I am forced to the conclusion that it is the South now which is principally responsible for the hold that the Anthony amendment has gained upon the people." And to Alabama anti Bessie Somerville, Clay observed sardonically that the failure of the Southern Democrats to realize that "White Supremacy . . . is an issue of little or no importance to more than a half-dozen states and the rest of the country will not consent to sacrifice great national issues and problems (like woman suffrage) to those half-dozen" was "not to the credit of those who insist upon Anglo-Saxon supremacy" in politics. Still trying to turn fear of the federal amendment into an opportunity for suffrage, she told Evans that "States Rights still may be saved, if the South is willing to make any sacrifice to do so," such as calling special sessions and "granting woman suffrage by state amendments in rapid succession, as in the plan suggested by Gov. Pleasant of Louisiana."[11]

To Breckinridge, the time had come and gone for the South to make the federal amendment unnecessary. She ridiculed Governor Pleasant's proposal, and applauded her governor's refusal to support it: "We are tired of Louisiana chivalry, that defeats a State amendment for woman suffrage one year and declares a passionate devotion to that method the next year when it is scared to death that we are going to get votes by federal amendment."[12]

Perhaps because she realized the federal amendment was certain to be ratified, Clay decided finally not to oppose the federal amendment before the Kentucky legislature, but simply to ask for submission of a state amendment. Indeed, she advised Bessie Somerville, president of the Southern Women's League for the Rejection of the Susan B. Anthony Amendment, not to send a representative to lobby against ratification in Lexington, saying it was unlikely that she could find a single person there to cooperate with her.[13]

By the opening day of the legislature, Breckinridge had the situation well under control. Kentucky broke its record of never approving a measure on the first day, and ratified January 3, 1920—in time for the grand celebration that evening that Breckinridge had prepared. At the victory celebration, Breckinridge paid tribute to Laura Clay, "who for a quarter of century when the cause of woman suffrage seemed but an incandescent dream, labored, toiled, spoke, spent herself and her wealth to advance that cause." Clay had "separated herself from the forces that led the fight in the past few years . . . due to her convictions about States' Rights." But Breckinridge urged that Clay's "separation" from the successful forces be forgotten and her contributions to the movement be remembered instead.[14]

No such harmony existed in Louisiana, where the Gordons and the states' rights suffragists combatted a coalition of supporters of the federal amendment, including both NAWSA and NWP emissaries and their affiliates. The legislature became the scene of a bitter three-way struggle that ended up producing no woman suffrage at all. States' rights suffragists helped antisuffragists defeat the ratification resolution in the Louisiana Senate July 7, 1920, but still failed to win a state suffrage measure. In this case the division among suffragists as to the proper method of enfranchisement ensured the failure of them all.[15]

In the suffrage movement's Armageddon in Nashville, suffragists and antisuffragists of all affiliations and strategies descended upon the city, one thousand strong, to do battle for the support of the Tennessee legislature. There Laura Clay and Kate Gordon (accompanied by Jean) became notorious in suffrage annals for actually lobbying against ratification of the Nineteenth Amendment. Determined to do everything she could to defeat "this hideous amendment," Clay was nonetheless extremely uncomfortable about going to Nashville. Having failed "to do anything at all in my own state to prevent ratification," she "felt very dubious about being able to do anything in another state." She also had a "great distaste to working with those who are avowedly opposed to suffrage" and hated being associated in the public mind with the despised antis. As time for the Tennessee trip drew near, she reconsidered her promise to the head of the National Association Opposed to Woman Suffrage to go to Nashville. But in keeping with a now-familiar pattern, she yielded to Kate Gordon's request that she go and oppose the amendment. As a representative of the SSWSC, Clay did not consider herself to be in Nashville "under the auspices of the anti-suffragists" but "under her true colors." Clay drew comfort from this distinction, but it was a distinction lost on others.[16]

Clay, Gordon, and the antis were up against suffragists who, according to Carrie Chapman Catt (herself in Tennessee for two full months), "laid aside their political differences and worked together in a manner worthy of imitation by the men of the State." Sue White returned to Tennessee from Washington and put to good use her skills in facilitating such cooperation. It had been White's policy as the leader of the National Woman's Party in Tennessee to work with, rather than against, the Tennessee Equal Suffrage League whenever the latter would cooperate. Supported by national leaders from both political parties, Sue White, the NWP, the Tennessee League, and the NAWSA all worked hard to wrest the call for a special session from Tennessee's governor, and then to convert legislators and hold their support against the best efforts of the liquor lobby and other groups who put considerable temptation before the legislators to oppose the amendment.[17]

II

When the Nineteenth Amendment was ratified, the champions of state sovereignty were bitter indeed. The indefatigable Gordon had remained confident until the end that she and her allies could defeat the amendment in Tennessee, preventing ratification until after the 1920 election, and thus buy time to solve the woman suffrage question through state action. She was devastated to learn that Tennessee had ratified and that the despised amendment had become law. "I left [Nashville]," she wrote to Clay, "assured that the battle was won and it was not till I reached Jackson Miss. and saw the headlines of an evening paper that I had doubt of the victory. I felt then as I do now that if a southern state had not been the medium of ratification no northern or western state would have put it over." Full of anger at the pressure brought to bear on these Southern legislators by national political leaders, Gordon concluded that "ratification by Tenn. was as fraudulent as the spirit that put over the 15th Amendment."[18]

Gordon and Clay were particularly disappointed in their erstwhile companions in the Southern suffrage movement. They believed that if Southern suffragists had followed their advice instead of that of the National and the NWP, Southern women would have emerged with what Clay and the Gordons considered a complete victory: enfranchisement by their own people signifying full recognition of women's political equality, and preservation of state sovereignty.

Kate Gordon and Laura Clay had struggled since the 1890s to find a way to convince politicians that woman suffrage was politically expedient, despite the widespread opposition in the South to expanding woman's role. Now, ironically, the two women condemned fellow suffragists for (they believed) accomplishing just that, for making Tennessee legislators compromise their principles and vote for the amendment despite the wishes of their constituents. In their view, it was entirely ethical for legislators to ignore regional conservatism on woman's role and support state suffrage measures, but it was despicable for them to cast aside their constituents' commitment to preserving the rights of the states to support the Nineteenth Amendment. In March 1920, Gordon wrote to Clay in despair: "I am so heartily sick of the whole situation and the way the suffragists have deserted all the things we contended for as the fruit of woman suffrage, that I am afraid I will be sympathizing with those arrant fools the anti's."[19]

In the last years of the suffrage movement, Clay and Gordon not only lost their fight against the federal amendment, but they lost much of the faith in women that had led them to work for suffrage in the first place. The majority of women, Clay and Gordon concluded, would not fight for their rights; indeed, women seemed to have little understanding of what the suffrage issue was about, and little knowledge of politics, period. In the midst of the frustrating Louisiana campaign of 1918, Gordon wrote to Boyer, "I am quite of the opinion that the Antis have summed us up correctly, and that women do not want to vote. The apathy, the indifference, the little understanding of suffrage as a basic right appalls me, the nearer I reach the goal." That same year a discouraged Laura Clay wrote to Kate Gordon, "You know I think your family contains some of the few women who have much political grasp of the woman suffrage question."[20]

Gordon had greatly admired the women with whom she had been associated early in her suffrage career, but the new breed of suffragists disgusted her. When one of her male allies reported being "overwhelmed that southern women are lined up to condone the 14th and 15th amendments," she said to Clay, "he does not know how little the rank and file of women know about the suffrage." Appalled by the cocktail-sipping, cigarette-smoking, pro-amendment suffragists who were her temporary allies in the 1918 Louisiana campaign, Gordon wrote to Clay: "O, but I am sick of woman suffrage, and almost every other kind of suffrage, and the only thing that supports me is a sense of gratitude to the women that blazed the path for us, and made possible the independence of women to-day. On the other hand, when I see how absolutely ignorant women undertake leadership, and play with the fire that they do, I am positively sick and disgusted with the whole thing."[21]

The Louisiana pro-amendment suffragists had committed what Gordon considered the ultimate outrage when they supported the

1923 re-election campaign of that "open advocate for every vicious influence possible," Mayor Behrman, in return for his last-minute conversion to the federal amendment. Though her "belief in the right of suffrage for women is as deep a conviction as ever," Gordon told Clay, she now "doubted seriously whether women could or would improve politics" and "would be very very chary of some of the promises held out as to what 'woman suffrage' would achieve."[22]

Indeed, as their despondency over the success of the federal amendment deepened, Clay and Gordon not only lost their conviction that woman suffrage would improve politics and the administration of public affairs, but also believed it might even be dangerous. Both expressed doubts that it would be wise to enfranchise women during the war. "That the great mass of women are absolutely indifferent argues strongly against this great inert mass being injected into a great political crisis and exploited for immediate gain by both the parties."[23]

Beginning in 1918, Clay and Gordon began expressing fears that various conspirators—German agents or Jesuits or both—were behind the success of the federal amendment, preying on the ignorance of "naïve" suffragists to inject masses of "untrained and unexperienced voters" into the American body politic who "would acquire the right to decide the policy of our nation in the great war." Writing to Anna Howard Shaw in April 1918, Clay said, "It is certainly a reason to be cautious to reflect that if these propagandists have the opportunity of working among millions of unsuspicious and untrained voters, no amount of native intelligence or sincere patriotism on their part will save multitudes of them from falling into the snares set for them." In a July 6, 1918, letter to Gordon, Clay suggested that since the federal amendment was so obviously "not the line of least resistance," especially given the declarations of the two parties, it was possible that German agents had influenced the NAWSA and especially the "naïve" National Woman's Party in their foolish emphasis on the federal amendment, in hopes that women voters would help the chances of "a German peace." Gordon was certain that the pope was pro-German and that the Jesuits were an active part of the German spy system in America.[24]

It seems clear that wounded pride clouded the judgement of these two suffrage pioneers during the last years of the woman suffrage movement in the South. Clay and Gordon had been rejected as leaders not only by the national organization but also by women they had personally converted to the suffrage cause and by the Southern suffrage movement they had played such a crucial role in establishing. While being asked to contribute to a fund to honor Shaw and Catt as heroines, they endured public criticism from women who they believed were undermining Southern civilization in their impatience for a suffrage victory.[25]

Clay and Gordon felt isolated in their opposition. In 1918, Clay told Boyer that the *Woman Citizen* (the *Woman's Journal*, renamed in 1917) was so filled with arguments for the federal amendment and "sarcastic remarks about those who are not favorable to it that nowadays I find difficulty in wading through it." To Shaw (who had sent her a souvenir from Susan B. Anthony's effects) Clay expressed bitterness that the NAWSA had departed from Anthony's "broadminded spirit" and old policy of urging both state and national suffrage. She complained that the National had previously encouraged the membership of many who were never in sympathy with the federal amendment, and led them to believe that each method would have "an equal and fair field for working out its success."[26]

In 1920, asked to compile material for *The History of Woman Suffrage*, Kate Gordon reflected on her own and Jean's "astonishing" contributions to the suffrage cause: "As a matter of fact," she told Clay, "we virtually carried the burden financially and educationally for not only Louisiana but in rousing most of the Southern states." This considered, she wrote to Alice Stone Blackwell, "It is an awful thing to feel that a life's work had borne such dead sea fruit."[27]

In their letters, Clay and Gordon commiserated over the amendment's success. "Do write to me, your fellow sufferer, when you can," said Clay to Gordon in the spring of 1920, "so that we can have at least the support of sympathy in what is one of the greatest trials of my life, as I doubt not it is of yours." When she was finally enfranchised after Tennessee's ratification, Gordon was so disconcerted that she could not even stand to write to her old colleague Clay for several years, and tried to bury herself in other kinds of reform work to get her mind off of what was—to her—defeat.[28]

III

Southern supporters of the Nineteenth Amendment, however, were delighted with its success. At the National's "Jubilee" convention in February 1920, suffragists savored the victory they knew was on its way. In her address, Madeline McDowell Breckinridge reflected the joy of suffragists whose states had ratified—particularly of Kentucky women who felt themselves empowered after years of struggling against the liquor interests and other antisuffragists in their state— when she recited a two-minute parody of "My Old Kentucky Home":

> The sun shines bright in my old Kentucky home,
> 'Tis winter, the ladies are gay,
>
> The corn top's gone, prohibition's in the swing,
> The colonel's in eclipse and the women in the ring.
>
> We'll get all our rights with the help of Uncle Sam,
> For the way that they come, we don't give a ____.

Weep no more, my lady, Oh, weep no more today,
For we'll vote one vote for the old Kentucky home,
The old Kentucky home, far away.[29]

The majority of Southern suffragists, those who had been enfranchised only through the "help of Uncle Sam" and without the consent of their states, were also happy and eager to put woman suffrage to work in support of further reforms. They were deeply disappointed, however, that they had gained neither state suffrage victories nor ratification of the federal amendment in their states. They bitterly acknowledged that they had failed to overturn the prevailing, traditional attitudes toward women and their participation in politics, a failure evident not only in the refusal of most states to ratify the Nineteenth Amendment and its formal rejection by some, but also in the sluggish way the amendment was implemented in several Southern states. Georgia, Virginia, and Mississippi did not allow women to vote in 1920, refusing to hold the special legislative sessions that were necessary to pass "enabling acts" setting up the mechanism for female participation in the November presidential election. Florida called such a session only after a State Supreme Court Justice reminded the governor that if the state failed to put the amendment into effect, the enforcement clause of the Nineteenth Amendment and perhaps of the Fifteenth Amendment might be invoked.[30]

The few victories in the region: primary suffrage in Arkansas (1917) and Texas (1918); presidential suffrage in Tennesseee (1919) and Kentucky (1920); and of course the ratification of the Nineteenth Amendment by Kentucky, Texas, Arkansas, and Tennessee; had all come through *legislative enactment*, not through state amendments approved by the majority of voters in public referenda. In Texas, the victory for primary suffrage resulted from the suffragists' brilliant exploitation of a schism in the Democratic Party; and when a woman suffrage amendment to the state constitution was placed before the male voters for approval a year later, they rejected it. Granted, this was a bizarre election, in which the enfranchisement of women was on the same ballot with the disfranchisement of "aliens" in an election in which women could not vote and "aliens" could. But it called into question the commitment of Texans to woman suffrage, created difficulties for the pro-suffrage faction in the legislature during the fight over ratification, and shook the confidence of the suffragists one month before the legislature ratified. Even after ratification of the Nineteenth Amendment, suffragists in two Southern states endured the rejection of state suffrage amendments. In November 1920, the all-male electorate of Mississippi rejected woman suffrage in a referendum the same day that women in most of the country voted for the first time. And in 1923, when the Kentucky League of Women Voters (as a gesture to Clay) launched a campaign to get the word "male" struck from the election clause of the state constitution, the measure sailed through the legislature without a dissenting vote but was defeated by the male *and female* voters by a vote of 56,441 to 45,308. Though suffragists in Kentucky, Arkansas, Texas, and Tennessee were thrilled with their victories, the notable lack of state suffrage victories made it clear that support for suffrage was quite limited in the Southland. Nowhere did the suffragists receive the ringing endorsement of female equality for which they had worked and hoped.[31]

Suffragists from the states that refused to ratify—or, worse, adopted the rejection resolution—felt this failure most keenly. At the same NAWSA convention in Chicago (1920) where Breckinridge spoke for the "victorious" suffragists, Pattie Ruffner Jacobs spoke for the defeated. "It only remains," she said, "for the outward and visible sign of our freedom to be put in the hands of Southern women by the generous men of other states, a situation which hurts our pride and to which we submit with deep regret but not apology."[32]

This remarkable address, entitled "Tradition Vs. Justice," reflected many important themes of the Southern suffrage movement, and spoke volumes about these elite, white Southern women like Jacobs who were so loyal to but critical of their region. It had been a bitter experience for these faithful daughters of the South to have the defeat of the Nineteenth Amendment celebrated in state after Southern state as a "Keeping of the Faith," and a "Triumph for Southern Civilization," and to see legislative champions of the amendment denounced as "traitors to their section." They became weary of the constant evocation of "loyalty to tradition" as justification for denying them the vote.[33]

Explaining the feelings of Southern suffragists to their co-workers from North and West, Jacobs insisted that Southern suffragists respected their heritage, but were convinced that the South was severely limited by this "tyranny of tradition," which was "difficult to explain" and to whose dominance Southern men seemed "particularly susceptible." "Traditions in themselves have no dignity," said Jacobs. "Our only interest in them is the fruitage they bear." And she insisted that "while many of the traditions of the old South were gracious and kindly, beautiful and honorable, if their product is injustice they are no longer admirable."[34]

Somewhat defensive before this mostly non-Southern audience, the same group that had heard Jacobs proclaim proudly in 1913 that it was insulting for outsiders to suggest that suffrage sentiment was weak in the South, Jacobs tried to explain if not justify the South's avid embrace of tradition, even as she lamented its resistance to change. While refusing to fault the South for the development of its hierarchical, tightly controlled, "aristocratic" society, she said the South had now "moved beyond the period in which the practises of repression created by the exigencies of a by-gone day can longer be justified." She considered it natural that democracy had evolved more slowly in the region as it had "further to go." One might also consider, said Jacobs, that the South was still affected by "the recoil due to pressure from a democratic age" (i.e., from the imposition of black male suffrage and reinstatement of white rule). She acknowledged that Southerners (herself included) were still "nursing our respect for the past" including "the old heritage of guardianship toward the unprivileged."[35]

But Jacobs insisted a state could not base present policy on "out-lived conditions," and while the "unprivileged" might still be in need of the protection of "guardianship," she clearly believed that such paternalism was inappropriate for Southern women like herself. Southern suffragists, she insisted, wanted, and believed that they deserved, to be among the decision makers in Southern society. They "had sickened of making constant and reiterated explanations of polit-ical blunders for which we are in no wise responsible," and wanted the power to help bring about justice as they saw it. Indeed, said Jacobs, for Southern women, administering "justice had become our tradition. Justice to all women, children, to the illiterates in our midst, justice to the women in industry still working unlimited hours, justice to all the hitherto unprivileged"—groups whose interests, suffragists believed, were not adequately protected by Southern men.[36]

What the suffragists found most frustrating was that, through the successful invocation of Southern tradition, the women of the region were being denied the opportunity to dispense justice by assisting in the governance of their society. They did not object to the vote's being restricted, but *they wanted to be among the elect.* Said Jacobs: "It is acutely distasteful to Southern suffragists not to be enfranchised by Southern men, for we of all people understand the symbolism of the ballot, especially in states where its use is restricted and professedly based upon virtue and intelligence." As Somerville had said back in 1914, "exclusion from the right to vote is a degradation . . . that can not be sugarcoated into anything else."[37]

Having worked so hard to gain enfranchisement through the "chivalrous" action of the men of their home states, nothing infuri-ated the suffragists so much as the antis' ratification-era claims that they were now willing to enfranchise women, but could not do so out of respect for states' rights. As Jacobs said:

> If these men who invoke the doctrine of states rights when it suits their purposes and who are still dominated by those old, unhappy, far-off memories of fifty years ago were sincere, we who live in the present might more readily forgive them. If they really wished the ballot to come to the Southern women by the state route, we would have had more ref-erenda. The test of their sincerity has been in repeatedly declining even that medium of relief to the voteless women. They are opposed to justice, not merely to its method of attainment.[38]

Participation in the suffrage movement had given Jacobs and the Southern leaders a bitter education about the strength of tradition in Southern society and the need to free themselves from its restraining power. "We know we have background and an honorable past," she said, "but we wish to occasionally be allowed to forget it, and to live in the present and build for the future." If keeping women rhetorically on a pedestal but actually in a state of dependence was a necessary component of traditional Southern society, they wanted tradition discarded. If supporting states' rights was *de rigueur* for loyal Southerners, not all, but most, Southern suffragists chose to think of themselves as Americans rather than renounce their only opportunity for full recognition as citizens.[39]

Looking back on the Southern suffrage movement of 1890 to 1920, it is clear that in most respects, its elite, white leaders offered no thoroughgoing indictment of their society. Their primary identification was with their states and region, and they shared many of the ideas of Southerners of their race and class. There were differences of opinion among them on the race issue, but even the most progressive believed that white political supremacy was necessary, at least until African-Americans "advanced" and were more "qualified" for the vote. While advocating assistance to blacks in the areas of education and health, none of these women openly defended the voting rights of black Southerners. Indeed, they publicly aligned their movement with the effort to return political power to those most "fit" to exercise it. Those who entertained views that might alienate potential supporters of their movement concealed or downplayed them for the cause; they took care to look and act like Southern Ladies and to avoid the appearance of "militancy." A few leading suffragists sympathized with organized labor, and one privately labeled herself a socialist, but the reforms they supported were designed only to ameliorate conditions and protect the "unprivileged"—not to reorganize the Southern economy. These suffragists were offering to assist in governing Southern society, to expand their traditional nurturing role in correspondence with the expansion of the functions of government. Rather than a threat to their society, the suffragists saw their movement as part of the natural development of Southern civilization, indeed, a means to perpetuate some of its finer qualities, such as the tradition of *noblesse oblige* that they perceived as losing ground among the leaders of the New South.

These leaders of the Southern suffrage movement advocated important changes, however, in the relations between the sexes. Throughout its thirty-year history, the suffrage movement in the South was a full-fledged women's rights movement, seeking an expanded and more equitable role for women within Southern society. Indeed, the suffragists succeeded in gaining improved legal and educational opportunities for women, as well as a significant amount of protective legislation that benefitted less-privileged women and children. None of these reforms, of course, was as threatening to the social and political order as woman suffrage. However beneficial, the reforms could still be seen as evidence of male protection of women and children. The request for the vote, on the other hand, represented a challenge to male authority and suggested that Southern men were less than successful in their cherished role as champions of Southern womanhood.

In the minds of the antisuffragists, the enfranchisement of women would have removed women from their unintrusive but enormously useful position on the pedestal. No longer the muse to Southern politicians, inspiring them to rule wisely for her sake, no longer the remote "White Goddess" whose defense legitimized acts of questionable legality and morality, woman would instead become an active participant in the unsavory world of politics, a well-intentioned but naïve meddler in a world she was ill equipped by nature and training to understand. The idea that enfranchised womanhood would clean up politics and protect the weak from exploitation won favor with progressive politicians but provoked powerful opposition as well. The suffragists' position was weakened further by the widespread perception that the entire women's rights movement was the creation of Northerners with no understanding of Southern traditions, who had forced unwelcome changes upon the South before and would not hesitate to do so again. Indeed, by opposing the Nineteenth Amendment, Southern politicians could register a protest of the Fifteenth Amendment, and did so, not unlike the conservative Southern politicians of the 1980s who, in opposing ratification of the Equal Rights Amendment, expressed their resentment at two decades of change "imposed" upon them by the federal government.[40]

The Nineteenth Amendment enfranchised Southern white women along with those of other sections, but for the Southerners the victory was quite incomplete. The victories "at home" that Southern suffragists so desired, state suffrage amendments that would signify the voluntary emancipation of Southern women by Southern men, never came. Clay and Gordon placed the blame for the federal amendment squarely on the shoulders of Southern Democrats whose failure to enfranchise women through state action had brought this potential calamity upon the South. But in deciding to oppose the federal amendment, these women chose to delay their own freedom rather than jeopardize state sovereignty. Most Southern suffragists, however, decided otherwise; in defying the tradition that demanded their subordination for the sake of "Southern civilization," they freed themselves. As Jacobs said, "By the thousands we have worked out our own salvation and have unshackled ourselves spiritually. We are not bound or gagged by any tradition which thwarts justice." These Southern suffragists did not want the role of "hostages to 'the Lost Cause,'" and they were determined not to play it.[41]

Epilogue

Having come so far with these eleven women, perhaps the reader would like to know what became of them *after* 1920. Most of them continued as political activists and reformers, working for "justice" as they saw it—though their definitions of it, or ideas about how to promote it, were often quite different. A number of them were involved in efforts to educate women about government and encourage them to use their newly won political rights. Some were actively involved in the 1919 conversion of the NAWSA to the League of Women Voters (LWV), through which, they believed, women could elevate the world of politics by means of nonpartisan activities. Others thought the League was a mistake of colossal proportions, believing that the whole idea behind the suffrage movement had been to integrate women into politics and that woman's influence should be injected directly into the political parties. None of them publicly defended the voting rights of African-American women who faced discrimination all over the South as they sought to register; and none of them was involved in the Southern interracial movement of the 1920s. Several ran for office, a few successfully. As one might expect, most Southern suffragists became Democrats. And as lobbyists, reformers, members of women's organizations and political parties, or as elected officials, they continued to advance the cause of women's rights.[1]

The premature deaths of Madeline McDowell Breckinridge

(November 1920 at age 48) and Lila Meade Valentine (July 1921 at age 56) prevented them from contributing their leadership skills to the ongoing movement for social reform supported by many Southern women in the 1920s. After Kentucky's ratification of the federal amendment early in 1920, Breckinridge played an active role in the March NAWSA convention in St. Louis, at which the National was transformed into the LWV; returning to Kentucky she hired a political scientist (a woman) to prepare lectures on citizenship, which Breckinridge published in the Lexington *Herald* and distributed to study groups she helped establish all over the state. She then left for Geneva, Switzerland, to attend the International Woman Suffrage Alliance. While touring the battlefield at Verdun, Breckinridge learned of Tennessee's ratification of the Nineteenth Amendment; she returned to the states determined to mobilize women voters to elect Cox and thus "fight world war" through the establishment of the League of Nations. Though her health (she suffered from tuberculosis most of her life) was worse than ever, she made extensive speaking tours throughout Kentucky as well as Missouri and Nebraska. Many of her friends attributed her sudden death from a stroke soon after the deeply disappointing election to these exhausting trips, believing that Breckinridge (like Woodrow Wilson) had sacrificed her life for the League of Nations.[2]

Lila Meade Valentine was also absorbed during her last year with plans to help women vote and vote wisely. Like her friend Breckinridge, Valentine was well aware that most women lacked the seasoned suffragists' understanding of government and politics. She persuaded the University of Virginia to sponsor a conference on government for women, and was heavily involved in planning civics lessons to be used in Virginia's public schools when she became very ill. She died on July 15, 1921. Unlike Breckinridge, Valentine never had the opportunity to cast a vote, since Virginia women were not allowed to vote until 1922. A plaque honoring Valentine as the leader of the suffragists was placed in the state capitol building in 1926. Yet this occasion only underscored the lingering resentment over the enfranchisement of women through the federal amendment. A letter expressing the objections of former members of the antisuffrage association appeared on the front page of the Richmond *News Leader*, saying (in part): that the proposed monument was not supported unanimously by Virginia women; that honoring the leader of the suffragists was inappropriate since their state had defeated the suffrage amendment at "the demand of the people of Virginia"; that even though "all who knew Mrs. Valentine loved and revered her," there had been many such women in Virginia who "fought for a cause that seemed to them just as great as suffrage" including the Confederate heroine and nurse Captain Sally Tompkins "who gave her all for the Confederacy!"

and had not "been so honored"; and that the capitol building was for Virginians who had made the state known worldwide "and kept her flag unsullied."[3]

Mary Johnston lived until 1936 (age 66) but did not continue to be politically active. Though interested in a variety of reforms and a member of many organizations promoting social change, woman suffrage was the only cause for which Johnston had ever taken time away from her writing for a sustained period. And by 1916 she had largely withdrawn from active participation even in this movement, though she gave Valentine both financial and moral support. But financial necessity and personal inclination drew Johnston back into full-time writing; she was in danger of losing her beloved mountain estate, "Three Hills," and she seemed to have the idealist's aversion to practical politics. Johnston continued to write the historical romances her fans loved, but she also experimented with modernist techniques and mystical themes in novels such as *Silver Cross* (1922). As mentioned above, during the 1920s she also published "Nemesis" (1923) and *The Slave Ship* (1924), revealing her somewhat unorthodox racial views. Johnston did not share Breckinridge's enthusiasm for the League of Women Voters. When informed of her election to a committee to convert the Virginia suffrage organization to a state LWV, she declined, saying that her own feeling was "against any re-segregation of women in the political and social life of the country." She explained:

> I am entirely in sympathy toward an extension of the life of the old suffrage leagues in the very recently enfranchised states for a year or two if needed, as a purely informative and advisory agency, until our women shall be over the first bewilderment and really inducted into political life. To this end the League of WV is as good a name as any. But further than this—that is, into a national, continuing body with a legislative programme—I am not personally willing to go.[4]

After 1920, the Gordon sisters became increasingly disillusioned with politics and immersed themselves "up to their eyes" in social work in New Orleans. After "the awful disappointment in Tennessee," wrote Kate to Laura Clay, "it was months before I could allow myself to think of the whole horrible experience." Their experience immediately thereafter in the 1920 municipal election (in which women voters who had favored the federal amendment supported Mayor Behrman's bid for re-election as repayment for his last-minute pledge to support ratification) contributed to their alienation. Women, it now seemed clear to the Gordons, would *not* improve or clean up politics; to obtain the civic improvements they wanted, the two sisters would just have to keep on haranguing inept or corrupt politicians at City Hall, same as before. For the last decade of their lives, they each achieved remarkable success with a favorite cause: for Kate it was the building of a tuberculosis hospital; for Jean, it was construction of the Alexander Milne Home for Destitute Orphan Girls (many of them "feeble-minded") on a tract of land adjoining Kate's facility. As Kate reported to Clay, "In the community I am now known as Tuberculosis Gordon and Jean as Feeble-minded Gordon. Take your choice." In 1923, Jean received the *Times-Picayune's* "Loving Cup," an annual award for extraordinary community service. The sisters managed to embroil themselves and the community in one more major controversy, however, when they demanded a full-scale investigation of the Community Chest they had helped establish years earlier. Jean died in 1931 at age sixty-six. Kate took over as director of the Milne home, "Jean's child," until her own death a year later at age 71.[5]

All of the other former leaders of the Southern suffragists took full advantage of their enhanced political opportunities right away, playing highly visible roles in political parties and government in the 1920s and 1930s. Laura Clay and Rebecca Latimer Felton, as senior, well-known, and respected representatives of the suffrage movement, benefitted from the desire of politicians to curry favor with women voters by means of symbolic gestures. Clay was selected as a delegate to the national Democratic Convention in 1920 where she was formally nominated for President of the United States. In 1922, Felton was appointed to succeed her friend Tom Watson in the United States Senate by a governor who had opposed woman suffrage. Though a temporary appointee (her tenure in the Senate lasted approximately one hour), Felton was sworn in with great ceremony, becoming at age eighty-two the "Junior Senator" from Georgia, the first woman senator, the darling of the press.[6]

Clay and Felton played more than symbolic roles in the politics of the 1920s, however. Clay declined to join the League of Women Voters and rejected their request for financial support, saying she was "not in sympathy with their mode of action. Now that we have the same voting power to affect legislation as men I believe that women should join with men for improved legislation, and not erect any division between the interests of the sexes." She decided to run for the state senate in 1923 (at age 74), saying that one of her aims was to get more women to vote. She lost, partly because she was running as a Democrat in a heavily Republican district, and partly because of her support for the parimutuel law (to legalize betting on horse races, etc.) in a conservative, rural area where gambling was regarded as sinful. She was in great demand among fellow Democrats as a speaker, and she stumped the state in 1928 for the party's presidential nominee, New York governor Al Smith, urging Kentuckians not to reject him because of his Catholicism or his opposition to prohibition.

Indeed, she insisted the Prohibition amendment had been a great mistake, and (to the surprise of her former associates in the WCTU) claimed she had always been "strong for temperance, but not for prohibition." In fact, Clay became a prominent opponent of the Eighteenth Amendment and was a member of the state convention that repealed it in 1933, celebrating the repeal as an example of the federal government's returning to the states the right "to govern their own internal and local affairs." Clay continued to fight for women's rights, particularly within the Episcopal Church. She finally got her Lexington diocese to give women full rights in 1920 and in 1924 was the first woman to be elected as a delegate to the Episcopal Synod of the District of Sewanee. At eighty-six, she struck one last blow for women's rights when she indignantly opposed a plan to pay male teachers more than females as a means of attracting more men into public school teaching. She died in 1941 at age ninety-two.[7]

Felton, of course, had been an avid participant in Georgia politics for decades prior to 1920, and she continued this activism well into the 1920s. She must have found it intensely irritating that the Georgia legislature took until 1922 to make provisions for women to vote, but she was nevertheless active in the campaigns of 1920. She was bitterly opposed to the League of Nations and to Wilson for his advocacy of it. Having suffered such grievous losses during the Civil War, Felton was greatly affected by the carnage and destruction of World War I; she feared that the League would just get more American boys killed fighting other nations' battles. She enthusiastically supported Tom Watson's isolationist campaign for the Senate, and favored the candidacy of Warren Harding. At his invitation she went to Florida (in October 1920) to confer with him on international affairs. Georgia politicians were well aware of her political influence, and her appointment in 1922 as Watson's successor was as much a tribute to her popularity with the late senator's supporters as a gesture to future women voters. But since a "real" senator would be elected before the Senate reconvened, Felton had to fight hard to achieve the distinction of being formally sworn in. There was nothing she loved so much as a fight, however, and this time she won the day—though she did not know until literally the last minute whether the Senate would accept her credentials. Naturally she had two speeches in her purse, one to celebrate this great victory for women's rights, the other to lambaste the Senate for its backwardness. The speech she actually delivered thanked her colleagues for accepting "this remnant of the old South," and predicted that future generations of women would contribute much to the Senate: "When the women of the country come in and sit with you, though there may be but very few in the next few years, I pledge to you that you will get ability, you will get integrity of purpose, you will get exalted patriotism, and you will get unstinted usefulness." Felton hated William McAdoo as Wilson's son-in-law and feared the Democrats' effort to get him elected President was a movement to get the United States to join the League of Nations after all. Though a fervent prohibitionist, she was even willing to take Al Smith over McAdoo, and antagonized the WCTU trying to get them to follow her lead. When the WCTU opposed Smith, she denounced them for mixing in politics! This was her last political battle. She died in 1930 at age ninety-five while in Atlanta for a meeting of the board of trustees of her beloved Georgia Training School for Girls.[8]

It is one of history's many ironies that the two suffrage leaders from Mississippi, Belle Kearney and Nellie Nugent Somerville, were both elected to public office the first year that women were eligible to serve, despite the fact that their state had been so hostile to woman suffrage. Indeed, they were the only two of these leading Southern suffragists elected to public office. Kearney lost her first political contest in 1922, a bid for the U.S. Senate, but thoroughly enjoyed the campaign—"the most delightful (year) of my public life." She was pleased that in the three-way race for the Democratic nomination she had helped defeat the hero of the "rednecks," the former Senator James K. Vardaman, and elect Hubert D. Stephens, a candidate more acceptable to the planter aristocracy. Apparently the candidates' suffrage records (Vardaman strongly pro-suffrage, Stephens against) mattered less to her than class solidarity. She also denounced Vardaman for his opposition to the League of Nations. It is interesting to note that Somerville did not support Kearney's candidacy. Though always cordial, the two women were much too different to be friends; and Somerville resented Kearney's tendency to remain away from Mississippi for long periods of time, return and launch a new and highly publicized campaign, and then leave it for others to manage. Soon after Kearney began her campaign, Somerville confided to a friend that Kearney was "too selfish and egotistical for real usefulness. . . . Needless to add she would never get my vote." Kearney filed for the state senate race just three months after Stephens' election. This time she won, the first woman in the South to be elected a state senator. Somerville, who was already a leader in the politics of her county prior to 1920, was elected to the Mississippi House of Representatives.[9]

The two women were sworn in amidst great fanfare, bouquets from Jackson's Shakespeare Club and the WCTU, roses from their male colleagues, and extensive press coverage; their staunch supporter, the *Woman Voter*, printed elaborate descriptions of their attire. Kearney announced her intention of remaining quiet in the senate unless absolutely necessary, to disappoint men who believed "that women want to have something to say upon every question," but found this resolution hard to keep. She tried to inject a more moral tone into the proceedings; one of her first acts was to move (success-fully) that each session of the senate open with prayer. She chided her fellow legislators for their occasional "indecent" jokes and made several attempts to get smoking banned in the senate chamber. She sponsored a number of bills aimed at "beefing up" prohibition legislation. Despite her own acceptance of evolution, she succumbed to pressure and voted in favor of a 1926 bill to prohibit the teaching of evolution in public schools—saying the bill would save Mississippi girls and boys from "materialism." Having pledged to work for women's rights, she sponsored legislation (unsuccessfully) to expand opportunities for women to serve in appointed offices in state government; she claimed all the women, children, and indigents of the state as "her constituents." An anti-lynching law she co-sponsored failed to get out of committee. Indeed, only four of her bills actually became law.[10]

Somerville, on the other hand, had a reputation as an unusually effective legislator; former governor Theodore Bilbo praised her for her "tact, diplomacy, and ability," qualities he found wanting in Kearney (and many found wanting in him). Somerville chaired the committee on eleemosynary (charitable) institutions, sponsored a number of social welfare proposals, and was responsible for major reforms at Mississippi's state mental hospital. As stated earlier, she opposed the federal child-labor amendment, owing to her disinclination toward federal intervention in state government plus the belief that the age of legal employment for children had been set too high for an agricultural state. Anne Firor Scott described Somerville's record as such "that the newspapers considered it a matter for comment when a bill she supported failed to pass." Somerville received a "surprise tribute" (with a somewhat mixed message) during the closing hours of her first session in the legislature. The *Clarion-Ledger* reported that Washington County's "lady member" was escorted to the podium, and as the representatives stood, Representative Joseph W. George commended Somerville for her outstanding work during the session and as "an exponent of southern womanhood, binding the old fashioned woman of the South, which he described as the greatest in all history, with the modern woman." He then gave her a silver vase, and "declared it peculiarly fitting that the first woman in Mississippi to advocate suffrage for women should be the first to sit in the House of Representatives." Perhaps because Somerville was so effective, she provoked strong opposition. She announced for re-election in 1927, but withdrew when it promised to be a nasty and probably unsuccessful battle; and she said that her district did not need a divisive political race the same summer they were trying to cope with the most disastrous flood in the history of the Mississippi Delta.[11]

Somerville was elected as a delegate (and Kearney an alternate) to the Democratic National Convention in 1924, where she was influential in getting the Mississippi delegation to support McAdoo, a "Dry." In this struggle over a nominee and throughout the decade, Somerville was dedicated to preserving and enforcing prohibition. Once again she served as president of the Mississippi WCTU, promoted prohibition enforcement through the state's Federation of Women's Clubs, and served as the state's representative on the National Committee for Law Enforcement. Kearney was also greatly agitated over the flagrant violation of prohibition and belonged to the National Woman's Democratic Law Enforcement League, which pledged to support only candidates who would take an oath to support fully the Constitution. Both women broke with the Democratic Party in 1928 and backed Hoover against Smith.[12]

After a few more years of lecture tours (billed as Senator Belle Kearney, Lecturer, Writer, Stateswoman"), Kearney returned to the plantation where she had been born, and remained an interested bystander to Mississippi politics until her death in 1939 (at age seventy-five). As a tribute to her prominent role in the state's history, state offices were closed, and her body lay in state in the capitol. Somerville, who believed that to be effective women must become directly involved in politics (she never forgave Catt for allowing the NAWSA to turn into the LWV, a development she privately regarded as "a fatal mistake"), had the satisfaction of seeing her daughter Lucy Somerville Howorth, a lawyer, elected to the legislature in 1932 and appointed to several positions of importance in the Roosevelt administration. Somerville was less pleased with other developments she witnessed as she grew older and the country changed, including the repeal of the Prohibition amendment; a movement to abolish the poll tax; the publication of new, revisionist histories of Reconstruction and the women's movement that gave the National Woman's Party considerable credit for the suffrage victory. By 1948 she considered herself an active "States' Rights Democrat." She was the last of these Southern suffrage leaders, first or second generation, to die—in 1952 at age eighty-eight.[13]

In the 1920s and 1930s, Pattie Ruffner Jacobs was active in the League of Women Voters *and* in party politics, not to mention as a reformer and government official. As the suffrage victory approached, Alabama Democrats named Jacobs the state's first National Committeewoman. She was also the first woman on the National Democratic Executive Committee and active in the National Association of Democratic Women. Back in Alabama, she promoted Cox's candidacy and made herself useful to Democrats by offering an "exposition of the league of nations (that) was the clearest yet heard on the stump." Jacobs was an enthusiastic participant in the League of Women Voters at the national and state levels, serving as the organization's first national secretary. Indeed, Jacobs and the Alabama LWV received much of the credit for the abolition of the convict lease system in their state in 1928. Alabama was one of the last Southern states to abolish the system, which one governor (who had tried and failed to abolish it) called "a relic of barbarism . . . a form of human slavery." Working together with the Jaycees and other civic groups and the United Mine Workers, Jacobs and the LWV exposed numerous atrocities until they finally got the legislature to act. Jacobs declared her candidacy for the state legislature in 1930, but later decided against running; no doubt her battle against the convict lease system had earned her many powerful enemies. She continued to be active in the fight against child labor and supported the child-labor amendment. She was on the other side of the prohibition controversy from Kearney and Somerville, serving as head of the Women's National Organization for the Repeal of Prohibition in her state.[14]

Jacobs was one of many former suffragists throughout the nation who kept progressive values alive in the 1920s and then had the opportunity to put some of these ideas into effect during the administration of Franklin Roosevelt—thanks to Eleanor Roosevelt. Jacobs became acquainted with Mrs. Roosevelt through her work with the LWV and through acquaintances in the Women's Bureau of Labor; the President appointed Jacobs head of the Women's Division of the Consumer Advisory Board of the National Recovery Administration (NRA) in 1933, and soon thereafter, head of public relations for the Tennessee Valley Authority in Alabama. She was still a TVA official when she died suddenly in 1935 (at age sixty).[15]

The youngest of these Southern suffrage leaders, Sue Shelton White, regarded the suffrage victory as but one important step in a long fight for full equality for women that was far from over; and as one of the authors of the Equal Rights Amendment, she helped launch another major chapter in the history of the women's rights movement in America. As early as December 1920, Alice Paul reported to the National Woman's Party Executive Committee that Sue White was studying discriminatory provisions in state legal codes and drawing up a "blanket bill" that "could be introduced in Congress and each legislature to sweep away these discriminations" that would be presented to the upcoming convention of the NWP as "a possible piece of work for the future." At the convention (February 1921) the NWP formally disbanded and immediately reconstituted itself under the same name, and devoted itself to removing these remaining legal disabilities of women. The "blanket bill" (which had undergone revision) was unveiled to the public at Seneca Falls, New York, at special ceremonies commemorating the launching of the women's movement there seventy-five years earlier. In a speech later that year, White insisted that the ERA (which she and the NWP called "The

Lucretia Mott Amendment") was necessary because of the injustices women still faced:

> In many states laws are such that the husband owns his wife's earnings, controls her property, fixes her legal residence, has the superior rights to the care and custody of the child, and in various ways exercises dominion over her. Young women find themselves barred from educational institutions supported by public funds, and girls attempting to enter the professions find obstacles that their brothers do not find. Such a condition can not, must not, continue. . . .
>
> We have commemorated the first equal rights meeting held 75 years ago. We can not be content to memorialize and leave the work then begun unfinished. No higher honor can be paid a prophet than to make the vision come true.

A close friend recalled that White was always very proud of her role in the history of the ERA, though very "disappointed with the way its passage has lagged."[16]

White was also one of several NWP leaders among the six officers of the Women's Committee for World Disarmament (WCWD), an organization that, according to Nancy Cott, was "the match that ignited public sentiment to shift the Harding administration's stance" on disarmament. Though there was already considerable public resentment at the postwar increases in the national defense budget, Harding's enthusiasm for naval buildups prevented him from responding to the British initiatives for naval disarmament. But working with the WCTU and other women's, church, and college groups, the WCWD instigated mass meetings around the country that generated floods of telegrams and petitions to Harding and to Congress and prompted Harding to call the Washington Disarmament Conference of 1921.[17]

Meanwhile, Sue White earned her living as secretary to Senator Kenneth McKellar of Tennessee (who had worked with her to secure Tennessee's ratification of the Nineteenth Amendment) and attended the Washington College of Law at night. In 1923 she received her long-coveted law degree. She lost her position with McKellar in 1926, however, apparently owing to her criticism of the Women's Bureau's promotion of protective legislation. In this way she was a victim of the bitter fight of the decade between the National Woman's Party, which opposed any laws giving special privileges to either sex, and women's rights advocates who (in this era before the New Deal provided protective legislation for both sexes) were still fighting to obtain and preserve legislation including maximum-hour and minimum-wage laws for women.[18]

White returned to Tennessee where she practiced law and began a new stage of her career as a Democratic organizer. Though earlier the stigma of her affiliation with the militant NWP had kept her out of the higher echelons of the state's Democratic Party, White broke with the NWP in 1928 over their endorsement of Hoover. At Eleanor Roosevelt's request, White helped organize a Tennessee Business and Professional Women's League for Al Smith in the 1928 campaign, also helping with the Midwestern division of the Democratic Party, through which she met the famous party leader Molly Dewson. White then worked with former governor of Wyoming Nellie Tayloe Ross, organizing Democratic women all over the country; and when Ross was appointed vice-chairman of the Democratic National Committee (with the responsibility of directing women's activities at national party headquarters), she took White with her to Washington as her executive assistant. Again critics tried to block White's appointment because of her former affiliation with the NWP and opposition to protective legislation for women, but instead White was appointed (in 1930) executive secretary of the Women's Division of the Democratic Party. And again White played an important historical role helping generate the sizable women's vote so important in the Roosevelt victory in 1932.[19]

After 1932, White held several posts in FDR's administration, beginning with administrative positions in the National Recovery Administration. When the NRA was declared unconstitutional, she joined the legal staff of the newly established Social Security Board, and helped lay the foundations of that program. She was proud to have gained for women in Federal Civil Service the right to continue to use their own names after marriage, and proud to have influenced President Roosevelt to appoint several very capable women to office, including her friend Judge Lucy Somerville Howorth. White remained with the Social Security Board (and its successor, the Federal Security Agency) until her death in 1943 at age fifty-six.[20]

Notes

Chapter 1: The Southern Lady: Hostage to "the Lost Cause"

1. Antisuffrage pamphlet, from antisuffrage literature sent to Laura Clay in June and July 1919 by Martin Lee Calhoun of Alabama, Laura Clay Papers, Special Collections and Archives, University of Kentucky Library, Lexington (hereafter cited as Clay Papers).

2. Quotation from A. Elizabeth Taylor, "The Last Phase of the Woman Suffrage Movement in Georgia," *Georgia Historical Quarterly* 43 (March 1959): 18.

3. For the history of the woman suffrage movement from the perspective of the participants, see Susan B. Anthony, Elizabeth Cady Stanton, and Ida Husted Harper, eds., *The History of Woman Suffrage*, 6 vols. (Rochester and New York, 1881–1922); Inez Haynes Irwin, *The Story of the Woman's Party* (New York: Harcourt, Brace, and Company, 1921); Carrie Chapman Catt and Nettie Rogers Shuler, *Woman Suffrage and Politics: The Inner Story of the Suffrage Movement* (1923; reprint edition, Seattle: University of Washington Press, 1970); and the National American Woman Suffrage Association, *Victory: How Women Won It* (New York: H. W. Wilson Company, 1940); Anna Howard Shaw, *The Story of a Pioneer* (New York: Harper Brothers, 1915). For general scholarly histories of the movement, see Eleanor Flexner, *Century of Struggle: The Woman's Rights Movement in the United States* (Cambridge, Mass.: Belknap Press, 1959); Aileen S. Kraditor, *The Ideas of the Woman Suffrage Movement, 1890–1920* (Garden City, New York: Doubleday and Company, 1971); Anne Firor Scott and Andrew M. Scott, *One Half the People: The Fight for Woman Suffrage* (Philadelphia: J. B. Lippincott Company, 1975).

4. For data on all full and partial suffrage victories prior to 1919, see NAWSA, *Victory: How the Women Won It*, pp. 161–166; on Southern opposition to the federal amendment, see Catt and Shuler, *Woman Suffrage and Politics*,

especially pp. 227–249, 316–342, 398–413, and 422–488; and David Morgan, *Suffragists and Democrats: The Politics of Woman Suffrage in America* (East Lansing: Michigan State University Press, 1972).

5. J. Morgan Kousser, *The Shaping of Southern Politics: Suffrage Restriction and the Establishment of the One-Party South, 1880–1910* (New Haven: Yale University Press, 1974); on the commitment of postwar Southerners to retaining traditional Southern values, see two fascinating studies of "the Lost Cause": Charles Reagan Wilson, *Baptized in Blood: The Religion of the Lost Cause, 1865–1920* (Athens: University of Georgia Press, 1980); and Gaines M. Foster, *Ghosts of the Confederacy: Defeat, the Lost Cause, and the Emergence of the New South* (New York: Oxford University Press, 1987). Foster argues convincingly that the "Confederate celebration" facilitated change in the South by providing a much-needed psychological balm for the wounded pride of white Southerners and enabling them to accept defeat and sectional reconciliation. Yet the celebration, which "prized order, deference to authority, and tradition," also had a conservative effect, bolstering white supremacy and "patterns of deference" in general, and helping "foster the cultural patterns that made political revolt or racial reform so difficult." (Foster, *op.cit.*, especially pp. 194–196.) This was certainly the case in regard to woman suffrage. On the opposition of certain industries, see Morgan, *Suffragists and Democrats*, pp. 155–178; see also Thomas L. Connelly and Barbara L. Bellows, *God and General Longstreet: The Lost Cause and the Southern Mind* (Baton Rouge: Louisiana State University Press, 1982).

6. On the development of traditional Southern ideas about the relations between the sexes and hostility to feminism in the prewar South, see Dorothy Ann Gay, "The Tangled Skein of Romanticism and Violence in the Old South: The Southern Response to Abolitionism and Feminism, 1830–1861," Ph.D. diss., University of North Carolina, 1975; antisuffrage literature, Clay Papers; antisuffrage literature in the Pattie Ruffner Jacobs Collection, Department of Archives and Manuscripts, Birmingham (Alabama) Public Library, hereafter cited as Jacobs papers. Note: part of this collection, including this antisuffrage literature, is material photocopied from the National American Woman Suffrage Papers, Manuscript Division, Library of Congress (hereafter cited as NAWSA Papers). Antisuffrage literature in the Lila Hardaway Meade Valentine Papers, then in the possession of Mrs. Ralph Catterall, Richmond, Virginia; now in the collection of the Virginia Historical Society, Richmond (hereafter cited as LHMV Papers).

7. Antisuffrage literature, Clay Papers; antisuffrage literature, NAWSA Papers; antisuffrage literature, LHMV Papers; Catt and Shuler, *Woman Suffrage and Politics*, esp. pp. 227–249 and pp. 462–488; Wilson, *Baptized in Blood*, passim.

8. Wilson, *Baptized in Blood*.

9. *Ibid.*, quotation, p. 7.

10. On Lost Cause rituals and institutions, see Wilson, *Baptized in Blood*, pp. 18–36; on "Lost Cause Education," see *ibid.*, pp. 139–160; and Foster, *Ghosts of the Confederacy*, pp. 180–191. Foster describes a number of professional historians who called for a more objective examination of Southern history, but failed to live up to their own ideal owing to a hostile public response, the desire to present their native region in a positive way to North-

ern readers, or the prospect of financial gain by joining in the Confederate celebration. *Ibid.*, pp. 180–186.

11. On religion and reconciliation, see Wilson, *Baptized in Blood*, pp. 58–78 and 161–182; quotation from Episcopalian Randolph McKim, p. 76. On the infatuation of Northerners with the Old South in the postwar period, see Paul M. Gaston, *The New South Creed: A Study in Southern Mythmaking* (Baton Rouge: Louisiana State University Press, 1970), pp. 167–171, quotation p. 172.

12. On the ideal Southern woman and her role in Southern society, see Julia Cherry Spruill, *Women's Life and Work in the Southern Colonies* (1938; reprint, New York: W.W. Norton and Company, 1972); Anne Firor Scott, *The Southern Lady: From Pedestal to Politics, 1830–1930* (Chicago: University of Chicago Press, 1970); Catherine Clinton, *The Plantation Mistress: Woman's World in the Old South* (New York: Pantheon, 1982); Suzanne Lebsock, *The Free Women of Petersburg: Status and Culture in a Southern Town, 1784–1860* (New York: W.W. Norton, 1985); Elizabeth Fox-Genovese, *Within the Plantation Household: Black and White Women of the Old South* (Chapel Hill: University of North Carolina Press, 1988); George C. Rable, *Civil Wars: Women and the Crisis of Southern Nationalism* (Urbana: University of Illinois Press, 1991). For an interesting discussion of the virtue and influence of the ideal Southern Lady, and her importance to the South's defense of its slave-based society, see Gay, "Tangled Skein," especially pp. 33–95. On the attributes of the Southern Lady being required of all "respectable women," see Jacquelyn Dowd Hall, *Revolt Against Chivalry: Jessie Daniel Ames and the Women's Campaign Against Lynching* (New York: Columbia University Press, 1979), pp. 151–152. In the ongoing debate concerning elite white women in the antebellum South, there seems to be general agreement about the *ideal* (as summarized here); historians do not agree, however, on many issues regarding the *reality* of elite Southern women's lives including the attitude of these women toward Southern society and their own roles in it.

13. Foster, *Ghosts of the Confederacy*, pp. 26–33, 124–125, and 135–139. In addition to traditional women, faithful blacks who had been body servants to Confederate soldiers were included in the annual UCV reunions as role models for younger blacks. *Ibid.*, p. 194.

14. Dr. Albert Bledsoe, "The Mission of Woman," *The Southern Review* (October 1871): 923–942, quotations pp. 941, 938.

15. *Ibid.*, pp. 941, 942.

16. See Gaston, *New South Creed*, pp. 153–186, quotation p. 153; Isaac F. Marcosson, *"Marse Henry": A Biography of Henry Watterson* (New York: Dodd, Mead, and Company, 1951), p. 218. Watterson wrote a well-known editorial, widely circulated by antisuffragists, entitled "The Most Momentous Question of Modern Times" saying "The *Courier-Journal* has for nearly fifty years fought the woman's battle." "If 'Votes for Women' were the end of it and all there is to it," he explained, "less account might be taken, for, under many conditions, women could by their votes do much good and womanly work. But 'Votes for Women' is the least part of it. Beneath lies—nay, yawns—an abyss of revolution, menacing not only government and politics, but the whole human species." Clay Papers.

17. Paul E. Fuller, *Laura Clay and the Woman's Rights Movement* (Lexing-

ton: University of Kentucky Press, 1975), p. 24. Watterson quotations from antisuffrage pamphlet "The Most Momentous Question of Modern Times," Clay Papers. On Lost Cause ministers' adulation of the Southern Lady, see Wilson, *Baptized in Blood*, pp. 46–48.

18. Quotation from Belle Kearney, *A Slaveholder's Daughter* (Abbey Press, 1900; reprint, New York: Negro Universities Press, 1969), p. 112; Scott, *Southern Lady*, pp. 80–102, 106–133; Rable, *Civil Wars*; Jean E. Friedman, *The Enclosed Garden: Women and Community in the Evangelical South, 1830–1900* (Chapel Hill: University of North Carolina Press, 1985). Suzanne Lebsock and others have questioned Scott's thesis that the war was a "watershed" that, as Scott said, "speeded social change and opened a Pandora's box," giving women many more options than they had prior to the war. Lebsock suggests that the war seems to have been a watershed only because historians have underestimated the antebellum opportunities and accomplishments of Southern women. Indeed, Lebsock insists that "the war itself was in some respects a setback for Petersburg's free women," and may have been so for Southern white women in general. She speculates (and challenges historians to explore the idea) that Southern white women's heightened sense of self-esteem derived from their expanded activites during the war did not take them very far when the war ended and the wounded pride of the male "losers" led them to insist on female deference. Rable's *Civil Wars* vividly describes the trials and tribulations of white women during the Civil War (though he lays to rest the idea of their unflagging support for the war effort and suggests that this was a postwar construction). He also challenges the watershed thesis and insists that the new responsibilities of women during the war and Reconstruction rarely led them to question the "dogmas" of Southern society, whether concerning race, class, or gender. Indeed, he says the hardships elite white women experienced made them eager for a restoration of the hierarchical society in which they enjoyed considerable privileges. Friedman takes an intermediate position between the "watershed" and the "continuity" theses, arguing that the Civil War introduced changes that would gradually lead women to a new consciousness and to seek reform.

19. Scott, *Southern Lady*, pp. 106–133, 134–163; Jean Friedman argues that the persistence of "kinship networks" that perpetuated conservative, evangelical values about gender relations kept the changes in women's work and education from having an immediate effect upon women's consciousness. The war did, however, loosen the grip of evangelical churches on their members, and women were able to play a more active role in the churches, including forming permanent foreign and home mission organizations that nurtured feelings of "group identity" and "established a core for the active reform groups that emerged in the 1880s." *Enclosed Garden*, p. 110–127, quotation p. 118.

20. Scott, *Southern Lady*, pp. 137–142. Josephine Bone Floyd, "Rebecca Latimer Felton, Champion of Women's Rights," *Georgia Historical Quarterly* 30 (June 1946): 84–85. The Presbyterian decree is cited on p. 84. Felton wrote a letter protesting the stance of that church, which was printed in the *Woman's Journal*, 27 May 1893. John Patrick McDowell, *The Social Gospel in the South: The Woman's Home Mission Movement in the Methodist Episcopal Church, South, 1886–1939* (Baton Rouge: Louisiana State University Press, 1982), pp. 15–19,

125–129; Bishop Candler's archrival described (and denounced) his anti-feminist activities in a 1919 letter to the editor of the Atlanta *Constitution*, "Some Reasons Why the General Assembly Failed to Ratify." She compared him to an autocratic Catholic priest, as she believed Candler (and Catholic priests) commanded too much influence over their flocks. Candler and other antifeminists, she said, should "move to Tokio where it would be easier to keep women enslaved." Letter to the Editor, Rebecca Latimer Felton Papers, University of Georgia Library, Athens (hereafter referred to as RLF Papers). Friedman, *Enclosed Garden*, pp. 113–120.

21. On the opposition of certain industries, particularly the liquor and cotton textile industries, to woman suffrage, see David Morgan, *Suffragists and Democrats*, Chapter Eleven, "Liquor, Cotton, and Suffrage," pp. 155–178; see also Catt and Shuler, *Woman Suffrage and Politics*, esp. pp. 266–279, 441–447. Catt bitterly referred to the "liquor interests" as "The Invisible Enemy," working in secret to control American politics, and said that "the combined liquor interests" (the liquor industry and their corporate allies) delayed the coming of woman suffrage for forty years! Describing the "nefarious intrigue" of corporate interests working against final ratification of the Nineteenth Amendment in Tennessee, Catt said that the "former 'whiskey lobby,'" the one-time railroad lobby that was alleged to have directed Tennessee politics for years, and "a newer, manufacturer's lobby" "worked openly as one man, although who paid the bills the public never knew," and "before the end all men checked as bribable . . . fell."

22. The quotation on support for prohibition is from Dewey W. Grantham, *Southern Progressivism: The Reconciliation of Progress and Tradition* (Knoxville: The University of Tennessee Press, 1983), p. 160. See also pp. 161–177 on prohibition in the South. Hall, *Revolt Against Chivalry*, pp. 23, 24; on Texas "Wets" and Ferguson, see Catt and Shuler, *Woman Suffrage and Politics*, pp. 256–258, 315, 329, 349. For the information on the Texas brewing industry, I am indebted to Judith McArthur, "Motherhood and Reform in the New South: Texas Women's Political Culture in the Progressive Era," Ph.D. diss., University of Texas, 1992, esp. Chapter Seven. Elna C. Green, whose dissertation on Southern antisuffragists is in progress (Tulane University), is quite correct that historians of the suffrage movement have all too often relied on the claims of suffragists for their evidence of "anti" activity. The subpoenaed material on the Texas brewers constitutes rare "direct" evidence of antisuffragists' covert political activity; Madeline McDowell Breckinridge and husband Desha believed that the liquor interests were largely responsible for the defeat of "school suffrage" for women in Kentucky in 1909 and for the defeat of many proposals for a state woman suffrage amendment. She frequently said that the liquor interests constituted a "Third House" in the legislature. See Melba Porter Hay, "Madeline McDowell Breckinridge: Kentucky Suffragist and Progressive Reformer," Ph.D. diss., University of Kentucky, 1980, pp. 121–122, 127–129, 146–149, 185–187.

23. Grantham, *Southern Progressivism*, pp. xix, xx, 178–217; see also George Tindall, *The Emergence of the New South, 1913–1945* (Baton Rouge: Louisiana State University Press, 1967), pp. 5–8, quotations from pp. 6 and 7; Morgan, *Suffragists and Democrats*, pp. 165–177.

24. Morgan, *Suffragists and Democrats*, pp. 165–177.

25. *Ibid.* Southern cotton men knew that their Northern competitors had

also fought woman suffrage, but thought that since Northern manufacturers were now being forced to accept protective legislation, they now wanted the woman suffrage amendment to succeed so that Southern competitors would also have protective legislation forced upon them.

26. *Ibid.*, quotations pp. 169, 170–171; for more information on David Clark and his conservative ideas and actions in regard to Southern labor relations, see Jacquelyn Dowd Hall, James Leloudis, Robert Korstad, Mary Murphy, LuAnn Jones, and Christopher B. Daly, *Like a Family: The Making of a Southern Cotton Mill World* (Chapel Hill: University of North Carolina Press, 1987).

27. Catt and Shuler, *Woman Suffrage and Politics*, pp. 132–159, 266–279 and 441–447. On the subterfuges of the liquor interests, Catt and Shuler observed, "The open campaign of self-defense conducted by the liquor forces can be respected as the unquestioned privilege and right of all who seek to convince public opinion. The point at issue is that the liquor interests did not rely upon open propaganda but upon secret maneuvers for results, and in this field no moral law, no democratic principle, no right of majorities was recognized" (p. 158). Morgan, *Suffragists and Democrats*, pp. 155, 172–173. The Breckinridges believed Henry Watterson was closely aligned with the liquor industry. Hay, "Madeline McDowell Breckinridge," p. 146.

28. Marcosson, *"Marse Henry,"* p. 218. On the liquor industry's covert political activity in Texas, see McArthur, "Motherhood and Reform in the New South," Chapter Seven.

29. See Kousser, *Shaping of Southern Politics*, especially pp. 11–44.

30. *Ibid.*, especially pp. 36–38 and 139–181, quotations p. 37. On the Mississippi Convention of 1890 and the "understanding clause," see pp. 139–144.

31. Kousser, *Shaping of Southern Politics*, pp. 238–265; Judith McArthur argues convincingly, however, that Texas suffragists were victorious because, under the skillful leadership of Minnie Fisher Cunningham, they found ways of exploiting a rift within the Democratic Party. Cunningham promised to mobilize women voters for Governor W. P. Hobby against former governor and virulent antisuffragist James E. Ferguson if Hobby's forces would get a bill passed giving women primary suffrage. Hobby's supporters complied, Cunningham delivered, Hobby was elected, and he became a staunch supporter of woman suffrage—support that helped make Texas one of the few Southern states to ratify. No doubt other Southern state Democratic parties were factionalized, but in no other instance did suffragists so skillfully exploit the situation. Judith McArthur, "Democrats Divided: Why the Texas Legislature Gave Women Primary Suffrage in 1918," paper delivered at the 1991 Southern Historical Association convention, Fort Worth, and drawn from her dissertation (previously cited), "Motherhood and Reform in the New South."

32. Kousser, *Shaping of Southern Politics*, p. 164.

33. *Ibid.*, p. 165; C. Vann Woodward, *Origins of the New South, 1877–1913* (Baton Rouge: Louisiana State University Press, 1971), pp. 323, 357–360.

34. Kousser, *Shaping of Southern Politics*, pp. 168–169, on cutbacks in black education, pp. 228–229. The phrase "Progressivism for Whites Only" is the frequently quoted title of Chapter Fourteen of Woodward's *Origins of the New South*, pp. 369–395.

35. Kousser, *Shaping of Southern Politics*, pp. 31, 32. The death or retire-

ment of many of the Republican champions of human rights was another important factor accounting for the party's dropping its protection of black voting rights in the South; Woodward, *Origins of the New South*, pp. 324–326.

36. Gay, "Tangled Skein," pp. 96, 97, and 125–132; Gerda Lerner, *The Grimké Sisters from South Carolina: Rebels Against Slavery* (Boston: Houghton Mifflin Company, 1967).

37. Gay, "Tangled Skein," pp. 125–132, quotation p. 125.

38. On early South Carolina suffragists, see Rosalyn Terborg-Penn, "Discrimination Against Afro-American Women in the Woman's Movement, 1830–1920," and her "Black Male Perspectives on the Nineteenth Century Woman," in Sharon Harley and Rosalyn Terborg-Penn, eds., *The Afro-American Woman: Struggles and Images* (Port Washington, N.Y.: Kennikat Press, 1978), pp. 27, 37–38; Barbara Bellows (then Ulmer), "Virginia Durant Young: New South Suffragist," M.A. thesis, University of South Carolina, 1979, pp. 51–52. On Virginia's first suffragists, see Charlotte Jean Sheldon, "Woman Suffrage and Virginia Politics, 1909–1920," M.A. thesis, University of Virginia, 1969, pp. 5–9; Catt and Shuler, *Woman Suffrage and Politics*, pp. 228–229. Between 1878 and 1919 when the amendment was finally approved by Congress (forty years and six months) the amendment was continuously pending, having been introduced in every session of Congress.

39. Catt and Shuler, *Woman Suffrage and Politics*, pp. 232–234, quotation p. 233.

40. *Ibid.*, p. 89; Morgan, *Suffragists and Politics*, p. 96.

41. Catt and Shuler, *Woman Suffrage and Politics*, pp. 229–232, quotation p. 230.

42. A proposal to enfranchise women who owned or whose husbands owned three hundred dollars' worth of property was considered by the Mississippi Constitutional Convention of 1890, as they looked for ways of countering black voting without risking congressional censure. See A. Elizabeth Taylor, "The Woman Suffrage Movement in Mississippi," *Journal of Mississippi History* 30 (February, 1968), esp. pp. 207–211; *Journal of the Proceedings of the Constitutional Convention of the State of Mississippi began in the City of Jackson on August 12, 1890, and concluded November 1, 1890*, pp. 79, 134. After Mississippi politicians considered the use of woman suffrage to solve "the negro problem," suffragists were sufficiently encouraged to promote this idea before subsequent disfranchising conventions, beginning with the next such convention in South Carolina in 1895. See Bellows, "Virginia Durant Young," pp. 54–88, quotation p. 75; see also Fuller, *Laura Clay*, pp. 62–71.

43. Nell Battle Lewis, "Negro Slavery Throws Dark Shadow Across the South to Keep Southern Women from Securing Their Freedom," *News and Observer* (Raleigh, N.C.), 3 May 1925; Hugh Talmadge Lefler and Albert Ray Newsome, *North Carolina, The History of a Southern State* (Chapel Hill: University of North Carolina Press, 1954, 1963), pp. 522–524; On Aycock see Oliver Orr, *Charles Brantley Aycock* (Chapel Hill: University of North Carolina Press, 1961), pp. 118, 119, quotation p. 174. The juxtaposition of images of pure white womanhood and rapacious black males may have been used to keep women in their place as well as to disfranchise black men. As Jacqueline Hall observed, "it may be no accident that the vision of the Negro as threatening beast flourished during the first organizational phase of the women's rights

movement in the South." Hall, *Revolt Against Chivalry*, p. 153. Anastatia Sims, *The Power of Femininity in the New South: Women's Organizations in North Carolina, 1883–1930* (Columbia: University of South Carolina Press, forthcoming) contains a fascinating discussion of the explosive combination of gender and racial issues that resulted in the Wilmington race riot of 1898.

44. For an example of Southern suffragists claiming race was not the real reason for opposition to suffrage, see Lila Meade Valentine, "President's Address," 1917, LHMV Papers.

45. Antisuffrage literature in NAWSA Papers; Sheldon, "Woman Suffrage and Virginia Politics," p. 20; Catt and Shuler, *Woman Suffrage and Politics*, pp. 463–465; Morgan, *Suffragists and Democrats*, pp. 144–153; antisuffrage literature in Clay Papers, especially James Callaway's "Will the States Consent to Blot the Stars from Old Glory, Leaving Only a Meaningless Square of Blue: A Message from the Old South to the Nation." On the failure of Northern feminists, even the relatively radical National Woman's Party, to demand the vote for African-American women after 1920, see Rosalyn Terborg-Penn, "Discontented Black Feminists: Prelude and Postcripts to the Nineteenth Amendment," in *Decades of Discontent: The Women's Movement, 1920–1940*, edited by Lois Scharf and Joan M. Jensen (Westport, Conn.: Greenwood Press, 1983); and Nancy F. Cott, *The Grounding of Modern Feminism* (New Haven: Yale University Press, 1987), pp. 68–72.

46. "South Rules in the Legislative Halls of Nation," Birmingham *News*, n.d., Pattie Ruffner Jacobs Scrapbook, Jacobs Papers; Tindall, *Emergence of the New South*, pp. 1–3.

47. On progress in the West and North, see Catt and Shuler, *Woman Suffrage and Politics*, pp. 174–195.

48. There were a number of calls for enfranchisement by white women of the "respectable classes" in the 1870s and 1880s, including Elizabeth Avery Meriwether (Tenn.), Elizabeth Lyle Saxon (Tenn. and La.), Lide Meriwether (Tenn.), and Caroline Merrick (La.), to name a few, but no sustained suffrage movement developed in the South until 1890. Merrick and Saxon gathered five hundred signatures for a woman suffrage petition they presented to the 1879 Louisiana Constitutional Convention. See Scott, *Southern Lady*, pp. 170–176. See also Kathleen C. Berkeley, "Elizabeth Avery Meriwether, 'An Advocate for Her Sex': Feminism and Conservatism in the Post–Civil War South," *Tennessee Historical Quarterly* 43 (Winter 1984): 390–407. The background and the motives of the Southern women who became leaders of the Southern suffrage movement are more fully discussed in Chapter Two. For detailed information about the development and progress of suffrage societies in the Southern states, see the many state studies, the majority written by A. Elizabeth Taylor, whose meticulous research laid the groundwork for all subsequent work on the subject: Lee Norcross Allen, "The Woman Suffrage Movement in Alabama," M.A. thesis, Auburn University, 1949; and Lee N. Allen, "The Woman Suffrage Movement in Alabama, 1910–1920," *Alabama Review* 11 (April 1958): 83–99; Mary Martha Thomas, "The New Woman in Alabama, 1890–1920," *Alabama Review* 43 (July 1990): 164–175; A. Elizabeth Taylor, "The Woman Suffrage Movement in Arkansas," *Arkansas Historical Quarterly* 15 (Spring 1956): 17–52; A. Elizabeth Taylor, "The Woman Suffrage Movement in Florida," *Florida Historical Quarterly* 36 (July 1957): 42–60; A.

Elizabeth Taylor, "The Origin of the Woman Suffrage Movement in Georgia," *Georgia Historical Quarterly* 28 (June 1944): 63–79; A. Elizabeth Taylor, "Revival and Development of the Woman Suffrage Movement in Georgia," *Georgia Historical Quarterly* 42 (December 1958): 339–354; A. Elizabeth Taylor, "The Last Phase of the Woman Suffrage Movement in Georgia," *Georgia Historical Quarterly* 43 (March 1959): 11–28; Paul E. Fuller, *Laura Clay and the Woman's Rights Movement* (Lexington: University Press of Kentucky, 1975), (more than a "state study," but it includes detailed information about the movement in Kentucky as he discusses Clay's involvement as a regional and national leader of the suffrage movement); Carmen Meriwether Lindig, "The Woman's Movement in Louisiana, 1879–1920," Ph.D. diss., North Texas State University, 1982, esp. Chapter Eight, "Louisiana Women and the Suffrage Movement," pp. 174–220; Kenneth R. Johnson, "Kate Gordon and the Woman Suffrage Movement in the South," *Journal of Southern History* 38 (August 1972): 365–392; Patricia Loraine Spiers, "The Woman Suffrage Movement in New Orleans," M.A. thesis, Southeastern Louisiana College, 1965; A. Elizabeth Taylor, "The Woman Suffrage Movement in Mississippi, 1890–1920," *Journal of Mississippi History* 30 (February 1968): 1–34; Mary Louise Meredith, "The Mississippi Woman's Rights Movement, 1889–1923: The Leadership Role of Nellie Nugent Somerville and Greenville in Suffrage Reform," M.A. thesis, Delta State University, 1974; A. Elizabeth Taylor, "The Woman Suffrage Movement in North Carolina," *North Carolina Historical Review* 38 (January and April 1961): 45–62, 173–189; Marjorie Spruill (Wheeler), "White Supremacy and the Southern Ideal of Woman: A Study of the Woman Suffrage Movement in North Carolina," honors thesis, University of North Carolina, Chapel Hill, 1973. On South Carolina, see Barbara (Ulmer) Bellows, "Virginia Durant Young: New South Suffragist," M.A. thesis, University of South Carolina, 1979; A. Elizabeth Taylor, *The Woman Suffrage Movement in Tennessee* (New York: Bookman Associates, 1957); A. Elizabeth Taylor, "The Woman Suffrage Movement in Texas," *Journal of Southern History* 17 (May 1951): 194–215; Anastatia Sims, "'Powers That Pray and Powers That Prey': Tennessee and the Fight for Woman Suffrage," *Tennessee Historical Quarterly* (Winter 1991): 203–225; Charlotte Jean Sheldon, "Woman Suffrage and Virginia Politics, 1909–1920," M.A. thesis, University of Virginia, 1969; and a wonderful resource combining Taylor's article on Texas suffrage, a wealth of primary sources, and two bibliographies—Ruthe Winegarten and Judith N. McArthur, *Citizens at Last: The Woman Suffrage Movement in Texas* (Austin: Ellen C. Temple, 1987).

49. Catt and Shuler, *Woman Suffrage and Politics*, pp. 88–89; on Laura Clay's vital role, see Fuller, *Laura Clay*, pp. 51–93.

50. Catt believed that the Southern states acted unconstitutionally in disfranchising blacks, but she also believed Congress had acted unconstitutionally in forcing black suffrage on the nation through the Fifteenth Amendment. She believed most blacks were ill prepared to vote and thus forced to rely upon whites who misled them. She thought the black vote was almost totally corrupt and, like the immigrant vote, a great detriment to American politics. Like most white suffragists, but especially Southern white suffragists, she bitterly resented the fact that black men had been enfranchised before white women. See *Woman Suffrage and Politics*, in which she wrote, "Whether the Negro, enfranchised a generation before his time, or the woman, enfran-

chised two generations after her time, suffered the greater injustice, it may take another century to demonstrate" (pp. 86–90, quotation p. 90). See Kraditor, *Ideas of the Woman Suffrage Movement*, pp. 138–171.

51. On the Atlanta convention, see Harper and Anthony, *History of Woman Suffrage* IV, pp. 236–251; Taylor, "Origin of the Woman Suffrage Movement in Georgia," pp. 68–79, quotation p. 74. On the New Orleans convention, see Shaw, *Story of a Pioneer*, pp. 310–314; *Journal of the Proceedings of the Constitutional Convention of the State of Mississippi August 12, 1890 to November 1, 1890*, pp. 79 and 134; Spiers, "Woman Suffrage Movement in New Orleans," pp. 21, 34–39.

52. For the reaction to suffrage in the 1890s, see the state studies listed above.

53. Taylor, "Origin of the Woman Suffrage Movement in Georgia," pp. 68–79, quotation p. 74; Shaw, *Story of a Pioneer*, pp. 309–310; Spiers, "Woman Suffrage Movement in New Orleans," pp. 34–39.

54. Catt and Shuler, *Woman Suffrage and Politics*, especially pp. 174–195.

55. On McKelway's aid to the NAWSA, see Morgan, *Suffragists and Democrats*, pp. 168–170; Grantham, *Southern Progressivism*, p. 209. On the distinguished careers as reformers of Breckinridge and Valentine, see Sophonisba P. Breckinridge, *Madeline McDowell Breckinridge: A Leader in the New South* (Chicago: University of Chicago Press, 1921); Hay, "Madeline McDowell Breckinridge"; Lloyd C. Taylor, Jr., "Lila Meade Valentine: The FFV as Reformer," *Virginia Magazine of History and Biography* 70 (October 1962): 471–487. On the urbanization and industrialization of the New South, see Don Doyle, *New Men, New Cities, New South: Atlanta, Nashville, Charleston, Mobile, 1860–1910* (Chapel Hill: University of North Carolina Press, 1990). On the ways urbanization and industrialization contributed to growing support for suffrage in the Progressive era, see Elizabeth Hayes Turner, "Women Progressives and the Origins of Local Suffrage Societies in Texas," paper presented at the Southern Historical Association meeting, 1991, and based on her Ph.D. diss., "Women's Culture and Community: Religion and Reform in Galveston, 1880–1920," Rice University, 1990; Scott, *Southern Lady*, pp. 106–133, 136–180; Sheldon, "Woman Suffrage and Virginia Politics," pp. 23, 27.

56. For the suffragists' account of the parade, see Catt and Shuler, *Woman Suffrage and Politics*, p. 242; "Women's Parade Jostled," Birmingham *Ledger*, 4 March 1913, Jacobs Scrapbook, Jacobs Papers; according to Gaines Foster, the crowd of Southerners greeted the Southern politicians in the parade with Rebel yells and "Dixie." Foster, *Ghosts of the Confederacy*, p. 193.

57. See Allen, "Woman Suffrage Movement in Alabama"; Trudy J. Hanmer, "A Divine Discontent: Mary Johnston and Woman Suffrage in Virginia," M.A. thesis, University of Virginia, 1972, p. 1; Taylor, "Woman Suffrage Movement in Mississippi"; Taylor, "Woman Suffrage Movement in Arkansas"; Taylor, *Woman Suffrage Movement in Tennessee*; and the other state studies listed above. See also Sophonisba Breckinridge, *Madeline McDowell Breckinridge*; and Hay, "Madeline McDowell Breckinridge." On successes before 1919, see tables in NAWSA, *Victory*, pp. 161–166. There had also been other more limited grants of suffrage prior to 1919. For example, in 1838, Kentucky had given widows with school-age children the right to vote in school elections, and in 1898 it extended this right to unmarried women taxpayers. The privilege was revoked in 1909.

58. Johnson, "Kate Gordon and the Woman Suffrage Movement"; Catt and Shuler, *Woman Suffrage and Politics*, pp. 313, 314; and Spiers, "Woman Suffrage Movement in New Orleans," pp. 46–54. In addition to the suffragists, two New Orleans newspapers and the Raleigh *News and Observer* blamed the defeat on Mayor Behrman. The Raleigh paper is quoted in "How the South Really Feels About Woman Suffrage," (Asheville, N.C.) *Southern Review* (4 May 1920), clipping in Clay Papers.

59. See state studies on anti activity in each state. See especially Pattie Ruffner Jacobs' Scrapbook, Jacobs Papers; and Lee Allen's thesis, "Woman Suffrage Movement in Alabama," on anti activity in Alabama—one of their strongholds. Other leading suffrage opponents in Alabama included the Montgomery *Advertiser* and the Birmingham *News*, Congressman Thomas Heflin (who spoke all over the nation against suffrage), Senator Oscar Underwood, and state Senator J. B. Evans. Macon, Georgia, was another anti stronghold, and James Callaway, editor of the Macon *Telegraph*, wrote much of the material widely circulated by Southern antisuffragists. See antisuffrage literature sent by Alabaman Martin Lee Calhoun to Laura Clay, June and July 1919, Clay Papers. Catt and Shuler reported that some of this literature, mailed from Selma, Alabama (and of a "vilely insinuating character") was sent to "every nook and corner" of Texas during the referendum of 1918. It was placed upon the desks of the representatives, who suspended all business to pass a resolution, with only five dissenting votes, condemning its circulation. Catt and Shuler, *Woman Suffrage and Politics*, pp. 314, 315. For Catt's and Shuler's views on antis and their relationship with corporate interests nationwide, see pp. 271–279.

60. For examples, see antisuffrage flyer entitled "A Southern Woman Speaks Her Mind: 'Our Men, God Bless Them': Superbly Brave Enough to Die for Us in France, Yet Not Good Enough to Vote for Us at Home! Oh, the Base Ingratitude of Some Women!: Were You Represented, Suffragette, On Flanders Field?"—and another, "Protect the Black Belt, and Remember the Lonely Farmers' Wives: Many Have Given Their Only Protector for Service in France." Antisuffrage literature, Clay Papers; Allen, (thesis), "Woman Suffrage Movement in Alabama," pp. 145–146; Taylor, *Woman Suffrage Movement in Tennessee*, p. 78; Taylor, "Last Phase . . . Georgia," p. 16. The Southern antisuffrage movement is at last receiving the attention this very interesting topic warrants. See Anastatia Sims, "Beyond the Ballot: The Radical Vision of the Antisuffragists," in *Votes for Women: The Woman Suffrage Movement in Tennessee, the South and the Nation*, ed. Marjorie Spruill Wheeler (Knoxville: University of Tennessee Press, forthcoming); and Elna C. Green, "Those Opposed: The Antisuffragists in North Carolina, 1900–1920," *North Carolina Historical Review* 42 (July 1990): 315–333. The article is based on research for her dissertation (in progress) at Tulane University.

61. Taylor, "Last Phase . . . Georgia," p. 18.

62. Antisuffrage literature, Clay Papers.

63. Sheldon, "Woman Suffrage and Virginia Politics," p. 20.

64. "Virginia Warns Her People Against Woman Suffrage," reprinted from the Richmond *Evening Journal*, 4 May 1915, Antisuffrage Papers, Clay Papers.

65. Morgan, pp. 73–82, 120–123; Catt and Shuler, *Woman Suffrage and*

Politics, pp. 237–240; quotation on Heflin, "Alabama Congressman Was Absent, and Another Goes to His Defense," Birmingham *News*, 6 July 1914; "Speech of Hon. Benjamin R. Tillman of South Carolina, August 18, 1913," NAWSA Papers. The South Carolina legislature first legalized divorce in 1872 during Reconstruction. The "Redeemers" promptly repealed the act (1878). Divorce was made unconstitutional in 1895. Not until 1948 was divorce again legal in the state. Suzanne D. Lebsock, "Radical Reconstruction and the Property Rights of Southern Women," *Journal of Southern History* 43 (May 1977), p. 195, n.2.

66. On Tillman on woman suffrage in 1895, see Bellows, "Virginia Durant Young"; quotations from "Speech of Hon. Benjamin R. Tillman," pp. 6, 8, 11, 12, NAWSA Papers.

67. Tillman speech, NAWSA Papers, quotations pp. 13, 15.

68. Catt and Shuler, *Woman Suffrage and Politics*, pp. 240–246; Morgan, *Suffragists and Democrats*, pp. 79–82, 113, 118–127, 134–144. Quotation from Senator Williams, p. 136.

69. Morgan, *Suffragists and Democrats*, pp. 105–114.

70. Catt and Shuler, *Woman Suffrage and Politics*, pp. 250–265, 280–299. Morgan, *Suffragists and Democrats*, pp. 107–110.

71. Catt and Shuler, *Woman Suffrage and Politics*, pp. 323–325, 340–342, 374, 392, 427, 465; Morgan, *Suffragists and Democrats*, pp. 134–144.

72. See Morgan, *Suffragists and Democrats*, pp. 117–137, esp. p. 136, where William Jennings Bryan's statement that he hoped "the Democrats of the South will not handicap the Democrats of the North by compelling them to spend the next twenty-five years explaining to the women of the country why their party prevented submission" is quoted. Of the senators who opposed the amendment in January 1918, two-thirds were Democrats; and of these, three-fourths had come from the South (18) and border states (5)—pp. 126, 127.

73. Morgan, *Suffragists and Democrats*, pp. 129–138; Catt and Shuler, *Woman Suffrage and Politics*, pp. 333–334.

74. Morgan, *Suffragists and Democrats*, p. 137–138, Pollock quoted p. 137; Catt and Shuler, *Woman Suffrage and Politics*. On p. 334 they discuss Pollock's speech, which "threw his State into an uproar of controversy in which abuse was more often heaped upon him than praise."

75. Morgan, *Suffragists and Democrats*, pp. 130–131, 137, 142, 175–177.

76. *Ibid.* Williams quoted p. 131.

77. *Ibid.*, pp. 138–142; Catt and Shuler, *Woman Suffrage and Politics*, pp. 340–341.

78. Catt and Shuler, *Woman Suffrage and Politics*, pp. 348–349, 353, 354, 374–375, 422–461, 462–488. Quotation from Catt, p. 353.

79. On the antisuffragists in various Southern states, see the state studies and Green, "Those Opposed."

80. Catt and Shuler, *Woman Suffrage and Politics*, pp. 463, 464; Morgan, *Suffragists and Democrats*, pp. 144–153. In Georgia, Representative J. B. Jackson expressed this explicitly in the legislative debate: "If you pass this Nineteenth Amendment you ratify the Fifteenth and any Southerner . . . (so doing) is a traitor to his section," p. 146.

81. "Thomas Nelson Page, Late Ambassador to Italy and Distinguished

Virginia Novelist, Warns Against Legislative Ratification of the Woman Suffrage Amendment," Antisuffrage leaflet dated 2 December 1919, NAWSA
Papers.

82. See antisuffrage literature, Clay Papers; antisuffrage literature,
NAWSA Papers; see also descriptions of legislative hearings and debates in the
state studies.

83. Lucille Wheeler, "When Women Battled for the Vote," Richmond
Times-Dispatch, 30 July 1947, p. 4-D, clipping, Benjamin B. Valentine Papers,
Valentine Museum, Richmond (hereafter referred to as Valentine Papers);
"Planks from the Suffrage Platform—as Stated by Mrs. C. C. Catt," Virginia
Suffrage Papers, Virginia State Library and Archives, Richmond. (This leaflet
fits the description of the flyer put on the desks of legislators, though is not
marked as such.)

84. J. B. Evans (Ala.), "Politics and Patriotism: War and Women," antisuffrage leaflet, Clay Papers; Senator H. M. Candler (Tenn.), Taylor, *Woman
Suffrage Movement in Tennessee*, p. 117. See especially "Some Facts About Suffrage Leaders: A Cause Is No Stronger Than Its Leaders," "Some Strange History," and "Anna Howard Shaw Said: 'What Is the American Flag But a Piece
of Bunting,'" Clay Papers; and "Catt and Woman-Suffrage Leaders Repudiate
the Bible" (a flyer that invited readers to peruse a copy of the *Woman's Bible* at
the Tennessee Antiratification Headquarters), and "The Dark and Dangerous
Side of Woman Suffrage," NAWSA Papers.

85. Catt and Shuler, *Woman Suffrage and Politics*, p. 353; Spiers, "Woman
Suffrage Movement in New Orleans," p. 56.

86. Antisuffrage literature, Clay Papers.

87. See Catt and Shuler, *Woman Suffrage and Politics*, Chapter 31, "The
States That Did Not Ratify," pp. 462–488. The full text of the proposed
"Proclamation of Defeat" is given on p. 463. Quotation from the *Clarion-Ledger*
from Taylor, "Woman Suffrage Movement in Mississippi," p. 231.

88. Catt and Shuler, *Woman Suffrage and Politics*, pp. 470, 471; Taylor,
"Woman Suffrage Movement in Mississippi," pp. 228–232.

89. On the search for the thirty-sixth state and the importance of winning the victory in time, see Catt and Shuler, *Woman Suffrage and Politics*, pp.
317, 396–423. The suffragists knew that Wilson's plea to the Senate had been
for woman suffrage as a war measure, and that many sympathized with the
suffragists because of the contributions of women to the war effort. The suffragists feared, however, that as the nation returned to normal, this public
sympathy for woman suffrage would wane and they might not win a federal
amendment after all. The recent failure of the Equal Rights Amendment,
which received the overwhelming endorsement of Congress and came within
three states of being ratified by the requisite three-fourths of the states,
demonstrates the shifting nature of public opinion and suggests that the fears
of the suffragists were well grounded. It is possible that a federal amendment
granting woman suffrage would have been delayed for many years or never
adopted at all, and that woman suffrage would have been granted gradually
by the states as they saw fit. On the debate over women's role in the South
since the 1960s, see Marjorie Spruill Wheeler, "Feminism and Antifeminism,"
Charles Reagan Wilson and William R. Ferris, *Encyclopedia of Southern Culture*
(Chapel Hill: University of North Carolina Press, 1989), pp. 1,543–1,545.

90. Catt and Shuler, *Woman Suffrage and Politics*, pp. 465–466; Sheldon, "Woman Suffrage and Virginia Politics," pp. 57, 58.

91. Catt and Shuler, *Woman Suffrage and Politics*, pp. 478–480; Spruill (Wheeler), "White Supremacy and the Southern Ideal of Woman," pp. 44–46. Quotation from *State's Defense* is cited in Green, "Those Opposed," pp. 327, 328; Raleigh *News and Observer*, 12 and 14 August 1920. The North Carolina Senate deferred action until 1921; the house voted down the ratification resolution 71–41 the day after Tennessee ratified.

92. Catt and Shuler, Chapter 30, "Tennessee," *Woman Suffrage and Politics*, pp. 422–461; Taylor, *Woman Suffrage Movement in Tennessee*, pp. 104–125; Sims, "'Powers That Pray and Powers That Prey.'"

93. Catt and Shuler, *Woman Suffrage and Politics*, pp. 449–456, quotation pp. 451–452. Catt and Shuler also claimed the antis threatened Harry Burn with exposure of an alleged bribe if he didn't change his vote, *ibid.*, p. 451; Taylor, *Woman Suffrage Movement in Tennessee*, pp. 119–122.

94. Taylor, *Woman Suffrage Movement in Tennessee*, pp. 122–125; Catt and Shuler, *Woman Suffrage and Politics*, pp. 456–461.

95. Morgan, *Suffragists and Democrats*, p. 131; quotations from anti legislator, Spruill (Wheeler), "White Supremacy and the Southern Ideal of Woman," pp. 19, 20; quotation about the antis' view of the feminist movement, James Callaway, "What Is Pedestal?" antisuffrage literature, Clay Papers.

Chapter 2: The Making of Southern Suffragists

1. "Equal Suffragists Hold Fine Meeting at Library," Selma, Alabama, newspaper, 29 January 1913, Jacobs Scrapbook, Jacobs Papers.

2. Jean Gordon, "New Louisiana Child Labor Law," *Charities* 21 (26 January 1908): 481. Cited in Margaret Nell Price, "The Development of Leadership in Southern Women," M.A. thesis, University of North Carolina, Chapel Hill, 1945, p. 109.

3. Catt and Shuler, *Woman Suffrage and Politics*, pp. 88, 89.

4. Many historians have taken notice of the fact that most of the prominent leaders of the Southern suffrage movement were from socially or politically prominent families. Many of their followers, however, came from the South's growing middle class. See Dewey Grantham, *Southern Progressivism*, pp. 207, 208.

5. Fuller, *Laura Clay*, esp. pp. 1–18; Hay, "Madeline McDowell Breckinridge," pp. 1–25; Sophonisba Breckinridge, *Madeline McDowell Breckinridge*; Scott, "Madeline McDowell Breckinridge," in Edward T. James and Janet Wilson James, eds., *Notable American Women*, 3 vols. (Cambridge: Harvard University Press, 1971) (hereafter referred to as NAW), Vol. I, pp. 231–233.

6. Scott, "Nellie Nugent Somerville," in Barbara Sicherman and Carol Hurd Greed, *Notable American Women: The Modern Period* (Cambridge: Harvard University Press), pp. 655, 656; Marjorie Spruill Wheeler, "An Oral History with Judge Lucy Somerville Howorth," Cleveland, Mississippi, 15 March 1983, and Hattiesburg, Mississippi, 6 March 1984. Volume 297, Part II, the Mississippi Oral History Program of the University of Southern Mississippi, 1984; Constance Ashton Myers, interview with Judge Lucy Somerville

Howorth, Monteagle, Tennessee, June 20–23, 1975, Southern Oral History Collection, Southern Historical Collection, UNC-Chapel Hill; clippings, Somerville-Howorth Family Papers, Schlesinger Library, Radcliffe. According to the *Picayune* (18 January 1897), "Few men in the state were better known or more popular than Col. Nugent. He had for a quarter of a century been a leading member of the state bar and no Mississippi lawyer appeared oftener before the Supreme Court or the federal courts, including the Supreme Court of the United States. . . . The Supreme Court of Mississippi adjourned in tribute."

7. Belle Kearney, *A Slaveholder's Daughter*, pp. 4–9, 20–39, 68; quotation from Nancy Carol Tipton, "It Is My Duty," M.A. thesis, University of Mississippi, Oxford, 1975, p 3. Kearney, who was known to exaggerate, gave this description of the family's summer excursion to a WPA interviewer in the 1930s.

8. L. E. Zimmerman, "Jean Margaret Gordon," and "Kate M. Gordon," *NAW*, II, pp. 64–68; Kathryn W. Kemp, "Jean and Kate Gordon: New Orleans Social Reformers, 1898–1933," *Louisiana History* 24 (1983): 389–401.

9. John E. Talmadge, *Rebecca Latimer Felton: Nine Stormy Decades* (Athens: University of Georgia Press, 1960); Joel Williamson, *The Crucible of Race: Black-White Relations in the American South Since Emancipation* (New York: Oxford University Press, 1984), pp. 124–130.

10. "Mary Johnston," *NAW*, II, pp. 282–284; Mary Johnston to Lila Meade Valentine, 29 September 1913, 27 October 1917, LHMV Papers. Wartime conditions undercut Johnston's financial position. After 1916 she grew increasingly dependent on her writing for her support and that of her sisters, and less able to contribute to the suffrage cause. After 1917 the sisters had to open Three Hills to paying guests. Lloyd Taylor, "LMV: FFV as Reformer," pp. 471, 472; obituary of B. B. Valentine, *The Evening Journal* (Richmond), 11 June 1919, Valentine Papers.

11. Lee N. Allen, "Pattie Ruffner Jacobs," *NAW*, II, pp. 266, 267; Pattie Ruffner Diaries, 8 August 1893, 21 September 1893, 24 September 1893, 2 October 1893, Jacobs Diaries, belonging to Mr. and Mrs. John L. Hillhouse, Jr. of Birmingham, Alabama. Mr. Hillhouse is Jacobs' grandson.

12. James P. Louis, "Sue Shelton White," *NAW*, III, pp. 590–592; [Sue Shelton White], "Mother's Daughter," in Elaine Showalter, ed., *These Modern Women: Autobiographical Essays From the Twenties* (Old Westbury, New York: Feminist Press, 1978), pp. 46–52, quotations pp. 47, 50.

13. Fuller, *Laura Clay*, pp. 1–5, 9, 10, 20, 21; Scott, "Madeline McDowell Breckinridge," *NAW*, I, p. 231; Talmadge, "Rebecca Latimer Felton," *NAW*, I, pp. 606, 607; Scott, "Nellie Nugent Somerville," *NAW Modern Period*, p. 654; Sue White's personnel information sheet, United States Civil Service Commission, Sue Shelton White Papers (hereafter cited as White Papers), Schlesinger Library, Radcliffe; Lee N. Allen, "Pattie Ruffner Jacobs," *NAW*, II, pp. 266, 267; James P. Louis, "Sue Shelton White," *NAW*, III, pp. 590–592. After the suffrage victory in 1920, White became an aide to a senator and worked her way through law school in the evenings. Lloyd C. Taylor, Jr., "LMV: FFV as Reformer," p. 471.

14. Fuller, *Laura Clay*, p. 4; Rebecca Latimer Felton, *The Romantic Story of Georgia Women* (Atlanta, 1930), pp. 31–33; "Mary Johnston," *NAW*, II, p. 282;

L. E. Zimmerman, "Kate Gordon," NAW, II, pp. 66–68; Pattie Ruffner Jacobs to Solon Jacobs, 26 August 1906, letter in the possession of John L. Hillhouse, Jr.; Lloyd C. Taylor, Jr., "LMV: FFV as Reformer," p. 473; Scott, "Madeline McDowell Breckinridge," NAW, I, p. 232; Kearney, *Slaveholder's Daughter.*

15. Felton, *Romantic Story*, pp. 30–33; on Hooker and Palmer, see NAW, II, pp. 212–214, and NAW, III, pp. 8–10; Mary Johnston, 1910–1911 suffrage speeches, "Speech IV" and "Speech to Women's College Alumnae, May 31," Mary Johnston Papers, Manuscripts Division, Special Collections Department, University of Virginia Library (hereafter cited as Johnston Papers); Pattie Ruffner Jacobs to Solon Jacobs, 26 August 1906, in the possession of John L. Hillhouse, Jr.; Kearney, *Slaveholder's Daughter*, pp. 208–217, 228, 229, 239–243, quotation p. 195.

16. Quotation from Lila Meade Valentine to Mary Johnston, 17 July 1910. The letter was accompanied by a British suffrage newsletter, "Votes for Women," containing the full debate on a suffrage bill in the House of Commons. Also Lila Meade Valentine to Mary Johnston, 3 June 1910, and Lila Meade Valentine to Mary Johnston, 26 May 1910, Johnston Papers; Miss Philippa Strachey, secretary to Lady Frances Balfour, London Society for Women's Suffrage of the National Union of Women's Suffrage Societies, 24 June 1910, LHMV Papers; Lloyd Taylor, "LMV: FFV as Reformer," pp. 481, 482; S. Breckinridge, *Madeline McDowell Breckinridge*, pp. 185–186.

17. Myers interview with Judge Lucy Somerville Howorth, pp. 24, 25.

18. Clay returned a check from the Tennessee suffragists saying she wanted no expenses or fee, that her visit was meant to be a donation to their work—Laura Clay to Florence Hughes, 21 November 1916, Clay Papers. According to Paul Fuller, between 1911 and 1917, Clay traveled to Ohio, Kansas, Michigan, Wisconsin, West Virginia, Iowa, Rhode Island, and New York—each time paying her own expenses as well as making a generous donation. Clay also was the executrix of a $5,000 fund left for suffrage work by her friend Laura Bruce. Fuller, *Laura Clay*, pp. 95, 96, 136. On Louisville, see p. 126; on NAWSA debt to Clay, see clipping from New York *Tribune*, 2 December 1913, Jacobs Scrapbook, Jacobs Papers. Clay contributed much and offered still more to Kate Gordon for the 1918 state suffrage campaign in Louisiana, but Gordon declined her last offer, saying Louisiana women should pay for it. Kate Gordon to Laura Clay, 26 September 1918, Clay Papers. On Clay's and Gordon's contributions to the SSWSC, see Kate Gordon to Laura Clay, 28 March 1914, Clay Papers; quotation from Madeline McDowell Breckinridge to Janet S. Harris, 20 November 1914, Madeline McDowell Breckinridge Papers (hereafter cited as MMB Papers), in Breckinridge Family Papers, Manuscripts Division, Library of Congress; Alva Belmont to Madeline McDowell Breckinridge, 29 December 1913, MMB Papers. On matching funds, Madeline McDowell Breckinridge to Laura Clay (1918), Clay Papers; Somerville, "Woman Suffrage in Mississippi," "1911 Report of State Work," Somerville-Howorth Family Papers; Myers interview with Lucy Somerville Howorth. Kate Gordon wrote to Clay in 1920 that she and Jean "virtually carried the burden financially and educationally" for Louisiana and "most of the Southern states," 8 February 1920, Clay Papers. Jacobs paid for Alabama's share of stock in the *Woman's Journal* in 1913 as the state suffrage association was too "tottering" to contribute. Pattie Jacobs to Miss Agnes Ryan, 30 June 1913, Jacobs Papers.

19. H. Augusta Howard to Laura Clay, 26 November 1894; Belle Kearney to A. H. Shaw, 5 January 1907; Shaw to Business Committee, 8 January 1907; Shaw to Laura Clay, 14 January 1907; Henry Blackwell to Laura Clay, 20 September 1907; Henry Blackwell to Laura Clay, 28 September 1907; Kate Gordon to Laura Clay, 1 October 1907; Kate Gordon to Henry Blackwell, n.d. (probably October 1907); A. H. Shaw to Business Committee (NAWSA) 5 November 1907. At a later date, Gordon experienced financial difficulties and had to accept payment for suffrage work. Laura Clay to Kate Gordon, 13 April 1914; Kate Gordon to Laura Clay, 19 August 1914; Laura Clay to Kate Gordon, 22 August 1914, Clay Papers.

20. Clipping, n.d., signed by Jacobs; and "Equal Suffragists Hold Fine Meeting at Library," Selma, Alabama, newspaper, 29 January 1913, Jacobs Scrapbook, Jacobs Papers.

21. MMB quotation from S. Breckinridge, *Madeline McDowell Breckinridge*, p. 210. For the quotation on the "pink tea stage" of the movement and the gathering of the elite for suffrage speech, see pp. 202–204. Fuller, *Laura Clay*, p. 43.

22. Mary Johnston to Lila Meade Valentine, "Sunday 1910" (probably January 3), LHMV Papers; Johnston quotation from Elizabeth Johnston, 1953 draft of a biography; Pauline Adams (Norfolk) to Mary Johnston, 23 September 1910, 6 November 1910, and 11 November 1910; Lila Meade Valentine to Mary Johnston, Johnston Papers; Hanmer, "Divine Discontent," p. 1.

23. Myers interview with Lucy Somerville Howorth, p. 32.

24. Clipping, Knoxville *Sentinel*, 1913, Nashville *Democrat*, January 1913, Clay Scrapbook, Clay Papers; Charlotte *News* quoted in Taylor, "Woman Suffrage Movement in North Carolina," p. 59; clippings on Jacobs from Jacobs Scrapbook, Jacobs Papers.

25. Sue Shelton White to Carrie Chapman Catt, 25 July 1918, White Papers.

26. Susan B. Anthony to Laura Clay, 13 March 1894; Carrie Chapman Catt to "Dear Girls," 1 April 1897, *National Suffrage Bulletin*, May 1897, Ella Harrison Papers, Schlesinger Library, Radcliffe; Anna Howard Shaw, "Report on Southern Trip," n.d., Mary Earhart Dillon Collection, Schlesinger Library, Radcliffe, hereafter cited as Dillon Collection. Laura Clay to A. H. Shaw, 10 May 1907, Clay Papers.

27. Kate Gordon to Catharine Waugh McCulloch, 1 June 1915, McCulloch Papers, Dillon Collection; Anna Howard Shaw quoted Belle Kearney in A. H. Shaw to Laura Clay, 4 January 1907, Clay Papers.

28. Clement Eaton, "Breaking a Path for the Liberation of Women in the South," *The Georgia Review* 28 (Summer 1974): 187–199, p. 197; Clay obituary, clipping from the Lexington *Herald*, 30 June 1941, Clay Papers; Lila Meade Valentine to Mary Johnston, 26 May 1910, Johnston Papers; quotation of Callaway from Floyd, "Rebecca Latimer Felton, Champion of Women's Rights," p. 86; Sue Shelton White, untitled notes on suffrage movement, p. 1., White Papers; "Mrs. Jacobs Has Narrow Escape While Speaking," "'Bomb' Thrown into Suffragist Meeting," and other clippings dated around 21 and 22 October 1913, Jacobs Scrapbook, Jacobs Papers.

29. Talmadge, *Rebecca Latimer Felton*, p. 105; clipping, Jackson *Clarion-Ledger*, n.d. (probably 1907), Somerville-Howorth Family Papers.

30. Desha Breckinridge to Madeline McDowell Breckinridge, 4 May 1913, MMB Papers.

31. Sheldon, "Woman Suffrage and Virginia Politics," pp. 18, 19. The speech was reprinted and widely circulated by the NAWSA. Mary Johnston to National Woman Suffrage Publishing Company, 10 October 1914, Johnston Papers.

32. See Grantham, *Southern Progressivism*, pp. 14–35, 207–208, 246, 256; Woodward, *Origins of the New South*, pp. 396–401; S. Breckinridge, *Madeline McDowell Breckinridge*, pp. 8, 9. Certainly reformers in other regions were also motivated in part by a sense of *noblesse oblige*, including the leaders of the Consumer's League and the Women's Trade Union League, for example. It is an interesting question whether or not this tradition was of any greater significance as a motivating force among Southern than among Northern Progressives.

33. Obituary from Richmond *Evening Dispatch*, 25 July 1921, cited in Lloyd Taylor, "LMV: FFV as Reformer," p. 487.

34. For a description of the traditional responsibilities of ideal upper-class white Southern men and women, see Gay, "Tangled Skein," pp. 6–95; and Scott, *Southern Lady*, pp. 4–44. On the expansion of woman's role in the late nineteenth century, see Scott, pp. 106–163.

35. Scott, *Southern Lady*, Chapters Five (pp. 105–133), Six (pp. 134–163), and Seven (pp. 164–184). Jean Friedman explained in *The Enclosed Garden* that this process of women's developing a new gender-based consciousness and public activism through voluntary associations occurred so much later in the South than in the North because of the South's rural and kin-based evangelical culture. It gradually weakened its hold on women after the Civil War as the South experienced "modernization."

36. Gordon also assisted in the establishment of the School of Applied Sociology in New Orleans, where she lectured in 1914 and 1915, and helped set up the city's first Federation of Non-Sectarian Charity and Philanthropy in 1914. L. E. Zimmerman, "Jean Gordon," NAW, II, pp. 64–66; Lindig, "The Woman's Movement in Louisiana," pp. 139, 140; see Kemp, "Jean and Kate Gordon," for information on Jean Gordon's work with the "feeble-minded," including her efforts to sterilize some of them in keeping with the theories of eugenicists.

37. Zimmerman, "Jean Gordon," NAW, II, pp. 64–66; Grantham, pp. 198, 199; James E. McCulloch, ed., *The South Mobilizing for Social Service* (Nashville: Southern Sociological Congress, 1913), pp. 679–691.

38. The Chattanooga *News* reported that Jean Gordon was "often called 'the Jane Addams of the South,'" "Women's Equal Suffrage Edition," Supplement to the Chattanooga *News*, 10 November 1914; Zimmerman, "Jean Gordon," NAW, II, pp. 64–66. For information about the Consumers' League, see William L. O'Neill, *Everyone Was Brave: A History of Feminism in America* (New York: Quadrangle, 1971), pp. 95–98; Grantham, *Southern Progressivism*, pp. 212, 213.

39. Lindig, "Woman's Movement in Louisiana," pp. 149–154. Taking advantage of the recent provision in the state constitution allowing women to vote by proxy, Kate Gordon pulled off the miraculous feat of gathering 300 such proxies from reticent New Orleans ladies on election day. The city's newspapers and mayor gave the Gordons, especially Kate, full credit for the victory; Zimmerman, "Kate Gordon," NAW, II, pp. 66–68.

40. Biographical data, Somerville-Howorth Family Papers; Scott, "Nellie Nugent Somerville," *NAW: The Modern Period*, pp. 655–656; Meredith, "Mississippi Woman's Rights Movement," pp. 28–34; on the work of the Methodist women, see McDowell, *Social Gospel in the South*.

41. In her scrapbook, next to a photograph of Martha Washington College, Somerville said she left Brookhaven College and went to Martha Washington in September 1878 "on account of the yellow fever in Mississippi." A clipping (n.d.) from the Jackson *Daily News* describes the massive evacuation of Mississippi families in the 1890s because of rumors of an impending yellow fever epidemic. Somerville-Howorth Family Papers. Shortly after the Mississippi Woman Suffrage Association was organized in 1897, suffrage activity was suspended because of a yellow fever scare and Somerville's flight to the safety of Cincinnati during the fall. Helen M. Reynolds to Ella Harrison, 27 November 1897, Harrison Papers; clipping, (1910), NNS Scrapbook, Somerville-Howorth Family Papers.

42. On the Civic Improvement Club, see Meredith, "Mississippi Woman's Rights Movement," pp. 48–57.

43. Kearney, *Slaveholder's Daughter*, pp. 131–269, quotation p. 118; Kearney carefully preserved Frances Willard's letters, which are now in the Belle Kearney Papers, Mississippi Department of Archives and History. In one letter from her London headquarters, Willard wrote to Kearney, "My Dear Belle, You are one of those on whom I count and regard as one of the very best oncoming workers. The general opinion is that you will be our Southern Leader." In response to Kearney's request that Willard recommend a speaking coach, Willard replied that Kearney "seemed already well equipped with one of the best voices I have ever heard anywhere, and a beautiful womanly manner." Since Willard was "particularly desirous that you (Belle) should be well furnished for your work," she recommended a Chicago "voice culturalist" to enhance Kearney's speaking performance. Kearney was also active in the social purity movement. She served at one time as a field secretary for the World Purity Federation, and published a novel in 1921 designed to warn young people of the dangers of venereal disease. Fuller, *Laura Clay*, pp. 33–38; Floyd, "Rebecca Latimer Felton: Champion of Women's Rights," pp. 81–83; on Willard and the WCTU, see Ruth Bordin, *Woman and Temperance: The Quest for Power and Liberty, 1873–1900* (Philadelphia, 1980); and *idem, Frances Willard: A Biography* (Chapel Hill: University of North Carolina Press, 1986).

44. Josephine Bone Floyd, "Rebecca Latimer Felton: Political Independent," *Georgia Historical Quarterly* 30 (March 1946): 28–31; Floyd, "Rebecca Latimer Felton: Champion of Women's Rights," pp. 88–95. This resentment of reformers by those they tried to help but sometimes failed to understand is thoroughly discussed in Link, *The Changing Face of Southern Progressivism: Social Policy and Localism, 1880–1930* (Chapel Hill: University of North Carolina Press, 1992).

45. Scott, "Madeline McDowell Breckinridge," NAW, I, pp. 231–233; S. Breckinridge, *Madeline McDowell Breckinridge*, especially Chapter Two; Hay, "Madeline McDowell Breckinridge."

46. J. Adams to MMB, 21 August 1903, MMB Papers; S. Breckinridge, *Madeline McDowell Breckinridge*, pp. 156–181; Hay, "Madeline McDowell Breckinridge," esp. pp. 35–46, 79, 90, 152; Scott, "Madeline McDowell Breckinridge," NAW, I, pp. 231–233.

47. Breckinridge objected to the Salvation Army mainly because it distributed charity indiscriminately (she believed) and thus encouraged dependence, but also because it was a large, profit-making corporation with a sizable overhead and scant disclosure of expenditures and received public funds, which was a violation of the principle of separation of church and state. In 1917, she filed suit against the Army, requesting an injunction to prevent the city from giving it money. The mayor retaliated by stopping all charitable expenditures in order to discredit Breckinridge and make her position unpopular. Hay, "Madeline McDowell Breckinridge," pp. 63, 64, 72, 73, 179–184.

48. Lloyd Taylor, "LMV: FFV as Reformer," pp. 473–474.

49. *Ibid.*, pp. 474–480.

50. Grantham, *Southern Progressivism*, pp. 246–253, quotation p. 247; Lloyd Taylor, "LMV: FFV as Reformer," pp. 476–479.

51. "Mary Johnston," NAW, II, pp. 282–284; Elizabeth Johnston, preface to an unpublished biography of Mary Johnston; Mary Johnston to B. M. Dutton, secretary of the Socialist Party of Virginia, [1911]. Johnston expressed fears that her views were too radical to be helpful to the *Woman's Journal* and gave them the right to omit any of her contributions they thought unsuitable, but Alice Stone Blackwell replied: "My own views of socialism are just about what you describe yours to be. . . . it is unlikely that anything with which you may favor us will be received otherwise than with appreciation and gratitude." Alice Stone Blackwell to Mary Johnston, 24 August 1900, Johnston Papers.

52. Mary Johnston, "Speech—Labor Convention, 1911"; Elizabeth Johnston, preface to unpublished biography of Mary Johnston, Johnston Papers; "Mary Johnston," NAW, II, pp. 282–284.

53. Lee N. Allen, "Pattie Ruffner Jacobs," NAW, II, pp. 266, 267; "Personal Recollections of Florence Armstrong," (close friend of Sue White for many years); Sue White, untitled notes on suffrage movement, White Papers. Clay's letter to Mary Dreir Robbins, in which she declined to join the National Women's Trade Union League, contained this statement: "I was born and reared in the country; and I have never known by observation the needs of women in the industrial masses. Hence I have never studied the problems of trade unionism: All the time I have been able to give for public work has been given to woman's suffrage." Laura Clay to Margaret Dreir Robbins, 19 February 1917, Clay Papers; see Fuller, *Laura Clay*, Chapters Three and Five. On Southern clubwomen's using "the power of femininity," see Anastatia Sims, *Power of Femininity*.

54. For examples of women's organizations endorsing woman suffrage, see the state studies. Sallie Southall Cotton, leader of the North Carolina Federation of Women's Clubs, described her organization's endorsement of woman suffrage in 1918 as follows: "The long delayed storm burst. For many years the expediency of adopting a resolution in favor of suffrage for women had been discussed at each convention but in respect to many who believed in it but thought the time for action had not come, it had not been brought before the Convention." The resolution was adopted amidst great applause and with only two dissenting votes. Sallie Southall Cotton, *History of the North Carolina Federation of Women's Clubs, 1901–1925* (Raleigh: Edwards and Broughton Printing Co., 1925), p. 127. Otelia Carington (Cuningham) Con-

nor Papers, Southern Historical Collection, University of North Carolina at Chapel Hill. In Mississippi, even the Daughters of the American Revolution and the United Daughters of the Confederacy were openly working for suffrage after 1916. Scott, *Southern Lady*, p. 180.

55. Lucinda Helm to Laura Clay, 21 May 1889, Clay Papers; Fitzgerald quoted in Taylor, "Last Phase . . . Georgia," p. 14; Friedman, *Enclosed Garden*.

56. Catt and Shuler, *Woman Suffrage and Politics*, pp. 88, 89.

57. Kemp, "Jean and Kate Gordon," pp. 389, 394.

58. Pattie Ruffner Diary, 25 March 1893 and 28 June 1893, Jacobs Diaries; untitled, undated clipping, and "To Women Who Vote: Mrs. Jacobs Labored to Give You the Right," Jacobs Scrapbook, Jacobs Papers.

59. Laura Clay Diary, 27 April 1864 and 15 July 1878, Clay Papers.

60. In the same entry, Clay wrote, "God has called me to the activity of Woman's Rights," Clay Diary, 26 July 1874, Clay Papers. Claudia Knott concludes from her study of the woman suffrage movement in Kentucky that evangelical Protestantism, rather than an obstacle to the development of a woman suffrage movement, was in fact the "central force" in creating suffrage sentiment and organization in Kentucky in the 1880s and 1890s and important even during the Progressive era. Clay and other Kentucky suffragists, says Knott, insisted that a "corrected interpretation" of the Bible would reveal God's true intention as equality between the sexes, and that acceptance of that interpretation should lead to conversion to the woman suffrage cause. Claudia Knott, "Evangelical Protestantism in the Kentucky Woman Suffrage Movement," paper presented to the Organization of American Historians convention, 1991, and based on her Ph.D. dissertation, "The Woman Suffrage Movement in Kentucky, 1879–1920," University of Kentucky, 1989. The letters and speeches of Clay, Somerville, Felton, and Kearney suggested very strong religious convictions. The other leading suffragists mentioned religion much less frequently. As for religious affiliation, Clay, Breckinridge, and Valentine were Episcopalian; Felton, Somerville, and White were Methodist; Jacobs was Presbyterian; and Kate and Jean Gordon were Unitarian. Mary Johnston was reared as a Baptist, but as an adult rejected conventional religion in favor of spiritualism and "Theosophy." See NAW, II, p. 283. Kearney's autobiography contains an interesting description of an early religious crisis. She was "converted" during a revival at age twelve and was reared as a Methodist. Around the age of fifteen, however, she began experiencing grave doubts, resulting from the poverty and misery she experienced and saw around her, a "natural tendency to question," and reading "material philosophers" including Herbert Spencer. Reconverted ten years later, shortly before meeting Frances Willard, she took Willard's entrance into her life as a divine calling to work for temperance and women's rights. See *Slaveholder's Daughter*, Chapters Five, Twelve, Thirteen and Fourteen.

61. Kearney, *Slaveholder's Daughter*, p. 189; Nellie Nugent Somerville, "President's Address at First Annual Woman Suffrage Convention, State of Mississippi," 28 March 1898, Somerville-Howorth Family Papers.

62. Fuller, *Laura Clay*, pp. 1–29.

63. White, "Mother's Daughter," in Showalter, *These Modern Women*, pp. 45–52; Florence Armstrong, Recollections of Sue White, White Papers.

64. Kearney, *Slaveholder's Daughter*, pp. 49, 70–72, 108–110.

65. Scott, "Nellie Nugent Somerville," *NAW Modern Period*, pp. 654–656; Myers interview with Judge Lucy Somerville Howorth, p. 7.

66. Kemp, "Jean and Kate Gordon," p. 189.

67. Zimmerman, "Jean Gordon," NAW, II, p. 66; Kemp, "Jean and Kate Gordon," p. 390, n. 5; Kate Gordon to Laura Clay, 22 March 1923, Clay Papers; Shaw, *Story of a Pioneer*, p. 309.

68. Hay, "Madeline McDowell Breckinridge," esp. pp. 177–178 and 217–218; Marie Stokes Jemison, "Ladies Become Voters," *Southern Exposure* 7 (Spring 1979): 51–52; Lloyd Taylor, "LMV: FFV as Reformer," pp. 486–487.

69. Myers interview with Judge Lucy Somerville Howorth, pp. 4, 5, 12, 15, 17–21. Somerville's son, Robert N. Somerville of Cleveland, was an ardent supporter of his mother's suffrage work. In 1914 he served on a committee formed to help get a state suffrage amendment through the legislature. Meredith, "Mississippi Woman's Rights Movement," p. 63. An article by Nellie Nugent Somerville in a Memphis newspaper said that "Mr. Robert Somerville, young attorney, was host and man of all work" when the MWSA met in Cleveland. Clipping, Somerville Scrapbook, Somerville-Howorth Family Papers. Lucy Somerville Howorth recalls helping her mother clip suffrage articles from newspapers and otherwise promote woman suffrage when she was just a small child. She knew many leaders of the suffrage movement, and invited Dr. Anna Howard Shaw to speak at Randolph-Macon in Lynchburg, Virginia. She attended the 1915 NAWSA convention in Washington, D.C.

70. Clay first joined the proto-feminist American Association of Women, from which she was recruited into the suffrage movement. Her records include AAW membership cards from 1877 and 1883–1886. LH? to Laura Clay, n.d., asking Clay to prepare a paper for upcoming Portland AAW convention; Ellen Lapham to Laura Clay, 17 October 1885, saying that Clay had been elected AAW vice-president for Kentucky; Caroline M. Brown to Laura Clay, 4 June 1886, Clay Papers; Frances Willard to Laura Clay, 13 October 1877, attempting to recruit Clay for the WCTU. For a while, leaders of both factions of the suffrage movement, the American Woman Suffrage Association (AWSA) and the National Woman Suffrage Association (NWSA), both founded in 1869, tried to recruit the talented young Kentuckian. Lucy Stone to Laura Clay, 23 September 1885, trying to get Clay to represent Kentucky at an AWSA national convention; Lucy Stone to Laura Clay, 30 April 1886; Lucy Stone to Laura Clay, 6 January 1887; Lucy Stone to Laura Clay, 28 October 1888; Lucy Stone to Laura Clay, 13 December 1889; Lucy Stone to Laura Clay, 25 July 1890; Henry Blackwell to Laura Clay, 2 June 1893; Nellie Nugent Somerville to Laura Clay, 16 February 1895. This is the first preserved record of correspondence between them. Somerville apologizes for not answering previous letters, reports on status of suffrage activity in the state in wake of a visit by Catt, and recommends other potential leaders from Mississippi, saying that she is personally "up to my eyes in WCTU work to say nothing of a family." See Clay's notebook concerning her work with the Southern Committee. Clay Papers.

71. Kearney, *Slaveholder's Daughter*, pp. 182, 183, 195–197, Anthony quotation, p. 185. A vivid account of the 1897 mission of NAWSA emissaries Ella Harrison and Mary Bradford in Mississippi is contained in Harrison's letters to her father in the Ella Harrison Papers; Somerville's version of the

recruiting mission and the formation of the MWSA is recounted in her letter to Laura Clay in which she is clearly resentful that Catt sent them in
without consulting Mississippi women, and "shocked" that the astounding
sum of $700 had been spent in the recruiting effort. Apparently she pre-
ferred Clay's method of organizing Southern women, identifying indigenous reformers and having *them* call suffrage meetings, to Catt's method of
sending in "outsiders." Somerville was, however, eager to see that the
recruiting trip not fail, and thus assisted them in calling the convention—
and accepted the presidency. Nellie Nugent Somerville to Laura Clay, 28
December 1897, Clay Papers.

72. Kemp, "Jean and Kate Gordon," p. 391; Harrison and Bradford spoke
in the Unitarian Church, of which Gordon was a member. Harrison wrote
that this was the only church in the city that would allow them to speak. Ella
Harrison to "Pa," 23 March 1897, Ella Harrison Papers; Kate Gordon to Laura
Clay, 28 March 1898, Clay Papers.

73. Carrie Chapman Catt to Mary Johnston, 1910. In her diary, Johnston described hearing Laura Clay speak on suffrage, Mary Johnston Diary
(1909), Johnston Papers. Glasgow's tea for Clay mentioned in Eaton, "Breaking a Path," p. 197; "Miss Jean Gordon to Speak on Suffrage," 1912. Clipping
described the effect of her 1911 visit to Birmingham, as does Myrtle Miles'
"Why the Suffrage Movement Should Win Favor Here," 6 December 1912.
On Mary Johnston in Birmingham, see "Mrs. Solon Jacobs Hostess at Tea,"
undated clipping, and "Says Far East Will Have Suffrage Soon," Philadelphia
Telegraph, 25 November 1912, Jacobs Scrapbook, Jacobs Papers.

74. Fuller, *Laura Clay*, pp. 22, 23, 81, 82. Gordon and Alice Blackwell
referred to one another respectively as "Nuzie" and "Massy," Kate Gordon to
Alice Stone Blackwell, 1 April 1907, NAWSA Papers. Henry Blackwell to Belle
Kearney, 25 August 1900, Kearney Papers. Blackwell and Kearney were co-
conspirators in her unsuccessful move to create a Southern Woman Suffrage
Conference in 1906 and attempt to get some form of suffrage from the Mississippi legislature in 1907. See Chapter Four, below. Somerville greatly admired
the Gordons, who helped her a great deal with the suffrage work in Mississippi. A 1911 report of the Mississippi Woman Suffrage Association reported
that Kate Gordon attended the annual convention, gave several addresses,
served on the committee on resolutions, and was issued thanks and a standing invitation to attend. Somerville Scrapbook, 1909–1912. Somerville's 1914
legislative report describes Kate Gordon coming to the state "on their
urgent request" when the Mississippi House of Representives voted to allow
suffragists to speak for a state suffrage amendment in the House: NNS Legislative Report, 1914. There are countless examples of such aid. Somerville-
Howorth Family Papers; Johnston quotation from Mary Johnston to Lila
Meade Valentine, 1 January 1910, LHMV Papers; Breckinridge quotation
from Madeline McDowell Breckinridge to Lila Meade Valentine, 20 August
1914, MMB Papers. She also urged Valentine to ask Alva Belmont for a contribution for suffage work in Virginia, saying "she's got plenty to blow." The
correspondence between Clay and Gordon extended between 1898 and 1923.
Clay Papers.

75. For example, in 1911, Breckinridge spoke of the Democratic Party's
being led once again by "the best element," and hoped that would mean they
were more receptive to woman suffrage. "The Prospect for Woman Suffrage

in the South," address to the NAWSA Convention of 1911, MMB Papers; Hay, "Madeline McDowell Breckinridge," pp. 58, 241.

76. Nellie Nugent Somerville, "Christian Citizenship," 1898, quotations pp. 1, 2; Somerville, "Presidential address to First Mississippi Woman Suffrage Association," 28 March 1898, handwritten. Somerville frequently quoted Frances Willard as saying, "The Ten Commandments are voted up and down on election day. . . . That belief is today the corner stone of the suffrage movement." Somerville, "Christian Citizenship," 1898; Somerville, "A Temperance Campaign in Mississippi," 30 May 1907, clipping; Del Kelso Mohlenoff, MWSA treasurer, recalled that Somerville, while working with WCTU, "became convinced that no great or lasting results could be attained in this or any other reform work unless backed by the consecrated ballot. Acting on this conviction she refused re-election to the office of State Corresponding Secretary of the WCTU and entered the suffrage work." Somerville-Howorth Family Papers. Somerville's daughter agrees that Frances Willard's endorsement of suffrage had a great deal of influence on her mother. Wheeler interview, March 1983.

77. Felton, "The Subjection of Women and The Enfranchisement of Women," No. 2, RLF Papers; Floyd, "Rebecca Latimer Felton: Champion of Women's Rights," pp. 81–83. For a fascinating discussion of Felton's views on Southern men's failure to protect women's interests, see LeeAnn Whites, "Rebecca Latimer Felton and the Problem of 'Protection' in the New South," in Nancy Hewitt and Suzanne Lebsock, eds., *Visible Women: Essays in Honor of Anne Firor Scott* (Urbana: University of Illinois Press, forthcoming).

78. Talmadge, *Rebecca Latimer Felton*, pp. 20–25; Floyd, "Rebecca Latimer Felton: Champion of Women's Rights," p. 86.

79. Floyd, "Rebecca Latimer Felton: Political Independent"; Rebecca Latimer Felton, *Country Life in Georgia in the Days of My Youth* (Atlanta, 1919), p. 93.

80. Grantham, *Southern Progressivism*, pp. 95–98, 279.

81. Lindig, "Woman's Movement in Louisiana," pp. 164, 165; M. M. Breckinridge, "Article for Colonel Polk Johnson's forthcoming history of Kentucky, What Kentucky Women Are Doing For The State," p. 2, MMB Papers; Jean Gordon to the editor of the *Times-Picayune*, 6 November 1918, clipping, Clay Papers.

82. S. Breckinridge, *Madeline McDowell Breckinridge*, pp. 34–42, quotation pp. 41, 42.

83. Breckinridge, "Public Schools and Southern Development," handwritten speech, n.d., MMB Papers.

84. Lindig, "Woman's Movement in Louisiana," pp. 140–142, quotation p. 140.

85. NNS, "Factories and Child Labor," clipping, n.d., Somerville-Howorth Family Papers.

86. Price, "The Development of Leadership in Southern Women," p. 109; Jacobs' address to the first annual meeting of the Birmingham Equal Suffrage Association, 1913, Jacobs Scrapbook, Jacobs Papers.

87. Taylor, "Last Phase of the Woman Suffrage Movement in Georgia," p. 14; Breckinridge, "Indirect Versus Direct Influence in Kentucky," MMB Papers.

88. Mary Johnston, 1910–1911 suffrage speeches; Johnston, "Woman's War," p. 25, Johnston Papers.

89. Kearney, *Slaveholder's Daughter*, pp. 112–113; Somerville, "How Mississippi Women Work for the Ballot," New Orleans *Daily Item*, 1910, clipping, Somerville-Howorth Family Papers.

90. Jacobs quoted in Taylor, "Woman Suffrage Movement in Florida," p. 50.

91. Breckinridge, "The Prospect for Woman Suffrage in the South," address made at National Suffrage Convention in Louisville, 1911, clipping, MMB Papers.

92. Lloyd Taylor, "LMV: FFV as Reformer," p. 481; Somerville, "Christian Citizenship," address before the Woman Suffrage Clubs, 13 November 1898, Somerville-Howorth Family Papers.

Chapter 3: Respectable Radicals: Southern Suffragists As Champions of Women's Rights

1. Kearney, *Slaveholder's Daughter*, p. 185.

2. Somerville, "Are Women Too Good to Vote?" clipping, ca. 1914, Somerville-Howorth Family Papers.

3. Since the publication of Nancy F. Cott's *The Grounding of Modern Feminism* (New Haven: Yale University Press, 1987), historians have quite rightly been more cautious in the use of the word "feminist." As Cott points out, the term has a particular, historically specific meaning as well as the more general meaning familiar to most modern readers. The term did not come into use in America until the 1910s. Even then it was embraced by (and used in reference to) a minority of women's rights advocates who were for the most part younger and more radical than the majority of suffragists, and many of them affiliated with the National Woman's Party. Politically leftist, "feminists" advocated major changes in the relationship between the sexes, including economic independence for women, egalitarian marriages, and a more open enjoyment of sexuality by women. They shunned the traditional association of the women's movement with Christianity and rejected the idea of woman's superior morality. Their credo, said Cott, was "self development" rather than "self sacrifice." Of the Southern suffragists, only Mary Johnston called herself a "feminist," though she felt the need to qualify her statement by saying she was not "simply a feminist" but a "humanist" as well. And though she shared some of the feminists' goals, her views were closer to the more traditional women's rights advocates on the issue of converting men to woman's standard of morality rather than "lowering" woman's standard. As Cott says, however, the word "feminist" has a contemporary meaning "not tied down to specific historical time," and it is this meaning that I wish to invoke as I use the term throughout this book. When I describe these suffragists as feminists, I mean to say that they had a well-developed sense of gender identification and sought to remove all of the constraints placed on women's development *because of their sex*. They sought much more than their own enfranchisement, including major reforms in woman's legal status and economic opportunities, as well as adjustments in the traditional relationships between the sexes in Southern society. See Cott, especially pp. 3–10. On Johnston, see Hanmer, "Divine Discontent," ii.

4. There are many references to the term "New Woman" in the papers of these women. For example, Rebecca Latimer Felton was proud to be called a

"New Woman of the new century," in Felton, *Romantic Story of Georgia Women*, p. 38, and "an old woman who has been a 'new woman' for fully thirty years." Felton, *Country Life*, p. 115. Madeline McDowell Breckinridge said that her woman's page in the Lexington *Herald* would have "a 'new woman' flavor." Hay, "Madeline McDowell Breckinridge," p. 9. On the "feminists" in contrast to whom these suffragists appear conservative, see Cott, *Grounding of Modern Feminism*, pp. 13–85.

5. Mary Johnston, draft of a speech to be given in Philadelphia, 1910–1911 suffrage speeches, Johnston Papers.

6. Lloyd Taylor, "LMV: FFV as Reformer," p. 483; quotation from LMV to Mrs. Townsend, 7 April 1914, Virginia Suffrage Papers; on the WTUL, see Lila Meade Valentine to J. Townsend, 25 February 1915, and Lila Meade Valentine to Mrs. C. E. Townsend, 13 October 1919; and on removing socialist literature, see Lila Meade Valentine to Mrs. Townsend, 2 July 1915, Virginia Suffrage Papers. Johnston quotation from Mary Johnston to B. M. Dutton, n.d., Johnston Papers.

7. Fuller, *Laura Clay*, pp. 75–77, quotation p. 71. On the *Woman's Bible*, see Flexner, *Century of Struggle*, p. 220.

8. The Alabama Equal Suffrage League was a member of the Woman's Peace Party and the National Peace Federation, and in 1915 actively supported a proposed conference of neutral countries to seek an end to the war in Europe. "What We Stand For," *Alabama Suffrage Bulletin*, 1, p. 2; and Pattie Ruffner Jacobs, "Equal Suffrage Activities Reviewed by a Suffragist," Birmingham *Age-Herald*, 30 November 1915, Jacobs Scrapbook, Jacobs Papers. Mary Johnston to Mary Branch Cabell Munford, 14 June 1917, declining Munford's request that she serve on the Virginia Committee of the Women's Council of National Defense, Johnston Papers; Mary Johnston to Lila Meade Valentine, 6 May 1917, LHMV Papers; Laura Clay to Mrs. South, 4 May 1917, Clay Papers; Fuller, *Laura Clay*, pp. 138, 139; S. Breckinridge, *Madeline McDowell Breckinridge*, pp. 244, 245; Orlean Lackey, "To Women Who Vote: Mrs. Jacobs Labored to Give You the Right," Birmingham *News*, n.d., Jacobs Scrapbook, Jacobs Papers; Myers interview with Judge Lucy Somerville Howorth, p. 66; clipping, n.d., Valentine Papers.

9. Kearney, *Slaveholder's Daughter*, p. 185; description of Kearney from Judge Lucy Somerville Howorth in Wheeler interview, 15 March 1983; Nellie Nugent Somerville to "Members and Friends of the Mississippi Woman Suffrage Movement," May 1897, Somerville-Howorth Family Papers.

10. Clipping, n.d., Somerville Scrapbook, Somerville-Howorth Family Papers; clipping, 6 December 1912, and clipping, [1918], Birmingham *Age-Herald*, Jacobs Scrapbook, Jacobs Papers.

11. Sheldon, "Woman Suffrage and Virginia Politics," pp. 31, 40; Taylor, "Revival and Development . . . Georgia," p. 354; Taylor, *Woman Suffrage Movement in Tennessee*, p. 54; Birmingham *News*, 30 September 1917.

12. Press release, Otelia Cunningham, president of the Equal Suffrage Association of North Carolina; and Otelia Cunningham to Woodrow Wilson, 30 October 1917, Connor Papers. Madeline McDowell Breckinridge, "What's Sauce for the Goose Is Sauce for the Gander," Lexington *Herald*, 24 March 1914; Breckinridge ridiculed North Carolina suffragists for their caution: "They are trying to get suffrage there in the most lady-like manner without having anybody find out they want it." S. Breckinridge, *Madeline McDowell*

Breckinridge, p. 210; Clay quoted in Knoxville *Sentinel*, 1 February 1913, Clay Scrapbook, 1913, Clay Papers. One of the most active groups of "militant" suffragists in the South was in South Carolina, but even there the NWP had far fewer members than the NAWSA affiliates. See Sidney R. Bland, "Fighting the Odds: Militant Suffragists in South Carolina," *South Carolina Historical Magazine* 82 (January 1981): 32–43.

13. Lila Meade Valentine, press release of the Equal Suffrage League of Virginia, 2 July 1917, and "Resolutions Adopted by the Equal Suffrage League of Virginia," 14 November 1917, Virginia Suffrage Papers; Allen, "Woman Suffrage Movement in Alabama," (thesis), p. 141.

14. Lila Meade Valentine to Mrs. Townsend, 7 April 1914, Virginia Suffrage Papers; on ideology of the NAWSA, see Aileen Kraditor, *Ideas of the Woman Suffrage Movement*; Mary Johnston, "Sentimental Idea Hurts Suffrage," *Woman's Journal*, 12 April 1913, Johnston Papers.

15. Examples of such suffrage literature, including the pamphlet "Woman in the Home" quoted here, can be found in the Equal Suffrage Association of North Carolina Papers, North Carolina Collection, University of North Carolina Library.

16. Scott, *Southern Lady*, pp. 183, 184; Pattie Ruffner Jacobs to the editor, 12 February 1912, Birmingham *Ledger*, Jacobs Scrapbook, Jacobs Papers; "Sentimental Idea Hurts Suffrage," *Woman's Journal*, 12 April 1913, Johnston Papers.

17. Kearney, *Slaveholder's Daughter*, pp. 118, 119.

18. Johnston, "Woman Movement in the South," suffrage speeches 1910–1911, Johnston Papers.

19. Fuller, *Laura Clay*, pp. 31, 32.

20. On the rights of Southern women in the latter part of the nineteenth century, see Eleanor Flexner, *Century of Struggle*, pp. 229, 230; and Suzanne Lebsock, "Radical Reconstruction and the Property Rights of Southern Women," pp. 195–216; Sandra Moncrief, "The Mississippi Married Woman's Property Act of 1839," *Journal of Mississippi History* 47 (1985): 110–125; Kearney, *Slaveholder's Daughter*, pp. 114, 117. Kearney knew Mississippi had been the first to pass a married women's property act, but cited the date as 1880 instead of 1839. Nellie Nugent Somerville, "President's Address, State Suffrage Convention, 1898," Somerville-Howorth Family Papers.

21. Minutes of the Second Annual Convention, MWSA, April 5–6, 1891; Nellie Nugent Somerville, "History of the Mississippi Woman Suffrage Association 1897–1919," p. 13, Somerville-Howorth Family Papers; Allen, "Woman Suffrage Movement in Alabama," (thesis), p. 25. See "Fruits of the ERA Club's Policy of Initiation and Agitation" listed on their stationery, Kate Gordon to Alice Stone Blackwell, 18 July ?, NAWSA Papers; on the need for male witnesses of the signatures in 1898, see Anna Howard Shaw, *Story of a Pioneer*, p. 314.

22. Sue Shelton White, untitled notes on the suffrage movement, White Papers; "Resolution Adopted by the Equal Suffrage League of Virginia," 14 November 1917, Virginia Suffrage Papers; Eaton, "Breaking a Path," p. 193; Madeline McDowell Breckinridge, "Kentucky Chapter Woman Suffrage History, 1900–1920," MMB Papers.

23. Lindig, "Woman's Movement in Louisiana," pp. 105, 106.

24. The University of Virginia became co-educational in the early 1970s. On the proposed co-ordinate college, see Anne Hobson Freeman, "Mary Munford's Fight for a College for Women Co-ordinate with the University of Virginia," *Virginia Magazine of History and Biography*, (October 1970): 482–491; Mary Johnston, "Speech on University Bill, Mother's Club, Mar. 30," 1910–1911 speeches, Johnston Papers.

25. Talmadge, *Rebecca Latimer Felton*, pp. 109–110; Taylor, "Revival and Development . . . Georgia," p. 341; Floyd, "Rebecca Latimer Felton: Champion of Women's Rights," pp. 91–93.

26. Floyd, "Rebecca Latimer Felton: Champion of Women's Rights," pp. 90–91.

27. Fuller, *Laura Clay*, pp. 163, 164, and 203.

28. Resolution adopted by the Alabama Equal Suffrage Association convention, 1915, Jacobs Scrapbook, Jacobs Papers; "Resolutions Adopted by the Equal Suffrage League of Virginia, November 14, 1917," Virginia Suffrage Papers; annual reports of the Mississippi Woman Suffrage Association, Somerville-Howorth Family Papers; Sue Shelton White, "Outline of Woman Suffrage and Progress of Women in Tennessee," White Papers; Taylor, "Revival and Progress . . . Georgia"; Floyd, "Rebecca Latimer Felton: Champion of Women's Rights"; Hay, "Madeline McDowell Breckinridge"; Madeline McDowell Breckinridge, "Kentucky Chapter Woman Suffrage History, 1900–1920"; and Breckinridge speech entitled "A New Hope," including quotation, MMB Papers.

29. Allen, "Woman Suffrage Movement in Alabama," (thesis), pp. 42, 43, 113; Taylor, *Woman Suffrage Movement in Tennessee*, p. 54.

30. For just a few examples, see "Resolutions Adopted by the Equal Suffrage League of Virginia, November 14, 1917," Virginia Suffrage Papers; Sue Shelton White, "Outline of Woman Suffrage and Progress of Women in Tennessee," White Papers; ERA Club stationery inscribed with list of the "fruits of the ERA Club's Policy of Initiation and Agitation," Kate Gordon to Alice Stone Blackwell, 18 July ?, NAWSA Papers.

31. Quotation from Mary Johnston, "Sentimental Idea Hurts Suffrage," *Woman's Journal*, 12 April 1913, Johnston Papers.

32. Nellie Nugent Somerville, undated speech, "Christian Charity"; *idem*, loose notes, ca. 1900, Somerville-Howorth Family Papers.

33. Clay, speech, "The Christian's Duty Is to be Free," delivered to the Mississippi Valley Woman Suffrage Conference, clipping from *The Woman's Standard*, Des Moines, Ella Harrison Papers; Johnston, suffrage speeches, 1910–1911, Johnston Papers.

34. Mary Johnston, "Speech: Woman's College Alumnae, May 31," suffrage speeches, 1910–1911, Johnston Papers.

35. McDowell, *Social Gospel in the South*, p. 134; Fuller, *Laura Clay*, pp. 162–164, quotation p. 163; Sue Shelton White to Molly Dewson, 23 November 1928, White Papers. On Felton as an advocate of equal rights for women in the church, see Floyd, "Rebecca Latimer Felton: Champion of Women's Rights," pp. 84, 85; and Felton, *Country Life*, pp. 62–65.

36. Kearney, *Slaveholder's Daughter*, pp. 40–41; White, "Mother's Daughter," in Showalter, ed., *These Modern Women*, p. 50.

37. Kearney, *Slaveholder's Daughter*, p. 49.

38. White, "Mother's Daughter," in Showalter, ed., *These Modern Women*, p. 51; Louis, "Sue Shelton White," NAW, III, pp. 590–592; Nancy F. Cott, "Feminist Politics in the 1920s: The National Woman's Party," *Journal of American History* 71 (June 1984): 43–68.

39. Scott, *Southern Lady*, p. 131; Kate Gordon to Laura Clay, 15 January 1918, Clay Papers.

40. Suffrage organizations in Virginia, Kentucky, and Alabama sponsored public lectures by Gilman. Virginia suffragists issued postcards bearing one of her poems. Virginia postcard found in LHMV Papers. On Gilman in Arkansas, see Taylor, "Woman Suffrage Movement in Arkansas," p. 37; clipping, 21 December 1913, Jacobs Scrapbook, Jacobs Papers; Both Breckinridge and Johnston arranged lectures for Gilman in their states. Breckinridge described Gilman to Clay as having "probably the keenest wit in the United States." Madeline McDowell Breckinridge to Laura Clay, 1 October 1913, MMB Papers. In one of her letters to Johnston, Gilman wrote, "You hold a high place in my pantheon of friends . . . I'm always meaning to tell you how much I appreciate your approval and friendliness." Charlotte Perkins Gilman to Mary Johnston, 1 August 1917. In another, Gilman suggested an idea for a novel. 13 February 1923; Gilman's influence is evident in Johnston's speeches assembled together as Suffrage Speeches, 1910–1911, Johnston Papers.

41. Clay quotation from Scott, *Southern Lady*, p. 131; Mary Johnston, *Hagar* (Boston: Houghton Mifflin, 1913), pp. 284, 285.

42. Johnston, *Hagar*, pp. 261, 300, 318.

43. White, "Mother's Daughter," in Showalter, *These Modern Women*, p. 52.

44. Gillian Goodrich, "Romance and Reality: The Birmingham Suffragists, 1892–1920," *The Journal of the Birmingham Historical Society* (January 1978), p. 11.

45. Laura Clay, folder of letters from 1905, Clay Papers; Hay, "Madeline McDowell Breckinridge," p. 222. Mary Johnston defended unmarried women as "good soldiers in the Woman's War," and spoke wistfully of their "brain children" who "are of great consequence in the future, but they do not fill the human arms." "The Woman's War," draft, p. 23, Johnston Papers.

46. John Talmadge in Horace Montgomery, ed., *Georgians in Profile* (Athens: University of Georgia Press, 1958), p. 288; Eaton, "Breaking a Path," p. 188; quotation on farm husbands and wives from LeeAnn Whites, "Rebecca Latimer Felton and the Wife's Farm: The Class and Racial Politics of Gender Reform," paper delivered at the Berkshire Conference on Women, June 1990.

47. Felton, *Country Life*, pp. 147–149; Eaton, "Breaking a Path," p. 188; Johnston, "Woman's War," draft, p. 20, Johnston Papers.

48. S. Breckinridge, *Madeline McDowell Breckinridge*, pp. 204, 205.

49. On Felton, see Talmadge, *Rebecca Latimer Felton*, pp. 113–118; Sims, *The Power of Femininity in the New South*; and Williamson, *Crucible of Race*, pp. 124–130. Mary Johnston would later write a short story entitled "Nemesis" about the "breakdown of civilization" in a small Southern town as a result of a lynching (see Chapter Four), Albert Spingarn to Mary Johnston, 7 May 1923, and Walter White to Mary Johnston, 28 December 1935, Johnston Papers; quotations from Kearney, *Slaveholder's Daughter*, pp. 95–97. Shortly

after the enfranchisement of women, a number of Southern white women led by a former suffragist, Jessie Daniel Ames of Texas, would publicly disclaim any "appreciation" of lynching, and demand its prevention by law enforcement agencies. For this remarkable story, see Jacquelyn Dowd Hall, *Revolt Against Chivalry*.

50. Nellie Nugent Somervile, notes for a speech, "Mother's Influence," 1900, Somerville-Howorth Family Papers; Tipton, "It Is My Duty," pp. 74, 75; Madeline McDowell Breckinridge, "A New Hope," MMB Papers.

51. Clipping, n.d., Somerville scrapbook, Somerville-Howorth Family Papers. In Texas, state suffrage president Minnie Cunningham acted as state chairman of the Texas Woman's Anti-Vice Committee to work for improvement of moral conditions in the vicinity of army camps, Taylor, "The Woman Suffrage Movement in Texas," p. 206; S. Breckinridge, *Madeline McDowell Breckinridge*, pp. 70–72. In 1913 Alabama suffragists engaged in a heated debate over a resolution to seek abolition of the so-called segregated districts (red light districts). Solon Jacobs, husband of Pattie Ruffner Jacobs, was strongly opposed, saying it was inexpedient and "not a subject for ladies to discuss on a parity with men. . . ." The association did, however, send representatives before the city commission seeking to have a vice commission appointed—an unsuccessful mission. Ethel Armes to Alice Stone Blackwell, 26 June 1913, Jacobs Papers.

52. Mary Johnston, "Woman's War," draft, p. 14, Johnston Papers; Floyd, "Rebecca Latimer Felton: Champion of Women's Rights," p. 94.

53. Madeline McDowell Breckinridge, speech, "New Hope"; and S. Breckinridge, *Madeline McDowell Breckinridge*, pp. 70–72.

54. Clipping, 1924 Scrapbook, Somerville-Howorth Family Papers; Wheeler interview with Judge Lucy Somerville Howorth, 15 March 1983.

55. Mary Johnston, "Woman's War," draft, p. 21; Johnston, "The Eugenical Point of View, Child Conference, May 25," 1910–1911 suffrage speeches, Johnston Papers.

56. Felton, *Country Life*, pp. 141–154; Johnston, *Hagar*, pp. 214–220; Belle Kearney, *Conqueror or Conquered: Or the Sex Challenge Answered*, 1921; 1911 Convention Report, MWSA, Somerville-Howorth Family Papers.

57. Madeline McDowell Breckinridge, "Direct Versus Indirect Influence in Kentucky," written for the New York *Evening Post*, 3 February 1914, MMB Papers.

58. Laura Clay Diary, 26 July 1874, Clay Papers.

59. Madeline McDowell Breckinridge, "The Prospect for Woman Suffrage in the South," clipping, Lexington *Herald*, October 1911, MMB Papers.

60. Nellie Nugent Somerville, "Are Women Too Good to Vote?" clipping, ca. 1914, Somerville-Howorth Family Papers.

61. *Ibid.*; Mary Johnston, "Speech: Woman's College Alumnae, May 31," suffrage speeches, 1910–1911, Johnston Papers.

62. On Cassius Marcellus Clay, see Fuller, *Laura Clay*, pp. 1–4, 14, 15; and the *Dictionary of American Biography*, I, pp. 169, 170; Laura Clay Diary, 25 October 1874, Clay Papers.

63. Mary Johnston, "Speech to Mother's Club, March 30," in suffrage speeches, 1910–1911; Mary Johnston, "Woman's War," draft, pp. 7, 11, 12, Johnston Papers.

64. Rosalind Rosenberg, "In Search of Woman's Nature, 1850–1920," *Feminist Studies* 3 (Fall 1975): 141–154; Rosalind Rosenberg, *Beyond Separate Spheres: Intellectual Roots of Modern Feminism* (New Haven: Yale University Press, 1982).

65. Marjorie Spruill (Wheeler), "Sex, Science, and 'the Woman Question': The *Woman's Journal* on Woman's Nature and Potential, 1870–1875," M.A. thesis, University of Virginia, 1980.

66. *Ibid.* Also see Margaret Fuller, *Woman in the Nineteenth Century*, 1948, and Antoinette Brown Blackwell, *The Sexes Throughout Nature*, 1875. Johnston's theories sound much like those of Blackwell and the other feminist defenders against the antifeminist "scientific" theories of the late nineteenth century. Blackwell, Thomas Wentworth Higginson, Julia Ward Howe, and others blended the romantic dualism of Fuller with the language of science used by Darwin, Spencer, etc., to form a defense of feminist goals based on a version of evolutionary theory.

67. Mary Johnston, "Woman's War," draft, pp. 6–14, Johnston Papers.

68. Clay quotation cited in a clipping from the Knoxville *Sentinel*, 1 February 1913, Clay Scrapbook, 1913; Clay, 1917 speech to a NAWSA conference to decide what the organization should do during the war, Clay Papers.

69. See Ted Ownby, *Subduing Satan: Religion, Recreation, and Manhood in the Rural South, 1865–1920* (Chapel Hill: University of North Carolina Press, 1990); Rebecca Latimer Felton, "On the Subjection and the Enfranchisement of Women," RLF Papers.

70. Laura Clay, draft of a speech, ca. 1919, Clay Papers.

71. "Who Takes Care of Mississippi Women," brochure signed by Somerville and published by the MWSA, Somerville-Howorth Family Papers.

72. Hay, "Madeline McDowell Breckinridge," pp. 139–140.

73. Mary Johnston, "Speech, Woman's Club Alumnae, May 31," 1910–1911 suffrage speeches, Johnston Papers.

74. Kraditor, *Ideas of the Woman Suffrage Movement*, Chapter Two, "Two Major Types of Suffragist Argument," pp. 38–63. A problem with this otherwise excellent study is exaggeration of the difference in suffrage arguments in the years before and after 1890. My own examination of the suffrage rhetoric in the *Woman's Journal* between 1870 and 1890 makes it clear that at least the Stone-Blackwell (AWSA) branch of the feminist movement used the "justice" and "expediency" arguments simultaneously; and certainly the Southern suffragists employed both types of arguments from 1890 through 1920.

75. Nellie Nugent Somerville to the editor of an unspecified Greenville, Mississippi, newspaper, 16 May ?, Scrapbook, Somerville-Howorth Family Papers; Laura Clay, Josephine Henry, and Sarah Sawyer for the KERA, "What the KERA Has Done and the Work for the Future," 1894, Clay Papers.

76. Floyd, "Rebecca Latimer Felton: Champion of Women's Rights," p. 86.

77. Pattie Ruffner Jacobs, "Tradition Vs. Justice," speech at the 1920 NAWSA "Jubilee Convention" in Chicago, reprinted in the *Southern Review* (Asheville, N.C.), May 1920, under the title "The Pulse of the South: How the South Really Feels About Woman Suffrage," clipping, Clay Papers; Mary Johnston, draft of a speech to be given in Philadelphia, 1910–1911 suffrage speeches, Johnston Papers.

78. Kearney, *Slaveholder's Daughter*; Pattie Ruffner Jacobs to Madeline

McDowell Breckinridge, 26 November 1914, MMB Papers. Jacobs sometimes gave a speech about "the contented woman" in which she insisted that indifference should not be taken for opposition. Allen, "Woman Suffrage Movement in Alabama," (thesis), pp. 122–123; Fuller, *Laura Clay*, p. 106.

79. Talmadge, *Rebecca Latimer Felton*, p. 129; S. Breckinridge, *Madeline McDowell Breckinridge*, pp. 186–188; Hay, "Madeline McDowell Breckinridge," p. 9.

80. McDowell, *Social Gospel in the South*, pp. 118, 119.

81. Mary Johnston, "The Woman Movement in the South," 1910–1911 suffrage speeches, Johnston Papers.

82. *Ibid.*; Kearney, *Slaveholder's Daughter*, p. 120.

83. Fuller, *Laura Clay*, p. 31.

Chapter 4: Southern Suffragists and "the Negro Problem"

1. From "Votes for Women," W. E. B. Du Bois, the *Crisis*, August 1914. Du Bois nevertheless supported woman suffrage because it was "just" and because he believed (like Southern antis) that the North's enfranchisement of all women would eventually force the South to do so or face a force bill. Du Bois also believed woman suffrage was important because African-American women were more likely to be educated than African-American men and "are moving quietly but forcibly toward the intellectual leadership of the race." (*Crisis*, September 1912). In a subsequent editorial (November 1917), Du Bois predicted that Southern white women would learn "political justice" faster than the men of their race. See Cynthia Neverdon-Morton, *Afro-American Women of the South and the Advancement of the Race, 1895–1925* (Knoxville: University of Tennessee Press, 1989), pp. 201–206.

2. Rebecca Latimer Felton, "The Subjection of Women and the Enfranchisement of Women," 15 May 1915, RLF Papers.

3. Kate Gordon to Laura Clay, 5 December 1907, Clay Papers.

4. For a thorough description and analysis of this campaign, see J. Morton Kousser, *The Shaping of Southern Politics: Suffrage Restriction and the Establishment of the One-Party South, 1880–1910* (New Haven: Yale University Press, 1974).

5. On the conservative motives for the enfranchisement of women in the West, see Alan P. Grimes, *The Puritan Ethic and Woman Suffrage* (New York: Oxford University Press, 1967).

6. Kate Gordon to Laura Clay, 30 May 1907, Clay Papers; Fuller, *Laura Clay*, p. 107; Mary Johnston to Lila Meade Valentine, 5 January 1913, and ? October 1915, LHMV Papers.

7. Belle Kearney, *Slaveholder's Daughter*, p. 97.

8. *Ibid.* pp. 62–64, 92.

9. Rebecca Latimer Felton, *Country Life*, pp. 10–11, 93; Talmadge, "Rebecca Latimer Felton," in Montgomery, *Georgians in Profile*, pp. 293, 294; Floyd, "Rebecca Latimer Felton: Champion of Women's Rights," pp. 83, 84; Joel Williamson, *Crucible of Race*, pp. 127–130.

10. Talmadge, "Rebecca Latimer Felton," in Montgomery, *Georgians in Profile*, pp. 292, 294; Kemp, "Jean and Kate Gordon," p. 393; Kate Gordon to Laura Clay, 30 May 1907, Clay Papers.

11. Nellie Nugent Somerville, "Italians in the Cotton States," article in

her 1906 scrapbook, Somerville-Howorth Family Papers; Belle Kearney, speech to the 1903 Southern States Woman Suffrage Conference Convention in New Orleans, clipping, November 1903, Kearney Papers. According to Dewey Grantham, many reformers of the Progressive era thought "black workers were unfit and unreliable and foreign immigration ought to be promoted." Grantham, *Southern Progressivism*, p. 300.

12. Laura Clay Diary, 26 July 1874, Clay Papers; Fuller, *Laura Clay*, pp. 54, 169, 170. Clay's father, Cassius Marcellus Clay, opposed the Reconstruction policies of the Republicans, supported Greeley in 1872 and 1876, and opposed integrated education at Berea College, which he helped establish. *Dictionary of American Biography*, pp. 169, 170.

13. Lila Meade Valentine to Mrs. Townsend of Norfolk, n.d., Virginia Suffrage Papers; Grantham, *Southern Progressivism*, pp. 126, 127. See the poem "A Southern Symphony" in a book of poems by Lila Meade Valentine's husband, Benjamin Batchelder Valentine, unpublished, collected by his brother Granville Valentine, and dated June 25, 1919. The poem was written in 1903–1904 by Ben Valentine, but I consider it indicative of Lila Valentine's views also, because of her handwritten comments on the manuscript: "This was written slowly during 2 years, partly in our library at 101 S. 3rd St., and during his summer vacation at the Warm. We had been for some time studying the negro question, secession, the war, and reconstruction. [Ben] felt impelled to make a true picture of life in the South and its reactions to these complex and tragic events, hence this poem. . . . He read it to many, both of the old South and the new South—all were equally impressed, with the truth and beauty of the survey." Valentine Papers. Lloyd Taylor, "LMV: The FFV as Reformer," pp. 471–487.

14. Pattie Ruffner Jacobs' papers provide fewer insights into her racial attitudes than is the case for the other younger suffragists. It is clear, however, that the ideas of Breckinridge, Johnston, and White resembled those of the relatively liberal Southern progressives Grantham described who were more aware of the need for new approaches to the South's racial problems and more hopeful about the future of race relations than most white Southerners. Their views were shaped by "compassion and paternalism." Their concern for the "uplift" of blacks was not as strong or as evident, however, as that of some Southern churchwomen, particularly of the Southern Methodist church, such as Lily Hardy Hammond, a champion of Paine College; Mary De Bardeleben, a "missionary" to American blacks; or Belle H. Bennett, sister of Clay's brother-in-law, and for many years president of the Woman's Home Mission Society. See Grantham, *Southern Progressivism*, pp. 234–239, and McDowell, *The Social Gospel in the South*, especially Chapter Four, "Extending the Kingdom to Blacks," pp. 84–115.

15. For descriptions of these women as Southern liberals, see S. Breckinridge, *Madeline McDowell Breckinridge*, pp. 54, 217–218, 259; "Personal Recollections of Sue Shelton White (1887–1943) by some of her friends and associates," 1959. Florence Armstrong, who shared a house with White for many years, observed, "She [White] had an ardent belief that 'Liberty and Justice for All' should really be for ALL and not for a select chosen race or level, not just in words but in reality, in everyday living." Also, Sue Shelton White, letter to the editor of *Harper's*, undated, White Papers; Elizabeth Johnston,

unpublished biography of Mary Johnston (1953), pp. 106, 107, Johnston Papers; S. Breckinridge, *Madeline McDowell Breckinridge*, pp. 54, 67, 72–75, 217–218, 259; Madeline McDowell Breckinridge to Dr. James H. Dillard, General Agent, Slater Fund, 13 April 1911.

16. On Vardaman, see "School Suffrage for Kentucky Women," speech, MMB Papers; Hay, "Madeline McDowell Breckinridge," p. 237.

17. Sue Shelton White, letter to the editor of *Harper's*, White Papers.

18. Mary Johnston, *The Slave Ship* (Boston: Little, Brown, and Company, 1924); Mary Johnston, *Hagar*; Mary Johnston to Lila Meade Valentine, 20 February 1915, LHMV Papers.

19. Elizabeth Johnston, unpublished biography of Mary Johnston, pp. 106, 107, Johnston Papers.

20. Johnston, *Slave Ship*; Walter White to Mary Johnston, 18 June 1923, and A. Spingarn to Mary Johnston, 7 May 1923, Johnston Papers.

21. Kearney, *Slaveholder's Daughter*, pp. 64, 92, 93; Rebecca Latimer Felton, *Romantic Story of Georgia Women*, p. 21; quotation from Felton, *Country Life in Georgia*, p. 79.

22. "Anti-tuberculosis Meeting," clipping, n.d., Somerville Scrapbook; Nellie Nugent Somerville, 1913 MWSA Convention Report, Somerville-Howorth Family Papers; Kearney, *Slaveholder's Daughter*, pp. 64–65.

23. Talmadge, *Rebecca Latimer Felton*, pp. lll, 128. Felton's opposition to child-labor legislation was partly owed to her fear such legislation would lead mill owners to hire black men and women instead of white boys and girls; Talmadge, "Rebecca Latimer Felton," in Montgomery, *Georgia Profiles*, pp. 293–294; Felton, *Romantic Story*, p. 21.

24. Kate Gordon to Alice Stone Blackwell, 18 July [1920], NAWSA Papers; Judge Lucy Somerville Howorth to Marjorie Spruill Wheeler, 26 December 1987 (the quotation related to Somerville is from Judge Howorth about her mother); Kearney, *Slaveholder's Daughter*, p. 96.

25. Wheeler interview with Judge Lucy Somerville Howorth. Judge Howorth said that the suffragists used these pragmatic arguments, but were also motivated by sincere humanitarianism; Kearney, *Slaveholder's Daughter*, pp. 95, 96.

26. Adella Hunt Logan, "Colored Women as Voters," the *Crisis*, Sept. 1912; Adele Logan Alexander, "How I Discovered My Grandmother: And the Truth About Black Women and the Suffrage Movement," *Ms.* (November 1983); Adele Logan Alexander, "Grandmother, Grandfather, W. E. B. Du Bois and Booker T. Washington," the *Crisis* (February 1983). On black women and suffrage, Cynthia Neverdon-Morton writes: "questions concerning the relative importance of promoting the vote for women generally versus continuing to work for both black male suffrage and their own rights as Afro-Americans and women . . . did receive some consideration by the black female intelligentsia, but were not subjects of continuous public debate. At no time did feminist views, largely articulated by white women, become more important than racial isses. It was not a matter of choice for black women; they understood clearly that advancement of women was meaningless if not accompanied by racial advancement." Yet, said Neverdon-Morton, black women found time to respond to both racial and gender issues. On their activities as suffragists and discrimination against them in the movement, see Neverdon-

Morton, *Afro-American Women of the South*, pp. 176–179, 202–206; and Kraditor, *Ideas of the Woman Suffrage Movement*, pp. 139–184.

27. Grantham, *Southern Progressivism*, p. 236. See Kousser, *Shaping of Southern Politics*, p. 1, for a full description of the myth about the nature of Reconstruction and the return to white supremacy so widespread in the South at the turn of the century; Nellie Nugent Somerville, "Lest We Forget," letter to the editor of the Memphis *Commercial Appeal*, 27 January 1946, written to protest revisionist views of Reconstruction, clipping, Somerville subject file, Mississippi Archives; Kearney, *Slaveholder's Daughter*, p. 16: see Chapter Two, "Changed Conditions," for her full description of Reconstruction. Mary Johnston, "Speech: Woman's College Alumnae, May 31," suffrage speeches, Johnston Papers; "Southern Symphony," Valentine Papers.

28. "Southern Symphony," Valentine Papers.

29. "The Prospect for Woman Suffrage in the South, Address of Mrs. Desha Breckinridge, Made at National Suffrage Convention in Louisville, October 29th, 1911," clipping from the Lexington *Herald*, n.d., MMB Papers.

30. Kousser, *Shaping of Southern Politics*; Laura Clay to Anna Howard Shaw, 30 October 1907, Clay Papers.

31. Rebecca Latimer Felton, pamphlet, "The Subjection of Women and the Enfranchisement of Women," 15 May 1915, Felton Papers. For Kearney's views, see the full text of her address to the 1903 NAWSA Convention in New Orleans, clipping from Charleston, S.C., *Sunday News*, Kearney Papers; Kate Gordon to Laura Clay, 6 November 1913, Clay Papers; Hay, "Madeline McDowell Breckinridge," p. 198.

32. Fuller, *Laura Clay*, pp. 54, 202 n. 45; Jemison, "Ladies Become Voters," p. 58; Madeline McDowell Breckinridge to Miss Mary Winser, Haverford, Pa., 1 January 1912, Clay Papers.

33. Madeline McDowell Breckinridge to Miss Mary Winser, 1 January 1912, Clay Papers.

34. S. Breckinridge, *Madeline McDowell Breckinridge*, pp. 217, 218; Adella Hunt Logan, the daughter of a black/Creek Indian mulatto and a wealthy white planter, received a bachelor's degree (1881) and master's degree (1905) from Atlanta University. Logan, who was light-skinned, occasionally attended suffrage meetings without revealing her racial identity. After a private meeting with Carrie Chapman Catt before a suffrage meeting in Atlanta in 1901, she wrote to a friend that she "could not resist the temptation to stay in the meeting a while, observing how the superior sister does things. You know a number of colored women would have done it more intelligently, and yet if [the white Southern suffragists] had known me, I would have been ordered out in no very gracious manner." Logan had the courage to publish her suffrage views in the *Crisis* and to support the views of W. E. B. Du Bois, which alienated her from family and friends in Tuskegee. This stressful situation, and her frustration with the racism and sexism with which she was constantly at war, led to a deepening depression and finally suicide. Alexander, "How I Discovered My Grandmother," and "Grandmother, Grandfather, W. E. B. Du Bois and Booker T. Washington." Jemison, "Ladies Become Voters"; Albert Spingarn to Mary Johnston, 7 May 1923, Johnston Papers; [White], letter to the editor, *Harper's*, White Papers.

35. Anna Howard Shaw, *Story of a Pioneer*, pp. 313, 314. There are numerous examples of the SSWSC stationery in the Clay Papers and other

manuscript collections of these suffragists. The Jacobs quotation is from Taylor, "Woman Suffrage Movement in North Carolina," p. 177.

36. Kearney, *Slaveholder's Daughter*, p. 185; Kate Gordon to Official Board (NAWSA), [July-August, 1911], cited in Fuller, *Laura Clay*, p. 202, n. 45. There is no way to ascertain if Gordon's speculations were correct. It is significant, however, that four of the six black delegates to the South Carolina constitutional convention of 1895 supported the woman suffrage proposal, even with property and educational qualifications meant to disqualify black women. Their leader indicated that even with its limitations, the suffrage proposal if passed would be a small victory for human rights, and that he hoped to "live to see both black and white women [voting] together." See Barbara Bellows (then Ulmer), "Virginia Durant Young: New South Suffragist," pp. 66, 78, 79. Adella Hunt Logan also lamented the opposition of "ignorant" men to the enfranchisement of women and was outraged that in California, a "heathen" Chinaman could vote while Mrs. Stanford, the founder of Stanford University, could not. Logan wrote, "Oh, the accident of sex! One humiliating feature of the case is that the right of suffrage is withheld from women largely by ignorant and vicious men. A large proportion of the best educated men are ardently in favor of the reform albeit not all find it expedient to express their sentiment." Adella Hunt Logan, "Woman Suffrage," *The Colored American Magazine* 9 (September 1906): 487–489. A November 1917 editorial in the *Crisis*, urging support for woman suffrage, lamented the fact that the majority of black men opposed woman suffrage, partly because of their resentment of the racism of white suffragists and partly because the black man "looked forward to the time when his wages will be large enough to support his wife and daughters in comparative idleness at home." Neverdon-Morton, *Afro-American Women of the South*, p. 204.

37. Lila Meade Valentine, "President's Address" to Equal Suffrage League of Virginia, 12 November 1917, LHMV Papers.

38. On the motives of the suffragists, see Chapters Two and Three. In the Kraditor/Scott controversy over the centrality of racism as a *motive* of white Southern suffragists, I agree with Anne Scott that "it is beyond any doubt that southern women wanted the vote primarily because of their concern about the place of women in the world, not because of their concern about the place of Negroes." Kraditor, *Ideas of the Woman Suffrage Movement*, p. 173; and Scott, *Southern Lady*, pp. 182, 183 and n. 33.

39. On Blackwell's letter to the Southern legislatures and for the full text of the letter, see Aileen S. Kraditor, ed., *Up from the Pedestal: Selected Writings in the History of American Feminism* (New York: Quadrangle, 1968), pp. 253–257; Lois Bannister Merk, "Massachusetts in the Woman Suffrage Movement," Ph.D. diss., Harvard University, 1961, p. 232.

40. Henry Blackwell to Laura Clay, 21 November 1885, Clay Papers; Fuller, *Laura Clay*, pp. 54–56. Aileen Kraditor dubbed the argument that the enfranchisement of women in the South, given the numerical superiority of whites to blacks and thus of white women to black women, would guarantee white supremacy, the "statistical argument." Kraditor, *Up from the Pedestal*, p. 253.

41. Merk, "Massachusetts in the Woman Suffrage Movement," pp. 233, 234.

42. On the Mississippi convention, see *Journal of the Proceedings of the Con-*

stitutional Convention of the State of Mississippi Begun in the City of Jackson on August 12, 1890 and Concluded November 1, 1890, pp. 79, 134. According to A. Elizabeth Taylor, the resolution provided that (to avoid appearing in person at the polls) women voters could authorize male electors to cast their votes for them. It also specified that enfranchisement did not authorize women to hold public office. The Vicksburg *Commercial Appeal* formally endorsed the resolution as an "eminently suitable method of disposing of a difficult problem . . . (that is) open to no constitutional objection." Taylor, "Woman Suffrage Movement in Mississippi," pp. 207–210; Fuller, *Laura Clay*, pp. 54–57. For evidence that consideration of the suffrage measure by the Mississippi convention inspired the national leaders to organize in the South, see Nellie Nugent Somerville's 1898 "Presidential Address" at the Mississippi Woman Suffrage Association convention. Somerville directly attributed the formation of their organization to the actions of the constitutional convention, "observed by our friends in NAWSA," who later sent organizers to the state in 1897. She announced a plan to send immediately letters of inquiry to the convention delegates who had favored woman suffrage. "President's Address, 1898 MWSA Convention," Somerville-Howorth Family Papers.

43. Fuller, *Laura Clay*, pp. 44, 56, 57; Taylor, "Woman Suffrage Movement in Mississippi," pp. 207–210.

44. Elizabeth Cady Stanton, *Eighty Years and More: Reminiscences 1815–1897*, (New York: Schocken Books, 1971), reprinted from 1898 original, pp. 255, 256; Lois W. Banner, *Elizabeth Cady Stanton: A Radical for Woman's Rights* (Boston: Little, Brown and Company, 1980), p. 100. On the increasing conservatism of the NAWSA on the race issue, see Kraditor, *Ideas of the Woman Suffrage Movement*, especially pp. 141–144. Of the prominent national leaders of the woman suffrage movement in the late nineteenth century, Anthony seemed the least afflicted by racism. Yet she was becoming ever more intent upon winning suffrage and eager for the NAWSA to disassociate itself from radical causes.

45. Carrie Chapman Catt and Nettie Rogers Shuler, *Woman Suffrage and Politics*, p. 230; Kraditor, *Up from the Pedestal*, pp. 257–262; Cott, "Feminist Politics in the 1920s, pp. 43–68.

46. Catt and Shuler, *Woman Suffrage and Politics*, pp. 227–231; Fuller, *Laura Clay*, pp. 57–59.

47. Clay's notebook records her correspondence with Southern Committee officers and her work as chair of the Southern Committee, 1892–1895, Clay Papers. Catt's efforts in the South were not as extensive as Clay's would have been had she been allowed to operate the Southern Committee as an autonomous unit, and Clay was unhappy that Catt did not reserve for exclusive use in the South the contributions made by Southern women for Southern suffrage work. See Laura Clay to Sarah Clay Bennett, [1898], and C. C. Catt to Laura Clay, 13 January 1899, Clay Papers.

48. The tour began in Lexington and continued in major cities and many small towns in Kentucky, Tennessee, Louisiana, Mississippi, Alabama, South Carolina, and Virginia. Susan B. Anthony to Laura Clay, 21 September 1894, Clay Papers. On the decision to hold the convention in Atlanta, and on the convention, see Taylor, "Origin of the Woman Suffrage Movement in Georgia," pp. 68–70. On the Atlanta convention, see Ida Husted Harper and Susan B. Anthony, *History of Woman Suffrage* 4: 236–251; Terborg-Penn, "Discrimina-

tion Against Afro-American Women in the Woman's Movement, 1830–1920," p. 24; on Douglass' record, see Benjamin Quarles, "Frederick Douglass and the Woman's Rights Movement," *Journal of Negro History* 25 (January 1940): 35–44; Bellows, "Virginia Durant Young," pp. 44–46.

49. Fuller, *Laura Clay*, pp. 63–72; Bellows, "Virginia Durant Young."

50. Fuller, *Laura Clay*, pp. 67–69; Taylor, "Woman Suffrage Movement in Mississippi," p. 209.

51. Fuller, *Laura Clay*, pp. 68, 69. On the measures adopted at the South Carolina convention, see Jack Temple Kirby, *Darkness at the Dawning: Race and Reform in the Progressive South* (Philadelphia: J.B. Lippincott Company, 1972), p. 151. For other suffragists' comments on this strategy, see Belle Kearney, 1903 address to the NAWSA Convention, Kearney Papers; Kate Gordon to Laura Clay, 6 November 1913, and Gordon to state presidents, 3 July 1913, Clay Papers. On the need of the disfranchisers to gain the support of the white masses for suffrage restriction, see Kousser, *Shaping of Southern Politics*.

52. Carrie Chapman Catt to Viola Neblitt, 16 November 1895, Clay Papers; Carrie Chapman Catt to Ella Harrison, 10 April 1896, Harrison Papers; "President's Address, 1898 MWSA Convention," Somerville-Howorth Family Papers.

53. Catt addressed the conventions in Louisiana and Virginia, accompanied by local suffragists. See accounts of these appeals at the constitutional conventions in Lindig, "Woman's Movement in Louisiana," pp. 147–149; Sheldon, "Woman Suffrage and Virginia Politics," pp. 10–11; *Official Proceedings of the Constitutional Convention of the State of Alabama . . . 1901* (Wetumpka, Ala., 1940) I: 322–331; II: 1388–1389, and III: 3855–3879. Also Allen, "Woman Suffrage Movement in Alabama" (thesis), pp. 12, 13, including quotation; and Goodrich, "Romance and Reality," pp. 4–21. On Kate Gordon, see Kemp, "Jean and Kate Gordon," p. 392.

54. Anna Howard Shaw, *Story of a Pioneer*, pp. 310–311; Lindig, "Woman's Movement in Louisiana," pp. 159–160; Kraditor, *Ideas of the Woman Suffrage Movement*, pp. 139, 140.

55. The text of Belle Kearney's address appears in a clipping from the Charleston, S.C., *Sunday News*, 12 April 1903, Kearney Papers.

56. *Ibid.*

57. *Ibid.*

58. Kousser, *Shaping of Southern Politics*, pp. 31, 32; Fuller, *Laura Clay*, pp. 94–112. On the period of diminished activity in the Southern states, see the various state studies.

59. Harriet Taylor Upton to Lida Calvert Obenchain, 4 September 1906, Clay Papers.

60. The last suffrage victory had been achieved in Utah in 1896. In 1910, the NAWSA began winning a string of crucial victories, beginning in Washington (1910), California (1911), Oregon (1912), Kansas (1912), and Arizona (1912). See NAWSA, *Victory*, Appendix 4; Fuller, *Laura Clay*, pp. 102–104.

61. Belle Kearney to Anna Howard Shaw, 29 October 1906; Shaw to Business Committee, 15 November 1906; Shaw to Belle Kearney, 15 November 1906; Shaw to Business Committee, 24 November 1906, Clay Papers.

62. Kearney was eager for Clay to attend the conference because of Clay's prestige with Southern suffragists. Shaw was torn between her desire to have Clay monitor and restrain Kearney and fear that Clay's participation

would be interpreted as an official NAWSA sanction: Anna Howard Shaw to Laura Clay, 15 November 1906; Shaw to Business Committee, 15 November 1906, Clay Papers. The conference created the "Southern Woman Suffrage Conference" and issued a statement urging Southern suffragists to seek presidential suffrage (which might be easier to obtain as it could be granted by legislatures without a constitutional amendment or a referendum) or constitutional amendments with an educational qualification. Clipping, "A Southern Suffrage Movement," from the *Woman's Journal*, 29 December 1906, Kearney Papers; Henry Blackwell believed the conference to be the beginning of a campaign that would make woman suffrage a national Democratic issue that would generate suffrage victories throughout the South and the West. H. Blackwell to Laura Clay, 28 December 1906, Clay Papers.

63. Northern and Southern suffragists generally believed Mississippi might be a promising state because of the 1890 convention incident, and because several prominent politicians, including Senator John Sharp Williams and James K. Vardaman, were for woman suffrage—though absolutely opposed to enfranchising black women. Kate Gordon wrote to Anna Howard Shaw that Mississippi women were very encouraged, as Vardaman "repeatedly committed himself to woman suffrage . . . in the recent senatorial campaign," and the Democratic gubernatorial nominee Edmund Noel had written Gordon, "coming out flat-footed for woman suffrage." Kate Gordon to Anna Howard Shaw, 15 October 1907; Henry Blackwell to Laura Clay, 11 September 1907; Kate Gordon to Laura Clay, 30 May 1907; Laura Clay to Kate Gordon, 17 September 1907; Laura Clay to Henry Blackwell, 17 September 1907; Laura Clay to Kate Gordon, 8 October 1907; Kate Gordon to Laura Clay, 11 October 1907; Laura Clay to Henry Blackwell, 22 September 1907; Kate Gordon to Laura Clay, 1 October 1907; Kate Gordon to Henry Blackwell, 1 October 1907, in which she says "I would not give ten cents towards securing presidential suffrage"; Clay Papers.

64. Clay's letter to Blackwell of 22 September 1907 fully explains her reasoning at this point. Included is the statement that "hitherto I have supposed that the 15th amendment forbade any discrimination in terms which could not be evaded. But recent manipulations of the suffrage makes it seem possible that a distinction be made." And she quoted a passage from Alexander McElway's article in the *Outlook*, September 14, 1907, p. 64, saying that the Fifteenth Amendment did not forbid any *extension* of the suffrage to any class. Clay stated "there is an opinion among some very well-informed people that there is a possibility of extending the suffrage to white women without a similar extension to black ones." She thought the constitutionality of the issue should be tested in Mississippi, and if it was upheld, "we may all hope to live to see the day when all Southern women would be enfranchised; and I do not think the North would linger behind." Clay Papers.

65. For Shaw's assessment of Kearney relative to Clay and Gordon, see Shaw to members of the Business Committee, 25 October 1907; see series of letters from Henry Blackwell to Laura Clay: 25 September 1907; 28 September 1907; 5 October 1907; 7 October 1907 (includes reference to black women's need for the vote); 10 October 1907, in which he says Mrs. (Harriet) Kells and Mrs. (Lily Wilkinson) Thompson expressed to Kearney "a preference for asking for full suffrage by government resolve for *white* women only"; 14 October 1907; 17 October 1907; and Belle Kearney to Henry Black-

well, 1 October 1907. Kate Gordon to Anna Howard Shaw, 15 October 1907. On Somerville, see Myers interview with Judge Lucy Somerville Howorth; and Laura Clay to Henry Blackwell, 5 December 1907, Clay Papers.

66. Kate Gordon to Anna Howard Shaw, 15 October 1907. Henry Blackwell opposed Gordon's suggestion of asking the NAWSA for help, saying "that would be a *divisive* suggestion, and would be a very dangerous step." 5 October 1907. In another letter he wrote, "Of course I cannot solicit my Northern friends and coworkers to contribute for white suffrage, nor should I approve of asking the National American for contributions on that basis. It must be a strictly southern movement by Southern women." Henry Blackwell to Laura Clay, 10 October 1907, 17 October 1907; Laura Clay to Henry Blackwell, 14 October 1907; Laura Clay to Anna Howard Shaw, 30 October 1907, Clay Papers.

67. Kraditor, *Ideas of the Woman Suffrage Movement,* pp. 161, 162; Alice Stone Blackwell to Laura Clay (copy to Gordon), 6 October 1907, Clay Papers.

68. Alice Stone Blackwell to Laura Clay (copy to Gordon), 6 October 1907; quotations from Chicago *Tribune,* 15 February 1907, from Fuller, *Laura Clay,* p. 107.

69. For Henry Blackwell's defense of seeking woman suffrage with an educational qualification in both North and South, see Anthony and Shuler, *History of Woman Suffrage* 4: 246; Anna Howard Shaw to Business Committee, 25 October 1907, Clay Papers.

70. Laura Clay to Henry Blackwell, 14 October 1907, Clay Papers. Clay expressed similar views in her letter to Anna Howard Shaw, 30 October 1907, in which she also said, "I am in favor of obtaining the right of white women to vote, if I can, even if the negro women will still have to wait awhile for the fit ones among them to vote. I do not think their chances for enfranchisement are delayed by this procedure, but to the contrary. This move may be the speediest for the enfranchisement of all women north and south."

71. Kate Gordon to Laura Clay, 11 October 1907, and 12 November 1907, Clay Papers.

72. Laura Clay to Kate Gordon, 12 December 1907; Laura Clay to Catharine Waugh McCulloch, 13 December 1907; Kate Gordon to Laura Clay, 14 December 1907, Clay Papers.

73. Kate Gordon to Anna Howard Shaw, 15 October 1907; Laura Clay to Henry Blackwell, 5 December 1907, Clay Papers. Throughout the suffrage campaign (to 1920), both Clay and Gordon continued to have warm relationships with many Northern leaders with whom they had ideological differences, including Alice Stone Blackwell. Their relations with Catt and Shaw, however, definitely soured.

74. Kate Gordon to state presidents, 3 July 1913; Kate Gordon to Laura Clay, 6 November 1913; Johnson, "Kate Gordon and the Woman Suffrage Movement in the South," p. 376–377. For the letter claiming credit for the SSWSC, see Kate Gordon to members of the official board, NAWSA, 23 June 1915, NAWSA Papers.

75. Kate Gordon to Catharine Waugh McCulloch, 19 August 1915, McCulloch Papers.

76. "The Prospect for Woman Suffrage in the South: Address of Mrs. Desha Breckinridge, Made at National Suffrage Convention in Louisville, October 29th, 1911," clipping from Lexington *Herald,* 1912, MMB Papers.

77. Mary Johnston to Lila Meade Valentine, 5 January 1913, LHMV Papers; Hanmer, "Divine Discontent," p. 48.

78. Statistics from Fuller, *Laura Clay*, p. 107; Nellie Nugent Somerville, "Arguments to Be Met: MWSA," "Report of Legislative Work, 1914"; letter to the editor, Greenville *Times-Democrat*, clipping, n.d., in Scrapbook, 1909–1912, Somerville-Howorth Family Papers.

79. Antisuffrage literature, NAWSA Papers.

80. Lila Meade Valentine to Mrs. Townsend, 10 April 1915; Valentine's "President's Address," 12 November 1917, Virginia Suffrage Papers.

81. See antisuffrage literature in the Clay Papers, sent to Clay in late June or early July, 1919, by Martin Lee Calhoun of Alabama; also antisuffrage literature, NAWSA Papers.

82. Kate Gordon to Southern suffragists, 31 May 1915, Virginia Suffrage Papers.

83. See pamphlets issued by the Equal Suffrage Association of North Carolina, North Carolina Collection, Wilson Library, University of North Carolina, Chapel Hill; Kate Gordon to Mrs. Jessie Townsend, 13 May 1915, Virginia Suffrage Papers. That disfranchisement had been realized and the statistical argument was a moot point did not prevent suffragists from using it occasionally. For example, as the NWP began to organize in the South, the NWP paper *The Suffragist* tried this tactic. See Bland, "Fighting the Odds," p. 35.

84. Quotation from Kraditor, *Ideas of the Woman Suffrage Movement*, p. 156; clipping, n.d., Jacobs Scrapbook, Jacobs Papers.

85. Mary Johnston to Lila Meade Valentine, 5 January 1913, LHMV Papers.

86. Mary Johnston to Lila Meade Valentine, 29 September 1913; Valentine to Johnston, 8 November 1915; quotation from Johnston to Valentine, October 1915, LHMV Papers.

87. Mary Johnston to Lila Meade Valentine, 5 January 1913, LHMV Papers.

88. Sue Shelton White to the editor, *Harper's* Magazine, n.d., White Papers.

Chapter 5: Women's Rights and States' Rights: Dissension in "the Solid South"

1. Kate Gordon to Ida Porter Boyer, 16 September 1918, Clay Papers.

2. Pattie Ruffner Jacobs speech, "Tradition Vs. Justice," given at the 1920 NAWSA "Jubilee Convention," Chicago, reprinted under the title "Pulse of the South." Clay Papers.

3. Mary Johnston to Lila Meade Valentine, 18 August 1912. Mary and her sister Eloise helped make the arrangements for a monument at Vicksburg to their father's old company. He was a major in the Confederate artillery and served under his cousin General Joseph E. Johnston. Elizabeth Johnston's 1953 draft of an unpublished biography of Mary Johnston, Johnston Papers; quotation from Anne Goodwyn Jones, *Tomorrow Is Another Day: The Woman Writer in the South, 1859–1936* (Baton Rouge: Louisiana State University Press, 1981) , p. 186.

4. Ellen Glasgow to Lila Meade Valentine, 1 July 1912, LHMV Papers.

5. Somerville quoted in Johnson, "Kate Gordon and the Woman Suffrage Movement in the South," p. 381.

6. Catt and Shuler, *Woman Suffrage and Politics*, p. 27.

7. For examples of 1890s-era support for the federal amendment and national as well as state legislation, see: "Minutes of the Mississippi Woman Suffrage Association Convention," 1899, Somerville-Howorth Family Papers; Taylor, "Revival and Development . . . Georgia," p. 341. Kate Gordon described the amendment as "a good form of suffrage agitation" as long as the amendment was not a real possibility, in the *New Citizen* 3 (January 1914): 4, Clay Papers. Examples of Southern suffragists' belief that a federal amendment was a long shot, 1912–1914, include: Valentine to Johnston in 1912, "woman suffrage can scarcely be expected to come about through federal action, but is distinctly a state issue." Lila Meade Valentine to Mary Johnston, 22 August 1912, Johnston Papers; Madeline McDowell Breckinridge said in 1914, "I still consider that the Washington end [work for the federal amendment] is more for purposes of agitation than with the hope of results; but I believe that if some of us press hard enough at Washington, there is much more hope of results at home." Madeline McDowell Breckinridge to Kate Gordon, 19 April 1914, cited in S. Breckinridge, *Madeline McDowell Breckinridge*, p. 215.

8. On the adoption of the NAWSA's "states' rights" policy toward its members, see Kraditor, *Ideas of the Woman Suffrage Movement*, pp. 139, 140; Kate Gordon, in the *New Citizen* 3 (January 1914): 4, Clay Papers; Fuller, *Laura Clay*, p. 140.

9. O'Neill, *Everyone Was Brave*, p. 128.

10. Morgan, *Suffragists and Democrats*, pp. 84–99.

11. *Ibid.*, pp. 89–90.

12. Fuller, *Laura Clay*, pp. 113–127, quotation p. 123. Clay ran afoul of Shaw when Clay persuaded the NAWSA's Executive Board to continue the 1908 Oklahoma campaign when Shaw wanted it abandoned. Shaw declared that she would have her own way more often and the other officers could "like it or lump it," and that she was "tired of being bossed and bullied by Miss Clay."

13. Fuller, *Laura Clay*, pp. 123–127.

14. Kate Gordon to Laura Clay, 29 June 1915, Clay Papers.

15. At the conference between Kate Gordon and Nellie Nugent Somerville, they decided to send out invitations to all Southern suffrage associations asking their cooperation in the formation of a federation of Southern suffrage associations loyal to the NAWSA but designed to promote suffrage work in the South. Judith Hyams Douglass, ERA Club vice-president, sent out these letters. Judith Hyams Douglass to Laura Clay, 13 February 1912; Laura Clay to Judith Hyams Douglass, 19 February 1912, Clay Papers. After the Louisville convention, Somerville did not attend any more national conventions until 1914. She believed that her displeasure with events at the Louisville convention led some in Shaw's camp to regard her as anti-administration. Somerville later defended herself against this claim, saying that she did not hold Shaw "responsible for all her officers may do." Nellie Nugent Somerville to Catharine Waugh McCul-

loch, 13 June ? (probably 1915), McCulloch Papers; Clay quoted in Fuller, *Laura Clay*, p. 128; Kate Gordon to Laura Clay, 30 September 1913, Clay Papers.

16. Fuller, *Laura Clay*, pp. 128–144, quotation p. 128.

17. On Sophonisba Breckinridge and Clay, see Fuller, *Laura Clay*, pp. 125, 128; Laura Clay to Alice Stone Blackwell, 30 January 1912, Clay Papers; Kate Gordon to Catharine McCulloch, 6 June 1911, McCulloch Papers; Kate Gordon to Laura Clay and Ida Porter Boyer, 2 February 1914; Kate Gordon to Laura Clay, 30 September 1913, Clay Papers.

18. One of Gordon's many statements along these lines was her "Open Letter to the Members of the National Woman Suffrage Association," the *New Citizen* 3 (January 1914): 4, Clay Papers. It was also published in the *Woman's Journal*. Kate Gordon to Ida Porter Boyer, 16 September 1918, Clay Papers.

19. Fuller, *Laura Clay*, pp. 153, 154. See copy of Clay's speech for the 1916 NAWSA Convention at Atlantic City, "Shall Work Be Dropped on the Federal Amendment and Efforts Confined to State Legislation?" Laura Clay to Catharine McCulloch, 13 December 1907, Clay Papers.

20. Laura Clay to Judith Hyams Douglass, 19 February 1912; Laura Clay to Kate Gordon, 30 July 1913, Clay Papers.

21. Reprinted in Dr. Anna Howard Shaw, "Woman's Suffrage: Suffrage in the 'Solid South,'" from *The Trend*, clipping in the McCulloch Papers.

22. Johnson, "Kate Gordon and Woman Suffrage," p. 369.

23. See clippings describing the organizational meeting and giving lists of officers, Kearney Papers.

24. On Gordon and her rival suffrage club, see Kate Gordon to Laura Clay, 23 July 1913, Clay Papers; also see Johnson, "Kate Gordon and Woman Suffrage," n. 9.

25. Kate Gordon to Laura Clay and Ida Porter Boyer, 2 February 1914; Kate Gordon to SSWSC officers, 11 February 1914, Clay Papers.

26. "Open Letter to the Members of the National Woman Suffrage Association," the *New Citizen* 3 (January 1914), 4. Clay Papers; see also Gordon's speech to the 1914 SSWSC convention, quoted at length in a supplement to the Chattanooga *News*, 10 November 1914.

27. See clippings describing the organizational meeting, Kearney Papers. Somerville is sometimes presented as more of an extremist on states' rights than she really was. When she opposed ratification of the Child Labor Amendment in 1924, she insisted she was opposed, not to a federal child labor amendment *per se*, but to the amendment "in its present form." Still, she acknowledged strong reservations about "turning over the childhood of the state to the federal government" under "such a sweeping grant of power." Clipping, Nellie Nugent Somerville scrapbook, Somerville-Howorth Family Papers. According to her daughter Judge Lucy Somerville Howorth, Nellie Somerville believed the amendment set the age of restriction too low. She seemed to believe the measure would regulate chores around home and farm, not just in factories. Wheeler interview with Judge Lucy Somerville Howorth.

28. Clippings, Kearney Papers.

29. See clippings describing the organizational meeting and Kearney's speech at the 1903 NAWSA Convention in New Orleans; literature advertis-

ing her as a lecturer; and the 1922 campaign brochure "Miss Belle Kearney and Her Life Work," all in the Kearney Papers. Also see Tipton, "It Is My Duty," pp. 27, 48, 49, 61, 64. Last quotations, pp. 48, 49.

30. Clipping, Kearney Papers; Mary Johnston, who was unable to attend the conference, commented to Valentine that the "Governor letter" seemed all right, but she believed it was a mistake to say at the close "'to support a National Amendment, *weighted with the same objections as the Fifteenth Amendment*' [her emphasis]. I see no use in calling that to the attention of these men." Mary Johnston to Lila Meade Valentine, 2 September 1913 (misdated 1893) LHMV Papers.

31. Clipping, Kearney Papers; "An Address by Miss Kate M. Gordon of New Orleans, delivered at the Southern States Woman Suffrage Conference in Chattanooga, November 10, 1914," SSWSC Press Bulletin, Clay Papers; Laura Clay to A. C. Prive, 28 November 1914, Clay Papers. The resolution was passed by the delegates to the convention calling on the NAWSA's Congressional Committee to "invest and promote the right of women to vote for U.S. Congressmen and Senators and Presidential Electors, by Congressional action," i.e., to support Clay's bill. It was signed by Clay, Medill McCormick, Kate Gordon, Nellie Nugent Somerville, Rebecca Latimer Felton, and Anna Howard Shaw, among others. Dated 23 November 1914, Clay Papers. See also the "Woman's Equal Suffrage Edition," a special edition of the Chattanooga *News*, issued by Chattanooga Equal Suffrage Association, 1 November 1914.

32. Somerville was being cautious and somewhat generous when she said of Gordon, "I think Miss Gordon has confused her own personal feeling, or her own personal comment with the deliberate action of the Conference. I am quite sure that Miss Gordon would not knowingly make a mis-statement any more than I would/but I must be shown the record, or the testimony of other persons present, before I will concede that I am mistaken." Comment on letter to members of the national board, 23 June 1915, Somerville-Howorth Family Papers.

33. Clipping from the New York *Tribune*, 2 December 1913, about the New York convention, Jacobs Scrapbook, Jacobs Papers; Kate Gordon to "The Officers of the SSWSC," 11 February 1914, Clay Papers; "Open Letter to the Members of the National Woman Suffrage Association," the *New Citizen* 3 (January 1914): 4. Clay Papers.

34. "Open Letter to the Members of the National Woman Suffrage Association," the *New Citizen* 3 (January 1914): 4, Clay Papers.

35. *Ibid*.

36. Kate Gordon to Laura Clay and Ida Porter Boyer, 2 February 1914; Kate Gordon to NAWSA officers, 13 April 1914; Kate Gordon to Laura Clay, 1 March 1914, Clay Papers.

37. Elinor Byrns, chair of the NAWSA National Press Bureau, 31 December 1913. Sophonisba Breckinridge and Jane Addams hoped that Shaw could be persuaded to step down from the NAWSA presidency if promised financial security, and were working through a Mrs. Leonard to try to arrange it. See Sophonisba Breckinridge to Madeline McDowell Breckinridge, 13 June 1914, 23 November 1914, and 4 November 1914, in which Sophonisba said that she and Jane Addams believed Madeline Breckinridge was "the very best presidential material in the country—that we thought you had the temper for the

position, judicial, and calm and fair; and that you had the brains and would have a great deal of support." Madeline McDowell Breckinridge to Sophonisba, 3 November 1914, MMB Papers. Melba Porter Hay explains that Madeline Breckinridge was willing to accept the NAWSA presidency if Shaw would step down but was hesitant to fight her for it. In caucuses before the Nashville convention, Shaw refused to step down and allow "Madge" to become president. Afterward it was understandably difficult for the two women to work together, so Breckinridge resigned from the NAWSA board. Hay, "Madeline McDowell Breckinridge," p. 159, *passim.*

38. Dr. Anna Howard Shaw, "Suffrage in the 'Solid South,'" in *The Trend,* clipping in the McCulloch Papers; clipping from the New York *Tribune,* 2 December 1913 about New York convention, Jacobs Scrapbook, Jacobs Papers.

39. S. Breckinridge, *Madeline McDowell Breckinridge,* pp. 209, 214–215; clippings, Jacobs Scrapbook, Jacobs Papers.

40. Laura Clay to Kate Gordon, 21 October 1914, Clay Papers; Madeline McDowell Breckinridge to Kate Gordon, 29 April 1914, Kate Gordon to Madeline McDowell Breckinridge, 15 May 1914, Madeline McDowell Breckinridge to Kate Gordon, 23 November 1914, MMB Papers.

41. Description of Breckinridge's attitude from Harriet Taylor Upton to Madeline McDowell Breckinridge, 27 February 1914, MMB Papers; and S. Breckinridge, *Madeline McDowell Breckinridge,* pp. 214, 215, quotation p. 215; Madeline McDowell Breckinridge to Mrs. E. M. Kahn, 15 April 1914, MMB Papers; Madeline McDowell Breckinrige to Kentucky congressional delegation, 21 December 1914, MMB Papers.

42. Jacobs' first reaction described in Kate Gordon to NAWSA officers, 13 April 1914, Clay Papers; Jacobs quotation in clipping from the Montgomery *Advertiser,* 21 November 1914, Jacobs Scrapbook, Jacobs Papers; Allen, "Woman Suffrage Movement in Alabama," (thesis) p. 75.

43. Clipping, Birmingham *News,* 21 December 1913, Jacobs Scrapbook, Jacobs Papers.

44. Clippings, Jacobs Scrapbook, Jacobs Papers; Pattie Ruffner Jacobs to presidents of Southern State Suffrage Organizations, ? ? 1914, MMB Papers.

45. Lila Meade Valentine to Jessie Townsend, 13 April 1914, Virginia Suffrage Papers; clipping, "Special Posters Asked For South," n.d., and "Alabama Suffragists Join Buy-A-Bale Ranks," 29 September 1914, Jacobs Scrapbook, Jacobs Papers. The idea was to demonstrate concern for falling cotton prices. Clipping, "Suffragists to Hold Meetings Next Month," 21 October 1914, MMB Papers; AESA minutes, 26 January 1913, cited in Allen, "Woman Suffrage Movement in Alabama."

46. Gordon wrote to Clay of her expectations for the Birmingham Conference, "I take it, from [Shaw's] invitation and from the fact that archdemon, Mary Ware Dennett, has written me that the National's policy is to be modified, that they intend to cooperate with the Southern Conference—and cooperation, of course, will mean financial assistance—in that event we will have Mrs. Boyer down here in the course of a month and really and truly launch the work of the Conference." Kate Gordon to Laura Clay, 1 March 1914; Mary Ware Dennett to Kate Gordon, 17 March 1914; Kate Gordon to SSWSC officers, 22 April 1914, Clay Papers; Allen, "Woman Suffrage Movement in Alabama" (M.A. thesis), p. 63.

47. Kate Gordon to officers of the NAWSA, 13 April 1914. In May, Gordon thanked Breckinridge for her support on the NAWSA board of the SSWSC resolution and blamed her rival organization in Louisiana for poisoning Jacobs against her (Gordon) and for the "ugly situation in Birmingham." The woman was seen "hob-nobbing" with Jacobs and Dennett. Shaw was unable to attend the conference because of illness. Kate Gordon to Madeline McDowell Breckinridge, 15 May 1914, MMB Papers.

48. Mary Ware Dennett to Kate Gordon, 17 March 1914, Clay Papers.

49. Kate Gordon to SSWSC officers, 15 May 1914, Clay Papers.

50. On Belmont's gift, see Kate Gordon to Laura Clay, 8 April 1914; Laura Clay to Belmont, 11 April 1914; Laura Clay to Kate Gordon, 13 April 1914; Alva Belmont to Laura Clay, 15 April 1914; quotation from Clay, 19 September 1914. Belmont defended her SSWSC contribution in a letter to Catt, 1 June 1915, NAWSA Papers.

51. Kate Gordon to SSWSC officers, 17 September 1914, Clay Papers.

52. The *New Southern Citizen* 1 (October 1914): 1, MMB Papers; Spiers, "Woman Suffrage Movement in New Orleans," pp. 40–44.

53. Laura Clay to Kate Gordon, 13 April 1914, Clay Papers. On Gordon's actions toward the U.S. Elections Bill, see Johnson, "Kate Gordon and Woman Suffrage," pp. 382–385.

54. Gordon wrote to Clay of her disappointment at being snubbed by the Alabama campaigners: "I have been astonished not to hear anything from Alabama. I was under the impression that they wanted the Southern women to do some campaigning for them. I have heard of none of our prominent suffragists being invited, but I read in the *Woman's Journal* that the National's organizers—Misses Engel and Thompson—are both employed there." Kate Gordon to Laura Clay, 25 January 1915; Kate Gordon to Laura Clay, 8 September 1914, Clay Papers. On the blacklisting episode, see clippings, Jacobs Scrapbook, Jacobs Papers; and Allen, "Woman Suffrage Movement in Alabama" (M.A. thesis), pp. 67–68; Johnson, "Kate Gordon and Woman Suffrage," pp. 379–380.

55. For examples of Southern suffragists' opposition to Alice Paul's tactics, see S. Breckinridge, *Madeline McDowell Breckinridge*, p. 218–220. Madeline Breckinridge wrote to a politician friend in 1914, insisting on NAWSA's nonpartisanship and saying she believed Paul's policy of opposing Democrats as the party in power to be "a bad mistake." Clay advised KERA president (and Clay's niece) Elise Bennett Smith not to invite Harriet Stanton Blatch, "a militant Congressional Union woman," to speak in Kentucky, saying, "I feel we are much better off not to bring that element into our State." Laura Clay to Elise Bennett Smith, 15 April 1916, Clay Papers. Southern suffragists' denunciations of the NWP became even more frequent and emphatic once NWP members began picketing the White House. See, for example, Lila Meade Valentine press release dated 2 July 1917: "the Equal Suffrage League of Virginia condemns the folly of the fanatical women who are picketing the White House" and concurred with Mrs. Catt and Dr. Shaw that the picketing was "unwise, unpatriotic and injurious to the cause of woman suffrage." "We utterly repudiate such methods," she continued, "and deeply regret that any citizen of the United States should seek to embarrass the President or the government at such a crisis." She asked that the public not unjustly "condemn

the suffrage cause as a whole because of the folly of a handful of women,"
just as the "essential rightness" of the claims of Ireland should not be con-
demned because of the "revolt of the Sinn Feiners last Easter." Press release, 2
July 1917, Virginia Suffrage Papers. The CU/NWP had an active contingent in
South Carolina, though similar tensions existed between them and the
NAWSA regulars. See Bland, "Fighting the Odds."

56. Nellie Nugent Somerville, "Legislative Report, May 1914," Somerville-
Howorth Family Papers; Lila Meade Valentine to Jessie Townsend, 13 April
1914, Virginia Suffrage Papers; Meredith, "Mississippi Woman's Rights Movement," pp. 69, 70; Kate Gordon to Laura Clay, 12 June 1915, Clay Papers.

57. Lila Meade Valentine to Jessie Townsend, 6 October 1916, Virginia
Suffrage Papers. On Valentine's distress at the CU organizing in Virginia, see
Mary Johnston to Lila Meade Valentine, 1 June 1915, LHMV Papers. In May
1915, Valentine was extremely angry with the CU members making use of
the Equal Suffrage League's office and resources without permission: "I have
been overwhelmed with work and perplexed about this Congressional Union
business which makes me sick at heart. Do you know that in spite of the decision against their organizing in Virginia by the State [ESLV] Board and the
Richmond Executive Committee of twentyfive, Miss Vernon and Mrs. Latti-
more I find have used our Headquarters after our office hours to further their
propaganda. They made use of our typewriter and our card index of city and
State members to send out the call to the Conference. . . . Such a proceeding we consider dishonorable in the extreme and if I had no other reason
against the existence of their Union in Virginia, this very unscrupulous
method of attaining their ends would constitute a strong one. I am sick at
heart to think that suffragists could stoop to such things." Lila Meade Valentine to Jessie Townsend, 29 May 1915, Virginia Suffrage Papers.

58. When consulted by Valentine about Gordon's 1913 conference
with Southern governors, Johnston said she could not attend, and that she
"personally, honestly object[ed] to the assertion that we fear, (hence inferentially will fight) the presence of the negro woman at the polls." Mary
Johnston to Lila Meade Valentine, 29 September 1913, LHMV Papers. Kate
Gordon to Mary Johnston, 5 November 1915, Johnston Papers. Alice Stone
Blackwell invited Johnston to an "informal peace conference to promote
harmony between national association congressional union Boston September 17," Alice Stone Blackwell to Mary Johnston, telegram, 9 September
1914, Johnston Papers. Mary Johnston to Lila Meade Valentine, 1 June
1915, LHMV Papers; Mary Johnston to Lila Meade Valentine, ca. 1914,
Johnston Papers.

59. Kate Gordon to Laura Clay, 29 June 1915; Kate Gordon to Lila
Meade Valentine, 29 June 1915; Kate Gordon to Medill McCormick, 13 July
1915, Clay Papers.

60. Morgan, *Suffragists and Democrats*, p. 95; Kate Gordon to SSWSC
officers, 11 May 1915, Clay Papers; Kate Gordon to Southern suffragists, 31
May 1915, McCulloch Papers.

61. Kate Gordon to Laura Clay, 29 June 1915, Clay Papers; Nellie
Nugent Somerville to Barbara Henderson, 2 February 1916, Somerville-
Howorth Family Papers; Kate Gordon to Laura Clay, 20 July 1916, and 6
November 1915, Clay Papers.

62. Laura Clay to Kate Gordon, 3 July 1915; Kate Gordon to the NAWSA board, 23 June 1915, Clay Papers.

63. Kate Gordon to SSWSC members, 16 July 1915, Virginia Suffrage Papers.

64. Nellie Nugent Somerville to Barbara Henderson, 2 February 1916, Somerville-Howorth Family Papers. On Johnston's resignation, see Lila Meade Valentine to Mary Johnston, 8 November 1915, Virginia Suffrage Papers. Valentine says, "I am sorry that you feel it necessary for I think it would have been better to have all opinions frankly represented in the Conference in order to gain a saner and safer point of view."

65. Resolution adopted by the 1915 state convention of Tennessee suffragists, Jackson, White Papers.

66. Cited by Wayne Flynt and Marlene Hunt Rikard, "Pattie Ruffner Jacobs: Alabama Suffragist, 1900–1930," paper presented at the Southern Association for Women Historians' Conference on Women's History, Converse College, June 1988.

67. Nellie Nugent Somerville, "Comment on Letter to Members of National Board," written in response to Kate Gordon's letter to the board, dated 23 June 1915, Somerville-Howorth Family Papers.

68. *Ibid.*

69. *Ibid.*

70. *Ibid.*

71. In Gordon's "Open Letter to the Members of the NAWSA," she said that to Southern women "the suffrage is greater than even the State right principle" and they would seek a federal suffrage amendment if forced to by the inaction of Southern men, the *New Citizen* 3 (January 1914): 4. Gordon also told Clay privately she would support the federal amendment if the Democratic Party made it necessary for her to get her suffrage that way. Kate Gordon to Laura Clay, 21 December 1916, Clay Papers.

72. Kate Gordon to Laura Clay, 6 November 1915, Clay Papers.

73. Lila Meade Valentine to Kate Gordon, 14 November 1915, Clay Papers.

74. Relations between Kate Gordon and Shaw had deteriorated to the point that Gordon vowed not to have Shaw in her house during Shaw's trip to New Orleans. Jean Gordon finally persuaded Kate to entertain Shaw, arguing that it was better to entertain Shaw than to throw the NAWSA president into the arms of their rival organization. Kate Gordon to Laura Clay, 2 February 1915, Clay Papers.

75. Nellie Nugent Somerville to Barbara Henderson, 2 February 1916, Somerville-Howorth Family Papers; Carrie Chapman Catt to Southern presidents, ll January 1916 (this one was a copy of Catt's letter to Mrs. Thomas J. Smith, Clay's relative and KERA president), Clay Papers. Another example of Catt's initial faith in Gordon is found in the papers of North Carolina suffrage president Otelia Cunningham, who reported that Catt urged the Southern presidents not to submit an amendment, but "to come together at the Southern Conference Meeting with Miss Jean Gordon [*sic*, should have said "Kate"] as President and vote upon the Southern State best prepared and ready for campaign work. This we consented to do but Miss Gordon has not yet informed us as to the date of the meeting." Draft, president's report, Connor Papers.

76. On Catt's trying to persuade Gordon not to seek the states' rights suffrage endorsement, see Kate Gordon to Laura Clay, 21 January 1918; Kate Gordon to SSWSC officers, 8 May 1916, Clay Papers.

77. Kate Gordon to SSWSC officers, 8 May 1916; Carrie Chapman Catt to presidents, 15 May 1916; Kate Gordon to presidents, 22 May 1916; Kate Gordon to Carrie Chapman Catt, 23 May 1916, Clay Papers.

78. Kate Gordon to Carrie Chapman Catt, 23 May 1916; In 1918, Gordon told Catt, "When you wrote me . . . the letter that you did I resented so bitterly your unwarranted attack that I determined to never voluntarily initiate any correspondence with you." Gordon broke the vow because of her determination to keep Catt and the NAWSA out of Louisiana during the 1918 state suffrage campaign. Kate Gordon to Carrie Chapman Catt, 3 July 1918, Clay Papers.

79. Johnson, "Kate Gordon and Woman Suffrage," p. 386.

80. If the states called special legislative sessions to set up constitutional conventions, they could enfranchise women through state action without having to submit the question to the voters in a referendum. Kate Gordon to SSWSC board, 6 December 1916; Kate Gordon to Southern governors, 13 December 1916, Clay Papers.

81. Kate Gordon to SSWSC officers, 7 July 1916, Clay Papers.

82. Laura Clay to Kate Gordon, 19 December 1916; Ida Porter Boyer to Laura Clay, 9 August 1916; Laura Clay to Kate Gordon, 26 January 1918; Clay Papers.

83. Kate Gordon to Laura Clay, 26 June 1916, Clay Papers. On Catt and the party conventions, see Catt and Shuler, *Woman Suffrage and Politics*, pp. 250–259.

84. Catt said, "No matter what the Republican and Democratic planks said, suffragists were in no mood to go to the States again and beg the vote from Negroes, immigrants and the liquor trade. The first step was to put their own house in order. [Hence] the Emergency Convention met at Atlantic City on September 4." Catt and Shuler, *Woman Suffrage and Politics*, pp. 258, 259; Carrie Chapman Catt to state presidents, 27 June 1916; Carrie Chapman Catt to Laura Clay, 19 July 1916, Clay Papers.

85. Laura Clay, "Shall Work Be Dropped on the Federal Amendment and Efforts Confined to State Legislation?" Prepared in the summer of 1916, Clay Papers.

86. Laura Clay to Kate Gordon, 12 July 1916; Kate Gordon to Laura Clay, 27 July 1916, Clay Papers; Fuller, *Laura Clay*, p. 144; Carrie Chapman Catt to Laura Clay, 12 December 1916, Clay Papers.

87. Catt and Shuler, *Woman Suffrage and Politics*, pp. 259–265, Wilson quoted on p. 260.

88. For a full description of Catt's "Winning Plan," see National American Woman Suffrage Association, *Victory*, pp. 123, 124; Carrie Chapman Catt to Laura Clay, 27 November 1916, Clay Papers.

89. NAWSA, *Victory*, pp. 123, 124, 129, 134, 162, 163; Carrie Chapman Catt to Southern presidents, 11 January 1916, Clay Papers. Breckinridge opposed the idea of Kentucky suffragists' seeking primary suffrage, as it would have the effect "of keeping women voters to a single party until full suffrage was obtained." Clipping, n.d. (1919), Clay papers. Gordon had tried

unsuccessfully to win a primary suffrage bill from the Louisiana legislature in 1912, but she was critical when the Arkansas suffragists won primary suffrage because of the NAWSA connection with the campaign. When Clay suggested that the SSWSC support a primary suffrage campaign in Oklahoma, Gordon said she thought it could win, but refused to support it because it would give momentum to the federal amendment. Johnson, "Kate Gordon and Woman Suffrage," pp. 390–391. On the victory for primary suffrage in Texas, see McArthur, "Motherhood and Reform in the New South."

90. S. Breckinridge, *Madeline McDowell Breckinridge*, pp. 228, 229; Mary Johnston to Lila Meade Valentine, 16 September 1916, LHMV Papers.

91. Alabama Equal Suffrage Association minutes, 7 May 1915, cited in Allen, "Woman Suffrage Movement in Alabama," p. 91; Lloyd Taylor, "Lila Meade Valentine: The FFV as Reformer," p. 482; Lila Meade Valentine to Mrs. Townsend, 30 January 1918, Virginia Suffrage Papers.

92. Meredith, "Mississippi Woman's Rights Movement," pp. 75, 79.

93. Somerville quoted in Johnson, "Kate Gordon and Woman Suffrage," p. 381.

94. S. Breckinridge, *Madeline McDowell Breckinridge*, pp. 215, 216; Equal Suffrage League of Virginia suffrage brochure, "Suffrage Ratification Map," Virginia Suffrage Papers.

95. Lila Meade Valentine, "President's Address," 1917, LHMV Papers.

96. "Democratic Party May Lose Support," clipping, n.d., White Papers.

97. Allen, "Woman Suffrage Movement in Alabama," pp. 94, 95; Carrie Chapman Catt to Laura Clay, 27 November 1918; Madeline McDowell Breckinridge to Mrs. South, 3 January 1918, Clay Papers; S. Breckinridge, *Madeline McDowell Breckinridge*, p. 230.

98. Laura Clay to Kate Gordon, 26 January 1918, and 30 January 1918; Kate Gordon to Laura Clay, 21 January 1918; Laura Clay to Catharine McCulloch, 30 November 1916, Clay Papers.

99. Clay now favored a proposed amendment to strike "sex" from the Fourteenth Amendment "as almost anything is better than persistence on the Susan B. Anthony Amendment." Laura Clay to Ida Porter Boyer, 31 January 1917; Kate Gordon to Laura Clay, 21 January 1918, Clay Papers.

100. Note: Wilson's decision was announced January 9, 1918; Laura Clay to Kate Gordon, 19 January 1918; Laura Clay to Sallie Clay Bennett, ? January 1918, and 8 February 1918. Clay also asked Catt to drop her opposition to a Kentucky campaign for a state suffrage amendment, and was very disappointed when this request was not granted. Laura Clay to Carrie Chapman Catt, 16 January 1918; Carrie Chapman Catt to Laura Clay, 22 January 1918, Clay Papers.

101. Kate Gordon to Laura Clay, 15 January 1918; Laura Clay to Kate Gordon, 19 January 1918, Clay Papers.

102. Kate Gordon to Laura Clay, 21 January 1918 and 1 February 1918; Laura Clay to Kate Gordon, 8 February 1918 and 30 March 1918; Kate Gordon to Laura Clay, 20 July 1918 and 31 July 1918, Clay Papers.

103. Laura Clay to Kate Gordon, 18 March 1918; Kate Gordon to Laura Clay, 15 January 1918, Clay Papers.

104. Kate Gordon to Laura Clay, 30 May 1918; Laura Clay to Kate Gordon, 4 June 1918, Clay Papers.

105. Wilson, they said, tried to prevent opponents from running against Senator Joseph E. Ransdell of Louisiana. Kate Gordon to Laura Clay, 13 August 1918 and 26 September 1918, Clay Papers.

106. The Senate vote in which the South cast nineteen of the thirty-four opposing votes confirmed their belief that the region would hold firm against the federal amendment. The vote was just two votes short of the two-thirds necessary for passage of a constitutional amendment. Flexner, *Century of Struggle*, p. 310; Laura Clay to Kate Gordon, 2 October 1918, Clay Papers.

107. Kate Gordon to Laura Clay, 16 June 1918. Gordon also urged Clay to launch a state suffrage campaign in Kentucky under SSWSC auspices. Kate Gordon to Laura Clay, 21 January 1918; Kate Gordon to Carrie Chapman Catt, 3 July 1918; Kate Gordon to Laura Clay, 26 March 1918; Carrie Chapman Catt to Kate Gordon, 11 July 1918, Clay Papers.

108. Kate Gordon to Laura Clay, 26 March 1918; copy sent to Clay by Gordon, 13 August 1918, Clay Papers.

109. Kate Gordon to Laura Clay, 2 July 1918; Jean Gordon to co-workers, 9 November 1918; Kate Gordon to Laura Clay, Ida Porter Boyer, and Caroline *Terror* Reilley, 30 May 1918, Clay Papers.

110. Kate Gordon to Ida Porter Boyer, 6 September 1918; Kate Gordon to Laura Clay, 13 November 1918, Clay Papers.

111. Jean Gordon to co-workers, 9 November 1918, Clay Papers.

112. Kate Gordon to Laura Clay, 13 November 1918. When congressional approval seemed imminent and inevitable, Gordon followed through on this idea, and, in cooperation with Senators Williams and Vardaman of Mississippi, Gay of Louisiana, and Underwood of Alabama, attempted to amend the federal suffrage amendment to make it less of a threat to white supremacy and states' rights.

113. Justina Wilson to Kate Gordon, 17 May 1918, NAWSA Papers; Ida Husted Harper to Kate Gordon, 18 November 1920, Clay Papers.

114. Kate Gordon to Ida Husted Harper, 9 December 1918, Clay Papers.

115. Loretta Ellen Zimmerman, "Alice Paul and the National Woman's Party, 1912–1920," Ph.D. diss., Tulane University, 1964, pp. 163–193, quotation p. 191; Sidney R. Bland, "Mad Women of the Cause: The National Woman's Party in the South," *Furman Studies* 26 (December 1980): 85–87; and *idem*, "Fighting The Odds: Militant Suffragists in South Carolina," which shows the NWP achieved some success in the state despite the organizer's comment. Note: the Congressional Union and its Western affiliate, the National Woman's Party, merged under the latter title in April 1917.

116. Irwin, *The Story of the Woman's Party*, pp. 292–298; Grantham, *Southern Progressivism*, p. 390; Sue Shelton White to Carrie Chapman Catt, 27 April 1918 and 9 May 1918, White Papers.

117. After hearing of White's aid to Younger, Catt had written to NAWSA officials in Tennessee telling them they must not trust NAWSA secrets to White. White wrote to Catt expressing her support for the NAWSA, but explaining what had happened regarding the NWP. Clearly White wanted to work with both organizations. Sue Shelton White to Carrie Chapman Catt, 27 April 1918; Carrie Chapman Catt to Sue Shelton White, 6 May 1918; Sue Shelton White to Carrie Chapman Catt, 9 May 1918, White Papers.

118. Madeline McDowell Breckinridge, "Kentucky Chapter Woman Suffrage History: 1900–1920," MMB Papers.

Chapter 6: Bitter Fruit: An Incomplete Victory, Courtesy of Uncle Sam

1. Kate Gordon to Alice Stone Blackwell, 18 July 1920, Clay Papers.
2. Pattie Ruffner Jacobs, "Tradition Vs. Justice," speech at the 1920 NAWSA "Jubilee Convention" in Chicago, reprinted in the (Asheville, N.C., newspaper) *Southern Review* (May 1920), under the title, "The Pulse of the South: How the South Really Feels About Woman Suffrage," clipping, Clay Papers.
3. Sheldon, "Woman Suffrage and Virginia Politics," p. 65.
4. Sue White referred to the South's "moss-backed traditions" in a letter to the editor of the *Patriot Phalanx*, undated clipping, White Papers.
5. Talmadge, *Rebecca Latimer Felton*, p. 108.
6. Taylor, "Revival and Development . . . Georgia," p. 339; quotation from Floyd, "Rebecca Latimer Felton: Champion of Women's Rights," p. 88; for the text of the resolution rejection, see Catt and Shuler, *Woman Suffrage and Politics*, p. 463.
7. Allen, "Woman Suffrage Movement in Alabama," p. 96; Allen, "The Woman Suffrage Movement in Alabama," (thesis), pp. 141–142.
8. Adele Clark to Carrie Chapman Catt, 13 August 1919; Carrie Chapman Catt to Adele Clark, 29 August 1919, Virginia Suffrage Papers. In 1920, the General Assembly passed a motion opposing ratification, and instead passed a resolution to amend the state constitution to provide woman suffrage. Sheldon, "Woman Suffrage and Virginia Politics," pp. 56–64.
9. Nellie Nugent Somerville, "History of Woman Suffrage," Somerville-Howorth Family Papers. Note: the Mississippi congressional delegation had voted solidly against the federal amendment in June 1919. See most of the text from Gordon's speech in a clipping from the Jackson, Mississippi, *Clarion-Ledger*, n.d., Clay Papers. Gordon boasted to Clay that she had been "in a nest of Antis" and had given "the strongest suffrage speech I ever made." Kate Gordon to Laura Clay, 19 March 1920, Clay Papers. Note: the Mississippi House of Representatives passed a rejection resolution. Later Mississippi suffragists were surprised when, with only one more state needed for ratification and under pressure from national Democratic leaders, the Mississippi Senate amended the House resolution to read "ratify" instead of "reject" and approved the change by a one-vote margin. The House, however, came back and overwhelmingly defeated the measure. Meredith, "Mississippi Woman's Rights Movement," pp. 79, 81.
10. Evidence of the good relations between Clay and Breckinridge appears frequently in their papers, however; one good example is a letter from Clay to her younger associate in 1918, in which she began an explanation of her opposition to Catt's national policy with the words, "There is no one, my dear Mrs. Breckinridge, in our K.E.R.A. whose sympathetic understanding, at least, of my position is more desired by me, whether or not you fully agree with it." Laura Clay to Madeline McDowell Breckinridge, 31 January 1918. Clay had withdrawn earlier from the KERA but Breckinridge and others had persuaded her to reconsider. Laura Clay to Mrs. South, 21 October

1918, MMB Papers; Laura Clay to the Lexington *Leader*, 12 June 1919, Clay Papers.

11. It is interesting to note that while Clay was writing letters to the Lexington *Herald* saying that the Nineteenth Amendment would resurrect the dormant Fifteenth Amendment, she was telling Alabama antis that the constitutions of the South had resolved "the negro problem." Quotation from Laura Clay to Judge J. B. Evans, 17 September 1919; Laura Clay to Bessie E. Somerville, 3 January 1920; Judge J. B. Evans to Laura Clay, 13 September 1919; Laura Clay to Martin Lee Calhoun. Note: while Clay thought the South could yet prevent the federal suffrage amendment, she searched for allies in Western states, appealing them to join the South as allies, each with a racial problem. Laura Clay to Senator Borah, 19 July 1918; Kate Gordon to Laura Clay, 20 July 1918; Fuller, *Laura Clay*, pp. 156, 157.

12. "Black for Anthony Amendment," clipping, n.d., MMB Papers. Breckinridge was supported by her husband in his editorials in the Lexington *Herald*. Desha Breckinridge said there was not much left of the "old idea" of states' rights, and compared the woman suffrage amendment to the Prohibition amendment and said it would be inconsistent to take one and not the other. He also said that the Fifteenth Amendment had never been fully enforced and it was unlikely this would change because of the woman suffrage amendment, and that the race problem was abating as the black population spread itself thin through recent migration. Clippings, MMB Papers.

13. Fuller, *Laura Clay*, p. 158; Laura Clay to Bessie E. Somerville, 3 January 1920, Clay Papers.

14. S. Breckinridge, *Madeline McDowell Breckinridge*, pp. 235, 236; Fuller, *Laura Clay*, p. 159. Note: in Kentucky, the amendment benefitted from the existence of a fully developed two-party system, as the two parties vied to be able to take credit for the victory. In most Southern states, women voters of the future would have no recourse in state elections other than the Democratic Party, regardless of the party's suffrage record.

15. Zimmerman, "Alice Paul and the National Woman's Party," pp. 317, 318; Spiers, "Woman Suffrage Movement in New Orleans," pp. 60–64.

16. Laura Clay to Kate Gordon, 31 July 1920; Fuller, *Laura Clay*, p. 160; Morgan, *Suffragists and Democrats*, p. 150.

17. Catt and Shuler, *Woman Suffrage and Politics*, p. 437. See White's obituary in *Equal Rights*, by Florence Boeckel, which read, "To Miss Sue White the political leaders of the state gave full credit for this historic success." White Papers. Many have spoken of White's efforts to promote cooperation between competing suffrage groups. See, for example, Louis, "Sue Shelton White," in NAW, III, p. 591. Further evidence that White was appreciated by the NAWSA affiliates in Tennessee is a letter written on the eve of the 1918 U.S. Senate vote by several officers of the Tennessee Equal Suffrage Association thanking White for her "energetic and effective work . . . intelligent and unceasing." Eleanor McCormack, president emeritus, and Mary P. McVergh, treasurer, to Sue White. Occasionally White became exasperated with NAWSA affiliates who seemed to expect her assistance while giving none to her for NWP-sponsored activities. White insisted that her assistance must be reciprocated to be continued: "It seems to be expected and desired that I work with those who absolutely refuse to render even the slightest assistance to me. This may or may not be regarded as a compliment. I don't know whether

it is because I am thought to be broad-minded myself or because I am taken for a fool. At any rate, circumstances seem to forbid the continuance of such a policy on my part." Sue Shelton White to Mary Lipe, 22 May 1918, White Papers.

18. Kate Gordon to Laura Clay, 22 March 1923, Clay Papers.

19. Kate Gordon to Laura Clay, 19 March 1920, Clay Papers.

20. Kate Gordon to Ida Porter Boyer, 6 September 1918; Laura Clay to Kate Gordon, 30 March 1918. Soon after enfranchisement, Clay told the leader of a Kentucky Democratic Women's Club that since experience is valuable in politics as in all else, "an attitude of respect for men's greater experience and of willingness to cooperate with them is very becoming to women until women have thoroughly studied the new applications of principles which are required in rightly dividing the things which are God's from the things which are Caesar's." Laura Clay to Miss Scrugham, Clay Papers.

21. Kate Gordon to Laura Clay, 5 February 1918; quotation, Kate Gordon to Laura Clay, 26 September 1918, Clay Papers.

22. Kate Gordon to Laura Clay, 22 March 1923, Clay Papers.

23. Kate Gordon to Laura Clay, 12 April 1920, Clay Papers.

24. Laura Clay to Mrs. South, 13 April 1918; Laura Clay to Anna Howard Shaw, 13 April 1918; Laura Clay to Kate Gordon, 6 July 1918; Kate Gordon to Laura Clay, 20 July 1918, Clay Papers.

25. A letter sent by Anne Dallas Dudley of Tennessee to Mrs. South, KERA president, was tactlessly forwarded to Clay with a request for a contribution. It was a letter seeking donations from Southern suffragists toward the purchase of "illuminated testimonials" of Wilson's Senate speech for Shaw and Catt. Dudley believed this was appropriate since the South had been "the seat of so much bitter opposition," and the testimonials would symbolize the "spirit of the New South" that had been "misunderstood" by Southern representatives in Congress. In truth, said, Dudley, "we are glad and proud to acclaim ourselves loyally an integral part of our nation today." Kate Gordon to Laura Clay, 8 February 1920, Clay Papers. Paul Fuller said that Clay greatly resented Catt's ability to direct the actions of Kentucky suffragists, Fuller, *Laura Clay*, p. 151. On the same subject, see Laura Clay to Kate Gordon, 30 November 1918; Laura Clay to Ida Porter Boyer, 28 March 1918; Laura Clay to Shaw, 13 April 1918, Clay Papers. Catt was so surprised that Clay would choose states' rights over the federal suffrage amendment that she wrote to Breckinridge for an explanation; Catt feared that Clay might not be "quite in her right mind to take the attitude she has." Hay, "Madeline McDowell Breckinridge," p. 205.

26. Laura Clay to Ida Porter Boyer, 28 March 1918; Laura Clay to Anna Howard Shaw, 14 April 1918, Clay Papers.

27. Kate Gordon to Laura Clay, 8 February 1920; Gordon was later very negative about the *History of Woman Suffrage* and Mrs. Harper. Kate Gordon to Laura Clay, 22 March 1923; Kate Gordon to Alice Stone Blackwell, 18 July 1920, Clay Papers.

28. Laura Clay to Kate Gordon, 15 April 1920, Clay Papers.

29. Madeline McDowell Breckinridge speech at the NAWSA "Jubilee Convention," February 1920, S. Breckinridge, *Madeline McDowell Breckinridge*, pp. 236, 237.

30. Taylor, "Woman Suffrage Movement in Mississippi," p. 233; Taylor,

"Last Phase . . . Georgia," p. 28. On Virginia, see the Richmond *News-Leader*, 24 September 1936. At the 1920 regular session of the Virginia General Assembly, they rejected the Nineteenth Amendment, but passed a bill giving women the right to vote if the Amendment was ratified within ninety days after the close of the session—which it was not; clipping, Valentine Papers. On Florida, see Morgan, *Suffragists and Democrats*, p. 152.

31. On the Texas referendum, see Ruthe Winegarten and Judith N. McArthur, eds., *Citizens at Last*, esp. pp. 36–48 and 183–198. On Kentucky, see Fuller, *Laura Clay*, pp. 165 and 203, nn. 10, 11. On Mississippi, see Taylor, "Woman Suffrage Movement in Mississippi," pp. 232, 233.

32. Pattie Ruffner Jacobs, "Tradition Vs. Justice," speech at the 1920 NAWSA "Jubilee Convention" in Chicago, Clay Papers.

33. On the use of the speech in an attempt to discredit Jacobs, see Allen, "Woman Suffrage Movement in Alabama," (M.A. thesis) p. 162. On the reaction to the defeat of the Nineteenth Amendment in Virginia, see Sheldon, "Woman Suffrage and Virginia Politics," p. 60; Taylor, "Last Phase . . . Georgia," p. 27.

34. Jacobs, "Tradition Vs. Justice."

35. *Ibid.* On Jacobs' 1913 speech, see clipping from New York *Tribune*, 2 December 1913, Jacobs Scrapbook, Jacobs Papers.

36. Jacobs, "Tradition Vs. Justice."

37. *Ibid.* Somerville, "Are Women Too Good to Vote?" clipping, ca. 1914, Somerville-Howorth Family Papers.

38. Jacobs, "Tradition Vs. Justice."

39. *Ibid.*

40. Wheeler, Marjorie Spruill, "Feminism and Antifeminism," in Charles Reagan Wilson and William R. Ferris, eds., *Encyclopedia of Southern Culture* (Chapel Hill: University of North Carolina Press, 1989).

41. Jacobs, "Tradition Vs. Justice."

Epilogue

1. On Southern women in the 1920s, see Scott, *Southern Lady*, Chapter Eight, "Women with the Vote." Scott describes how Southern white women, now armed with the vote, continued to promote progressive reform; she finds those most active in politics to be very progressive, partly explained by the fact that, given the "deep conservatism of the majority of southern women," a woman who was "bold enough to assume a role unusual for women was also likely to be radical on social questions generally." p. 194. On discrimination against African-American women trying to register in 1920, see Morgan, *Suffragists and Democrats*, pp. 152–153; and Glenda Gilmore, "Gender and Jim Crow," Chapter Eight. On the interracial movement and the Association of Southern Women for the Prevention of Lynching, led by a white former suffragist from Texas, Jessie Daniel Ames, see Hall, *Revolt Against Chivalry*.

2. See S. Breckinridge, *Madeline McDowell Breckinridge*, pp. 236–259; M. Breckinridge, "Kentucky Chapter Woman Suffrage History, 1900–1920," MMB Papers; Anne Firor Scott, NAW, I, pp. 231–233; Hay, "Madeline McDowell Breckinridge," pp. 209–212, 218–221, and on her health, pp. 6–8 and 66–71. According to Hay, Breckinridge suffered from ill health all her life, though con-

cealing this as much as possible from the public. Afflicted with tuberculosis, which led to the amputation of her lower leg, she had had an artificial limb since her teens. Furthermore, she suffered a stroke in the winter of 1903-04 that temporarily paralyzed one of her hands. Her tuberculosis worsened in 1910, but she seemed to drive herself more than ever, seemingly conscious that she had little time in which to work for the causes she believed in.

3. Lloyd Taylor, "LMV: FFV as Reformer," pp. 486, 487; clipping, Richmond *News-Leader*, 27 February 1926, LHMV Papers.

4. NAW, II, p. 283; Jones, *Tomorrow Is Another Day*, pp. 184–186, quotation p. 185; Johnston, *Slave Ship*; Johnston, "Nemesis," copy of a short story from *Century* magazine, Johnston Papers. Johnston declined to serve on the LWV committee, citing ill health and too much work, as well as reservations about the organization. Mary Johnson to Edith Cowles, executive secretary, ESLV, 1920, Johnston Papers.

5. Kate Gordon to Laura Clay, 22 March 1923, Clay Papers; L. E. Zimmerman, NAW, II, pp. 64–67; Kemp, "Jean and Kate Gordon." Kemp says that Jean, though she "cared tenderly for her charges," believed that the "feeble-minded" should not reproduce, and had 125 of these "child women" sterilized over a thirteen-year period.

6. Clippings, Clay scrapbook, Clay papers; Talmadge, *Rebecca Latimer Felton*, pp. 139–149.

7. Clay obituary, Lexington *Herald*, 30 June 1941, Clay Scrapbook; first quotation from Clay to Miss Lloyd (LWV), 26 November 1921; other quotations from Fuller, *Laura Clay*, pp. 162–166.

8. Talmadge, *Rebecca Latimer Felton*, pp. 137–160; Floyd, "Rebecca Latimer Felton: Champion of Women's Rights," pp. 99–104, quotation p. 102.

9. In the first primary, Kearney received 18,303 votes, compared to 74,597 for Vardaman and 65,980 for Stephens. Tipton, "It Is My Duty," pp. 83–117, Somerville quotation pp. 89, 90. See also Anne Scott's articles on these two women in *Notable American Women*: "Belle Kearney," NAW, II, pp. 309–310; and *NAW Modern Period*, pp. 654–656; Scott, *Southern Lady*, pp. 203–205.

10. Clipping from the (Jackson, Mississippi) *Woman Voter*, 11 January 1924, Somerville-Howorth Family Papers; The *Woman Voter* (1922–1924), was a fascinating feminist newspaper run by Minnie Brewer, daughter of former governor Earl Brewer. See Vinton M. Price, "The *Woman Voter* and Mississippi Elections in the Early Twenties," and Dorothy Shawhan, "Women Behind the *Woman Voter*," both in the *Journal of Mississippi History* 49 (May 1987): 105–114 and 115–128; Tipton, "It Is My Duty," pp. 124–137.

11. Tipton, "It Is My Duty," p. 126; Scott quotation from *NAW: Modern Period*, p. 655; Scott, *Southern Lady*, pp. 203–205. On Somerville's view on the child-labor amendment, see Wheeler interview, p. 15, 16. Quotation from a *Clarion-Ledger* clipping, n.d., Somerville-Howorth Family Papers. On her decision not to run for re-election, see Myers interview with Howorth, pp. 50, 51.

12. Miscellaneous clippings, 1924, Somerville scrapbook, Somerville-Howorth Family Papers; Anne Firor Scott, NAW, II, p. 310; Tipton, "It Is My Duty," pp. 139–144.

13. Tipton, "It Is My Duty," pp. 138–150; Myers interview with Howorth, p. 33. Somerville assisted the LWV and other women's organiza-

tions with voter-education programs for women, knowing they needed assistance with the deliberately daunting process of registering to vote in Mississippi, but that was the extent of her support of the League; see Joanne Varner Hawks, "Like Mother, Like Daughter: Nellie Nugent Somerville and Lucy Somerville Howorth," *Journal of Mississippi History* 45 (May 1983): 116–123; Nellie Nugent Somerville, "Lest We Forget," letter to the editor of the Memphis *Commercial Appeal*, 27 January 1946, written to protest revisionist views of Reconstruction, clipping Somerville subject file, Mississippi Archives. Somerville objected to a 1944 Memphis *Press-Scimitar* article on the ERA in which the NWP was credited with the 1920 suffrage victory. Somerville notebook, Somerville-Howorth Family Papers; Scott, *NAW: Modern Period*, pp. 655, 656; Wheeler interview with Howorth.

14. See clippings in Jacobs Scrapbook. The quotation praising her speaking ability is from the Birmingham *Evening Journal*, 26 October 1920, Jacobs Papers. See also Jemison, "Ladies Become Voters," pp. 58, 59; and Lee N. Allen, NAW, II, p. 267. On the convict lease system in Alabama, and quotation from the former governor, see Tindall, *Emergence of the New South*, pp. 212, 213.

15. Bill Chafe observes that the women reformers "constitute a human bridge joining the indirect political influence of the settlement-house generation with the formal political practice of a reform administration in the 1930s." William H. Chafe, *The Paradox of Change: American Women in the 20th Century* (New York: Oxford University Press, 1991), pp. 34–44, quotation p. 36; Jemison, "Ladies Become Voters," p. 59.

16. On White's role in the earliest stage of the ERA's history, see Cott, *Grounding of Modern Feminism*, pp. 66–68, quotation p. 67. The Equal Rights Amendment unveiled at Seneca Falls (which had gone into many drafts) read: "Men and women shall have equal rights throughout the United States and every place subject to its jurisdiction," and was introduced in Congress on December 10, 1923. The ERA that passed Congress but failed to be ratified in the 1980s read, "Equality of rights under the law shall not be denied or abridged by the United States or by any state on account of sex," and was introduced in Congress in 1943. See Cott, *op.cit.*, pp. 120–126 and 324–325, n. 13. For White quotation, see her 1923 speech, "Women Owe Debt to Pioneers of 1848, Says Sue White," clipping, White Papers; Dr. Florence Armstrong, "Personal Recollections of Sue White," White Papers.

17. Cott, *Grounding of Modern Feminism*, pp. 244–246.

18. James P. Louis, NAW, III, pp. 591–592; Louis, "Sue Shelton White"; on the NWP *vs.* proponents of protective legislation, see Chafe, *Paradox of Change*, pp. 45–60, and Cott, *Grounding of Modern Feminism*.

19. Louis, NAW, III, pp. 591–592.

20. *Ibid.*; Dr. Florence A. Armstrong, "Personal Recollections of Sue White," White Papers.

Bibliography

Manuscript Collections and Interviews

Madeline McDowell Breckinridge Papers. In the Breckinridge Family Papers, Manuscript Division, Library of Congress, Washington, D.C.

Laura Clay Papers. Special Collections and Archives, Margaret I. King Library, University of Kentucky, Lexington.

Otelia Carrington (Cuningham) Connor Papers (#3228). Southern Historical Collection, University of North Carolina, Chapel Hill.

Mary Earhart Dillon Collection. Schlesinger Library, Radcliffe College, Cambridge, Massachusetts.

Equal Suffrage Association of North Carolina Papers. North Carolina Collection, University of North Carolina, Chapel Hill.

Rebecca Latimer Felton Papers. Special Collections Division, Hargrett Rare Book and Manuscript Library, University of Georgia, Athens.

Ella Harrison Papers. Schlesinger Library, Radcliffe College, Cambridge, Massachusetts. Reprints in Nellie Nugent Somerville Papers, Mississippi Department of Archives and History, Jackson.

Pattie Ruffner Jacobs Diaries. Property of Mr. and Mrs. John L. Hillhouse, Jr., Birmingham, Alabama.

Pattie Ruffner Jacobs Papers. Department of Archives and Manuscripts, Birmingham Public Library, Birmingham, Alabama.

Mary Johnston Papers (#3588). Manuscripts Division, Special Collections Department, University of Virginia Library, Charlottesville.

Belle Kearney Papers (#Z/778; Z/778.1). Mississippi Department of Archives and History, Jackson.

Lindsey-Orr Papers (#Z/1726). Mississippi Department of Archives and History, Jackson.

Catharine Waugh McCulloch Papers. Schlesinger Library, Radcliffe College, Cambridge, Massachusetts.

Constance Ashton Myers Interview with Judge Lucy Somerville Howorth, June 20, 22, and 23, 1975, Monteagle, Tennessee (#4007). Southern Oral History Collection, Southern Historical Collection, University of North Carolina, Chapel Hill.

National American Woman Suffrage Association (NAWSA) Papers, Manuscripts Division, Library of Congress.

Nellie Nugent Somerville Papers. (Copies of selections from the Somerville-Howorth Family Papers, Schlesinger Library, Radcliffe College.) Mississippi Department of Archives and History, Jackson.

Somerville-Howorth Family Papers. (Papers of Nellie Nugent Somerville and her daughter Lucy Somerville Howorth and their family.) Schlesinger Library, Radcliffe College, Cambridge, Massachusetts.

Sue Shelton White Papers. Schlesinger Library, Radcliffe College, Cambridge, Massachusetts.

Benjamin Batchelder Valentine Papers. Valentine Museum, Richmond, Virginia.

Lila Hardaway Meade Valentine Papers (MSS1V2345a). Division of Manuscripts and Archives, Virginia Historical Society, Richmond, Virginia.

Virginia Suffrage Papers. Virginia State Library and Archives, Richmond, Virginia.

Marjorie Spruill Wheeler Interview with Judge Lucy Somerville Howorth. 15 March 1983, Cleveland, Mississippi, and 6 March 1984, Hattiesburg, Mississippi. Volume 297, "An Oral History with Judge Lucy Somerville Howorth," Part II (1983), of the Mississippi Oral History Program of the University of Southern Mississippi.

Secondary Sources

Alexander, Adele Logan. "How I Discovered My Grandmother: And the Truth About Black Women and the Suffrage Movement." *Ms.* (November 1983): 29–33.

———. "Grandmother, Grandfather, W.E.B. Du Bois and Booker T. Washington." *Crisis* (February 1983): 8–11.

———. "African-Americans in the Woman Suffrage Movement and the Ladies from Tuskegee Institute." In Marjorie Spruill Wheeler, ed., *Votes for Women*, q.v.

Allen, Lee Norcross. "The Woman Suffrage Movement in Alabama." M.A. thesis, Auburn University, 1949.

Allen, Lee N. "The Woman Suffrage Movement in Alabama, 1910–1920." *Alabama Review* 11 (April 1958): 83–99.

Arendale, Marirose. "Tennessee and Women's Rights." *Tennessee Historical Quarterly* 39 (Spring 1980): 62–78.

Banner, Lois W. *Elizabeth Cady Stanton: A Radical for Woman's Rights.* Boston: Little, Brown and Company, 1980.

Bellows, Barbara (then Barbara Ulmer). "Virginia Durant Young: New South Suffragist." M.A. thesis, University of South Carolina, 1979.

Berkeley, Kathleen Christine. "'An Advocate for Her Sex': Feminism and

Conservatism in the Post–Civil War South." *Tennessee Historical Quarterly* 43 (Winter 1984): 390–407.

Bland, Sidney R. "Mad Women of the Cause: The National Woman's Party in the South." *Furman Studies* 26 (December 1980): 82–91.

———. "Fighting the Odds: Militant Suffragists in South Carolina." *South Carolina Historical Magazine* 82, (January 1981): 32–43.

Bordin, Ruth. *Frances Willard: A Biography*. Chapel Hill: University of North Carolina Press, 1986.

Breckinridge, Sophonisba P. *Madeline McDowell Breckinridge: A Leader in the New South*. Chicago: University of Chicago Press, 1921.

Buechler, Steven M. *The Transformation of the Woman Suffrage Movement: The Case of Illinois, 1850–1920*. New Brunswick: Rutgers University Press, 1986.

Buhle, Mari Jo, and Paul Buhle, eds. *The Concise History of Woman Suffrage, Selections from the Classic Work of Stanton, Anthony, Gage and Harper*. Urbana: University of Illinois Press, 1978.

Catt, Carrie Chapman, and Nettie Rogers Shuler. *Woman Suffrage and Politics: The Inner Story of the Suffrage Movement*. 1923. Reprint, Seattle: University of Washington Press, 1970.

Chafe, William H. *The Paradox of Change: American Women in the Twentieth Century*. New York: Oxford University Press, 1991.

Clarke, Edward H. *Sex in Education: A Fair Chance for the Girls*. Boston, 1873.

Clinton, Catherine. *The Plantation Mistress: Woman's World in the Old South*. New York: Pantheon Books, 1982.

Coleman, Elizabeth D. "Penwoman of Virginia's Feminists." *Virginia Calvacade* (Winter 1956): 8–11.

Connelly, Thomas L., and Barbara L. Bellows. *God and General Longstreet: The Lost Cause and the Southern Mind*. Baton Rouge: Louisiana State University Press, 1982.

Cott, Nancy F. *The Grounding of Modern Feminism*. New Haven: Yale University Press, 1987.

———. "Feminist Politics in the 1920s: The National Woman's Party." *Journal of American History* 71 (June 1984): 43–68.

———. *The Bonds of Womanhood: "Woman's Sphere" in New England, 1780–1835*. New Haven: Yale University Press, 1977.

Cotton, Sallie Southall. *History of the North Carolina Federation of Woman's Clubs, 1901–1925*. Raleigh: Edwards and Broughton Printing Company, 1925.

Degler, Carl N. *At Odds: Women and the Family in America from the Revolution to the Present*. New York: Oxford University Press, 1980.

Doyle, Don. *New Men, New Cities, New South: Atlanta, Nashville, Charleston, Mobile, 1860–1910*. Chapel Hill: University of North Carolina Press, 1990.

DuBois, Ellen Carol. *Feminism and Suffrage: The Emergence of an Independent Women's Movement in America, 1848–1869*. Ithaca: Cornell University Press, 1978.

Eaton, Clement. "Breaking a Path for the Liberation of Women in the South." *Georgia Review* 28 (Summer 1974): 187–199.

Felton, Rebecca Latimer. *Country Life in Georgia in the Days of My Youth*. Atlanta, 1919.

———. *The Romantic Story of Georgia Women*. Atlanta, 1930.

Flexner, Eleanor. *Century of Struggle: The Woman's Rights Movement in the United States*. New York: Atheneum, 1974.

Floyd, Josephine Bone. "Rebecca Latimer Felton: Champion of Women's Rights." *Georgia Historical Quarterly* 30 (June 1946): 81–104.

———. "Rebecca Latimer Felton: Political Independent." *Georgia Historical Quarterly* 30 (March 1946): 14–34.

Flynt, Wayne, and Marlene Hunt Rikard. "Pattie Ruffner Jacobs: Alabama Suffragist, 1900–1930." Paper read at the Southern Association for Women Historians Conference on Women's History, Converse College, June 1988.

Foster, Gaines M. *Ghosts of the Confederacy: Defeat, the Lost Cause, and the Emergence of the New South.* New York: Oxford University Press, 1987.

Fox-Genovese, Elizabeth. *Within the Plantation Household: Black and White Women of the Old South.* Chapel Hill: University of North Carolina Press, 1988.

Freedman, Estelle. "Separatism as Strategy: Female Institution Building and American Feminism, 1870–1930." *Feminist Studies* 5 (Fall 1979): 512–529.

Freeman, Anne Hobson. "Mary Munford's Fight for a College for Women Coordinate with the University of Virginia." *Virginia Magazine of History and Biography* (October 1970): 481–491.

Friedman, Jean E. *The Enclosed Garden: Women and Community in the Evangelical South, 1830–1900.* Chapel Hill: University of North Carolina Press, 1985.

Fuller, Paul E. *Laura Clay and the Woman's Rights Movement.* Lexington: University of Kentucky Press, 1975.

Gay, Dorothy Ann. "The Tangled Skein of Romanticism and Violence in the Old South: The Southern Response to Abolitionism and Feminism, 1830–1861." Ph.D. dissertation, University of North Carolina, Chapel Hill, 1975.

Gaston, Paul M. *The New South Creed: A Study in Southern Mythmaking.* Baton Rouge: Louisiana State University Press, 1970.

Gilman, Charlotte Perkins. *Women and Economics: A Study of the Economic Relation Between Men and Women as a Factor in Social Evolution.* Boston: Small, Maynard, 1898.

Gilmore, Glenda Elizabeth. "Gender and Jim Crow: Women and the Politics of White Supremacy in North Carolina, 1896–1920." Ph.D. dissertation, University of North Carolina, Chapel Hill, 1992.

———. "Gender and Jim Crow: Sarah Dudley Pettey's Vision of the New South." *North Carolina Historical Review* 68 (July 1991): 261–285.

Gluck, Sherna, ed. *From Parlor to Prison: Five American Suffragists Talk About Their Lives.* New York: Vintage Books, 1976.

Goodrich, Gillian. "Romance and Reality: The Birmingham Suffragists, 1892–1920." *Journal of the Birmingham Historical Society* 5 (January 1978): 4–21.

Grantham, Dewey W. *Southern Progressivism: The Reconciliation of Progress and Tradition.* Knoxville: University of Tennessee Press, 1983.

Green, Elna C. "Those Opposed: The Antisuffragists in North Carolina, 1900–1920." *North Carolina Historical Review* 67 (July 1990): 316–333.

Grimes, Alan P. *The Puritan Ethic and Woman Suffrage.* New York: Oxford University Press, 1967.

Hall, Jacquelyn Dowd. *Revolt Against Chivalry: Jessie Daniel Ames and the Women's Campaign Against Lynching.* New York: Columbia University Press, 1979.

————. James Leloudis, Robert Korstad, Mary Murphy, LuAnn Jones, and Christopher B. Daly. *Like a Family: The Making of a Southern Cotton Mill World.* Chapel Hill: University of North Carolina Press, 1987.

Hanmer, Trudy J. "A Divine Discontent: Mary Johnston and Woman Suffrage in Virginia." M.A. thesis, University of Virginia, 1972.

Harley, Sharon, and Rosalyn Terborg-Penn, eds. *The Afro-American Woman: Struggles and Images.* Port Washington, New York: Kennikat Press, 1978.

Hawks, Joanne V., and Sheila L. Skemp, eds. *Sex, Race, and the Role of Women in the South.* Jackson: University Press of Mississippi, 1983.

Hawks, Joanne Varner. "Like Mother, Like Daughter: Nellie Nugent Somerville and Lucy Somervile Howorth." *Journal of Mississippi History* 45 (May 1983): 116–123.

Hay, Melba Porter. "Madeline McDowell Breckinridge: Kentucky Suffragist and Progressive Reformer." Ph.D. dissertation, University of Kentucky, 1980.

Hays, Elinor R. *Morning Star: A Biography of Lucy Stone.* New York: Harcourt, Brace and World, 1961.

Hersh, Blanche Glassman. *The Slavery of Sex: Feminist-Abolitionists in America.* Urbana and Chicago: University of Illinois Press, 1978.

Irwin, Inez Haynes. *The Story of the Woman's Party.* New York: Harcourt, Brace, and Company, 1921.

James, Edward T., *et al. Notable American Women: A Biographical Dictionary.* Volumes 1–3. Cambridge: Harvard University Press, 1971.

Jeffrey, Julie Roy. "Women in the Southern Farmer's Alliance: A Reconsideration of the Role and Status of Women in the Late Nineteenth Century South." *Feminist Studies* 3 (Fall 1975): 72–91.

Jemison, Marie Stokes. "Ladies Become Voters: Pattie Ruffner Jacobs and Women's Suffrage in Alabama." *Southern Exposure* 7 (Spring 1979): 48–59.

Johnson, Kenneth R. "Kate Gordon and the Woman Suffrage Movement in the South." *Journal of Southern History* 38 (August 1972): 365–392.

Johnston, Mary. *Hagar.* Boston: Houghton Mifflin, 1913.

————. *The Slave Ship.* Boston: Little, Brown and Company, 1924.

————. "The Woman's War." *Atlantic Monthly* (April 1910).

Jones, Anne Goodwyn. *Tomorrow Is Another Day: The Woman Writer in the South, 1859–1936.* Baton Rouge: Louisiana State University Press, 1981.

Jones, Jacqueline. *Labor of Love, Labor of Sorrow: Black Women, Work and the Family, from Slavery to the Present.* New York: Basic Books, 1985.

Kearney, Belle. *A Slaveholder's Daughter.* Abbey Press, 1900. Reprint, New York: Negro Universities Press, 1969.

————. *Conqueror or Conquered: or the Sex Challenge Answered.* Cincinnati, Ohio: S. A. Millikan Company, 1921.

Kemp, Kathryn W. "Jean and Kate Gordon: New Orleans Social Reformers, 1898–1933." *Louisiana History* 24 (1983): 389–401.

Kirby, Jack Temple. *Darkness at the Dawning: Race and Reform in the Progressive South.* Philadelphia: J. B. Lippincott Company, 1972.

Knott, Claudia. "Evangelical Protestantism in the Kentucky Woman Suffrage Movement." Presented at the Organization of American Historians Convention, Louisville, 1991.

Kraditor, Aileen S. *The Ideas of the Woman's Suffrage Movement, 1890–1920*. Garden City, New York: Doubleday and Company, 1965, 1971.

———. ed. *Up from the Pedestal: Selected Writings in the History of American Feminism*. Chicago: Quadrangle Books, 1968.

———. "Tactical Problems of the Woman-Suffrage Movement in the South." *Louisiana Studies* (Winter 1966): 289–307.

Kousser, J. Morgan. *The Shaping of Southern Politics: Suffrage Restriction and the Establishment of the One-Party South, 1880–1910*. New Haven: Yale University Press, 1974.

Lebsock, Suzanne. *The Free Women of Petersburg: Status and Culture in a Southern Town, 1784–1860*. New York: W.W. Norton and Company, 1985.

———. "Radical Reconstruction and the Property Rights of Southern Women." *Journal of Southern History* 43 (May 1977): 195–216.

———. *"A Share of Honour": Virginia Women, 1600–1945*. Richmond: Virginia State Library, 1987.

———. "Woman Suffrage and White Supremacy: A Virginia Case Study." Paper presented November 10, 1988, to the Southern Association for Women Historians, Norfolk, Virginia.

Lerner, Gerda. *The Grimké Sisters from South Carolina: Pioneers for Woman's Rights and Abolition*. New York: Schocken Books, 1971.

Lindig, Carmen Meriwether. "The Woman's Movement in Louisiana, 1879–1920." Ph.D. dissertation, North Texas State University, 1983.

Link, William A. *The Changing Face of Southern Progressivism: Social Policy and Localism, 1880–1930*. Chapel Hill: University of North Carolina Press, 1992.

Logan, Adella Hunt. "Woman Suffrage." *Colored American Magazine* 9 (September 1905): 487–489.

———. "Colored Women as Voters." *Crisis* (September, 1912).

Louis, James P. "Sue Shelton White and the Woman Suffrage Movement, 1913–1920." *Tennessee Historical Quarterly* 22 (June 1963): 170–190.

Marcosson, Isaac. *"Marse Henry": A Biography of Henry Watterson*. New York: Dodd, Mead and Company, 1951.

McArthur, Judith N. "Motherhood and Reform in the New South: Texas Women During the Progressive Era." Ph.D. dissertation, University of Texas, 1992.

———. "Democrats Divided: Why the Texas Legislature Gave Women Primary Suffrage in 1918." Paper presented at the Southern Historical Association Convention, Fort Worth, November 1991.

———. "Gender Politics: Women Voters and the Texas Primary of 1918." Paper presented at the Southern Association for Women Historians' Conference, Chapel Hill, June 1990.

McCulloch, James E., ed. *The South Mobilizing for Social Service*. Nashville: Southern Sociological Congress, 1913.

McDowell, John Patrick. *The Social Gospel in the South: The Woman's Home Mission Movement in the Methodist Episcopal Church, South, 1886–1939*. Baton Rouge: Louisiana State University Press, 1982.

Meredith, Mary Louise. "The Mississippi Woman's Rights Movement, 1889–1923: The Leadership of Nellie Nugent Somerville and Greenville in Suffrage Reform." M.A. thesis, Delta State University, 1974.

Merk, Lois Bannister. "Massachusetts in the Woman Suffrage Movement." Ph.D. dissertation, Harvard University, 1961.

Mitchell, Samuel Chiles. *An Aftermath of Appomattox.* Privately printed, n.d. Copy in Benjamin B. Valentine Papers, Valentine Museum, Richmond.

Moncrief, Sandra. "The Mississippi Married Woman's Property Act of 1839." *Journal of Mississippi History* 47 (1985): 110–125.

Montgomery, Horace, ed. *Georgians in Profile.* Athens: University of Georgia Press, 1958.

Morgan, David. *Suffragists and Democrats: The Politics of Woman Suffrage in America.* East Lansing: Michigan State University Press, 1972.

National American Woman Suffrage Association. *Victory: How Women Won It: A Centennial Symposium, 1840–1940.* New York: H.W. Wilson Company, 1940.

Neverdon-Morton, Cynthia. *Afro-American Women of the South and the Advancement of the Race, 1895–1925.* Knoxville: University of Tennessee Press, 1989.

O'Neill, William L. *Everyone Was Brave: A History of Feminism in America.* New York: Quadrangle/The *New York Times* Book Company, 1969.

Orr, Oliver. *Charles Brantley Aycock.* Chapel Hill: University of North Carolina Press, 1961.

Ownby, Ted. *Subduing Satan: Religion, Recreation, and Manhood in the Rural South, 1865–1920.* Chapel Hill: The University of North Carolina Press, 1990.

Price, Margaret Nell. "The Development of Leadership in Southern Women." M.A. thesis, University of North Carolina at Chapel Hill, 1945.

Prince, Vinton M. "The *Woman Voter* and Mississippi Elections in the Early Twenties." *Journal of Mississippi History* 49 (May 1987): 105–114.

Quarles, Benjamin. "Frederick Douglass and the Woman's Rights Movement." *Journal of Negro History* 25 (January 1940): 35–44.

Rable, George C. *Civil Wars: Women and the Crisis of Southern Nationalism.* Urbana and Chicago: University of Illinois Press, 1991.

Rosenberg, Rosalind. *Beyond Separate Spheres: Intellectual Roots of Modern Feminism.* New Haven: Yale University Press, 1982.

———. "In Search of Woman's Nature, 1850–1920." *Feminist Studies* 3 (Fall 1975): 141–154.

Rossi, Alice S., ed. *The Feminist Papers: From Adams to de Beauvoir.* New York: Columbia University Press, 1973.

Scott, Anne Firor. *The Southern Lady: From Pedestal to Politics, 1830–1930.* Chicago: University of Chicago Press, 1970.

———. "The 'New Woman' in the New South." *South Atlantic Quarterly* 6 (Autumn 1962): 473–483.

———. "Women, Religion, and Social Change in the South, 1830–1930." *Religion and the Solid South*, Samuel S. Hill, ed. Nashville: Abingdon Press, 1972.

———. *Making the Invisible Woman Visible.* Urbana and Chicago: University of Illinois Press, 1984.

Scott, Anne Firor, and Andrew M. Scott. *One Half the People: The Fight for Woman Suffrage.* Philadelphia: J. B. Lippincott Company, 1975.

Shadron, Virginia. "Out of Our Homes: The Woman's Rights Movement in the Methodist Episcopal Church, South, 1890–1918." M.A. thesis, Emory University, 1976.

Shaw, Anna Howard. *The Story of a Pioneer.* New York: Harper Brothers, 1915.

Shawhan, Dorothy. "Women Behind the *Woman Voter.*" *Journal of Mississippi History* 49 (May 1987): 115–128.

Sheldon, Charlotte Jean. "Woman Suffrage and Virginia Politics, 1909–1920." M.A. thesis, University of Virginia, 1969.

Showalter, Elaine, ed. *These Modern Women: Autobiographical Essays from the Twenties.* Old Westbury, New York: The Feminist Press, 1978.

Sicherman, Barbara, and Carol Hurd Green. *Notable American Women: The Modern Period.* Cambridge: Harvard University Press, 1980.

Sims, Anastatia. *The Power of Femininity in the New South: Women's Organizations in North Carolina, 1883–1930.* Columbia: University of South Carolina Press, forthcoming.

———. "'Powers That Pray and Powers That Prey': Tennessee and the Fight for Woman Suffrage." *Tennessee Historical Quarterly* (Winter 1991): 203–225.

———. "Beyond the Ballot: The Radical Vision of the Antisuffragists." In Marjorie Spruill Wheeler, ed.

———. "The Woman Suffrage Movement in Texas." Senior thesis, *Votes for Women,* q.v. University of Texas, 1974.

Singal, Daniel Joseph. *The War Within: From Victorianism to Modernist Thought in the South, 1919–1945.* Chapel Hill: University of North Carolina Press, 1982.

Sosna, Morton. *In Search of the Silent South: Southern Liberals and the Race Issue.* New York: Columbia University Press, 1977.

Spiers, Patricia L. "The Woman Suffrage Movement in New Orleans." M.A. thesis, Southeastern Louisiana College, 1965.

Sproat, John G. *"The Best Men": Liberal Reformers in the Gilded Age.* New York: Oxford University Press, 1968.

Spruill, Julia Cherry. *Women's Life and Work in the Southern Colonies.* 1938. Reprint. New York: W. W. Norton and Company, 1972.

Stanton, Elizabeth Cady. *Eighty Years and More: Reminiscenses, 1815–1897.* 1898. Reprint, New York: Schocken Books, 1971.

Stanton, Elizabeth Cady, Susan B. Anthony, and Ida Husted Harper. *The History of Woman Suffrage.* 6 vols. Rochester, New York, 1881–1922.

Talmadge, John E. *Rebecca Latimer Felton: Nine Stormy Decades.* Athens: University of Georgia Press, 1960.

Taylor, A. Elizabeth. "The Woman Suffrage Movement in Arkansas." *Arkansas Historical Quarterly* 15 (Spring 1956): 17–52.

———. "The Woman Suffrage Movement in Florida." *Florida Historical Quarterly* 36 (July 1957): 42–60.

———. "The Origin of the Woman Suffrage Movement in Georgia." *Georgia Historical Quarterly* 28 (June 1944): 63–79.

———. "Revival and Development of the Woman Suffrage Movement in Georgia." *Georgia Historical Quarterly* 42 (December 1958): 339–354.

———. "The Last Phase of the Woman Suffrage Movement in Georgia." *Georgia Historical Quarterly* 43 (March 1959): 11–28.

———. "Tennessee—the Thirty-Sixth State." Marjorie Spruill Wheeler, ed. *Votes for Women,* q.v.

———. "The Woman Suffrage Movement in Mississippi." *Journal of Mississippi History* 30 (February 1968): 1–34.

———. "The Woman Suffrage Movement in North Carolina." *North Carolina Historical Review* 38 (January and April 1961): 45–62 and 173–189.

———. *The Woman Suffrage Movement in Tennessee.* New York: Bookman, 1957.

———. "The Woman Suffrage Movement in Texas." *Journal of Southern History* 17 (May 1951): 194–215.

Taylor, Lloyd C., Jr. "Lila Meade Valentine: The FFV as Reformer." *Virginia Magazine of History and Biography* 70 (October 1962): 471–487.

Terborg-Penn, Rosalyn. "Discontented Black Feminists: Prelude and Postcript to the Passage of the Nineteenth Amendment." Lois Scharf and Joan M. Jensen, eds. *Decades of Discontent: The Women's Movement, 1920–1940.* Westport, Connecticut: Greenwood Press, 1983.

———. "Discrimination Against Afro-American Women in the Women's Movement, 1830–1920." *The Afro-American Woman: Struggles and Images.* Sharon Harley and Rosalyn Terborg-Penn, eds. Port Washington, New York: Kennikat Press, 1978.

Thomas, Mary Martha. "The New Woman in Alabama, 1890 to 1920." *Alabama Review* 43 (July 1990): 164–175.

Tillman, The Hon. Benjamin R., of South Carolina. "Speech in the Senate of the United States, August 18, 1913." Washington, Government Printing Office, 1913.

Tindall, George B. *The Emergence of the New South: 1913–1945.* Baton Rouge: Louisiana State University Press, 1967.

Tipton, Nancy Carol. "'It Is My Duty': The Public Career of Belle Kearney." M.A. thesis, University of Mississippi, 1975.

Turner, Elizabeth Hayes. "Benevolent Ladies, Club Women, and Suffragists: Galveston Women's Organizations, 1880–1920." Ph.D. dissertation, Rice University, 1990.

———. "Women Progressives and the Origins of Local Suffrage Societies in Texas." Paper presented at the Southern Historical Association Convention, Fort Worth, November 1991.

———. "Southern Suffragists and the Progressive Period." Paper presented at the Organization of American Historians, Louisville, April 1991.

Wall, Joseph Frazier. *Henry Watterson: Reconstructed Rebel.* New York: Oxford University Press, 1956.

Wheeler, Marjorie Spruill. *Votes for Women: The Woman Suffrage Movement in Tennessee, the South, and the Nation.* Knoxville: University of Tennessee Press, forthcoming.

———. [Spruill]. "Sex, Science, and the Woman Question': The *Woman's Journal* on Woman's Nature and Potential, 1870–1875." M.A. thesis, University of Virginia, 1980.

———. "Mary Johnston, Suffragist." *Virginia Magazine of History and Biography* 100 (January 1992): 99–118.

———. "Feminism and Antifeminism in the South." *Encyclopedia of Southern Culture.* Charles Reagan Wilson and William R. Ferris, eds. Chapel Hill: University of North Carolina Press, 1989.

———. [Spruill]. "White Supremacy and the Southern Ideal of Woman: A Study of the Woman Suffrage Movement in North Carolina." Honors thesis, University of North Carolina, Chapel Hill, 1973.

Whites, LeeAnn. "Rebecca Latimer Felton and the Wife's Farm: The Class and
    Racial Politics of Gender Reform." Paper delivered at the Berkshire Con-
    ference on Women, June 1990. Revised version forthcoming in *Georgia
    Historical Quarterly*.
————. "Rebecca Latimer Felton and the Problem of 'Protection' in the New
    South." Nancy Hewitt and Suzanne Lebsock, eds. *Visible Women: Essays in
    Honor of Anne Firor Scott*. Urbana: University of Illinois Press, forthcoming.
Williamson, Joel. *The Crucible of Race: Black-White Relations in the American South
    Since Emancipation*. New York: Oxford University Press, 1984.
Wilson, Charles Reagan. *Baptized in Blood: The Religion of the Lost Cause,
    1865–1920*. Athens: University of Georgia Press, 1980.
Winegarten, Ruthe, and Judith N. McArthur. *Citizens at Last: The Woman Suf-
    frage Movement in Texas*. Austin: Ellen C. Temple, Publisher, 1987.
Woodward, C. Vann. *Origins of the New South, 1877–1913*. Baton Rouge:
    Louisiana State University Press, 1971.
————. *The Strange Career of Jim Crow*. New York: Oxford University Press,
    1974.
Zimmerman, Loretta Ellen. "Alice Paul and the National Woman's Party,
    1912–1920." Ph.D. dissertation, Tulane University, 1964.

Index

Printed in the United States
2652

9 780195 082456